LANDING ON
THE EDGE OF ETERNITY

LANDING
ON THE EDGE OF
ETERNITY

TWENTY-FOUR HOURS AT OMAHA BEACH

ROBERT KERSHAW

PEGASUS BOOKS
NEW YORK LONDON

LANDING ON THE EDGE OF ETERNITY

Pegasus Books, Ltd.
148 W 37th Street, 13th Floor
New York, NY 10018

First Pegasus Books paperback edition November 2020

First Pegasus Books edition November 2018

Interior design by Maria Fernandez

Library of Congress Cataloging-in-Publication Data is available.

ISBN: 978-1-64313-350-8

10 9 8 7 6 5 4 3 2 1

Printed in the United States of America
Distributed by Simon & Schuster
www.pegasusbooks.com

*This book is dedicated to my Father, Lesley Kershaw, Légion d'Honneur,
who landed in the second wave on Gold Beach on D–Day,
and to my Mother, whom he met in Hamburg, 1945.*

CONTENTS

SOME OF THE VOICES FROM OMAHA

THE GERMANS

Oberleutnant Bernhard Frerking, commanding the 1st Battery of Artillery Regiment 352, had his forward artillery observation post located at strongpoint WN 62 at Colleville-sur-Mer. One of his soldiers claimed, "he kept human feeling awake in me during an inhuman war."

Gefreiter Franz Gockel manned a water-cooled Polish machine gun at WN 62. He felt "like God in France," but was surprised at the primitive state of the "Atlantic Wall."

Oberstleutnant Ernst Goth commanded 916 Regiment, responsible for the forward sector of Omaha Beach. He was confident his men were well trained enough to give a good account of themselves.

Oberleutnant Hans Heinz was Goth's Ordinance officer, a Stalingrad veteran who also had misgivings about the much-vaunted Atlantic Wall. A veteran *Feldwebel* had confided they could hold off successive waves of invaders, but once the ammunition ran out it would all be over.

Kurt Keller was a private in the reconnaissance unit of Fusilier Battalion 352. He was an ardent Nazi and disapproved of his NCO's amoral relationships with the local French women. He was convinced the invasion would not succeed, declaring, "Where the German soldier stands, nobody gets through!"

Machine Gunner Wilhelm Kirchhoff, with Werfer Regiment 84, occupied a cliff-edge trench near the observation bunker on top of Pointe du Hoc. "Now we're in for it," his officer had confided when they saw the massive invasion fleet.

Generalmajor Dietrich Kraiss was the astute Russian Front veteran commander of the 352nd Infantry Division. He had trained it up to "crack" status, far superior to the "static" infantry divisions positioned left and right of Omaha Beach. The Americans did not know his division was there.

Oberstleutnant Karl Meyer commanded Grenadier Regiment 915, which was Kraiss's operational *Kampfgruppe* reserve. During the early hours of the D-Day morning it was sent off in the wrong direction to combat American paratroopers that had landed well to the west of Omaha Beach. It would prove difficult to turn back.

Unteroffizier Henrik Naube manned a machine gun at WN 73 on the cliffs overlooking the Vierville draw. He thought the prospect of the Allies invading Germany one day to be unimaginable.

Gefreiter Heinrich Severloh was Oberleutnant Frerking's aide and manned a machine gun at WN 62. Severloh did not fit into the Wehrmacht concept of blind obedience; he was an individual. His effectiveness behind the gun that day was to earn him the dubious title "the Beast of Omaha."

Grenadier Karl Wegner manned a machine gun at beach level inside a bunker at WN 71 at Vierville-sur-Mer. After mistakenly declaring a fishing boat to be the invasion, he was nervously determined to conduct himself well. He could not believe the size of the fleet when it did appear.

Gefreiter Gustav Winter was the 75mm gunner inside a "concrete panzer" turret at WN 66, covering the beach at Saint-Laurent-sur-Mer at the center of Omaha Beach. He was an ex–panzer crewman, whose fingers and nose had been seriously damaged by frostbite in Russia. He was transferred to this lonely outpost with his loader, a young Czech-German boy, "who was not very bright, but very enthusiastic."

Oberstleutnant Fritz Ziegelmann was chief of staff to General Kraiss, the cerebral foil to the astute and decisive practical general. Operational research had convinced him the invasion was on that night, and he had placed the division on alert. When American paratroopers landed in strength to the west, the division reserve was prematurely committed in the wrong direction.

THE FRENCH

Albert André was pressed by the Germans to work on the unfinished beach defenses in the center of Omaha Beach the previous afternoon, fitting a tank turret to WN 66. He did not think, with all the activity, that pressed labor would be required that day.

Michel Hardelay had to assist the Germans with the demolition of his own house at Vierville-sur-Mer to make room for beach defenses. His neighbor had ridiculed his attempts to build a family shelter trench, convinced the Allies would never land here. Hardelay was not so sure.

Suzanne Hardelay was a young child when the invasion came. The first thing she saw at Vierville was American legs striding past her basement.

Victorine Houyvet was a thirty-one-year-old schoolteacher living at Vierville. The first American she saw shot at her through the window while she was pulling her skirt on, hardly an auspicious introduction to the liberators.

Jean Marion, the French Underground chief at Grandcamp was aware the invasion was pending. "There's so many ships out there," he told his wife, "there's no room for the fish."

Louise Oxéant had set off with her ten-year-old son that morning on a donkey to milk her neighbor's cows. The delayed bombing release for the approaching US air force Liberator armada intent on destroying the German defenses at Omaha would place her right in the eye of the storm.

Edmond Scelles was sixteen and lived at Saint-Laurent-sur-Mer. They had forty German soldiers billeted at their farm, and the alarm had been called. They moved out to occupy their beach positions seemingly totally confident.

THE AMERICANS

Private John Barnes was aboard LCA-911 with A Company the 116th Regiment heading toward Vierville off Omaha Beach. He had agreed to carry the heavy section flamethrower. Conditions were indescribable; everyone was seasick from the turbulence and they were constantly drenched by cold spray. The boat was alarmingly low in the water.

General Omar Bradley commanded the 1st US Army from aboard the cruiser USS *Augusta* ten miles offshore. He was concerned at the sea state, which would make his soldiers seasick and would compromise the launch of his DD tanks, vital to overcome the defending beach bunkers. Amazingly the Germans had not discovered their presence. He was frustrated and concerned he had no control of events onshore. Within three hours of landing he faced the dilemma whether or not to continue in the face of catastrophe.

Robert Capa was a celebrated combat war photographer working for *Life* magazine, who would land with E Company the 16th Regiment at Colleville, at the east side of Omaha Beach. He had chosen this hot spot because his maxim was, "if the pictures are not good enough, then you're not close enough."

Brigadier General Norman Cota was the unassuming assistant 29th Division commander, who landed one hour after the first wave. He possessed the inspirational command steel to get men moving off the beach.

Captain Joe Dawson commanded G Company of the 16th Regiment, which managed to land as a cohesive company group and was the first to climb the bluffs near Colleville. They achieved a decisive penetration of the German defenses.

Private Sam Goodgal with Sergeant Raymond Crouch were paratroopers from the 101st (US) Airborne Division who were mis-dropped into the sea off Pointe du

Hoc that night. They were already on the beach when Rudder's Rangers landed and joined in the assault.

Lieutenant Coit Hendley was in command of LCI(L)-85, which approached the beach late in the morning opposite WN 62. At twenty-three he had enjoyed the carnival atmosphere in England prior to the invasion with his WREN girlfriend Sylvia, who worked with naval communications. She believed his ship had sunk; his father saw the listing wreck in newsreels of the invasion back home in the United States.

Major General Clarence Huebner commanded the "Big Red One" 1st Infantry Division responsible for establishing the beachhead at Omaha. He was ten miles offshore and had no control or visibility of his subordinate units on the ground. By mid-morning he was contemplating failure.

Private Hu Riley landed near war photographer Robert Capa with F Company the 16th Regiment. This was his third landing under fire and was to prove the worst. He was to be immortalized by Capa's photograph of "the face in the surf," struggling, barely afloat, and under fire at the water's edge.

Lieutenant Colonel James Rudder commanded the Ranger group that assaulted the seemingly unassailable cliffs at Pointe du Hoc to destroy a German battery. He was to lose nearly two-thirds of his force and the guns were not there.

Seth Shepard was a combat photographer aboard LCI(L)-92, heading toward Colleville. He was visibly impressed by the epic size of the invasion fleet and thought they would doubtless succeed. Within minutes of landing his ship was turned into a fireball.

Private David Silva landed with the 29th Division opposite WN 62 near Colleville. The war was the first time he had left home. It is conceivable he was hit by Heinrich Severloh's machine gun fire. Severloh was to meet him after the war to ask forgiveness.

Sergeant Robert Slaughter landed with D Company the 116th regiment in the second wave, which was as much a disaster as the first. He got his friends to autograph his copy of Eisenhower's "Great Crusade" speech before they set off. He was in shock at the devastating casualties they lost that day, and remembered this was just the first day of many fighting days to come in Europe.

Lieutenant John Spalding commanded a platoon with E Company the 16th Regiment that landed alone, in the sheltered lee from German fire between Colleville and Saint-Laurent-sur-Mer. They were the first Americans to scale the bluffs behind Omaha that day.

Sergeant Donald Wilson landed with F Company the 16th Regiment. He was a veteran of three landings under fire and knew what he was doing. He was totally unimpressed with the secrecy surrounding their sea approach, and chewed an apple on the landing craft run-in to bolster and impress his green troops. He was soon pinned down in the grisly surfline with the rest of his few surviving men.

ABBREVIATIONS AND GLOSSARY

2 IC	Second in command
Bocage	Hedgerow terrain
CO	Commanding Officer
DD	Duplex Drive (amphibious tank)
DUKW	Amphibious Vehicle. The "duck" was a thirty-one-foot, six-wheeled amphibious truck that could carry twenty-five fully equipped soldiers or 5,000 lbs of stowed cargo. Slow at sea, it could reach up to fifty mph on land.
Heer	German for Army. "Heeresgruppe" Army Group
Kampfgruppe	Battle Group
Kriegsmarine	German Navy
LCA	Landing Craft Assault. British built, designed to carry thirty-five men (thirty-two with equipment) and 1,700 lbs. It was just under forty feet long, thirteen tons, and capable of six knots.
LCI (L)	Landing Craft Large. These were 160 feet long and could land 188 men on lowered bow ramps, or transport 75 tons of cargo.
LCM	Landing Craft Mechanized. These were up to 56 feet long, the smallest landing craft able to land a tank, and capable of nine knots. It could carry sixty demolition engineers and their equipment.
LCR	Landing Craft Rocket
LCT	Landing Craft Tank. The largest version was 119 feet long and could carry three 50-ton tanks or 150 tons of cargo.
LCVP	Landing Craft Vehicle and Personnel. The so-called "Higgins boats" were about thirty-six feet long, could make nine knots, carried thirty-two to thirty-five men, and weighed eighteen tons.

LST	Landing Ship Tank. These were 328 feet long and could land 500 tons, generally becoming hospital ships after unloading to take the wounded back to England.
Luftwaffe	German air force
Nebelwerfer	German automatic rocket launcher
OB West	Oberkommando West [Supreme Command West]
OKW	Oberkommando der Wehrmacht. [German Armed Forces Supreme Command]
Panzerschreck	Bazooka
Panzerjäger	Anti-tank
PAK	Panzerabwehrkanone[anti-tank gun]
Ranks	

Comparative German US Officers

Generalmajor	Major General
Oberst	Colonel
Oberstleutnant	Lieutenant Colonel
Major	Major
Hauptmann	Captain
Oberleutnant	Lieutenant
Leutnant	2nd Lieutenant

Comparative NCO ranks

Hauptfeldwebel	Sergeant Major
Oberfeldwebel	Master Sergeant
Feldwebel	Sergeant
Unteroffizier	Corporal
Obergefreiter	Private first class
Grenadier	Private
SP	Self-Propelled
WN	*Widerstandsnest* [strongpoint]

Omaha - D Day

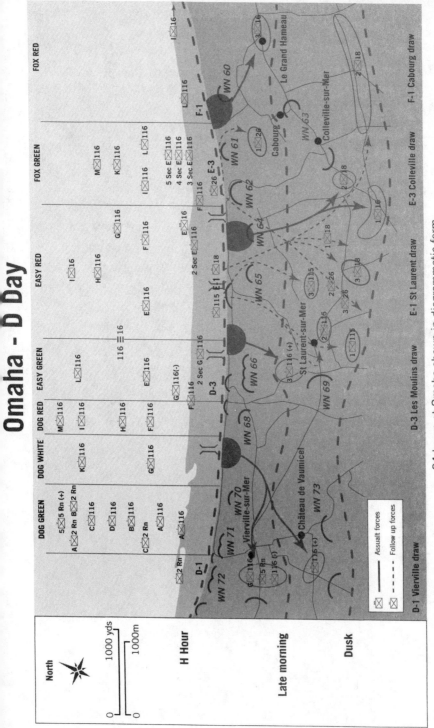

24 hours at Omaha shown in diagrammatic form.

Kampfgruppe Meyer Missed opportunties

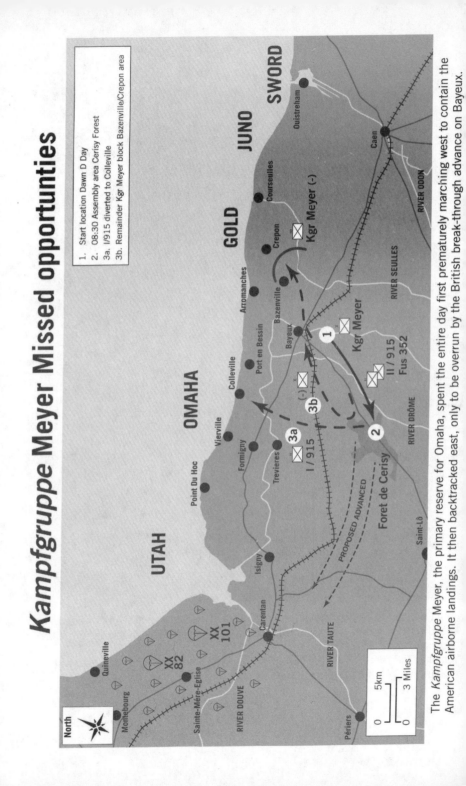

1. Start location Dawn D Day
2. 08:30 Assembly area Cerisy Forest
3a. I/915 diverted to Colleville
3b. Remainder Kgr Meyer block Bazenville/Crepon area

The *Kampfgruppe Meyer*, the primary reserve for Omaha, spent the entire day first prematurely marching west to contain the American airborne landings. It then backtracked east, only to be overrun by the British break-through advance on Bayeux.

24 Hours at Pointe du Hoc

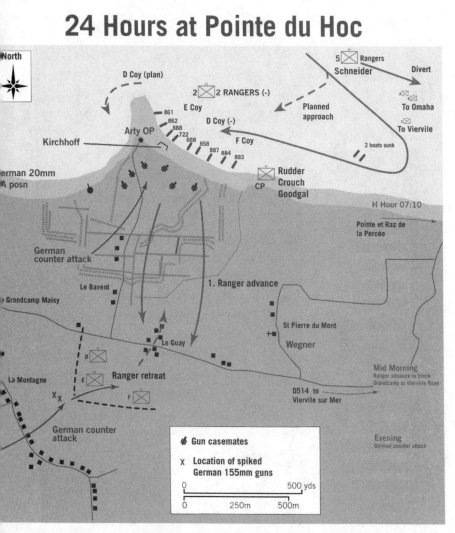

The German 155mm battery at Pointe du Hoc had already been neutralized by air attacks. The epic Ranger assault penetrated the headland, found and destroyed the guns and blocked the German reinforcement road from Grandcamp to Vierville at Omaha. They were not relieved until D+2, by which time the remnants had been compressed around Rudder's HQ.

Locations of voices from Omaha

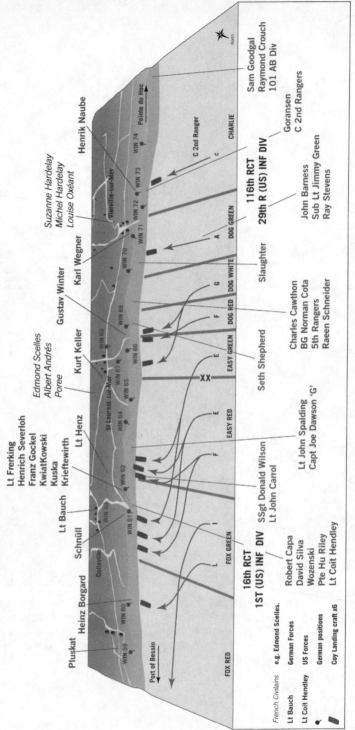

The wind and tide pushed the landing craft eastwards, where many bunched up in the less well defended German center, still under construction.

First waves Omaha

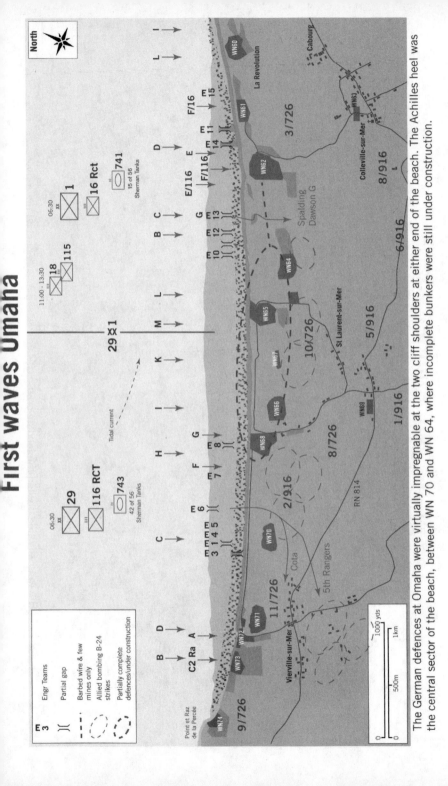

The German defences at Omaha were virtually impregnable at the two cliff shoulders at either end of the beach. The Achilles heel was the central sector of the beach, between WN 70 and WN 64, where incomplete bunkers were still under construction.

Attack and counter attack

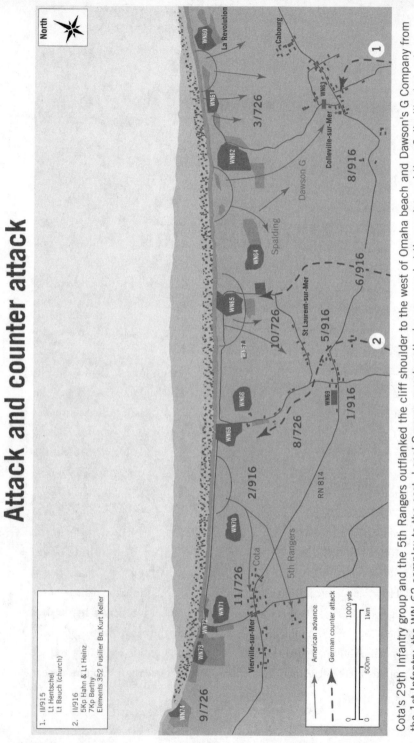

1. II/915
    Lt Hentschel
    Lt Bauch (church)

2. II/916
    5Kp Hahn & Lt Heinz
    7Kp Berthy
    Elements 352 Fusilier Bn.Kurt Keller

Cota's 29th Infantry group and the 5th Rangers outflanked the cliff shoulder to the west of Omaha beach and Dawson's G Company from the 1st Infantry, the WN 62 complex to the east. Local German counter-attacks appeared at the center and then Colleville, but only piece-meal, never arriving in greater than company strength.

INTRODUCTION

A fter a tense weather forecast conference on June 5, 1944 at South-wick House near Portsmouth, General Dwight D. Eisenhower, the supreme commander of allied forces, scrawled a hastily composed note. *"Our landings in the Cherbourg-Havre area have failed to gain a satisfactory foothold and I have withdrawn the troops,"* he wrote. He crossed out the start of the next sentence three times. *"My decision to attack at this time and place was based on the best information available."* It was his decision. *"The troops, the air and the navy did all that bravery and devotion to duty could do."* Eisenhower was about to visit one of the tented camps of the 101st (US) Airborne Division, before they took off to Normandy. *"If any blame or fault attaches to the attempt,"* he carried on, *"it is mine alone."* He was now to confront soldiers who would face the consequences of his "go" decision. That this was an anxious moment is reflected by the date he wrote beneath: "July 5th." It was actually the 5th of June.

Eisenhower folded the note and tucked it inside his wallet and set off to meet the American paratroopers at Greenham Common near

Newbury. Several weeks later the notelet was still inside his wallet and he passed it to his naval aide Commander Butcher, for posterity.

Two hours after H-hour on Omaha Beach the next day the prophecy rang ominously true. General Omar Bradley, commander of the American First Army, scanning the distant shoreline through binoculars aboard the USS *Augusta*, relived Eisenhower's dilemma. Fragmentary reports coming from offshore reported the first wave had foundered and that a catastrophe was unfolding along that gray, indistinct line of beach. Twinkling flashes and bulbous clouds of black smoke boiling up from burning tanks and listing landing craft in the obstacle-strewn surf suggested failure. The remorseless conveyor belt of successive waves heading for the maw of this fiercely fought bridgehead had to be momentarily halted. Bradley needed to decide whether to redirect the landing effort to the British Gold Beach further east, where headway was being made toward Bayeux, or carry on. Nobody was aware the supreme commander had already tucked away a note that formed the basis for a press statement covering just such an eventuality. Bradley agonized over what he should do.

Groundbreaking research by American historian Joseph Balkoski has convincingly suggested that some 4,700 casualties were inflicted on American forces landing at Omaha on D-Day: more than were lost at Pearl Harbor at the outset of the war and among the costliest single day's losses for the subsequent battles that would rage on the mainland of Europe. It has taken decades to realize the full extent of the damage inflicted, almost five times higher than the next worse loss suffered at D-Day on Juno Beach. Was General Eisenhower reluctant to admit that his hastily scrawled note, only to be released in the event of catastrophic failure, was almost in this league? Did it need to be concealed from the American public? Captain Charles Cawthon, who landed shortly after 7:00 A.M., nevertheless remembered at the time, "*I do not recall any questioning of a frontal assault on prepared defenses from the unstable base of the English Channel*."[1] Such an assault was an echo of the sterile tactics of the First World War.

Hollywood, beginning with Darryl F. Zanuck's rendition of Cornelius Ryan's *The Longest Day,* first brought the heroism of the assaults at Omaha and Pointe du Hoc vividly into the American consciousness. It also played to the global tensions of the Cold War. President Jimmy Carter was the first of five US presidents to visit the site. Addressing immaculately arrayed lines of bright white crosses against an emerald green setting at the cemetery at Colleville, above the beach, he declared, *"We are determined with our noble allies here, that Europe's freedom will never again be endangered."* With Cold War resonance, he encapsulated the significance of the Omaha battle to the American psyche. America's first physical entry onto the strategic heartland of northwest Europe was at the cost of a grievous bloodletting. In an age less cynical than our own, freedom meant so much more in an emotionally charged sense, juxtaposed against another totalitarian menace, Soviet hegemony seeking to dominate Europe. Successive Hollywood feature films and countless TV documentaries culminated in 1998 with Steven Spielberg's *Saving Private Ryan,* which offered both a poignant and viscerally gritty portrayal of the Omaha Beach landings. The critical and commercial acclaim the film engendered seemed to lead to a resurgence of American interest in the Second World War.

Four more successive American presidents sought to wrap themselves in the patriotic aura of reflected glory from Omaha Beach. President Ronald Reagan followed Carter at the fortieth anniversary when he spoke at Pointe du Hoc, emphasizing that the Rangers were *"the champions who helped free a continent."* President Bill Clinton took up the theme in the same place ten years later, saying, *"Like the soldiers of Omaha Beach, we cannot stand still. We cannot stay safe by doing so."*

The beach seemed to be turning into a European equivalent of the site of Abraham Lincoln's Gettysburg Address. President George W.

Bush came twice to the cemetery, announcing at the sixtieth anniversary how "*a strange turn of history called on young men from the prairie towns and city states of America to cross an ocean and throw back the marching mechanized evils of fascism.*" He was echoed by the fifth to appear, President Barack Obama, on June 6, 2014. He probably unknowingly stood meters from the site, alongside French president François Hollande, at the spot where Lieutenant John Spalding crested the German-held bluffs for the first time. "*This sacred place of rest for 9,387 Americans,*" President Obama said, should be "*seared into the memory of history,*" insisting it "*was democracy's beachhead.*" The battle on the Omaha Beaches resonates symbolically with Americans to tangibly demonstrate their attachment to Europe. [2]

Landing on the Edge of Eternity is a story therefore well worth the telling. Its narrative has over the years become increasing emotionally embellished by films and the media. Second World War veterans are often embarrassed to be collectively addressed casually as "heroes." The accolade is clear, but not everyone was a hero. They, more than others, are acutely aware of the soul-baring human frailties revealed in combat. Most were scared and carried on with a dogged determination that saved the day for the American landings, which were beset by some problematic planning. Some were rendered helpless and incoherent to orders because of the visceral shock they endured on landing. They were not in a fit state to do any more than survive. Others committed acts of extraordinary bravery, which had to be witnessed by superiors to be recognized for decorations, so many accomplishments that day went unrecorded. The assault at Omaha was committed frontally against well entrenched and prepared positions, defended by the most powerful infantry division stationed anywhere near the coast at the time. These were also brave men, despite fighting for a malign cause, and were also prepared to die. In between were French civilians, rarely written about, who died in the thousands.

One of the difficulties in an account following human stories over a twenty-four-hour period is to reconcile time and date discrepancies within different personal reminiscences. Wehrmacht and French civilian time was one hour later than Allied. Fading memories can often seek confirmation from alternative secondhand accounts in good faith.

The surviving 352nd Infantry Division telephone log is a remarkable document, preserving an authentic aura of firsthand immediacy. Recording this information in the din and confusion of a wartime headquarters, alongside vagaries in translation, makes it difficult at times to decide whether the time given for an event is a log of the action that occurred, or is the relaying of orders to expedite that activity. The log does authentically convey what all witnesses experience in conflict, namely confusion over what is really going on.

Eyewitness accounts have created a maze of contradictory information about the Omaha landings, influenced by strongly held views and the emotion implicit in the story they are telling. Recent documentary TV coverage often asks individuals to summon detail from the fringe of living memory. For this reason I have attempted to get as close to the origin of these events as is possible. Much of the recent German eyewitness material is at variance to earlier American accounts. In order to narrate a comprehensible story, it is advisable to simplify interesting but otherwise confusing detail with fair assumptions. My own personal memories of conflict come in snapshot form, and this has been the approach here. There are few certainties in the chaos of combat. Discussion about what happened after the event can be controversial, even minutes afterward, never mind decades later.

Films and TV documentaries tend to glorify the Omaha tale, told through iconic heroes, almost akin to Homer's *Iliad* account. Objective truth is so much more difficult to achieve. There were heroes yes, but also human frailty in abundance. Successive American presidents saw it as representing the nation's consciousness of who they are. American soldiers were brave, generous, and resolute in sacrificing thousands of their lives to free people they had never met.

The assault on Omaha's beaches was exactly what German propaganda foresaw should be the consequence of trying to breach Hitler's invincible "Atlantic Wall." The first hours appeared to realize the Allies' worst fears. If this resistance and intensity of firepower had been replicated on the other four beaches, the story of D-Day might have had a different outcome.

PROLOGUE
1:00 A.M. JUNE 6, 1944

As many as five to six Douglas C-47 Dakota aircraft were visible in the opaque blue sky viewed through the open moonlit fuselage door. They flew in "Vs" of nine aircraft at seven-second intervals. Little lavender blue lights were all that could be seen from the aircraft interior. Parachute transports, 822 in all, had risen majestically into the night sky from airfields in southern England. With as many as five hundred planes on the same track, it was easy for crews not paying attention to overrun the aircraft ahead. Serial 10, which contained Company I of the 3rd Battalion, 506th Parachute Infantry Regiment from the American 101st Airborne Division, flew inside this enormous stream, which droned south for fifty-seven miles before turning to port over a beacon launched in the English Channel below. The formation flew by the islands of Guernsey and Jersey before wheeling left again to cross the Cotentin Peninsula at fifteen hundred feet from the south. As they changed direction even more flights were taking off from English airfields. The date was June 6, 1944, D-Day, one hour past midnight, the start of the "Crusade" to liberate Nazi-occupied Europe. American paratroopers flying on board knew that to get back home to the United States, they would have to fight their way through France and Germany.

The men packed inside—constricted by parachute harnesses, overweight equipment, and weapons—slept, smoked, and thought of loved ones. Some joked a little but most sat in silence. A few were on their knees, lost in thought, not praying but coping with eighty to one hundred pounds of equipment by balancing it on canvas bench seats. Once they cleared the Channel Islands nervousness and tension increased, as they somberly looked out of open doors at the khaki-colored C-47s flying alongside, with their distinctive black-and-white D-Day striped markings on wings and rear fuselages. Cold winds came rushing and blustering through these doors and swirled around the rear of the aircraft. Private Leonard "Sam" Goodgal and Sergeant Raymond Crouch numbered three and four in their roster. The unit mission was to parachute onto Drop Zone D outside the small town of Les Drogueries and capture two wooden bridges spanning the Douve River. The American 101st and 82nd Airborne Divisions were tasked to secure the right flank of the Allied invasion. Their unit, the 101st, was to seize exits leading inland from Utah Beach, the westernmost landing point. The battalion and company objective to seize the Douve River bridges would enable American tanks to achieve the vital link up between Utah and Omaha beach, twenty-three miles apart, separated by the Vire River estuary.

Goodgal and Crouch had received no end of pep talks before taking off. General Eisenhower had told them "you are about to embark upon the Great Crusade," pointing out, "your task will not be an easy one" and the enemy "will fight savagely." British General Sir Bernard Montgomery breezily announced "good hunting on the mainland of Europe," which predictably elicited a lot of black humor from soldiers' responses. The most memorable advice came from their own commanding officer, Colonel Wolverton, who after a few preliminaries simply said:

> "Men, you know that I am not a religious man, but I want you
> to pray with me now. I want you to get down on your knees,
> and don't look down but look up to God with open eyes."

"There was not a dry eye in the battalion," Sergeant Robert Webb remembered, and it left Goodgal "fired up" for the operation, having alleviated some of his nervousness.

As the massive aerial armada made landfall, a vision of moonlit peaceful farmland passed serenely below before being abruptly extinguished by turbulent clouds. A huge bank of cumulonimbus had risen up across the flight path of the two divisions, immediately obscuring crew vision. The tightly compacted aircraft formations flew straight into it with pilots instinctively breaking away horizontally and vertically. Planes began to yaw and plunge, losing their tight V formation and fighting to maintain course as crews cringed at the prospect of colliding. Aircraft had just minutes to drop from the fifteen-hundred-foot approach to the seven hundred feet required for the run in to the drop zone. The flak that rose up to meet them when they came in sight of the coast clustered even more thickly as they lost altitude.

Veteran paratroopers stood up and began hooking up static lines as soon as they heard the distinctive noise of spent shrapnel rattling against the fuselage sides. They were left staggering for balance, or fell over when pilots took violent evasive action. Aircraft emerged from dense cloud into clear moonlight only to discover they were either completely alone or too close to other planes. Formations were scattered all over the Normandy countryside. Crouch and Goodgal's aircraft plunged steeply, panicking troopers as loose equipment clattered perilously around them. Goodgal, hanging onto his static line felt, "this is it, I'm going to be killed right here." "Jump! Jump!" the men at the back of the line screamed as the aircraft yawed and rose and fell as the pilot fought to regain control. Each upward and downward surge first lightened and then buckled legs under the excessive weights they were carrying.

As the aircraft finally leveled off a juddering impact was felt to starboard, which knocked men to the floor in a tangle of arms, legs, and equipment caught up in strop lines. Men laden with mortars and machine guns were too heavy to pick up. Lieutenant Floyd Johnston and Sergeant Neil Christiansen were the "chief" and jumpmaster, and were number one and two on the static line. Christiansen, who could see out of the door, told Crouch, next in line, that the starboard engine was on fire. The flickering glow from the flames was reflecting at the rear of the fuselage. At that moment the aircraft crew chief shouted they had overshot the drop zone and the pilot was going to go around again. But the C-47 was yawing to the right and already beginning to vibrate and shake as the starboard engine lost power. All the paratroopers pressed up toward the door yelling "Jump! Jump!" Clearly it was now or never, and a green light replaced the red glow over the door. "Get the hell out of here!" Crouch shouted at Johnson and Christiansen as they scrambled out the door. The fiery trail from the blazing engine was ejecting debris from the other side.

G force from the howling downward spiral of the plane was pressing the men backward up against the pilot's cabin. Crouch and Goodgal had virtually to climb the angled fuselage floor against the rush of air to get out. Crouch fell out and hit the screaming slipstream in an unaerodynamic posture that snatched away the leg bag and weapon from his parachute harness as he tumbled in the sky. Everything was lost in the inky blackness, lit only briefly by the blazing aircraft passing over his head. The opening shock of the parachute brutally strained his groin and limbs, but at least it had opened. Looking up he saw his 'chute had deployed, and another had popped open just above him. All around was cracking and zipping tracer fire. A flak gun was pounding upward nearby and a searchlight beam gyrated crazily about in the night sky. Looking down Crouch saw moonlight reflecting off water and seemingly a cliff edge, running off in both directions. They were on the coast. Out to sea the receding whine of the fiercely burning C-47 dropped lower and lower.[1]

The German gunners of the 2nd Battery *Heeres-Küsten* Coastal Artillery Regiment 1260 at Pointe du Hoc, four and a half miles west of Omaha Beach, were decidedly skittish. Two bombing runs by twin-engine aircraft had hit them on Sunday afternoon. The damage was so bad the *Organization Todt* decided to suspend all further construction work, it was too dangerous. The preceding day thirty-five American B-17 bombers had hit the site after 9:00 A.M. Over a hundred tons of bombs were dropped with at least fifty detonations inside the battery perimeter. Nineteen-year-old machine gunner Wilhelm Kirchhoff with Werfer Regiment 84, who had recently arrived to reinforce the battery, had managed to reach one of the underground shelters near the cliff edge, while twenty-five-year-old artillery observer *Unteroffizier* [lance corporal] Rudolf Karl took shelter in the concrete observation cupola on the Pointe du Hoc headland. Damage was again heavy. One of the gun pits and three personnel bunkers were struck, but they remained intact. Kirchhoff had spent the rest of the day clearing debris from communication trenches and bunker entrances.[2]

When a flaming twin engine aircraft appeared over the battery after midnight, all hell broke loose. Kirchhoff barely had time to duck down inside his machine gun emplacement, situated on the cliff edge, before the eastern and western flak emplacements began banging away. They spat up ragged lines of fiery tracers as searchlights tried to lock onto the stricken aircraft. Shouting and popping small arms fire rang out when parachutes were momentarily caught in the glare of the searchlights. Machine gun and rifle fire intensified as the parachutes descended, their one chance to get at the cursed Allied airmen. At least two parachutes appeared to land in the vicinity of the battery perimeter, maybe more out to sea.

Sergeant Crouch was in trouble. He had no weapon, and was under German small arms fire coming up from the ground. They "must have been cross-eyed" he later maintained, "because I could hear the bullets as they snapped past my head, but they never hit me." Shooting did not die down until he floated beneath the level of the cliff edge. He realized with some trepidation that he was going to land in the sea, and inflated his automatic "Mae West" life jacket just as he splashed into the water. Overcoming initial panic from the shock of the cold water he managed to struggle out of his parachute harness, before he realized he could actually stand up. He was in waist-deep water.

Leonard Goodgal looked up after the shock of his parachute opening, but saw no other jumpers get out of the plane. Three 'chutes were ahead, two descended into the dark landmass while the third, just in front, was about to enter the water. He activated the release mechanism on his parachute harness as he splashed down and shot up to the surface, propelled by panic and the jolt of the cold water. Unlike Crouch nearby, his equipment and rifle were still attached to his parachute. "Is that you Sam?" he heard the other shout as he struggled out of his harness. They were both lucky.

A few miles to his right, on the top of the cliff face, Unteroffizier Henrik Naube with the 352nd German Infantry Division had come on duty shortly after midnight. He was manning the machine gun position at the western corner of the cliffs at the strongpoint [*Widerstandsnest*— WN] 73, overlooking Omaha Beach at Vierville-sur-Mer. "There was heavy bombing to the south again and a very high level of aircraft noise," he recalled. Flak fire was curling across the sky "from points in a semicircle inland of us," mixed with a succession of distant explosions. "We all agreed that something was up, something was going to happen soon," he recalled. It was a moonlit night and they were able to fleetingly distinguish many "twin-engine types" of aircraft, but could not decide whether they were bombers or something else:

> "Several times, we saw an aircraft on fire, heading out across the sea toward England, and in some cases these burning planes descended and appeared to hit the sea in the distance."

Most of the aircraft were coming out of the hinterland and crossing the cliffs to their left before heading out to sea over Pointe du Hoc and also farther beyond, over the Vire estuary.[3]

The two American paratroopers wading ashore found they were trapped. Ahead lay the English Channel, whereas behind them was a sheer cliff, more than a hundred feet high, which overlooked a narrow stony beach. They had no idea where they were, except in the wrong place. On top of the cliffs were Germans, who had only just narrowly missed killing them. It was shortly after 1:00 A.M. June 6. They began to look for shelter and take stock of their situation. They had in fact landed along the narrow beach that ran from Omaha Beach to the German coastal battery that had fired at their stricken aircraft, at Pointe du Hoc.

Eleven miles south was the picturesque Château du Molay, which was the headquarters of General Dietrich Kraiss, the commander of the 352nd German Infantry Division. At around 1:00 A.M. his chief of staff, *Oberstleutnant* [lieutenant colonel] Fritz Ziegelmann picked up his telephone to receive a call from the staff of 84 Corps, his superior head-quarters. It was succinct and to the point: "Enemy parachute troops have landed near Caen. Alarm Stage II." Caen was over thirty miles away to the east. Ziegelmann notified the commanding general, he was not par-ticularly surprised. Having recently been posted from the Quartermaster Department of the Seventh Army, he was well aware of the developing situation, which he had been monitoring for some time. He was the consummate professional German General Staff officer. The Luftwaffe had reported ever increasing concentrations of landing craft in southern English ports since April and May. "I was of the opinion," he recalled, "that commencing with May, we could expect the invasion at any time." He was in agreement with his wily veteran commander General Kraiss, a Knight's Cross holder, who had excelled as an infantry division commander in Russia. Since his arrival at the newly established 352nd Division, he had trained it up to a "good–above average division." Leave for commanders and General Staff officers had been canceled since April, with the very real expectation of a coming invasion. Kraiss was responsible for the "Bayeux Sector" of the Normandy coastline, which included the so-called French *Plage d'Or* or Gold Beach. This was the four and a half mile expanse of sandy beach which the Allies referred to in code as "Omaha Beach."

Ziegelmann had shared his thoughts and analysis with Kraiss against a background of growing air attacks against the road and rail network in France and Belgium. In the 352 Division sector alone, twenty-seven carrier pigeons were shot down between March 20 and May 20, one of the regular courier conduits between the French Resistance and the Allies. Ceaseless air attacks had been occurring in the 84th Corps forward sector along the Norman coastline. Kraiss was especially alerted by the capture of a French resistance leader in Brittany, who under torture made statements about an invasion in a few days time. "All these things," Ziegelmann assessed, "gave me a feeling of certainty that the invasion would come soon." Tonight he was particularly suspicious of reports of large numbers of low-flying enemy aircraft coming in from the south and departing to the east and west.

By 2:00 A.M. Ziegelmann had placed all units on alert by telephone. About two hours later Oberstleutnant Ernst Heyna contacted him from his 914 Regiment headquarters at Neuilly-la-Forêt that thirty to fifty parachute aircraft had dropped paratroopers south of Brevands in the Vire estuary. Some had landed near Cardonville, near the gun positions of Artillery Regiment 352, which was just fifteen miles from

Ziegelmann's headquarters. One American *"Oberleutnant"* [first lieutenant] had apparently even landed next to the perimeter of the Pointe du Hoc coastal battery, "and after a short firefight was taken prisoner." The 352 Division's soldiers were now awake and streaming into their coastal bunkers and defense positions.[4]

Behind the Plage d'Or, soon to be called Omaha Beach, were four village communities. Cabourg, a small hamlet to the east, was linked to the villages of Colleville-sur-Mer, Saint-Laurent-sur-Mer, and Vierville-sur-Mer in the west. All were accessible from the east-west lateral minor road the *Route Nationale* 814, (RN 814, today the RD 514). These villages, no more than a kilometer from the beach, followed the curved outline of the bay between Cabourg in the east and Pointe et Raz de la Percée in the west. Vierville, with a population of about three hundred inhabitants, and Saint-Laurent were former holiday seaside resorts, whereas Colleville was a farming village. Each of the communities were accessible from the beach through five "draws," or shallow ravines, created by natural erosion, providing access to the RN 814 inland approach road. German defenders filed into emplacements that blocked these beach exits, and further emplacements along the curve of the bay. French civilians still lived in the villages.

The enduring memory for the French was that this day began with noise. Hundreds of airplanes could be heard flying south to northeast over the Cotentin Peninsula. "A ceaseless storm," one witness described, created by the constant drone of engines and the distant rumble and crack of antiaircraft artillery. Thousands of Normans were awakened from their deepest sleep by the obvious commotion going on around them. Ambulance driver Cécile Armagnac at Cherbourg, the northernmost point of the peninsula, recalled "unusual noises" to the south, with:

> ". . . repeated and significant groups of airplanes passing over toward the east; machine gunning and antiaircraft fire close

by; uninterrupted droning and humming toward the distant south; muffled rumbling—perhaps bombs; a halo of light, not unlike dawn."[5]

Rumors abounded that Cotentin Peninsula was isolated, that it was not possible to get through to Saint-Lô. Madame Destorses, living in Maisy, the coastal town between the future landing beaches at Utah and Omaha, was "awakened by the sound of airplanes turning and scraping the roofs." All this activity was surprising because up until now Normandy had been spared much of the intense bombing that had been going on in the Pas-de-Calais area, where an invasion was anticipated. Refugees had come from Paris and other towns in northeast France, and moved into the Normandy countryside for safety. Madame Destorses's husband Marcel watched a large red column of smoke rising into the night sky over the city after one particularly loud explosion and announced, "it looks like les Perruques has been hit again." Their young sons came out in their night clothes after a nearby blast smashed their windows. "The floor trembles like a tree shaken by a storm," she recalled, and "dust falls everywhere." She cradled her eighteen-month-old son, who had begun to wail, in her arms. "The bombs fall in bursts with a frightful noise," she recalled, while her boys "are in their pajamas with their feet bare, paying no mind to the fact they are walking on broken glass." She knelt by her son Yves's cradle. "I pray with all my soul!" she remembered. "Be so good, my Lord, to bless our house with your presence tonight!" The air around stank of gunpowder.[6]

Fernand Broeckx was woken up at Colleville-sur-Mer at about 2:00 A.M. by the bombing in Maisy, over ten miles farther west. "We were not too alarmed," he recalled, but the noise was sufficiently loud to get him up. "I went back to bed, but I was not able to get to sleep." Michel Hardelay, aged thirty-one and living at Vierville nearby, was also alerted to "the enormous roaring of the Maisy bombing, near Grandcamp." He got up to look out of the window, "but we could not locate the exact spot from Vierville." German searchlights were sweeping the sky to the west and "in the light beams, we noticed some little white spots falling slowly like snow flakes, way off in the distance." He later discovered they "were leaflets telling the population living by the shore to leave immediately." "What was going on?" Everybody asked the pervasive question, "Is this it?" *Le Débarquement*, the coming invasion, was a complete unknown, until now a vague and threatening phenomenon.[7]

Bomb shelters were rare in France and even more so in Normandy. Unlike more responsive governments in England and Germany, nobody took the trouble in defeated France. The occupying authorities were more intent on shoring up the Atlantic Wall to repel the anticipated Allied threat; French civilians were not their concern. For the past four years, hostile aircraft flying across France had been regarded as a German problem. They were the problem, not what to do with the French. However, the intensification of Allied bombing raids across the French transportation network heightened awareness of local vulnerabilities and that of families. Estimating the altitude of bombers and then the likelihood of overshoots was no longer enough.

Michel Hardelay had left it all rather late and had begun digging a shelter two days before, "a plan that I had already postponed many times." Listening clandestinely to radio advice on the BBC had encouraged him to begin collecting and salvaging building materials. His neighbor, intrigued by the emerging trench, asked, "What are you doing there?" "You can see," Hardelay replied, "I am building a shelter for my mother, the maid, and myself." He offered to enlarge the dig to accommodate five people if his neighbor wanted to help, but the neighbor snickered and shrugged his shoulders, saying they "won't land here," and left Hardelay to it. "He must have been sorry he did not accept my offer forty-eight hours later," he remembered.

Sixteen-year-old Edmond Scelles was not particularly concerned at the sudden influx of German troops into Saint-Laurent-sur-Mer. "On

June 5 the Germans were already alerted," he recalled, but "every year there used to be some big exercises that were supposed to happen around this time." Prieuré Farm, where he lived, set back from the beach, provided accommodation for forty German soldiers. They had requisitioned the top rooms, leaving his parents two rooms and a large kitchen below. Edmond had to sleep in the stable. The Germans were up and about tonight, obviously on maneuvers, he thought.

At 3:00 A.M. Hardelay, who had returned to bed at Vierville, was woken up again by the approaching roar of low-level aircraft. "I jumped to the window," he recalled, because he heard "a whistling, and saw a flash coming from two bombs that exploded at the ridge of the cliff." Six more bombs struck the cliffs, without apparently killing anyone or damaging anything. This time, "I got dressed completely and went to urge my mother and the maid, awakened by the explosions, to do the same." He was agitated, going to and fro from the window every fifteen minutes to check what was going on, "to be ready for any eventuality." At least, he thought, his rudimentary trench shelter had been completed.[8]

Below the cliffs on the stony beach beyond Vierville, the wet, exhausted, and shivering Sergeant Crouch and Private Goodgal wondered what to do next. The two undiscovered paratroopers had somehow to climb the one-hundred-foot cliff towering above to rejoin their regiment. They too heard the sound of heavy bombers overhead and the reverberating cracks of bombs hitting the cliff top, showering them with shale. Crouch thought "the whole cliff was going to come down" on top of them. It was the spur to move on, and they headed westward along the stony shore. Crouch sang "Pistol-Packin' Mama" under his breath as they trudged along, looking for the path that would get them out. They appreciated they needed to increase the pace, because it would soon be light and patrolling Germans might discover them. They had no idea that the promontory sticking out into the sea ahead was Pointe du Hoc.[9]

ONE
THE FAR SHORE
1:00 A.M. TO 4:30 A.M.

The Plage d'Or
1:00 A.M. to 4:00 A.M.

Come on Hein," artillery Oberleutnant Bernhard Frerking woke his orderly, "it's starting." It was shortly after midnight, June 6, 1944. Frerking commanded the 1st Battery of Artillery Regiment 352. His twenty-year-old aide *Gefreiter* [corporal] Heinrich Severloh recognized the seriousness of the alarm and got moving, level 2 callouts meant "imminent danger" of landings. Little more was said. A horse was hitched to their traditional Norman charrette, a two-wheeled carriage, and they set off for Widerstandsnest WN 62. They had about three miles to cover from the Legrand family estate house at Houtteville, the battery's position, to their artillery observation post at the eastern end of the Plage d'Or, or Omaha Beach. The cool night air was filled with the threatening drone of Allied aircraft flying in from the sea farther west. "I was happy to be with him," Severloh remembered, "as we had a good relationship." Things from now on would never be the same. The Legrand farm had "felt like home, I felt really comfortable there," he remembered. Severloh was fiercely independent-minded, not the stereotypical Wehrmacht conscript. "Everything they said in the barracks was a load of crap, none of it was true," he recalled. He was scathing about the unthinking discipline required of conscripts:

> "Shut up, when you talk to me, that was the usual treatment. Leave the thinking to the horses, they've got bigger heads. It was 100% blind obedience and there was no tolerance for back talk and it was punished immediately."[1]

Any illusions he might have had about the conduct of the war were expunged by his experience on the Russian Front, where he narrowly cheated death from fever and frostbite. Frerking his new chief, was tolerant, humane and paternal toward his men.

Frerking's battery was one of three 105mm batteries set back from Omaha, with a fourth 150mm heavy battery sited between Grandcamp-les-Bains to the west and the beach. Their commander Major Werner Pluskat had been playing cards in the headquarters mess at a chateau near Étréham, four miles from the coast. Alerted by the noise of antiaircraft fire he had telephoned division headquarters to find out what was going on. Prevailing gloom over the imminence of invasion was dispelled the night before when a troupe of German girls from a theater entertainment group entertained the mess. The soldiers' concert was canceled with the alert, so the girls found themselves dancing and singing for the officers instead. Several, as Pluskat described "made time" with his officers, and why not? Everyone appreciated that 1944 would be the decision year, young lives were likely to be cut short and casual sex was an expression of life. Frerking, unable to contact Pluskat, suspected he might still be with the ladies.

Pluskat was undecided whether or not to get ready, "nobody at either regiment or headquarters seemed to take the whole thing seriously," he recalled. Eventually his regimental commander got back to him. "It seems that the invasion is beginning," he was laconically informed, "you'd better get all the men to their battle stations right away." Allied intelligence had no knowledge of the existence of his four batteries. At 2:00 A.M. Pluskat reached WN 59, his advance bunker headquarters overlooking the cliffs at the eastern end of Omaha Beach. "Everything was terribly quiet and terribly silent," he remembered, "there was absolutely nothing to be seen." Turning to his ordnance officer Lieutenant Theen, he remarked "just another false alarm."[2]

German soldiers filed into their battle positions with the practiced ease of men who had rehearsed this on countless occasions over the previous two months. Box loads of ammunition were broken open, shells stacked alongside crew-served heavy guns, and machine gun belts made ready. Unteroffizier Ludwig Förster burst into the underground shelter at WN 62 housing men of the 3rd Kompanie 726 Regiment bellowing, "Alarm, the highest alarm level!" Eighteen-year-old Gefreiter Franz Gockel recalled, "we had been turned out so often, we couldn't be bothered." Most of the men in the foul-smelling bunk accommodation turned over and tried to go back to sleep. Förster insisted: "Men, this time it's serious, *Sie Kommen*! They're coming!" That got them up, "the tiredness was gone," Gockel recalled. Machine guns, artillery pieces, and mortars were loaded. "We were soon standing at our posts combat ready."[3]

The nondescript "Beach 313," identified by Allied planners and later code named Omaha Beach, lay in the middle of the German 84th Corps sector, the forward corps of the Seventh Army in Normandy. It was manned by the 352nd Infantry Division, reinforced by the 726th

Regiment, with the 716th Division to its right, covering proposed British landing beaches. To its left was the 709th Infantry Division covering the coastline to Cherbourg, including the earmarked American "Utah Beach." The Seventh Army with fourteen infantry divisions and one panzer division safeguarded nearly one thousand miles of Normandy coastline to the west. By contrast Fifteenth Army's eighteen infantry and two panzer divisions covered the much smaller 340 miles of the Pas-de-Calais east of the Seine, where the invasion, encouraged by Allied deception, was really expected. This anticipation was reflected by its threefold superiority of heavy guns and concrete casemates. Fifteenth Army had 132 heavy guns in its sector of which 93 were in casemates, Seventh Army had 47 heavy guns in Normandy with only 27 under concrete.[4]

General Dietrich Kraiss commanded the Omaha sector and coastline west to the Vire estuary. Omaha was not the focus of his defense effort; that lay farther west, the concentration of force around *Stützpunkt* [base] Vire, in between the Utah and Omaha beaches. The strongpoint was packed with field and coastal artillery alongside five infantry battalions, which aimed to protect the port of Grandcamp-les-Bains and the Vire estuary itself. The German OB (High Command) West was convinced the Allies would need to attack a port—such as Cherbourg, Le Havre, Dieppe, Boulogne, Dunkirk, or Antwerp on the northern coast of France—to reinforce success.

The tactically astute Kraiss, a Russian Front veteran, could tell at a glance that the lethal configuration of geography immensely aided defense at the former tourist beach at the Plage d'Or. It nestled between the high shoulders of two stretches of cliffs, with the Plateau du Calvados east and Pointe et Raz de la Percée west. These sandstone cliff ramparts transitioned to a line of formidably steep grass-covered bluffs in between, 150 to 200 feet above sea level, set back from wide flat beaches. The bluffs were impassable to tanks or trucks. The only exits leading up from the beaches were via five ravines or draws, enabling access to the plateau and road network beyond. The Allies had labeled them as objectives: F-1 in the east through E-3, E-1, D-3 to D-1 in the west. The D-1 exit at Vierville was the only paved road leading up from the beaches, while the most substantial E-3 draw came through Colleville-sur-Mer. The German tactical defense concept was simply to close off all five draws with strongpoints and gun emplacements, with beach obstacles, mines, anti-tank ditches, and two huge concrete anti-tank barriers to prevent access to the road network beyond.

The local French had seen a transformation of their geography since the first arrival of the Germans on the beaches in June 1940. Vierville and Saint-Laurent-sur-Mer had been popular seaside resorts for visiting Parisians. Originally a narrow-guage railway had brought vacationers from the romantic village of Littry near Bayeux, ten miles inland. Even by the nineteenth century there was a grand casino on the beach with its exclusive restaurant and three-story hotel. The Hôtel du Casino became a rest center for German troops, the Château à Thann, the local German *Kommandantur* [headquarters]. Elegant villas alongside the promenade seawall between Saint-Laurent and Vierville formed the incongruous backdrop for Luftwaffe pilots sunning themselves on the beautiful beaches in the summer of 1941. Michel Hardelay remembered "concerts by the regulated music, sea or sunbathing" in Vierville:

> "I saw them laying down on deck chairs, having drinks served on the beach by waiters wearing white gloves, listening to music or news, not hesitating to bring cable all the way from the house to the beach in order to get electricity."

After the failure of the German offensive on Moscow Hardelay observed the first "green mouse" amid bright blue Luftwaffe uniforms, as army engineer officers started to survey the beaches. "The German pilots warned us that an engineering unit was coming to institute a 'few changes.'" Demolition of seaside villas began and accelerated following the fall of Stalingrad in early 1943. The Germans began to construct Widerstandsnest WN 70 on the land just above Hardelay's house, with its sea view. "They allowed us to use the path leading to our garden," at first he recalled, and then by the beginning of 1944, "the access to our garden became completely forbidden, when the Germans started to mine the area above the cliffs."

"Vierville was pretty before the war," Edmond Scelles in the nearby village of Saint-Laurent recalled, "but everything was destroyed." To add insult to injury, "the Germans requisitioned the French to destroy their own houses."[5]

In March 1942 the 716th Infantry Division arrived along this stretch of the Norman coastline, to provide much of the muscle that was to transform the picturesque Plage d'Or into Erwin Rommel's "Devil's Garden" of mined obstacles in the surf, covered by concrete bunkers. Fifteen Widerstandsnest, or strongpoints, were strung like beads between the cliff shoulders either side of the beach. They started at WN 60 to WN 63 in the east, covering access to Colleville. The cluster of emplacements between WN 64 to WN 68 in the center barred access to Saint-Laurent, with another strong group at WN 70 to WN 74 blocking the paved road leading up from Vierville to Route Nationale 814.

Initially the 716th *Bodenstandige,* or static infantry division, was responsible for the fifty-six-mile sector from the Orne estuary at Ouistreham in the east to the Vire estuary at Carentan in the west. These static division soldiers were older men with an average age of thirty-five to forty-five, or very young soldiers. The 716 Division was constantly combed of its young men to field replacements for units badly mauled in Russia. Like all static divisions, whose heavy equipment was essentially horse-drawn, every regiment lost one battalion to make up for losses on the Russian front. They were replaced by wounded convalescents and men with stomach or ear complaints, unsuited for hard campaigning.

Gefreiter Gustav Winter, in the division's 726 Regiment, was ironically an ex–panzer trooper manning a tank turret positioned on top of a concrete box dug into the shifting sand. His *Betonpanzer* or "concrete tank" as he called it, was set back from the beach in the WN 68 strongpoint, covering the ravine, or draw, leading up from the beach to Saint-Laurent.

Winter covered the sea front and beach. "I suffered very badly from frostbite during that first winter in Russia in 1941," he recalled, having ridden in both the French and opening Russian *Blitzkrieg* campaigns. "I lost fingers on each of my hands," in temperatures of -20 °F and -30 °F, "because my gloves were torn, also the tip of my nose, and my toes were damaged as well. . . . I was no longer the handsome panzer boy," he confessed. Although he was transferred to be a training instructor, "it was felt that my frostbite wounds would unsettle the cadets," so now he was on the coast in a panzer environment of sorts. "I learned to use the gun controls with my eight fingers well enough," and unit fitters had adapted the gun controls to include additional grips. "My loader was a Czech-German boy who was not very bright, but very enthusiastic."

By 1944 40% of Pvt. Winter's static infantry division included *Volksdeutch*, ethnic Germans from the occupied territories. Gefreiter Heinrich Severloh at WN 62 had trained with such men, Poles and Upper Silesians, who did not speak a word of German. They were always one order behind, reliant on watching what everybody else did and then imitating the activity. "Despite the frequent comical situations, I found it really tragic," he remembered. "I felt really sorry for the Poles." Nevertheless, "they were regular fellows and good comrades." Winter agreed, "We were a happy crew," he reminisced, "Just the two of us."[6]

Serving alongside the old were the very young. Hitler's decision not to send the youngest soldiers to Russia after the debacle at Stalingrad meant that many seventeen-to-eighteen-year-old soldiers conscripted in the 1925 conscript waves were sent to France. Hans Selbach and Franz Gockel ended up in WN 62, just north of Colleville. Selbach came in

July and Gockel in October 1943, after just seven weeks recruit training. Gockel's mother had written to him just before Christmas:

> "You are so young and have only lived with your parents and have no idea of the danger threatening young men. Retain what you have learned."

She was thankful he was at least in France. "God protect you," she concluded.[7]

In March 1944, Rommel, the commander OB west moved General Dietrich Kraiss's 352 Infantry Division forward from Saint-Lô to take over part of the 716 Division sector. Rommel knew the Normandy countryside well, having campaigned through it with his 7th Panzer Division advancing on Cherbourg in June 1940. The static division area of responsibility shifted eastward, toward the coastal area around Caen. Two battalions of Infantry Regiment 726 were retained in their present positions along the Omaha sector under 352's command. They were reinforced with two battalions from the new division's Regiment 916. Sited to their west were 914 Regiment and 915 Regiment, which became the 84 Corps reserve under Oberstleutnant Meyer, positioned inland. This was a substantial size quick reaction force, which included the division's contingent of armored self-propelled assault guns. The reinforcement was a threefold increase of strength along Omaha Beach and was completely missed by Allied intelligence. Kraiss had prepared his division for likely operations in Russia. Such was the intensity of training imposed on his fledgling division that its men were convinced they were earmarked for the Russian Front that summer.

The new arrival was of entirely different character and lineage to the unit it replaced. The 352nd Division was the most powerful infantry unit in Normandy. The newly constituted division had been formed from the torso of the 321st Division, burned out in the Dnieper and Desna winter battles of early 1943. "Torso" because the core of the headquarters, support, and artillery units had remained intact, reinforced by survivors from the mauled 268 Infantry Division and Grenadier Regiment 546. These were veteran soldiers. Unlike static units, the 352nd was equipped with modern German-produced 105mm and 150mm artillery pieces as well as twenty-eight *Stürmgeschütz III* and *Marder* self-propelled assault guns. Although most of the division's infantry were freshly conscripted Germans, 20% of its strength was battle hardened. Unlike the youngsters among the 726 Regiment personnel and 8% ethnic Germans and an Ost (Russian recruited battalion), the new unit was acknowledged *Ostharte*, tough enough to serve in the East. At its core were experienced *Russland Kämpfer* [Russian fighters] from the old *Obergefreiter* [senior lance corporal] who knew how to handle an MG 42, cook a chicken, and avoid undue risks to experienced thirty-five-year-old battalion commanders. This brought a different quality of combat cohesion to the Omaha sector. The 352nd Division retained a hint of its *Friedensheer* [peacetime] character, with former regular army men among its senior NCOs. It had recruited from the Niedersachsen area, with men known to be calm, dependable, and even a little *stur*, or stubborn in a crisis. The division was at full strength with 12,734 men, even though 505 of its officers were new and inexperienced.

Patrols were already out after midnight, covering the beach and bluffs. Gefreiter Heinz Bongard standing watch at WN 60, set above the cliff at the easternmost point of the beach, could see the entire four mile stretch of Omaha Beach by day. By night, with a full moon reflecting on the water, and with the tide in, he could see the dark outline of the curvature of the bluffs merging into shadow toward Pointe et Raz de la Percée, just beyond Vierville. Clusters of cascading flares, searchlights, and distant flashes could be seen in that direction.

On the other side of the F-1 draw Bongard could pick out the shadowy outline of the WN 61 emplacement. Inside the bunker were a high-velocity 88mm anti-tank gun and 50mm gun. This, with two 75mm guns, two more in WN 62 beyond, with a pair of 50mm guns represented a formidable concentration of flat-fire trajectory weapons reaching out into the middle of Omaha Beach. They intersected with another powerful 88mm and two 75mm guns shooting out toward them from the cluster of strongpoints at WN 71 to 73 at Vierville on the far western side of the beach. The two cliff-high shoulders of the beach had clusters of high-velocity anti-tank and powerful field guns that intersected in the middle of the beach, forming a perfectly contained killing area in between.

Patrols generally departed from WN 62, which was the most formidable bastion to the east of the beach. "When we walked the patrols," remembered *Gefreiter* [corporal] Hans Selbach:

"We sometimes had to go the whole three and a half miles to Vierville. At low tide they went along the forward edge of the beach, and at high tide along the bluffs."

The route was a tour of the Omaha defenses between Colleville, Saint-Laurent, and Vierville, along restricted pathways hemmed in by minefields. Each patrol of four men was led by an NCO. On this evening the patrols heard the unremitting drone of bombers passing overhead, mainly to the west. By day there were telltale condensation trails etched across the sky from high-flying reconnaissance aircraft. "The reconnaissance flights came nearly every day, also at low level to take photographs of our strongpoints," Selbach remembered. "They were better informed than us." Soldiers based at WN 62 followed an exacting routine of two watches each night and one or two long beach patrols every week, interspersed with digging and practice-drill alarms that came with ever increasing frequency.[8]

Patrols had to be alert. Six weeks before seven naval artillery spotters had disappeared into thin air, with all their radios and technical equipment, from the isolated villa where they were stationed on the beach. Two of these *Kriegsmarine* [Navy] gunners often passed WN 62 in the mornings to pick up milk and rations. It was not until their Port-en-Bessin headquarters asked for checks that realization dawned that something was amiss. It was assumed they had been spirited away by Allied commandos. There had been incidents on the beach in September 1942. An alert had been followed by a brief firefight and bodies on the beach. Albert André, one of the Saint-Laurent locals saw the prisoners taken on the beach. "The Germans had a black dog that woke them up," he recalled. "They had him decorated with an Iron Cross."

The patrol route followed a narrow track to WN 66, which overlooked the ravine leading up to Saint-Laurent, blocked by a massive concrete wall, with a narrow man-sized chicane. They then made their way back across the bluffs. Each patrol leg was a check of the defenses and sticking carefully to the route was paramount because of mines. Oberschütze Bruno Plota, a mortar man from WN 62 had previously taken two watch dogs on patrol, during which Treff, a privately owned dog, went off route and was torn apart by a mine explosion, which set off alarms along the entire beach. The other dog, Raudi, a Wehrmacht hound and Plota's great favorite, panicked and ran off, only to be nearly cut in half by another mine blast. Plota had to bind the whimpering Raudi to a wooden post so that Lieutenant Claus, his superior officer, could come up and shoot the dog and put it out of its misery. It was a botched affair, which made the tragedy worse. Despite a shot to the head, the dog turned aggressive in its death throes and pulled on the line, barking fiercely, raising fears of yet another mine explosion. Claus's pistol jammed, and he had to reload again before finally dispatching the dog. The bloodied remains among the mines had to wait for the incoming tide before nature could clear up the mess. It was a salutary reminder of the effectiveness of the obstacle belt.

Soldiers were well aware of the imminence of invasion. "We had no doubt the English and the Americans would make their move into Europe," Gefreiter Heinrich Severloh remembered. "But everyone was hoping it would be somewhere else, not where we were." Soldiers rarely reflected on the war, they were more concerned about when and where they might eat or sleep. "The war seemed far away in Normandy," Severloh remembered. Tension was, however, palpably rising. Just three days before, 84 Corps had declared invasion was "imminent," then on June 4 soldiers were told the invasion would come inside twenty-four hours. The Germans had no idea that General Eisenhower, the supreme allied commander, had postponed the date for twenty-four hours due to inclement weather. The 352nd Division was then informed it could stand down for a day to relieve pressure, almost immediately followed by a contradictory message that a landing was imminent. Skepticism was now universal; the weather was stormy. In any case it was generally accepted that the allies had to land near a port.[9]

Patrols moving beyond WN 62 had to traverse an isolated 830-yard stretch of undefended tortuous bluff line, with no emplacements, marked only by a single coil of barbed wire. When they reached WN 64 they passed a churned-up area that was like a huge building site. WN 64 was still at its foundation stage, box outlines marked by wooden shuttering and steel rods, prepared to receive poured concrete. Some 486 workers were milling about this site most days, primarily paid Moroccan labor alongside locally pressed Frenchmen. A single 75mm gun stood in an open emplacement, waiting to be installed. The 50mm gun bunker at WN 65 beyond had only been completed at the end of April. The ground about was scored by construction works. The defenses guarding the E-1 ravine in Allied plans leading up to Colleville were half complete. Emplacements shielding Saint-Laurent farther along at WN 66 and WN 68 were still being worked upon. WN 66 had only been started in April and the 50mm gun earmarked for WN 68 was in an open emplacement. Incomplete installations meant emplacements at WN 67 and 65 could not be mutually supported.

Sixteen-year-old Albert André had been pressed the afternoon of June 5 to work on WN 66. He remembered the casemate lacked a roof, gun, and gun turret, "but it had already been camouflaged to look like a passable imitation of a beach villa." Its gun turret was loaded on the back of a French wood-burning gas truck that was stuck fast in a pothole. Two other pressed French locals were trying to push it out, but "were hardly making very strenuous efforts." A huge concrete anti-tank wall blocked the Les Moulins D-3 draw where he was working. One of the two emplacements overlooking it was still encased in wooden shuttering, its concrete not yet poured. The 50mm gun was in an open pit mounted on a turntable, protected only by its steel gun shield, while another anti-tank gun and two mortars nearby were in open emplacements. At about 3:00 P.M. two American Lightning twin-fuselage fighter aircraft strafed the beach, stopping Germans planting anti-invasion stakes in the sand and causing all construction work to close down. *"Tommy kommt,"* one of the Polish ethnic German NCOs told André. Everyone had the impression something was about to happen. The demoralized Germans sent all the pressed labor home. This central area under construction, between the two primary strongpoint clusters east and west of Omaha Beach, was its Achilles' heel. It meant eight of twenty-five anti-tank or field guns were still exposed in the open, which was 44% of the emplacements between Colleville in the east and Saint-Laurent in the center. WN 66 never got its tank turret.[10]

Patrols were wary of the local French, although in the 352nd Division area there was little interference from them prior to the invasion. "The Normans were people like us," Franz Gockel appreciated shortly after arriving in 1943. "Reserved, but correct . . . Do not treat them like overwhelming victors, we were advised."

Kraiss had ordered his men to be proper and polite at all times in their dealings with the locals. This was not so difficult. The majority of his young grenadiers were from farming areas in Germany and had much in common with the Norman farmers. *Obergefreiter* [senior lance corporal] Josef Brass, who served with 321 Pioneer battalion at Le Touquet south of Calais remembered, "Our units were never attacked by the *Maquis* [Resistance] because we were a combat unit with machine guns and support weapons." They may have been disliked, but, "for the most part," Brass commented, "the French people were amiable toward us." Maquis victims tended to be "usually older men of supply and garrison units" and others "foolish enough to venture down dark lonely roads to get robbed and killed."[11]

Désiré Lemière was the local postman and a member of the *Alliance* French resistance group. He daily bicycled through the villages of Saint-Laurent and Colleville observing German routine, which was passed on to London. One of the "watering holes" for German patrols from WN 62 and off-duty personnel was the Pommier family's grocery store and café on the Rue Principale, the main road through Colleville. The Café Violard in the vicinity of the church served wine, coffee, and beer from the small courtyard adjoining the grocery. It was a favorite haunt for soldiers from the 3rd and 4th companies of Grenadier Regiment 726, who garrisoned the WN cluster on the east side of Omaha Beach. This was also where one met the local girls. Just one month before, Lemière had been arrested by the Gestapo, having been betrayed by local collaborators. Three of his associates, another postman from Trévières village to the south, and the chief of the Saint-Laurent post office were arrested and executed. Désiré Lemière was languishing in Caen prison. Brutally interrogated by the Gestapo most days, he was returned to prison with clothing splattered with fresh blood. "Don't worry," he had written on a piece of sugar wrapping smuggled out to his family, "I'll manage to come back, don't be worried." They never saw him again. He had barely twenty-four hours to live.[12]

Pleasant recreation for Germans in Colleville village or around the Casino in Vierville was an irritating confusion of curfews and restrictions for the local French inhabitants. Since October 1941 a coastal band varying in width from fifteen to twenty kilometers had been declared out of bounds to all except permanent residents. "Because of the curfew, we were not allowed to go to the beach," remembered Edmond Scelles, living at Saint-Laurent-sur-Mer, "that was closed. . . . The limit was the Saint-Laurent post office, we were not to go any farther." The area by the massive concrete anti-tank wall blocking the reentrant leading up from the beach was especially sensitive. "We could not go farther down," he recalled:

> "It was forbidden and it was guarded. The whole sea front was mined and the whole beach covered with stakes and mines all around them."

A pass was required to enter the area, "because the Germans were very much afraid of sabotage." There were also "a lot of blockhouses that were not finished." Similar damaging restrictions were visited on the inhabitants of Vierville-sur-Mer. Michel Hardelay remembered that the paved road leading up the draw from the beach was "closed off with an anti-tank wall and a chicane leaving a passage of seventy-five centimeters." The blockhouse for the 88mm gun was built on the site of the demolished hotel and beaches' general store, and "most of the façade on the sea side was kept intact as camouflage." The wonderful Plage d'Or, a great favorite with the Parisian tourists, was resculpted in front of their eyes. Hardelay noticed:

> "A tamaris hedge above the edge of the road was preciously kept intact on the sea side, because it was blocking out the view of the beach, the anti-tank wall, and merged with the blockhouse doorway."

The remodeling was done with lethal intent, to deceive naval observation off the coast. Hardelay was particularly embittered by having to demolish his own house, built by his parents, alongside other pressed locals. Virtually the entire regional tourist and local infrastructure was destroyed along this part of the coast to provide unobscured fields of fire. Fifty-three houses were demolished or partly destroyed in the Omaha bay alone. "There was just one house that stayed up in Saint-Laurent," Edmond Scelles remembered. "Next to the beach." It was frustrating to see that those that survived were for the benefit of the Germans. Hardelay recalled the *Rinascente* house on top of the Vierville cliff was kept as a U-boat radio-relay station. "A casino hotel that was accommodating soldiers coming for rest breaks and was also used as a relay for patrols" was left standing, he remembered. Life fundamentally changed for the inhabitants of the three village communities set inland from Omaha Beach. Labor was requisitioned at will, German troops billeted in their homes, and their beautiful Plage d'Or fenced off as a "forbidden zone." Michel Hardely described the effect:

> "Because we were living in the 'forbidden zone' by the shore, each house had to show on the inside of the front door a piece of paper stipulating how many people were living in the house and their names, certified by the German authority, and everybody had to have an *Ausweis* [identity card] to prove that they were living in the forbidden zone.[13]

Franz Gockel at WN 62 could, on the contrary, write to his mother: "I feel like God here in France. Every day I see the sea." he enthused, and was living in "a lovely region." Even his washing was done for him, accommodated by a very friendly family with "a clean room that was cosily furnished." When the underground shelter was completed at WN 62 he had to move inside and occupy a bunk bed. There was no electricity, "only the flickering light of candles, and the weak glow from oil lamps that smelled bad." Like all soldiers, they made themselves comfortable. They wrote letters in the evening and busied themselves with personal administration while an old wind-up gramophone played scratchy music from one of the triple bunk beds in the background: *"If you once gave your heart away"* and *"When the white lilies bloom."* "We had all heard these records more than a hundred times," Gockel remembered, "perhaps more."[14]

Gefreiter Kurt Keller based inland with the 915 Regiment's counterattack reserve described France as a "land flowing with milk and honey," echoing the universal *Landser* [equivalent of British "Tommy"] view that you "lived like God in France." Gefreiter Gustav Winter, manning the "concrete panzer" at WN 68 covering Saint-Laurent, couldn't believe his luck after what he'd endured in Russia and claimed, "apart from the uncertainty, we in the infantry had a comfortable life before the invasion came." He felt the relationship with the French was "generally friendly."

> "The local French people were not supposed to come close to the bunkers, but in reality they would come and trade with us, offering food."

Cigarettes, bootlaces, and lamp oil were exchanged for bread, milk, cider, eggs, and "even fresh meat, which was unavailable to Wehrmacht lower ranks." Soldiers focused on food, sex, and sleep, often in that order. "We would say fill your belly on French ham and cider," Winter remembered, "because tomorrow you may be transferred to the East, where there is only biscuits and snow to eat." The French, he observed, "would complain bitterly about the allied bombing," which was hitting towns and villages along the transport network. "Many of us had lost relatives in the city bombing in Germany, so we sympathized."

Gefreiter Heinrich Severloh, the batman to his battery commander at WN 62, had a close relationship with the Legrand family, with whom they were billeted in Houtteville. "I believe I can say that I was, despite my German uniform, genuinely well liked." He assessed that the relationship with the French "could be described as good." And observed, "in many parts of daily life," such as working farmland, "there was a very positive willingness to cooperate on both sides." Many French farmers were prisoners of war in Germany, so "many German soldiers, with their horses, were ordered to help with the cultivation of the fields and other work on the properties."[15]

For young soldiers "the subject of French women was the number one talking point." admitted seventeen-year-old Franz Gockel. They were especially curious "to hear about experiences" from older soldiers. Madame Renard, who took in his washing, was a very respectable lady with two vivacious daughters. Gockel was attracted to the seventeen-year-old daughter of the dairy farmer that supplied WN 62 with its daily milk. The pretty Yvonne "was much courted." Gockel's age conferred certain advantages. When a thirty-five-year old Unteroffizier complained "you always get butter, why don't I?" Gockel could respond because "you are at least fifteen years too old!" Newly arrived seventeen-year-old Wehrmacht youngsters were completely out of their depth with the young women. Lieutenant Hermann Claus, Gockel's highly popular commander, made the most of his young life. Having been wounded in Russia, he had seen much death. "He was very young, blond, handsome, and spoke French," and the women found him very attractive. One of Gockel's seventeen-year-old friends was shocked when he had to bring firewood for his superior's stove and found him shamelessly sitting with his girlfriend, both naked, on the bed. Gockel fondly remembered "his French cleaning woman, standing on the balcony and laughing, waving a pair of lace panties that had been left behind." "For all Landsers," Gockel recalled, "France was the promised land, but the loose morals between the occupiers and French women was much talked about." Older soldiers felt responsible for the youngsters and offered sage advice about the dangers of sexually transmitted diseases, and Gockel remembered "shocking examples of VD treatments were shown to us."[16]

Older soldiers did not necessarily follow their own advice, because the official established Wehrmacht brothel at Bayeux beckoned both the curious and reckless. Brothels were required by regulation to be "hotel like" in their atmosphere, for young officers, with dining facilities populated by "ladies of higher 'quality'." Landsers were segregated by rank and status. A medical *Feldwebel* [sergeant] issued a pass following an embarrassing examination to confirm a clean bill of health. The pass identified a specific brothel by name, number, and location, and contained a section where the female partner was obliged to sign her name, all in the interest of sanitizing any source of infection. Equipped with an official condom and a small spray of disinfectant the Landser could advance with the army and Führer's approval, but not until his pass was checked by the unsympathetic *Kettehunde* [chain-dog], German military policeman at the door. (The nickname originated from the chain gorget that military police wore around the neck.)

The Wehrmacht took a dim view of any man infected with venereal disease, regarded as a self-inflicted injury, which could earn a transfer to the Eastern Front, or at worse to a penal battalion. Reckless sexual behavior did have military consequences for the WN strongpoints securing Omaha Beach. Lieutenant Claus, the commander of WN 62, was infected in May and ended up in Caen hospital, as also did the deputy commander of WN 60, *Oberfeldwebel* [master sergeant] Ludwig Pie (another blond favorite with the ladies, who had ironically infected Claus's sexual partner). Obergefreiter Siegfried Kuska, the 50mm gunner at WN 62, got into trouble after being overattentive to the lady who provided the daily milk and butter, facing serious consequences when she officially complained. He could have been transferred, but was saved when the charge was dropped after the woman developed acute appendicitis and unexpectedly died. Women could be dangerous.

Gefreiter Kurt Keller with 915 Regiment disapproved of the loose morals of his *Spiess* or company sergeant major, who had a penchant for inviting girls down from Caen. "This life was very comfortable," he commented, "but not my thing." Loose women were not for him; he was wedded to the Führer. "I had volunteered to be a soldier because of my ideological commitment." he insisted, "and had to fight heroically as my supreme leader expected." Before the invasion, this appeared a safer option. Although the famed Atlantic Wall had not measured up to the expectations presented by the newsreels, when he was required to work on beach obstacles, he did subscribe to the Führer's slogan, "where the German soldier stands, nobody gets in!" He was convinced the coming invasion would be repelled. "What we lacked in matériel we made up for in spirit," he recalled. "My confidence in victory was limitless."[17]

The Norman French had long come to regard the German army billeted on them at the coast as a shadow of the mechanized *Blitzkrieg* warriors of 1940. "The Germans did not have any equipment," remembered Edmond Scelles in Saint-Laurent, "they used to travel on their bikes." Commanders often rode up to visit companies on horseback. Scelles had forty German soldiers billeted at his farm. He remembered one of them crying on one occasion, and asked the others "what's up with your friend?" "Big disaster" was the response, "Russia." Two or three young men were quite often abruptly selected for transfer as reinforcements to the Eastern Front. Jeanette Legallois remembered German soldiers coming to her parents' farm in Sully, southeast of Omaha Beach in 1944:

> "There were many very young soldiers among them. They were well equipped and appeared smart. They had boyish faces, and their slung rifles trailed along the ground, because they were so short. If they wore helmets, they could hardly see from under them."

The heroic symbolism of victory in 1940 made the Wehrmacht feel they were the lords of Europe. They no longer looked the part.[18]

"Where the German Soldier Stands Nobody Gets In!"
3:00 A.M. to 4:30 A.M.

T he unfinished construction works at the center of Omaha Beach were a constant reminder for security patrols that preparations for the invasion were not as complete as the official propaganda would have them believe. *Invasionsangst*, or so-called "Invasion Anxiety," was a tangible phenomenon among the troops. Gefreiter Gustav Winter's concrete panzer position at WN 68 was set amid the unfinished construction zone. He recalled some of the other men manning bunkers "thought about the invasion too much and become weighed down with the thought." Not only that, "we were isolated there on that damn plateau of dunes" with little to do except scan a featureless dark sea, "not knowing what devilish things might appear out there." Tension was cumulative. "The waiting was very unnerving," claimed Unteroffizier Henrik Naube at WN 73 to his left. How the allies might land raised:

". . . questions that plagued us with no answers. And every day, the sea in front of our Widerstandsnest looked exactly the same, giving us no clues at all."

One soldier with the 352 Pioneer [Engineer] Battalion was shot on April 18 after injuring other soldiers in an allegedly self-inflicted detonator explosion.[19]

Newly arrived Lieutenant Hans Heinz, a battalion ordnance officer with Regiment 916 and a Stalingrad survivor, was dismayed at his first sight of the Atlantic Wall. "At first we could not find it," he recalled during an inspection visit of the Omaha coastal sector with his commander. "We went right over the wire without even tearing our trousers." They came across a brash Landser from the 726 Regiment, who had been there since 1940. "If the Tommies decide to invade and disturb our holy peace," he arrogantly remarked, "we will roll out our gun and teach them how to be scared." The veteran Heinz was unimpressed, like his commander. "We found no cheer or solace in this remark," he remembered. There was so much to do.

Invasionsangst was not just a feature of the front. The main talking points back home in the Reich was the anticipated invasion and the effects of the Allied air "terror bombing" offensive. Top secret SS and SD situation reports briefed weekly to Himmler and the top Nazi hierarchy in May mention the flurry of invasion reporting in the German press, labeled "*Invasionitus*." Field Marshal Erwin Rommel's publicized visits to the Atlantic Wall inspired public confidence; his Afrika Korps desert exploits had received a lot of public attention in German newsreels. Reports of ships massing in southern England had inspired rumors that the invasion had already started near Calais. There were also concerns in Hamburg that North Sea coast landings could encircle the city, or speculation that the invasion was simply a massive bluff. Others thought the Allies would never allow the Soviets to win the war alone. "Something must happen soon" was the prevailing sentiment reported in mid May, "as we cannot continue like this." Many believed the forthcoming invasion would result in a severe Allied reversal, and was welcomed, because the war would then decisively turn in Germany's favor.

Hitler's minister for propaganda, Joseph Goebbels, had even started to believe his own broadcasts. "When I looked at Atlantic Wall photographs," he had written in his diary the year before, "I had the feeling that we were sitting inside an absolutely secure fortress in Europe." Field Marshal Gerd von Rundstedt, the supreme commander west, cynically labeled it the "Propaganda Wall." German soldiers were tense but broadly confident about the likely outcome of an invasion. One *Hauptmann* [captain] with a transport unit at Nancy wrote home that he was "a little nervous where they might bite," but claimed the Allies "sing like frogs, they have a loud croak, but won't jump into the water." The invasion in any case would trigger the release of the much vaunted high-tech "revenge weapons." An Oberleutnant [lieutenant] standing by with the V2 flying bombs at Peenemünde asked, "Are the Gentlemen coming or not, and where?" because his view was that "invasion and revenge will follow on from each other." He felt they ought to be already bombarding the Allied ports and assembly areas in England with the secret weapons. Another NCO at a Lyon fighter base wrote home that "our Landser on the Channel and Mediterranean do not fight with beans and water pistols," he cockily claimed, because "the jump onto the European mainland for the Tommies and Yanks is going to be a lot more serious than parading in front of their General Eisenhower." Even so, a corporal in the 90th Panzergrenadier Division admitted "this waiting and hoping, guessing and wishing is awful," because, "our nerves are steadily going kaput with it all." In June 1944 half of 112 German POWs questioned at a camp in the United States believed Germany would emerge victorious in this war. Worst of all, people thought, would be if nothing happened at all and the invasion did not come.[20]

Lieutenant Heinz remembered when his men rescued a German reconnaissance pilot, who had nursed his flak-crippled aircraft across the Channel, only to crash in their sector. When they hauled the pilot out he had said, "Over there [England], the harbors are full of ships, ship on ship. . . . We thought the pilot must be in shock, because then, must—*Ja*—Hermann [Goering] come with his Luftwaffe, because he would never get a better target." But nothing happened. "Not a single plane came over, not on this day, and not during the following day."

"Terror bombing" at home, in the Reich, was a real concern. Franz Gockel, like many of the men in WN 62, had seen it close at hand.

His father, a roof repairer, had fixed damage in Dortmund from nearby Hamm-Rhynern, where they lived. His period with the RAD [*Reichsarbeitsdienst*, the German Labor Service], which had come before Wehrmacht conscription, was spent clearing rubble from the devastated streets of Dortmund. He had also participated in the cleanup after the Möhne dambuster raid of May 1943, when over a thousand Germans and foreign workers had been swept away by the flood. Recovering bodies from beneath the crust of dried mud had "been a shock for us," he recalled, the priest who had baptized him as a child had also perished.

Tension had risen in Germany on May 13 after an official *Wehrmacht Bericht* [armed forces report] suggested increasing air attacks were an indicator that the invasion was imminent. Secret SS reports noted "the number of women who lose their nerve at the sound of an air raid alert is constantly growing." Women were going "crazy," trying to immediately leave factories and go home to look after children, with "tears in their eyes" when told to remain. Soldiers dreaded receiving official police or town hall letters because they invariably contained bad news. The absence of home mail for a long period often meant a soldier's family had been killed and no bodies recovered or identified. "Bomber leave" for such compassionate cases was halted on April 29 after the increased tension on the coast. *Soldatenheim* [soldier's homes] were set up in most localities to assist in the location process, somewhere to stay and rest. More often than not, soldiers lost leave time waiting for trains that never came, or ended up being requisitioned by the local military to clear up bomb debris after raids. "I had lost several relatives in the daylight and night bombing of Berlin," Gustav Winter at WN 68 remembered. "So I was angry about this, yes, I was very bitter. Many of my comrades felt the same way."[21]

Soldiers filing into their bunkers and emplacements along Omaha Beach that night were apprehensive, but felt everything was still in play. The state of the defenses on the *Plage d'Or* in particular suggested that despite the unfinished construction in the center, they were capable of stopping a landing in its tracks. They were confident in their commanders. Unteroffizier Henrik Naube, perched on the cliff top at the westernmost shoulder of WN 73 overlooking the Vierville exit recalled "the concept of the Allies actually invading Germany seemed unimaginable at the time, it must be said." At the opposite end of the beach at the eastern cliff shoulder at WN 60 Franz Wilden was "full of confidence that with an invasion the Führer would activate the Luftwaffe and Navy." They had no concept of what the Allies would be able to throw at them.[22]

Young Franz Gockel in WN 62, like all German schoolboys, had followed the progress of the Blitzkrieg through Poland, France, and Russia by proudly sticking colored pins on newspaper maps plastered onto bedroom walls. His generation, the newly arrived conscript waves of 1925, were the first to have spent their school years tutored by National Socialism. Gockel had seen the dark side of the regime before he joined. Anton, a well-liked Polish laborer in the village, had been publicly hanged for consorting with a German girl, who then was forced to have an abortion. Gefreiter Kurt Keller with the *Fusilier* [reconnaissance] Battalion of Regiment 915 in reserve, seven and a half miles inland, was confident they would throw any invader back into the sea. Committed like many of his contemporaries to the Fuhrer's "Thousand Year Reich," he was determined to "fight to the last for the honor of Germany and for our freedom not to become the slave of foreign rulers." Keller's folk hero for joining was the courageous Landser who had fought to the death against impossible odds at Stalingrad. He shook his brother's hand through the railway carriage when he departed leave in Germany and assured him "they were so strong in Normandy that no English would be able to land."

Gustav Winter at WN 68 was equally convinced of the strength of their cause, bitterly complaining about "Americans [who] had so much space in their prairies and mountains." The British "had India and all those places in Africa," and yet they wanted "to take France from us, and stop us fighting the Reds." Only two years ago the Wehrmacht held from Brittany in the west to the Caucasus Mountains in the east, from the North Cape of Norway to North Africa in the south. This area was shrinking into southern Europe, and the Russians were moving west, but still a long way from Germany, from the simple Landser's perspective. Gefreiter Stefan Hinevez with the 709th Division, manning a "Tobruk" concrete shelter west of Omaha, at Utah Beach on the other side of the Vire estuary believed:

> "The loss of France would be a dreadful blow if it happened, because it would give the western Allies a platform to attack German soil in partnership with the Bolsheviks in the East."[23]

There was every reason to believe that the high-tech "revenge weapons" being developed would give the Allies a bloody nose. No amphibious invasion going in either direction across the English Channel had succeeded since 1066, including the German preparations in 1940.

Success in the coming battle was as much dependent on tactics as it was on their resilience. There were about 450 soldiers in the fifteen strongpoints beaded along the waterline: three 726 Regiment infantry companies and a heavy weapons company. Just under a mile inland were two more companies from 916 Regiment around Saint-Laurent and Colleville-sur-Mer, and another two at Formigny and Surrain, two miles inland from the same regiment. Both regiments were heavy weapons companies, with infantry and anti-tank guns forward on the beach. All this represented about 800 to 1,000 troops either on or just set back from the waterline. There was a tank destroyer unit of twenty-eight self-propelled assault guns grouped with 915 Regiment's two infantry battalions about seven miles inland, with the division's Pioneer Battalion located nearby on standby.

The tactical dilemma was whether to fight the main battle on the beach, as proposed by Rommel, or with reserves from farther inland. As Commander Army Group B (OB West), he was responsible for the German defense of the Atlantic Wall. It was at his direction that the 352nd Division was moved closer to the coast and during subsequent inspections he pushed subordinate commanders into deploying ever more assets to cover the waterline. Not only was he familiar with this part of Normandy, having advanced through it at the head of the 7th Panzer Division in 1940, he was also influenced by what he had seen in North Africa and Italy. Allied air superiority and naval gunfire would not enable traditional Eastern Front counter-strokes to be conducted with impunity against Allied units that had landed in strength.

On January 29 Rommel visited WN 62 and immediately spotted the parallels with the Allied landing beach at Salerno in Italy. Gazing along the beach between Colleville and Vierville he declared, "this bay must be fortified as quickly as possible against an attempted invasion by the Allies." He was testy about the two Czech 76.5mm field guns he saw standing in the open on concrete platforms beneath camouflage net poles. "You have been here for three years," he asked the uncomfortable local company commander, Hauptmann Ottermeier, "and what have you achieved?" Gefreiter Franz Gockel remembered that sixty paid Morrocan laborers turned up with locally pressed labor and built two new emplacements, upper and lower concrete casemates for the two 76.5mm guns in six weeks. Unteroffizier Henrik Naube at WN 73 farther along remembered Rommel as "a very energetic and active man; he walked very briskly and spoke rapidly." He fired off detailed questions at their officer "about the ammunition we had in the post; how old the weapons were," and so on. Rommel exuded impatient energy, "he was quite a short man," Naube recalled, "but with a powerful presence." He came back to check that the work had been done at the beginning of May. He greeted his old friend Oberstleutnant Ernst Goth, the commander of Regiment 916, shortly after it had taken over the Omaha sector. "Goth," he announced, calling him over, "they're going to come here, by you!"[24]

Rommel had not served in Russia, so his revisionist view of fighting the main battle on the waterline was viewed askance by veterans who believed their experience related to the decisive theater of the war. The real war, they felt, was waged against the Russians, and company commanders were ill at ease with Rommel's enthusiasm for a strongpoint defense of the water's edge. The concept had never worked in Russia, because they had always been too far apart. In the East the forward zone of defense acted as a "shock absorber" to break up the coherence of attacks, before reaching the main defense zone, where the decisive battle was waged. Strong forces were retained in the rear combat zone, to unexpectedly hit the enemy's flanks or rear once his momentum had been dissipated on the main position. The *bocage*, or hedgerow countryside inland of Omaha, was difficult to maneuver and attack across, being more suited to defense.

Rommel argued the obstacle belt in the surf covered by beach strongpoints was the main defense line. Allied air and naval gunfire superiority, not felt in the dispersed open spaces of Russia, made counterattacks questionable under such conditions. The widest fields of fire were sought on the beaches, even at the expense of camouflage and concealment. Positions were to be held, even if overrun and then restored, which was the purpose of the companies deployed at Colleville and Saint-Laurent, just under a mile inland, and the other two companies in depth, two miles from the water's edge. Company commanders wanted to occupy reverse slope positions to mask themselves from direct naval gunfire. Rommel insisted on concentrating firepower forward on the obstacle belt in the surf. Oberstleutnant Ziegelmann, General Kraiss's chief of staff, "was reproached" by Rommel during his last May visit, "because I did not bring the reserves close enough to the coast. . . . He wished every soldier to be able to concentrate his fire on the water." Both Kraiss and his Corps Commander Erich Marcks, who had fought in Russia, had reservations about this tactical concept, and as Ziegelmann remembered, "also had the opinion that we must find a compromise solution."

Veteran Landsers were also uneasy. Obergefreiter Peter Lützen had fought to within eighty kilometers of Moscow in 1941 and arrived at WN 62 in 1943. Just before Hauptmann Ottermeier, the highly decorated World War I veteran commander of WN 62, was retired a week before, he asked the experienced Russian veteran: "Truly Lützen, what do you think about our Atlantic Wall?" "The heavy weapons should be deployed to the rear, and not forward like everywhere here," the soldier responded. "*Ja*," the Captain agreed, "that's what it was like in the First World War too, the heavy weapons were always behind." Lieutenant Heinz with Regiment 916 had a similar conversation with one of the strongpoint veteran Feldwebels. He was with a visiting major from the 84 Corps staff, coordinating ammunition resupply. At most of the emplacements he was "mostly getting the correct if uninspired answers," until one of the Feldwebels gave an unexpectedly frank assessment:

> "Herr Major, we have enough ammunition to stop the first, second, third, fourth, and maybe even fifth wave of Tommies. But after that they're going to kick the door in on top of us and then all is lost!"

The bewildered supply officer stepped back and assured the Feldwebel that he would get his ammunition, but Heinz later reflected "again and again in the days that would come I would hear those words. I can still hear him to this day."[25]

Rommel had created a similar "Devil's Garden" of obstacles that he had established across his desert front at El Alamein in the autumn of 1942. As good as the tactic was, such lines could be overwhelmed by brute force. Only about 20% of the 352 Division soldiers had ever experienced such awesome firepower.

Morale in the devastated coastal battery position at Pointe du Hoc, covering Grandcamp port and the Plage d'Or was not good. It and the batteries at Maisy four and a half miles west, and Longues, eight miles east, could fire farthest into the Channel. Since building work began in November 1942 and the installation of six French World War I vintage Grand Puissance 155mm guns, Pointe du Hoc had not been a good place to serve. The first hit-and-run raid by a fighter-bomber had come at the end of April 1943. In the autumn of 1943,Lieutenant Ebeling, a revered and much loved battery commander was transferred to the Russian front for deciding not to engage three small British warships. They appeared off the coast of Colleville, at the extreme eastern edge of his range. When admonished by his irate battalion commander for not opening fire Ebeling had responded, without suitable reverence, that "I can't hit sparrows with these guns." This was a factor of army fire control, inferior to the naval battery at Longues, and less suitable for engaging sea targets. Unteroffizier Emil Kaufmann, a gunner on the site recalled they "were in tears" when Eberling left. The battery assistant chief, Oberleutnant Brotkorb, took over.

The severe winter of 1943–44 on the windswept promontory that year was decidedly uncomfortable. All formations in France were ruthlessly combed for personnel to reinforce units in Russia and the authorized battery strength of 146 shrunk to about 85 men by the early summer of 1944. Men were replaced by older reservists or wounded convalescents, unsuitable for the harsh conditions in Russia. "Toward the end of 1943 increasingly older soldiers came to the strongpoint," now labeled WN 75, Kaufmann recalled, "up to 50-year-olds." Morale sank because "they thought about their families at home and were always very homesick." The French resistance sector chief for Grandcamp nearby also recognized "a different caliber of troops" began to arrive. They were fearful, "terrorized," confiding to the French locals "we're going to be chopped up."[26]

Two waves of American A-20 Havoc bombers suddenly hit the site during the early evening of April 25, 1944, as the troops were queuing for supper at the Guelinel farm canteen, just south of the battery. The raid was devastatingly accurate; two of six kettle (open) concrete emplacements were destroyed, including one of the six 155mm guns, with two damaged. Two men were killed and three wounded. Such was the damage that the crews moved the guns that night to a tree-lined sunken lane one mile to the south, outside the battery position, and used nets to camouflage them from aerial observation. Only half the guns were now deployable, and they were separated from their fire control bunker forward on the Pointe promontory. Telegraph poles were set up with wooden supports inside the emplacements and covered with camouflage nets. André Farina in Jean Marion's resistance cell spotted this and attempted to relay the information to London via carrier pigeon. The bird never arrived and was thought to have been brought down by a German sentry with a shotgun.

Gefreiter Kurt Keller with the inland 915 Regiment recalled his astonishment in May working on beach obstacles near Vierville "that the mighty gun bunkers of the huge strongpoint at Pointe du Hoc were standing empty." All he saw on visiting was a number of machine gun nests covered in camouflage nets, and only barbed wire securing the sea side of the cliffs. "This did not correspond with my previous perception of an impregnable Atlantic Wall," he admitted.[27]

The deception ruse for Allied intelligence remained successful. The battery position was bombed again on May 13 and strafed by P-47 Thunderbolts eight days later. The Guelinel farm housing the battery's canteen and horses was destroyed, and all Organization Tödt construction work ceased. Yet another medium bomber raid churned the site over on Sunday, June 4, dropping a hundred tons of bombs. The site appeared cursed to the German artillery crews.

Gefreiter Heinrich Severloh clattered along the roads and tracks driving his one-horse charrette with his battery chief Lieutenant Bernhard

Frerking to their observation post atop WN 62. The clouds had disappeared, "and the sallow light of the full moon illuminated the rough, uneven landscape of Normandy." The three mile journey took nearly an hour, through Surrain, Saint-Laurent, and Colleville villages, made increasingly urgent by the dull, yet alarming drone of hundreds of bombers flying in from the sea to their west, beyond Pointe du Hoc. They had to detour across the plateau bluffs, because the valley leading to the dark hill mass of WN 62 was completely blocked by barbed wire and mines. Access was through what is now the Normandy American Cemetery. Feldwebel Beerman was waiting for them at the strongpoint entrance, which was reached shortly after 1:00 A.M. He drove the charrette away as a soldier closed the gateway with barbed wire and mines, in effect raising the drawbridge for one of the strongest defense positions along the Plage d'Or.

Frerking went to his small concrete observation post (OP) overlooking the beach. He was quietly confident. Only eight days before he had conducted the final live firing exercises to calibrate his guns to drop three hundred meters beyond the waterline and obstacles. A reassuring series of water spouts jetted up from the sea, precisely where he wanted them. They had even taken photographs. The fire boxes were plotted on maps and labeled—*Ursula, Anna, Frieda*—and so on. All Frerking had to do when the enemy entered the boxes, covering dead ground and the entrances to the ravines, was to call for fire by name: "Fire *Dora!*" Severloh meanwhile moved to his open machine gun emplacement just beyond the OP where his MG 42 was already positioned. He loaded a belt and readied the weapon for firing. From east to west, all along the fifteen strongpoints beaded along the waterline of the Plage d'Or, emplacements were being similarly manned.

To the right of Severloh's WN 62 emplacement were WN 60 and 61, a key 88mm and 75mm gun concentration commanded by 3rd Company Commander Lieutenant Edmond Bauch. He had just taken over from the recently retired Hauptmann Ottermeier. One of his first acts on meeting the assembled company two weeks before was to announce the imminence of the invasion. The soldiers noticed he was drunk. Having survived the harsh Russian Front and arrived in the land of "milk and honey," he was told combat was about to break out here. Although the soldiers empathized with his predicament, they did not take the forecast too seriously. Some were taken aback by his cynical advice that, "if possible, do not take prisoners under ten men." Veteran Obergefreiter Peter Lützen reassured his comrades that "we know that already from Russia," he pointed out, "and that's where Bauch has come from." Heinz Bongard, manning the highest point of the eastern beach defenses at WN 60, remained unfazed. "We weren't worried, we were still young and cocky."

Franz Gockel was positioned on the east side of the WN 62 hill mass, with a water-cooled Polish machine gun inside an earth-covered bunker. He covered the beach and could provide mutual support to WN 61 on the other side of the draw leading up to Colleville. His position was linked by a zig-zag trench to Obergefreiter Siegfried Kuska's 50mm anti-tank gun, protected by steel shields in an open emplacement that snugly fit into a natural fold in the ground that covered the beachfront before Oberfeldwebel Friedrich Schnüll's 88mm gun. Schnüll, a competent and experienced gun commander fired across Kuska's arc to link with a sister 88mm firing out from WN 72 in Vierville, intersecting at the midpoint of the flat expanse of beach just under two miles away. Kuska was a good man to have alongside. He had lived for a time in the Soviet Union and taken a Russian wife. She stayed behind when he came back to join the Wehrmacht, and had fought in the Polish and Russian campaigns. Once a Feldwebel, he was demoted after an altercation with an officer. Peter Lützen described him as *Ein harter Hund*: "a tough case," treated with enormous respect by all the WN 62 NCOs.[28]

"Still nothing could be seen on our coastal sector," Gockel recalled. "Everything was quiet. . . . Was it another false alarm?" he began to think. "Time passed slowly," and they began to feel cold because they were wearing light fatigue uniforms, as they were due to be digging out and improving the trench network that morning. "We shivered at our weapons" in the cold night air, he remembered, and the cook came around ladling out welcome hot red wine, "which sharpened us up again." They longed for the "damned alarm" to be rescinded and return to their stuffy accommodation. Frequent aircraft overflights "led to an increase in inner tension and the calm weighed heavily."

On the west side of the WN 62 slope was the lower 7.65mm casemate, commanded by thirty-five-year-old Obergefreiter Heinrich Krieftewirth, a father figure to many of the soldiers. In the bustling haste of the callout Krieftewirth had left his false teeth floating in a cup on the table beside his bunk. Hans Selbach, one of his ammunition carriers, was standing watch in the forward MG position of the strongpoint, which "gave the best view of the sea." Before coming on watch at midnight, he and his companions had used the fading light to bathe in the sea. Droning aircraft were commonplace most nights, but the company headquarters report that the invasion had begun seemed to almost tangibly confirm it as fact.

Lieutenant Hans Heinz the Ordnanz officer was in the presbytery headquarters of the II Battalion 916 Regiment, opposite the grocery shop at Formigny, three miles inland from the beach. They had been there a month, controlling two companies on the coast and two further to the rear, in readiness as a counterattack reserve. Heinz had erected an observation post on the high ground southwest of Colleville, in sight of the sea. Whenever there was an alert, and there had been many, he would move forward to his vantage point. On a good day he could see as far as the Vire estuary to his left and that of the Seine to his right. He was irritated when the alert came. Despite reports about paratroopers, subsequent reports indicated they were decoy dummies that exploded on impact with the ground. The earlier unsettled weather hinted he was wasting his time when he moved to the tree with his runner, but the companies were already moving into position. He had a look, but all he could see was an offshore mist—nothing.

Gefreiter Gustav Winter's concrete panzer turret stood in the midst of the construction zone in the center of the Plage d'Or. Of five strongpoints between WN 64 to 70, three were partially constructed and there was a largely undefended 880-yard stretch between the building site area and WN 62 on the right. Soldiers manned a mix of open gun emplacements and concreted finished individual Tobruk mortar and MG shelters. "On this night there was moonlight," remembered Winter, "but all I could make out was clouds over the horizon of the sea." As he arrived with his Czech-German loader they assumed all the activity "was an especially heavy bombing raid." "We never saw much happening on the sea at all," and "it was rare to observe one of our 'S-Boats' [gunboats] and we only occasionally glimpsed a proper warship"—always British or American, never the Kriegsmarine. Their officer rode up on horseback and warned them about "suspicious activity to the east, involving gliders and such things, and to be completely vigilant." This raised the ante somewhat, so they made ready with final checks on the gun, then came out of the turret to see if anything was going on around them:

> "There were flares in the sky, I don't know where from, and they lit up the underside of the clouds, and I could see many planes moving through the clouds, which worried me."

It was quiet; the 20mm flak gun behind them remained motionless. "I had a very bad feeling now," he recalled, "and I felt very exposed out there" amid the incomplete emplacements. "I suppose that all the other crews in the bunkers around me were thinking the same thing—what the devil is happening?"[29]

On the other side of the D-3 ravine to the right of his position was WN 66, mounted on top of a series of precipitous bluffs. Behind it was the André family farm, where a number of German soldiers were billeted. Access to the strongpoint was through the steep La Pissotière lane, connecting to Saint-Laurent. Albert André had been working on WN 66 that afternoon. Driven off by an American fighter-bomber strafing attack, he had retired early to bed. His parents, however, heard a commotion during the night and saw the Germans dashing out of the house, laden with packs, shouting "*Alarm, Alarm!*" They had been informed about Wehrmacht maneuvers that morning and thought little of it. As the Germans sped down the lane they were ambushed, stabbed, and clubbed to death by a group of alleged paratroopers or raiders who had dropped off course. They died soundlessly. "The eleventh one came back," Albert André's parents told him, "My mother saw him through the keyhole, leaving again and collapsing on the [garden] wall, his face covered in blood." He had forgotten his pack.[30]

Diagonally across the bay from the WN 62 trio of formidable strongpoints was another cluster of bunkers, WN 70 to 73, covering the Vierville exit from the Plage d'Or. The 88mm bunker at WN 72 fired at right angles, due west along the beach, linking to its opposite number at WN 61 on the other side. Its sidewalls were 6.5 feet thick, with steel reinforced concrete, able to withstand an eight-inch naval shell strike. A stone wall up to 2.15 feet thick cloaked the muzzle blast from the sea, obscuring the flash of the gun from ships standing offshore. An additional 75mm bunker at WN 73 with three 75mm and a 76mm Skoda gun at WN 74 covered the beach from east to west with powerful anti-tank and field gun artillery fire. Both the east and west cliff shoulders of the Plage d'Or were virtually impregnable.

Machine gunner Karl Wegner with Regiment 914 was a recent reinforcement to WN 71. After being unceremoniously roused by a hefty kick against his bunk by section commander Unteroffizier Radl he moved into position with his loader Willi Schuster. They made the gun ready and peered out into the Channel for targets. "It was dark and there were no ships in sight, not a single one," he recalled. "Was it another drill or test alarm?" Wegner had never been in combat, "so I was pretty nervous." The previous dawn there had been a scare in the early morning darkness when he had detected a boat heading "straight at us." It was not German and should not be French, because access to their beach was severely restricted. He called Radl forward and nervously handed over the binoculars. To his dismay he chortled and announced "not much of a fleet, that is if the Tommies are using fishing boats." One of Wegner's nightmares was that "my friends would be mad at me for disturbing their precious sleep." Even so, Radl commended his alertness, announcing the Frenchman would be in serious trouble for ignoring the restriction, but "I felt such an idiot," Wegner confessed. Tonight was different: *Raus, Raus!* Out! Radl had bellowed amid the sound of hobnailed boots clattering across concrete. He was with them now, quietly relaying in low tones that enemy paratroopers had landed around the Carentan Canal, and other companies from the 914th Regiment were engaging them.

Unteroffizier Henrik Naube atop the cliff position at WN 73 likewise saw nothing, although "there were various flames and explosions in the sky on the land side." The moonlit night enabled them to "see large numbers of aircraft in the sky at times, between the rain clouds. . . . I think that most of us were simply sick of the tension of waiting, waiting," he recalled. There was a palpable sense of foreboding, reinforced when an officer appeared, who "ordered us to be completely prepared for a possible sea landing." Some men weakly attempted a show of bravado. "Let them come soon," they said, "which made other men wink and laugh." Something was definitely going on and there was discussion whether the planes were twin-engine parachute types or bombers:

"I recall seeing one of these planes at low altitude followed
very closely by another plane, which we thought to be a glider

under tow. These two planes descended rapidly and disappeared into the sea."[31]

Oberstleutnant Ziegelmann at the 352 Division Headquarters in the Château du Molay-Littry was increasingly convinced the invasion was on. Eight separate reports from midnight to 3:00 A.M. had spoken of paratroopers and troop-carrying gliders. To their right 716 Division was reporting a similar level of activity. Then at 3:14 A.M. the Kriegsmarine headquarters at Cherbourg reported "enemy sea targets located 11 kilometers [just under 7 miles] north of Grandcamp." That was heading toward them. He immediately passed the information to Artillery Regiment 352, whose four batteries were located three to five miles inland. At a quarter past two General Kraiss alerted his inland reserve, Oberstleutnant Karl Meyer's 915 Regiment to assemble and begin to move westward. Their task was to advance "in several columns and small groups" to crush the landed parachute groups, that were already beginning to impede the communications and routes to the left neighbor 709 Infantry Division. This was the primary inland reserve for the Plage d'Or, and the battle had yet to start.

At 4:20 A.M. Ziegelmann received a call from the alerted 352 artillery forward observers on the beach. They could hear suspicious sounds out to sea, "noises which probably originate from naval units." Major Werner Pluskat, the artillery regiment commander, was viewing from his cliff top bunker at WN 59. "All he could hear," he remembered, "was some explosions in the distance" and "some shots" behind his location. He had heard nothing from regiment or division about the "course of the paratrooper battle which he knew was going on somewhere."[32]

Looking through his powerful binoculars "just as the long gray fingers of light began to creep across the sky," Pluskat recalled, "he stepped back in amazement." He shook his head and looked again through the bunker aperture and "saw the horizon filled with shipping of all kinds."

It was unbelievable. "It seemed impossible to him that this fleet had gathered there without anybody being the wiser, without anybody giving a warning." They had to be twelve miles out, but there had been no sea mine explosions from the coastal mine belt and no trace of any Luftwaffe air activity. Where had this fleet come from?

The ships were out of range of the 155mm battery at Pointe du Hoc. Heinz Bongard standing on top of the WN 60 cliff emplacement just west of Pluskat near Sainte-Honorine viewed the field from the highest point on the Plage d'Or, 200 feet up, 30 feet higher than his left neighbor WN 62. He too "could make out the huge fleet on the horizon in sketchy outline" he remembered, "because it is not so dark at night over the sea than it is on land." The ships kept out of 155mm range, ironically menaced by only six harmless telegraph poles sticking out of the camouflage net curtains draped over the bunker apertures at Pointe du Hoc.

They dared not come any nearer.

TWO

FORCE "O"

MIDNIGHT TO 3:30 A.M.

=====================================

The Funnel
Midnight to 3:00 A.M.

At midnight the invasion ships had moved out of *Area Z* southeast of the Isle of Wight, a circle on the charts appropriately named *Piccadilly Circus* before executing a complicated turn to the southeast. The number of ships and boats under way was breathtaking; accounts vary between 6,500 to 7,000 vessels. The precise number is still not known, but one estimate reckons 6,483. Within a period of about twelve hours, 284 major combat vessels, 4,024 landing craft and landing ships, and 2,175 converted liners, merchantmen, and LCTs executed this 90 degree turn which put them into a narrow channel called "the spout," which poked through the German coastal mine belt. Force "O," headed by Captain Lorenzo Sabin had set off from Portland, Weymouth, and Poole in Dorset, four huge columns, one hundred yards apart in convoy. With an overcast sky and strong winds the sea got rougher as they ventured into the English Channel, the small boats heaving and tossing as the great ones steadily advanced. By the time the tricky turn to starboard came up in the darkness the sea pitch began to moderate. Short June nights meant much of the 120-mile voyage would be conducted in vulnerable daylight. The fleet changed course at dusk—11:00 P.M.—it would start to become light again within five to six hours.

There were five shipping channels in the constrained funnel. The Force "O" fast ships swept into channel three at twelve knots while slow convoys ploughed through channel four at five knots. These designated mineswept lanes were forty miles long, but only four hundred yards wide. Skippers tended to focus on the blue light of the vessel in front rather than on the red and green dan buoys passing alongside. The preplanned, rigidly enforced maneuver created tightly bunched columns of slow moving vessels that stretched for twenty miles, like "a gigantic twisting dragon," as one officer described it. Large LCTs (Landing Craft Tank) were difficult to handle in such conditions, with high, light bows they were almost impossible to steer a tight course in a strong wind. When one executive LCT officer asked whether the green bouys should be on their right or left they realized the entire line of LCTs was outside the mineswept lane. Lieutenant Coit Hendley captaining US Coast Guard LCI(L) 85 remembered, "the wind was still blowing and the Channel was still choppy" following the storms that had postponed sailing the day before. Traffic snarl-ups and collisions were a real danger in such conditions with this density of boats. Lookouts had to be especially watchful to pick out the marker buoys indicating swept channels. The moon was obscured by high overcast clouds, but some light did filter through the haze. "As we plodded through the rough water, into the evening and night," Hendley recalled, "we waited for the air attacks, the E-Boat attacks or the submarines."[1]

Chaos hung like a sword of Damocles over the fleet throughout the passage. Rear Admiral John Hall commanding Force "O" recalled how vulnerable many of his subordinate commanders felt about the length and unwieldy nature of the maritime force. Although the passage of the mine belt was a tense affair, Allied minesweepers only found twenty-nine mines they had to neutralize when moving through the five-mile-thick German barrier. None were inside the two Force "O" swept channels. "The enemy missed a golden opportunity," Hall recalled, "by not attacking the assault convoys while they were in the vulnerable formation and restricted waters of the swept channels." Despite the density of shipping, the huge crowd of vessels sailed broadly to schedule. American Admiral S. E. Morison commented the crossing was "so remarkable" it suggested "divine guidance." There was no sign of the enemy, no Luftwaffe overflights nor the notorious Cherbourg E-boat Flotilla that had caused extensive damage when it got among an exercise convoy off Slapton Sands six weeks before. It sunk two LSTs and severely damaged another. The E-boats had chosen not to make routine patrols because of the severe weather. "A determined torpedo plane attack positively could not have been stopped," Admiral Hall admitted. "It would have been extremely serious." Newly invented German pressure mines might have seriously impaired the naval operation, but Hitler had determined to keep them back, as a post-invasion countermeasure. The Allies would only have been able to counter them with "suicide barges." Yet off to their right they could see the reassuring beam of the 236-foot gray stone Barfleur lighthouse sweeping out to sea from the tip of the Cherbourg peninsula. Astonishingly the Germans had not switched it off, thinking nothing would move in these marginal weather conditions.[2]

Combat photographer Seth Shepard was assigned to US Coast Guard Infantry Landing Craft LCI(L)-92, commanded by Lieutenant

Robert Salmon. Watching the fleet form up had been a memorable sight, "all the LSTs had a large barrage balloon flying above them," he recalled, "and the LCIs looked top-heavy with the mass of troops on deck":

> "We all watched the memorable sights of the vast flotillas of ships stretching in every direction. As we stood out into the channel our group formed into what seemed like three end- less columns of LCIs. Then later as we left the bay astern our three columns were joined by a flanking fourth column of the famous little 83-foot Coast Guard cutters, and a long line of huge transports beyond. On the horizon were destroyers and other escort vessels."

They continued their stormy progress in the brisk wind, "and it was definitely chilly topsides." A massive swarm of seventy-four P-38s flew high overhead in the clouds, "the largest concentration of planes at one time we had seen." Every view from the ship assumed epic proportions. "All evening bunches of Spitfires had flown over." With twilight setting in, "we began to ease away from the high cliffs of southern England." Few crew members consciously appreciated they were part of one of the greatest undertakings in history, but they were captivated by the spec- tacle. "Everyone was exceptionally calm and ready," Shepard remembered. Failure was not an option; their flotilla carried 170,000 invasion troops. In 1588 the fabled Spanish Armada had consisted of about 130 ships carrying 8,000 soldiers. "Off our port quarter now," Shepard observed, "we could make out in the evening haze more ships of task forces and amphibious flotillas coming out of other harbors." It seemed as if more and more men and matériel were spilling into the Channel from every outlet along the coast. "Chief Campen pointed out to me the growing number of LCTs coming out from land," he recalled. "There were so

many it was impossible to count them all as they dotted the horizon."
Realizing that from now on there would be few opportunities for rest,
he headed for his "sack":

> "I couldn't go right off to sleep but the last thing I remember
> was the one shaded light hanging down over the mess table,
> swinging back and forth and sending its faint rays over the
> tiers of three bunks, most of them filled with sleeping forms,
> relaxed and trusting and not knowing what hell they would
> be facing in less than ten hours."[3]

After transiting the funnel, the columns moved to their initial positions in readiness for the landings, dropping anchor from 2:30 to 3:00
A.M. The soul of Force "O" was its fifteen high-value troopships, eight
manned by the British Royal Navy and seven by the US Navy and Coast
Guard. They constituted the kernel of the force, the first 10,000 infantry
due to storm Omaha Beach. Landing craft were slung on davits on the
port and starboard sides. "Although the channel was full of vessels, there
was not a light to be seen on any of them," remembered pharmacist's
mate first class Roger Shoemaker on the attack transport USS *Henrico*.
Overhead "there was a continuous blanket of low clouds and a hazy
atmosphere with a reddish-purple sunset." By the time the *Henrico* was
nosing through the funnel he was asleep.

War photographer Robert Capa had taken pictures of the *Henrico*'s
departure from Weymouth. He had established his reputation photo-
graphing the Spanish Civil War, and China in 1938, and was already
celebrated for the iconic images he had produced of this war in Europe
and the Mediterranean. "Our boat is in motion and in ten hours we are
going to debarque on the beaches of France," he had penned to 35mm
caption notes dispatched to London. Another read, "the troops are on
the deck counting the ships around us and looking at the last mainland,

they are a bit quieter now." He remembered a resigned somber atmosphere reigning onboard. "H-hour is approaching," he commented. "Some of them are reading, most of them silent." *"Channelitus* got really serious," Private David Silva with the 116th Regiment recalled, "the greatest sound was silence." "All during the trip across the channel almost all of us stayed below," recalled Private Anthony Ferrara with the 116th Regiment, earmarked for the first wave. "There was really nowhere to go and no feeling to get away from the companionship of our buddies."[4]

"An invasion ship is a lonely ship," remembered Sergeant Ralph Martin, below decks on an LST. "You sit and sweat and nobody says anything because there is nothing to say." Breaching Hitler's Atlantic Wall would be an iconic moment. General Eisenhower's tinny address, played through countless ships' loudspeakers, called it a "Crusade," but there were few illusions about the approaching cost. The supreme commander's speech played alongside patriotic orations from Prime Minister Winston Churchill and President Franklin Roosevelt were often accompanied by hoots of cynical derision. "We all thought, isn't that nice?" one staff officer recalled, "if you had a couple of violins, you could put it to music." Bland assessments of casualties among the leading waves led some men to think they were being regarded as expendable. "You look around and you wonder who will be dead soon," Sergeant Martin considered:

> "Will it be that tall, tough looking sergeant who is busy checking his M1; or the guy stretched out in his upper bunk who keeps praying aloud all the time; or the kid sitting next to you who wet his pants? Who will be dead soon?"

Sketchy rumors circulated around the green 29th Division that the North African and Italian experiences suggested platoon and company commanders would not last long in combat. Martin was writing for the Army weekly *Yank*, which though occasionally melodramatic by contemporary conflict reporting standards, often hit the spot for the nervous soldiers reading it.

> "Then the thought comes, swelling inside of you, a huge fist
> of fear socking at your gut, hammering and hammering . . .
> Maybe it's me. Maybe I'll be dead soon . . ."

The veteran Capa, appreciating that sleep was unlikely to come easily, instead played craps and card games for "funny money," the occupation francs issued to the troops. "At 2:00 A.M. the ship's loud-speaker broke up our poker game," he remembered; and as "we placed our money in water-proof money belts," they "were reminded that the Thing was imminent."[5]

Lieutenant John Carroll, aboard with the 116th Regiment advance headquarters team, recalled that conditions on the *Henrico* were "very hampered and very limited":

> "There was a lot of talking when we first went aboard; by
> the second night, when we definitely knew we were going in
> on D-Day the following morning, everything became quiet.
> Men got out pencil and paper and started to write to their
> loved ones at home. Most of the crap games disappeared,
> the card games disappeared to a larger extent, and the men
> started to become quite sober about what they were about
> to go into."

Roger Shoemaker woke up after midnight, "as I felt the ship's pro-peller vibration slow down, then speed up again." For about thirty minutes he heard "the clattering sound of the anchor chain as the anchor went down in the water and was drawn up again." The *Henrico* was slowly coaxed into its disembarkation position.

> "When the anchor went down for the last time, I overheard the officers saying that we were right where we were supposed to be. Given the number of ships involved, and the fact that this was all accomplished under blackout conditions, it was a pretty amazing feat of navigation."[6]

Davits were made ready for the launch of landing craft. The telegraph poles protruding through the camouflaged net apertures of the German bunkers at Pointe du Hoc eleven miles away had succeeded in their aim. Whether the guns were in situ or not, a two- to three-hour, energy-sapping, nauseous ride lay ahead.

On a swathe of airfields across the flatlands of Norfolk and East Anglia, aircrews were awoken and alerted around midnight. They got dressed, freshened up with a splash of cold water, and walked to combat messes for the proverbial powdered scrambled egg breakfast. Radio operator Edwin Ehret with the 91st Bomb group at Bassingbourn remembered, "they had cheese mixed with them, which almost camouflaged the awful distaste we had for the ETO food." After that it was "out into the extra cool June night air again for the mile trek to the briefing hut." Invasion rumors had been bandied about and the invigorating walk "started to bring our reasoning powers into focus." What might be the target for tonight? B-24 Liberators were being tanked up with 2,400 gallons of high octane fuel with 100 pound fragmentation bombs stowed in the bomb bays. Berlin—the Big B—or maybe even the invasion? Crews sat down on rickety wooden benches in the briefing huts and expectantly waited for the briefing officers to draw back the curtains over the large maps on the wall. "Something big was in the wind," appreciated Ehret. "The base photographer was busy with flash bulbs and camera, taking shots of us waiting for briefing." Likewise Sam Stone at Snetterton Heath Norfolk observed a major with a clipboard checking off the names of aircrew entering the briefing room. "This had never occurred before, so we knew something unusual was up." The curtain was drawn, revealing a red ribbon going into the Normandy area and another coming out on a different heading. "D-Day started for me at about 02:00," he recalled.

It began three hours earlier for Second Lieutenant Ben Isgrig from Arkansas, a bombardier with the Eighth Air Force 448th Bomb Group. His colonel, Gerry Mason announced: "This is it, our target was Omaha Beach." The mission was to neutralize the enemy's coastal defenses and frontline troops. P-47 Thunderbolt pilot Second Lieutenant Quentin Aanenson, woken shortly before midnight, "knew it was something serious," because "we could tell by just the atmosphere." "Gentleman, this is it," he recalled the two briefing officers saying as they removed the map curtain, "the invasion of France has begun." He would fly fighter escort over Omaha. "I remember the feeling I had," he recalled, "that I can't believe I'm actually here." "I saw the first reaction of the crews," remembered Lieutenant Colonel Philip Ardery with the 2nd Combat Wing of the 2nd Bomb Division, "a show of genuine enthusiasm":

> "When it was announced that at last the invasion was begin-
> ning, a cheer stopped the briefing officer for almost a minute.
> The crews were cheering as they might have cheered the end
> of the war."

Briefings did not lack drama. At the start of Sam Stone's 337th Bomb Group, they were told "anyone who divulges any of the information given at this briefing will be shot."[7]

An entire bomb division from the Eighth Air Force was allocated to General Bradley's Force "O" to bomb thirteen identified strongpoints along the four-mile length of Omaha Beach. Seventy-five squadrons from the 2nd Bomb division would hit the targets with an average of six squadrons each, totaling 450 B-24 bombers in all. Their 862 tons of bombs would theoretically smash the German defenses into oblivion in about twenty minutes. This operation was risky at best and catastrophic at worst, with the vagaries of weather and the technical limitations of 1944 bomber accuracy accompanying the first amphibious waves. They were predicted to be just three thousand yards from the bomb line at the appointed H-hour. "The weather here is the most discouraging of factors," Lieutenant General Carl Spaatz, commanding the US Strategic Air Forces in Europe acknowledged during planning in January. "I am sure" that what General Bradley is proposing—the partially bald commander confessed—"will result in the loss of the remaining hairs on my head, or at least will turn what is left of the red to white." The Commander of the US First Army's strict and unforgiving timetable to pack his beaches with men and matériel as soon as possible meant there was little prospect the Eighth Air Force could deliver what he wanted. The shortcomings of Allied area bombing accuracy would not allow it.

Senior army and air force officers were acutely aware of the shortcomings. During a recent live practice bombing exercise on a beach in southern England, Generals Eisenhower, Montgomery, and Bradley, alongside Air Commanders Spaatz, Tedder, and Leigh-Mallory had a very close shave. Colonel John DeRussey, an Eighth Air Force liaison officer at the exercise remembered "the Field Order definitely stated bombs were to be held up after the deadline." After it passed, Eisenhower, anxious to view the results, promptly went to the beach just as another bombing group came over and dropped its load, "causing consternation and embarrassment." On another occasion, the mission dropped short, despite explicit orders to delay release "and ricocheting fragments splattered around the observation post, causing all the observers to hit the ground." A fleet of bombers traveling at 180 knots, several thousand feet high, immediately after sunrise with poor visibility and high chance of fog or heavy cloud, could accidently wreak havoc on invasion forces below.[8]

Bradley also insisted on no beach cratering. General Leonard Gerow's V Corps's innumerable jeeps, trucks, and tanks had to exit the five Omaha beach draws swiftly to push inland to Saint-Lô. The air force solution was to drop mostly light 100-pound high explosive and fragmentation bombs, but these would have no effect against hardened gun emplacements. Blast impacts from instantaneous fuses would be lethal for troops caught in the open and reasonably destructive against minefields, obstacles, and barbed wire. "Direct hits on gun emplacements would not be in excess of 2% of the tonnage dropped," a later report affirmed, aiming primarily "at the demoralization of front line troops." In short, bombing's results would be limited to ineffective.

When radio operator Sam Stone finally stowed his gear on arrival at the aircraft pan at Snetterton Heath, he offered the bored airplane guard a cigarette. The soldier, weary at the routine pacing back and forth, complained, "It seemed he would be doing this forever," seeing "no end in sight." If the invasion might happen soon, "he would feel his efforts were not in vain." Stone felt an irrepressible urge to tell him, and decided, "I better leave before I spilled the beans." He climbed into the aircraft radio room to get away and await the arrival of the rest of the crew. Presently, he heard the sound of sobbing from the waist of the aircraft. He found himself comforting the crying "short, hard-drinking, self-centered" top turret gunner, which was completely out of character. He assured him they would make it back, but Jimmy the gunner announced, "I'm not crying for us, I'm crying for all the poor bastards that are going to die today." It was generally accepted the first waves to assault the Atlantic Wall were on suicide missions. Stone was stunned at the unexpected response, and felt the need to move off, "overcome by my own emotions."[9]

Field Order 328 directed that thirty-six Liberators, divided into six successive waves of six aircraft each, would bomb each of the thirteen Omaha Beach targets. Takeoff for the twelve participating bomb groups was between 1:55 to 3:00 A.M., which meant each group had just seventeen minutes to get its thirty-six aircraft airborne. "Just on 02:20," remembered 2nd Lieutenant Ben Isgrig, "Captain Smith in the control tower told the crew of the chequered caravan at the edge of the runway to 'give 'em the green light.'" Once the bomb group's lead pilot opened his throttle and roared down the runway and off into the darkness, the rest stared intently at their watch faces counting down to zero out loud. "A steady rain was falling and we could hardly see to taxi, much less fly," remembered Allen Stephens with the 785th B-24 Bomb Squadron, "but there was no holding back." They throttled away at twenty-second intervals, and, "by the time we cleared the end of the runway, we could barely see the lights of the airplane ahead of us." They climbed using instruments with a strictly prescribed speed of 155 mph and rising at 300 feet per minute. "When we broke out on top of the cloudbank," Stephens recalled, "we could see B-26s and all kinds of other airplanes circling around." He was awed by what "was really a beautiful sight."[10]

Liberator aircrews feared the night more than the Germans. Flying up close was hazardous enough by day, at night it was infinitely worse, likened to driving through a tunnel with no headlights. Despite the full moon, heavy cloud cover at 2,500 feet considerably diffused its glow. Wing lights and an occasional Aldis lamp flickering from the odd rear gun turret was the only way to warn off other aircraft through the gloom. Circling above airfields as later flights took off was known as the "racetrack course." Cloaked in darkness, pilots executed sharp turns in close proximity to other aircraft climbing and forming up at the same time. Copilots timed approaching turns by counting down from zero using wristwatches. On zero the B-24 sharply banked with everybody on board tensed up hoping the other Liberators were following suit. B-17 Flying Fortresses were able to fly tighter formations, whereas the Liberators tended to join the tight bomber streams in much looser and scattered formations. Lieutenant Colonel Lawrence Gilbert with the 392nd Bomb Group admitted:

> "Most B-24 pilots will tell you that it was a difficult aircraft to hold in formation. It was physically demanding and after twenty to thirty minutes at altitude, you were worn out."

Climbing with fully laden bomb bays was never easy. Freezing air at between 8,000 to 10,000 feet accumulated ice on wings and engines, adding more weight to the aircraft. If the pilot did not decrease the rate of climb, the Liberator could go beyond its weight limit and lose momentum. The veteran 389th Bomb Group deputy lead ship crashed twenty miles north of its takeoff point beyond Hethel airfield, probably because of uncorrected ice buildup. Ten men had been killed even before the raid had begun.

Hazards multiplied when Liberator bomb groups of thirty-six combined to become four combat wings of 108. These clusters in turn coalesced to form the 450 aircraft of the 2nd Bomb Division. Ironically, they were all flying northeast, *away* from the channel coast to form up, because they shared their limited airspace with 1,350 combined Liberators and Fortresses who all had to fly along a ten mile wide corridor this night. "We flew inland to Manchester," recalled Wallace Patterson with the 448th Bomb Group before turning "south to the channel."[11]

Like the menacing noise identified by Normandy's inhabitants, the circling and forming B-24s created a steady throbbing across the skies of Norfolk and East Anglia, which grew in intensity throughout the night. Slumbering farmers and villagers below were woken up, puzzled by this orchestrated sound heading northeast. Nevertheless, they were confident that someone in Germany was going to be in for it. The direct flying time to Normandy was little more than an hour. Many of these aircraft had now been flying for well in excess of three.

GIs: Government Issue
1:30 A.M. to 3:00 A.M.

I n the two years following Pearl Harbor, only eleven American divisions had met the Germans in battle in North Africa, Sicily, and Italy. Hundreds of Wehrmacht and Soviet divisions were meanwhile locked in battle on the Eastern Front. The two American divisions from the US V Corps, aboard the fifteen attack transports bound for Omaha Beach, were confident of success, but they were entirely different from each other. They would assault the four-mile-wide beach with two regiments forward, on the left would be the 16th from the 1st "Big Red One" Infantry Division, and on their right the 116th Regiment, from the 29th "Blue and Gray" Infantry Division. The "Big Red One" was the oldest division in the US Army and had seen continuous regular service since 1917. By 1941 it had fought in North Africa and a more recent bitter nine-month campaign in the Mediterranean. Its veterans were grumbling that someone else in the Army ought to do some fighting for a change, pointedly looking at the 29th Division, a National Guard formation, which had not yet seen combat. So far as the hard-bitten men of the 1st were concerned, the US Army consisted of the "Big Red One" and eight million replacements.

By contrast the 29th Division, which had been training in England since October 1942, was called "England's Own." Many of its soldiers had worn the American uniform in the UK longer than English units that had trained and immediately departed to fight the North African desert, Burma jungle, and Mediterranean campaigns. The Omaha grouping was an "odd couple," twenty-seven years of continuous history versus three years of training and inactivity. One division was populated with a core of crusty old professionals, with regular army antecedents. The other consisted of inexperienced but highly trained citizen-soldiers, who were ex–national guardsmen, tinged with idealism at what lay ahead. The 29th was immaculately turned out and did everything by the book, enthusiastic about fighting without having heard a shot fired in anger. Cynical elements in the 1st Division were quick to respond to the keen "Twenty-Nine Let's Go!" unit chant by hooting "Go ahead, twenty nine, we'll be right behind you!" The National Guard, "Blue and Gray," primarily from Virginia and Maryland, like the relationship between the British Regular and Territorial Armies, were very sensitive to criticism.

Many of the veterans from the "Big Red One" thought their part in a third invasion to be unfair. During the Mediterranean campaign the 1st had earned a hard fighting reputation in the line, but were hard-drinking, rebellious, and irreverent outside of it. After capturing Oran during the Tunisian fighting they were banned from its bars, resenting the "typewriter commando" rear services, who were granted full access. Such parochial self-pity and a blatant disregard for discipline contributed to the removal of its charismatic commander Major Terry de la Mesa Allen and his replacement by Major General Clarence Huebner, a consummate and demanding professional. Private Huston "Hu" Riley, due to land with the first wave of the 16th recalled the "kind of joke around the company" as they waited to disembark:

> "You did such a good job in North Africa and Sicily that we
> are going to send you in the first wave again."

Riley aboard the *Henrico* thought the choppy water below, into which their flat-bottomed landing barge would shortly launch, was far from inviting. He was the F Company lifeguard and swim instructor, but had accomplished little in the cold waters of British estuaries in April and May. "I know I froze my buns off getting in and out of the water at that time of the year," and "I was sure most of these guys only saw water on Saturday night."[12]

Training for the invasion was so intense and repetitive it became mind numbing. Captain Edward Wozenski commanding ("Easy") E Company in the 16th felt, "we were overtrained," culminating in a number of live fire exercises at Slapton Sands on the Devon coastline. "We had number one man in number two boat team going for aperture number three in pill box number seventeen," he remembered. Five major exercises were conducted at Slapton during March, April, and May, with soldiers live-fired in by two cruisers and up to nine destroyers. "Big Red One" veteran GIs with three D-Day landings in North Africa, Sicily, and Salerno under their belts tended to be "a rather sober and subdued group" according to one eyewitness. They had seen it all before, and were looking forward to the 29th Division taking it on. One GI described it as "we all felt like fugitives from the law of averages."

The 29th was equally vexed and frustrated with the training preparation, which since 1942 had outlasted the rest. When an American evangelist erected a sign in Ivybridge proclaiming, "Where will you spend eternity?" one disgruntled wag scrawled "*In England*" across it. Men were, however, confident. They had been processed through gigantic sausage-shaped roadside staging areas and seen countless vehicles of all shapes countless vehicles of all shapes, such as Hobart's specially adapted armored vehicles, "The Funnies." The fantastic preparations underpinning this huge operation seemed to exude a tangible might. Colonel Paul Thompson commanding the 6th Engineer Brigade remembered, "I had the peace of mind of the pro golfer who knows that he has brought with him all that is necessary to win." Beneath the uneasy air of anticipation lay an overriding emotion of "it's finally here." "Let's get this damn thing over with" proclaimed one combat engineer with the 106th Group:

> "If we're gonna get killed, let's get killed. If we're gonna go home—let's go home. But we want to end this thing. Do what we gotta do and get it over with."[13]

The men of Force "O" were a microcosm of the two million US soldiers who stood by for the invasion in 1,100 locations in the UK, occupying 100,000 requisitioned buildings, 160,000 Nissen huts, and even more tents. They were men who hailed from the Depression years of the 1930s—tough, pragmatic, and used to hardship. Roy and Ray Stevens were platoon sergeants, twin brothers from a family of fourteen siblings who had grown up in the small town of Bedford, Virginia, during these bleak economic times. The two were inseparable and had abandoned their studies to buy a small farm to supplement the family's income, which was why they also joined the National Guard. Many soldiers in the 29th Division had signed up to the National Guard as much from economic necessity as patriotism. Thirty-four Bedford boys would land at D-Day that morning. Most were surprised when they were incorporated into the regular US Army. The Stevens brothers were both in A Company the 116th Regiment and would go in with the first wave. There had been a general American reluctance to go to war, despite considerable distaste for what Hitler was doing to Europe. The war and overseas events had seemed so very far away, but now it had plucked men from their very close-knit communities.

Private David Silva with E company the 116th Regiment admitted, "for me of course patriotism was high, everybody did their part." But he had been as distant from what was going on in Europe as everyone else. "The only thing that I knew was that there was a war going on over there," he recalled, "and as far as we could judge and see from the news, Hitler was taking over many countries." Silva arrived in England in 1943, destined for the 29th Division. They had come to sort out the mess the Europeans had caused among themselves. He was soon homesick. "I'm going away from home for the first time," he admitted:

> "The only time I went away was to see an uncle or aunt or something like that, maybe sixty to seventy miles at the most."

He landed in Scotland disembarking from the liner RMS *Queen Elizabeth*, where they had immediately to deal with the vagaries of the English weather. George Rarey, an American fighter pilot, wrote home to his recent bride Betty Lou in November 1943 about his first impressions on arrival:

> "An Englishman on the *Queen Elizabeth* had told us that if we could not see the mountains as we approached the British coast, it was a sign that it would soon rain. If we couldn't see the mountains, it was already raining."[14]

England was different; there was a blackout at nights, which only occurred on the eastern and western seaboards of the United States. They drove on the wrong side of the road and had a bizarre currency of "arf crowns" and "bobs." "England's language cannot adequately portray England's weather," complained one 29th Division GI. "It must be lived in to be appreciated." Rigorous training was conducted in dreary weather, "week in, week out, it was all the same, clouds, fog, rain, perhaps a few minutes of sunshine in a few days." Homesickness was rife; by 1943 the average GI received fourteen letters each week and wrote one per day unless in combat. The language was strange. "Motor and petrol" meant automobile and gasoline; "sweets and biscuits" were candy and cookies. It became embarrassing when a "bum" was a tramp or layabout, and could be positively excruciating if an American invited an outraged British woman to sit on her "fanny" instead of her backside. Labyrinthine English country lanes became virtually un-navigable, because all the signposts had been removed during the 1940 invasion scares. Farmers suspicious of odd-speaking spies would not volunteer information. Even finding the pub may not prove beneficial because British beer was warm and flat, "like talking to yourself," remarked one 29th Division GI. Despite all this, the women were pretty and GIs universally liked by the children. After initially viewing each other askance, it became accepted that not all GIs spat tobacco juice in public and not all the English were arrogant snobs. Relationships were forged that would last generations.[15]

By 1944 two million GIs were sharing limited space with 1.7 million British soldiers, 150,000 Canadian troops, and 60,000 from other nations. With increasing speculation and no invasion, anxieties and frustrations were vented outside camp. By 1944 there were outraged reports throughout Britain about GI heavy drinking and boorish behavior. As with the German soldiers in Normandy, girls were the number one talking point powering testosterone-fueled competition. GIs exuded an aura of wealth and luxury, resulting in jibes about being "overpaid, overfed, oversexed, and over here." British Tommys could not match this affluence and were labeled by their adversaries as "underpaid, underfed, undersexed, and under Eisenhower." American uniforms were well cut and of superior cloth to the British serge khaki, they had regular white teeth and exotic Hollywood accents that appealed to the local girls, *and* they had money to burn. Officers with brown jackets and fawn-colored trousers were more glamorous. Some 70,000 British women would marry their Yank boyfriends after the war and travel back to the US with them.

"Hello Yank, looking for a good time?" soon became a much-parodied wartime joke. Brazen so-called "Piccadilly Warriors" swarmed about the entrance to the American Rainbow Corner at a corner in Shaftesbury Avenue. High-level official letters sent to the Metropolitan Police Commissioners expressed concern at the "vicious debauchery" conducted in blacked-out Leicester Square. "Piccadilly Commando" antics discussed at the Home Office level resulted in a leaflet titled *How to Stay Out of Trouble* issued by the US Provost Marshall, with stern warnings about "females of questionable character." These became the GIs' indispensible guide for those who wished to track them down. Allegedly over 20,000 illegitimate babies provided silent testimony to the influx of US servicemen labeled the "Sweet Invasion."

Tensions between ethnic and non-ethnic German soldiers in Normandy were replicated to some extent by the segregation between white and black US servicemen in England. The perplexing term "color bar" emerged in Devon and Cornwall villages and towns where they had never been heard before. Bernard Peters, a local living at Truro recalled fistfights, stabbings, and even shootings when the two ethnic groups clashed. "They hated the way our girls took to the black soldiers and were very surprised that the English did not resent them." Senior US army officers appeared to have a poor opinion of black American troops, feeling they were incapable of combat service. British bigotry occasionally surfaced but on the whole the locals were mystified at the extent of racism still evident in sections of American society. America was after all the promised land, portrayed in Hollywood films as a place of freedom and equality for all. The British did not understand or suspect the social fissures lurking beneath the surface. Fistfights could break out when white soldiers saw black GIs date white girls. Also misunderstood was the very young average age of the girls the GIs dated, many between fourteen to sixteen years old. This was because most girls left school and began full-time employment at fourteen. Today they would be considered children.[16]

As Lieutenant Coit Hendley navigated LCI(L)-85 through the mineswept narrow channel of the Funnel into the Force "O" approach lanes he was transitioning from one personal high point in his life to a historically memorable one. The pre-D-Day months since his arrival in England the previous October had been "a continuous emotional binge that I never since have experienced," he remembered. He met his wartime girlfriend WRNS (Women's Royal Naval Service, nicknamed "Wrens") Sylvia Grashoff, "and began having a marvelous time":

> "Everything was more real than reality. Friendships were intense. Whiskey tasted good. There was a grand purpose that

the men who served in Vietnam many years later could not possibly have felt. Battered England was heroic. We believed in heroes."

"Those were good days," he later reflected. All around him, "the magnitude of what was happening was apparent." He saw southern England transformed into an "armed camp."

During the last week of May, "the canvas bag arrived," it was sealed and marked *top secret* and weighed fifteen pounds. All ships in port were sealed. Now on this dark night he was lining up LCI(L)-85 for its beach approach. Onboard were 220 army and navy men, a beach battalion, whose task was to go ashore behind the assault waves and organize and coordinate the logistic flow of men and cargo onto the beach. He noticed the men on board "were rather grim about the whole thing." He had taken them ashore twice already during division-size exercises on Slapton Sands. Hendley was phlegmatic about what he was required to do, "one thought of death abstractly," he recalled, "getting killed was what happened to others, not to you."[17]

War photographer Robert Capa aboard the transport USS *Henrico* had reveled in the swirl of parties, nightclubs, and poker games that made up the carnival atmosphere in London during the spring of 1944. Capa often lost quite heavily. One of his companions, future Pulitzer Prize–winning playwright William Saroyan, with a US Army Signal Corps propaganda film unit, claimed he did not mind. One of his superstitions was so long as he lost at cards, he would be safe in battle and in love. "It's when I start winning that I'll worry." he confided to friends. He had already lost the love of his life, the "little red fox" war photographer Gerda Taro, crushed by a tank during the Spanish Civil War in 1937. Now he was having a fling with "Pinky," a married British girlfriend in London. "A woman only had to look at you twice on a tube and you knew you were laid," recalled his friend Warren Trabant, serving with

American counterintelligence. Capa was the consummate professional war photographer. He had given lectures that spring to the official US Army photographic unit in preparation for the invasion. You had to travel light and only carry equipment that will not impede mobility, he taught. "When you're in the fighting," he advised, "you don't go where there's fire, you go where there are pictures."[18]

Soldiers felt vulnerable at sea. Previous Allied amphibious landings in North Africa and the Mediterranean had proved dicey. Those at Sicily, Salerno, and Anzio had erupted into crises when the constantly underestimated Wehrmacht's capacity to regenerate after surprise attack—retaliating with the dreaded panzers—often threatened to drive the invaders back into the sea. Sergeant Donald Wilson with the 16th Regiment of the "Big Red One" remembered their arrival in England after Sicily was supposed to be top secret. "We hardly looked the part," he remembered. "Most were deeply tanned, at least hands and faces from the sun of North Africa and Sicily." Many were also toting German army souvenirs and rifle stocks engraved with place names and dates of battle engagements. Although freely viewed by people on the sidewalk as they marched four abreast and flanked by MPs to the railway station on disembarkation, there were comments and wisecracks. All the windows of the railway coaches were blacked out and "the Army was content" with their stealthy arrival. The next day they were in the small hamlet of West Bay on the Dorset coast, making friends with the local children and handing out "the usual candies, gum, and so on," and one thirteen-year-old lad had casually mentioned our "coming from Sicily." "So much for big secrets," recalled Wilson with some disgust.[19]

Pharmacist's Mate Roger Shoemaker had watched Wilson's unit come aboard the *Henrico* the day before:

> "My impression was that there were no 'skinnies or shorties' in this group. They were all near six feet tall, weighed from

190 to 220 pounds and were solid muscle. They had more equipment on than I had ever seen on an army private before."

Donald Wilson heartily agreed they carried too much; between sixty and eighty pounds of weapons and equipment. So much so, the veteran recalled:

> "My own view was that this amount of weight was a detriment to our ability to maneuver. As a practical matter, each soldier was expected to emerge from up to his neck in the surf, then run zig-zag across a vast expanse of sand. Not bloody likely as the Brits would say!"

Like many of his division comrades Wilson confided, "I would miss the little harbor, the quaint cottages with their tiny front gardens," both "good times and good fellowship" would be left behind. Gone was "the West Bay Hotel with its piano and dart board, and 'ration day' and the fish and chips." They much admired the British "who treated us so well, who lived such simple lives, and yet were, apart from the war, seemingly content." They moved out at an early hour, "people silently lined the way waving and giving the victory sign." This was supposed to be the best kept secret of the war, yet here they were, some running alongside "tossing cookies and pastries to us":

> "They had not done this on any of our other departures, so it was clear they *knew,* just sensing it as we did, that the time was at hand."[20]

As veterans, there was a hard-bitten element in the ranks who had a realistic idea of what to expect. "For the most part," Wilson recalled, "the prevailing attitude within the company was a mixture of one part apprehension and three parts confidence." For the men in the 29th Division transports, death had been a rare occurrence over the previous twenty months. Ten men from the 175th Regiment were killed in an air raid over Bournemouth in May 1943. Like some of the "Big Red One" soldiers, the "Blues and Grays" felt exposed at sea. During the Atlantic crossing aboard the *Queen Mary* in October 1942 men had seen the shocking collision with the antiaircraft cruiser escort *Curacao*. Zig-zagging at 28.5 knots, "the gray ghost," as the newly painted liner was nicknamed, sliced through the armored bulkheads of the naval ship like cardboard and only 101 of her 439 crew were saved. The liner had not paused. She was a prime asset and propaganda target for U-boats, so she carried on at full speed. Fear and anxiety lurked on board the invasion fleet, the German U-boat and E-boat arms had fearsome reputations. General Eisenhower had ordered an information block on the Slapton Sands disaster when 639 lives were lost to E-Boats on Exercise *Tiger*. Few people in Force "O" knew about the tragedy, but the senior commanders did.

Sergeant Donald Wilson spent most of his time on the upper deck of the *Henrico*, "marveling at the amount of activity taking place, literally as far as the eye could see in almost any direction." This was his third invasion and "that it was happening in broad daylight, not really far from fortress Europe, was absolutely astounding." They could see no Luftwaffe or any sign of hostile naval activity. "Surely they must know, but where were they?" Despite feeling vulnerable the sight of all these ships evinced an aura of power and invincibility that gave him confidence. "Surveying this panorama convinced me that victory would ultimately, unquestionably be ours," he recalled. Shortly after the *Henrico* reached her approach point off the coast Wilson was warned off for breakfast. "The alarm gongs did sound off at precisely 02:00, startlingly loud," he remembered. They had two hours before disembarking. *Henrico* crewmember Roger Shoemaker "jumped out of my rack" and wolfed down a quick breakfast.

At 4:00 A.M. he heard the bell clanging again to man all debarkation stations. Wilson, watchful and alert, particularly now that they were just off the enemy coast, was unimpressed. "I recall thinking that noise should be kept to a minimum since we must be near the Normandy coast," he recalled with some exasperation. "I wanted our arrival to be a complete surprise."[21]

"Strictly Power" The Plan
2:30 A.M. to 3:30 A.M.

The original COSSAC [Chief of Staff to the Supreme Allied Commander] D-Day plan was a three-division amphibious landing supported by two air-dropped parachute brigades. Landings would be across the eventually agreed British beaches and Beach 313. COSSAC expanded the conceptual idea to a greatly enhanced Normandy *Overlord* invasion, adding one more American beach, *Utah*, and expanding the airborne insertion to three divisions, one British securing the east flank and two American on the west side. This made the assault at Beach 313, renamed *Omaha*, the cornerstone of the entire invasion, as it was the link between the British beaches and *Utah*, on the other side of the Vire estuary.

It was intended that two infantry divisions, the 1st and 29th, would land on Omaha Beach on D-Day and advance five miles inland. They were to connect with the British beaches on their left and be ready to link with Utah the following day. The landings would be preceded by a 446-strong Liberator air raid dropping 1,088 tons of bombs over the beach defenses. This would be followed by a heavy naval bombardment from two battleships, the *Texas* and *Arkansas*, three cruisers, eight destroyers, and nine landing craft firing five-inch rockets. Tanks would either land at H-hour or swim ashore as DD [Duplex Drive] variants, supported by even more tanks firing from landing craft. The force would bludgeon itself ashore in an overwhelming display of force and firepower that would incapacitate any German defenders left alive on the beach.

Omaha Beach was divided for planning purposes into halves, each two miles wide. The 116th Regiment from the 29th Division would land on the right, or western half, at Dog Green, White, Red, and Easy Green. Concurrently the 16th Regiment from the 1st Division would come ashore on their left, the eastern side, at Easy Red, Fox Green, and Fox Red at the end below the cliffs. These seven beach sectors were replicated by white painted lines on the wooden floors and walls of the Gymnasium below decks on the attack transport USS *Chase* for briefing purposes. A number of veterans well remember these floor briefings over the painted diagram of the plan. On the wall was a piecemeal panorama of reconnaissance photos stuck together, showing the beach terrain. Lieutenant Coit Hendley, skippering LCI(L)-85, remembered how, "at one end, a scale drawing of the area to be assaulted was painted on the wall, with the beach sectors and landmarks indicated." All the ships' positions and courses to the beach were marked, and "even the buoys were painted in." Robert Capa shot pictures of the scene, including a close-up of infantry company and platoon commanders studying a large, highly detailed sponge-rubber model of the beaches and immediately inland. His handwritten photo captions noted, "the whole day the model is occupied," and assault groups, "as well as high officers and the navy men who are bringing them in" are able to benefit from "the results of months and months of work, and every gun and obstacle is shown." Artillery observation officer Captain Oscar Rich with the 5th Artillery Battalion was especially impressed in the detail. "Trees were there, the trails, the roads, the houses, the beach obstacles—everything was there." With everything to scale, "it was actually like being in an airplane, about 500 feet above the beach," so that observers could see "the whole thing in true perspective." Surgeon Captain Norval Carter with the 115th

Regiment recalled, "it is so fascinating not only to sit and listen to the plan, but also to watch the facial expressions of the officers" captured in Capa's photographs:

> "No smiles except one officer. Everyone is dead serious. Faces immobile and deeply lined. Young men look old. No fear shown, no nervous finger tapping, just quiet, deeply thoughtful immobility."

Capa did not simply frame the scene for his camera, he was also interested in the various company missions indicated on the model. True to his philosophy, "you don't go where there's fire," but "where there are pictures," he decided he should accompany E Company with the 16th Regiment. He had been with them at Sicily where he took a photo that "was one of my best during the war." There was an option to go with Colonel Taylor's regiment advance headquarters, but they would be behind the assault wave. He decided to accompany E Company onto Easy Red with the first wave. "If your pictures aren't good enough," Capa maintained, then "you're not close enough."[22]

During the buildup to the invasion, the V Corps divisions earmarked to land on Omaha were told by intelligence officers that the only resistance they would meet on D-Day would be from the German static 716 Infantry Division. This might mean one thousand men in the beach sector, comprising mainly Poles, Russians, and other nationalities press-ganged into service by the Wehrmacht. The poor caliber of this division suggested it was unlikely to engage in prolonged combat or be able mount any major counterattacks against the beachhead.

The imperative driving the Omaha landing, like everywhere else, was speed, and speed would be achieved through firepower and overwhelming force. The operation was commanded by General Sir Bernard Montgomery's 21st Army Group, to which Major General Gerow's V Corps, part of

Bradley's 1st (US) Army, belonged. The strategic setting was that the Germans held fifty-eight to sixty divisions in France to match an Allied invasion potential of thirty-seven standing by on the UK mainland. Montgomery's operational plan was based on the imperative swiftly to win the race to dominate the invasion foreshore. A combination of six amphibious landing divisions and three airborne divisions securing the flanks was expected to oppose five German divisions on D-Day. This figure would double by D+1 day with maybe thirteen German divisions entering the battle by D+5 days. After that it was anyone's guess, depending upon Allied deception, but it was estimated that twenty-four German divisions could be engaged against the Allied bridgehead within eight days. Major General Gerow's planning therefore aimed quickly to secure a lodgment, to win this buildup race, cost what it may. His superior General Bradley would constantly apply pressure to get results. He saw the battle in terms of an imperative to establish a bridgehead sufficiently strong enough to contain the anticipated feared German panzer counterattacks.[23]

As a consequence of this urgency, the Omaha tactical landing plan became prescriptive rather than creative. There was little room for maneuvering to establish beach-landing tables, which read like a mathematical formula of echeloned assault waves of infantry, quickly followed by supporting heavy equipment with artillery and tank firepower. Examination of the landing tables for the first six hours reveal serial infantry waves and then everything from amphibious tanks to supplies, naval salvage parties, antiaircraft battalions, engineer battalions, infantry rangers, trucks, amphibious tractors, and even Piper Cub light observation planes. The sequence of landing assumed short, sharp skirmishes on the beach transitioning to a conveyor belt of matériel and equipment that had to come ashore without disruption. Tight schedules barely allowed a minute between waves. It is clear from the tabular format that the fighting would be over within an hour, enabling follow-up assets to quickly move inland to set up for the anticipated German counterattacks. Any deviation from the in-built complexity of the landing sequence could result in chaos.

Two regimental combat teams were to land, over 1,500 infantry, two battalions abreast on a two-company front. The difficulty was that company command organizations were constrained to landing in six boats containing thirty-two men each, not the traditional combat structure. An indication of the conveyor-belt mindset was the meticulous arrangement agreed for each landing craft. The boat-section commander led off with his radio operator and five riflemen. Next came the barbed wire cutting team followed by machine gun, bazooka, mortar, and flamethrower teams with demolition teams behind them. The landing tactic was a drill. Light maneuver elements disembarked first followed by progressively heavier combat teams. Dividing the assault companies into six separate boat sections both taxed and complicated internal company command. General Gerow was aware of this. "The whole success of the operation may depend on the speed with which commanders can get out their orders," he advised, "and the familiarity of subordinate commanders with the tasks that may be assigned to them." The inexperienced 29th Division:

> "Must not look at these problems from an academic standpoint. They are very real situations involving the lives of men, and every effort must be made to solve them along realistic lines."

What this meant in practice, encapsulated in the conveyor-belt dynamic of the constrained beach landing tables, was the development of drills to cope.

Tactical maneuvers on the beach were impeded by the amount of equipment each man had to carry. This was configured to both assault the beaches and be sufficiently heavy to maintain durability, while fighting off German counterattacks in the beach lodgment phase. "I had the firm belief in traveling light," Sergeant Donald Wilson recalled. "Once I was in the field I got rid of both weight and bulk, i.e., blanket, gas mask, and extra food rations were 'lost' rather quickly." When Wilson boarded his landing craft he remembered, "I felt overloaded and cumbersome and waited for the opportunity to ditch the unnecessary items." The 1st Division veterans were already ditching superfluous items. They needed to be light to fight. The green 29th Division, dependent on training guidance, had little idea of what was to come. Personal equipment weights would multiply when they got wet in the surf.[24]

Very little is said in the multiplicity of Omaha veteran accounts about tactical objectives on the beach, bunker bypass options or pre-planned flanking moves to capture identified German strongpoints. Subordinate commanders may well have been overwhelmed by the amount of detail offered to them in maps and charts. It is difficult to disentangle the outline and tactical significance of the WN strong-points from the plethora of intricate detail showing mines, wire, and beach obstacles. The plan appears to be based upon landing in an identified "area" and dealing with resistance within its confines by applying bunker-busting drills learned at Slapton Sands. The V Corps invasion plan expressed by General Gerow in his outline appears com-paratively simple. There are "well organized strongpoints" on the beach and heights beyond, of about "one infantry battalion, reinforced" in strength. The preliminary air and naval bombardment "will effect some destruction of these defenses, but we are relying on infantry assault teams to finally take them out."

Attacks would focus on the draws or ravines leading up from the beach. These gaps in the dunes were easily detectable from the sea and the only way to get vehicles and heavy equipment out through the bluffs enclosing the beach to the roads beyond. The Germans anticipated that the main effort would be against these draws, which they carefully registered as machine gun and artillery killing zones. No mention is made in American plans of scaling the bluffs with infantry. It was assumed that with only a battalion defending, there would be numerous gaps in the resistance belt, so tanks and vehicle-mounted weapons could blast their way through. The US manual on amphibious operations according to Lieutenant Colonel Lucius Chase, a training adviser, was "fortified areas are avoided in the initial assault and taken from the rear. . . . Our feeling was," he remembered, "nice work, if you can get it!"[25]

The plan of attack was therefore general. Those going into the assault were not questioning the concept and felt confident. Captain Charles Cawthon with the 116th Regiment believed, "the Allied command had assembled a blasting, shredding, and tearing force of awesome proportions." The response to violent defense was to increase the level of violence in the attack until it was overcome. "We are not being cute, no gimmicks, no flanking movements" confided Colonel George Taylor commanding the first wave 16th Regiment assault, to *Chicago Tribune* correspondent John "Jack" Thompson. "We are coming straight at him with everything we have. This is strictly power." The overall German defense stance, concentrating German firepower within a cluster of strongpoints on the cliff shoulders, either side of the four mile-wide beach, appears to have been missed, or perhaps lost in the intricate detail of the intelligence maps. When Taylor was asked "what would happen if the Germans stopped the 16th cold on the beach?" he responded:

"Why, the 18th Infantry is coming in right behind us. The 26th Infantry will come on too. Then there is the 2nd Infantry Division already afloat. And the 9th Division. And the 2nd Armored. And the 3rd Armored. And all the rest. Maybe the 16th won't make it, but someone will."[26]

The general and overly prescriptive nature of the Omaha assault scheme, based on an impractically ambitious tight landing and unloading plan, presupposes a disturbingly cynical disregard for likely casualties. The acceptance is akin to First World War attrition norms and would be out of place today. There was, however, a general acceptance—and this should be viewed in the context of the bloody fighting that had already occurred in Russia, the Pacific, and the Mediterranean—that the cost of breaching Hitler's Atlantic Wall was likely to be high. Veteran accounts are littered with fearful anticipation of coming losses. The first waves were regarded as virtually "suicidal." Corporal Herbert Krieger in the 29th Division was told by his commander Colonel Eugene Slappey after their attack briefing that "most of you men are not coming back." "Not very encouraging," he remembered, "but we went about our tasks anyway." They were further discouraged by the gravedigging unit that set up alongside them in their roadside marshaling area in England. "Being part of the first wave," Private John MacPhee with the 16th Regiment recalled, "we were told that we would probably all be killed." This ramped up the tension, so that "the night before was like waiting to go to the electric chair."

Men were phlegmatic or fatalistic, appreciating they had little or no control over their wartime destinies. Richard Ford, a 2nd Lieutenant with the 115th Regiment, heard they would land later on from LCI(L)s and recalled, "we were just thankful that we were not on the first wave." Robert Guise was in the same regiment, a veteran wounded in Tunisia and then in Sicily. He had barely returned from the hospital and was aboard the USS *Samuel Chase* transport thinking about his third invasion. Despite "an awkward quiet," he was unquestioning, doing "our share in preserving freedom for not only the French, but for mankind." Vincent Bognanni with the 115th was equally fatalistic after being shown "mock-up models of the area we were to invade and what to expect.... They pulled no punches," he recalled. "They expected heavy casualties."

Morale remained high; it would always be the other man that was hit, "most of us couldn't wait to get on the assault boats." Ignorance among the green troops of the 29th Division remained a form of bliss. "I think that part of this was because we didn't know what death was up to this point," Bognanni recalled. "It was like a big game."

The plan was a frontal attack, delivered in echelon until it broke through. The tactical plan was subordinate to the operation plan, which required large amounts of equipment and matériel to be landed, to block the anticipated panzer counterattacks. Yet inland from the beaches, the nature of the bocage, or hedgerow country, was totally unsuited to maneuver armored and many other vehicles, but was well suited to infantry defense. The Allies, however, had decided to land with a preponderance of armor and vehicle-borne equipment on essentially infantry terrain. The nearest German panzer units in reserve were the *Panzer Lehr* Division, which would have to march 75 to 125 miles to reach the invasion area and the 12th SS *Hitlerjugend* Panzer Division, with units between 45 to 120 miles away. "In bare recital, the Omaha Beach defenses were impregnable," Captain Charles Cawthon with the 29th Division remembered, "the weight of our attack overwhelming." In his opinion he thought, "on balance, we believed the odds favored the overwhelming."[27]

To some extent, American soldiers fell victim to their innate patriotic "wilco" penchant not to question authority, regardless of the fallibility of the plan. "No mission too difficult," was the 1st Division catchphrase. Captain Charles Hangsterfer with the 16th Regiment recalled despite the anxieties, "no sacrifice is too great" and "duty first" always. Even though the 1st Division had experienced a series of close call landings, morale was intact:

> "We were all scared, but we felt that all we had to do was to turn our shoulder around, show them our Big Red One—and they would all run away."

Crucial to the beach-landing plan was the rapid clearance of beach obstacles. General Gerow, the V Corps commander, had anxiously observed the thickening up of the obstacle belt before Omaha in the weeks leading up to D-Day. Previous Mediterranean and Pacific beach assaults had never had to deal with the same density of bunkers, barbed wire, and mined beach obstacles that there were on Omaha Beach. Gerow managed to procure twelve engineer battalions to land alongside his infantry, nearly 10,000 sappers, virtually a division in its own right. Two were to land with the first wave, the rest progressively over the next few hours. It was an enormous risk to attempt to breach the obstacle belt under fire as the first wave went in. Unlike the British, US combat engineers had few armored vehicles apart from some tankdozers. The British had Sherman tank flail minesweepers and a number of Churchill tank obstacle-crossing variants such as bridge-layers, collectively termed "Funnies." Unable to logistically support Churchill variants the Americans had placed an order four months before based on Shermans for flail tanks, flamethrowers, and other anti-mine devices. They had not arrived in time because British production capacity was barely sufficient to cover British and Canadian needs. In fact, the Americans passed over eighty Sherman DD [duplex-drive] to the British, because they were short.

One armor protection option from the US could have been the *Alligator*, or armored amphibious tractor, already used in the Pacific. There were only three hundred of them in the European theater and just a few "water-buffalo" LVT-4 vehicles. They could carry eighteen soldiers and could have at least supported the engineer effort. But since they were mostly used in the Pacific theater, they were not seriously considered a first wave option on D-Day. Major General Charles Corlett had commanded the US 7th Division assault on the Japanese-occupied Kwajalein Atoll and pointedly asked Eisenhower and Bradley why this fresher technology could not be employed with initial assault at Omaha. "I was pretty well squelched for my question," Corlett recalled:

"I soon got the feeling that American generals in England considered anything that had happened in the Pacific strictly "bush league stuff," which didn't merit any consideration."

Nevertheless, one British general who listened to his presentation on the Kwajalein invasion blurted out: "By Jove! If we have an island to take, you ought to do it!" This was scant comfort to Corlett, who had been made to feel like the "son-of-a-bitch from out of town." The American engineers would have to tackle the obstacles from rubber dinghies.[28]

The heavy cruiser USS *Augusta* was a rakish beauty alongside the snub-nosed LSTs she passed at an easy fifteen knots. She had flanked the Utah-bound convoys out of Plymouth to reach the Force "O" rendezvous point south of the Isle of Wight. Well after midnight she entered the fast lane mine swept channel heading for Omaha. She was General Bradley and Admiral Alan Kirk's Force "O" flagship. The general had briefed one of the onboard correspondents in the army war room, a metal-lined shed constructed on the after deck, ordinarily used by the cruiser's spotter aircraft. "You've got to remember," he said, "that just as soon as we land this business becomes primarily a business of build-up." His concern was less the assault, more the maintenance of a bridgehead to hold off the inevitable German counterattacks. "For you can always force an invasion," he insisted, "but you can't always make it stick."

Before retiring to his cabin at 11:00 P.M. Bradley had been astounded that the Germans had, so far, missed the invasion fleet. "Seems hard to believe," he had remarked to Admiral Kirk, "maybe we're going to have Sicily all over again." They had also held their breath there, but "the enemy had slumbered on until we piled up on his beaches." The thought of achieving it again in the narrow confines of the English Channel just did not seem possible. "On a clear day," he remembered, "aircraft at 10,000 feet over Le Havre could look clear across to Southampton," but E-boat patrols had been canceled, German mine layers restricted to port, and the Luftwaffe grounded. "In this capricious turn of the weather," Bradley recalled, with stormy weather and a clear spell developing, coming up the Bay of Biscay, "we had found a Trojan Horse."

Bradley was well aware of the high strategic stakes underpinning the invasion. Japan, it was becoming apparent, had exceeded both her power and resources. Ultimately she would be defeated, "She could not win the war," he said, and the Pacific Islands campaign was edging ever nearer to the Japanese mainland. Germany was different. Despite profuse bleeding in Russia, Africa, and Italy, "Germany had not lost her offensive strength":

> "'We could still not free our minds from the fear that Stalin might make a deal and leave us to face the Axis alone. If we were to fail on the *Overlord* invasion, we might never get a second chance."

The Germans knew it too. Repelling the invasion might well alter the course of the war in their favor.

"It was 3:35 A.M.," Bradley remembered, "when the clanking bell outside my cabin called the crew to battle stations." The "Trojan Horse" weather that had cloaked the fleet's approach made him feel uneasy about three problems. The only creative element of the Omaha landing plan was the technological surprise offered by the top secret DD swimming tanks, never seen before. The thin canvas screens enabling them to float on water based on the Archimedean principle of weight, volume, and mass looked likely to swamp in the marginal wind and wave conditions. "We had bargained on the shock effect of these tanks," he reflected. "It would hurt badly to lose them." The weather also looked likely to prevent spotter aircraft directing naval gunfire, crucial to smash through German defenses at the water's edge. Moreover, he did not underestimate the debilitating effect of the choppy conditions, likely to be "distressingly cruel to GI stomachs." They were boarding landing craft eleven miles out. "A heavy surf," he worried, "might defeat our troops with seasickness before they landed."[29]

Bradley never mentioned any particular concerns in his memoirs about the anticipated resistance at Omaha relative to any of the other beaches. Eisenhower's postponement the day before, frustrating though it was, enabled a final look at the latest 21st Army Group intelligence assessment in the Weekly Neptune Review, which was released at 09:00 hours on June 4. The reports, prepared by Brigadier Edgar "Bill" Williams, Montgomery's intelligence chief, were not reassuring reading. "The chief gaps in our knowledge of the enemy in the Neptune area," the report began, "are the strength and location of the 21st Panzer Division" and "the location of the 352 Division." Both were potentially hard-hitting, rugged regular combat divisions, equally menacing in attack or defense. "The evidence about 352 Division is . . . flimsy," the report continued. Williams thought he had identified a significant reinforcement of Omaha and Gold Beaches by German units as early as April 23, situated together on the same coastal sector south of Bayeux. By the middle of May a clearly frustrated Williams was writing:

> "It is a most unsatisfactory state of affairs that we cannot specifically identify all the elements which go to make up the sector we are proposing to assault."[30]

ULTRA—the code name for the signals intelligence produced at Bletchley Park, which had penetrated the German top-secret cipher codes, had identified the locations of fifty-six of fifty-eight German divisions in France prior to D-Day. The two missing were the 21st Panzer, around the area of the Orne River estuary, and the 352 Division covering the Vire River estuary along the coast beyond Omaha to south of Bayeux. Vagaries of "fading" radio transmissions due to bad weather and face-to-face meetings by German commanders amid strict radio silence, had contributed to this. Allied bombing had not been so effective destroying telephone lines to make radio traffic necessary.

Williams was receiving sufficient human intelligence from the French Resistance to feel uneasy or uncertain at best about the density of German defenses securing Omaha. By June 4 he was developing an instinctive *feel* that units like the 352, hitherto "read as layback, have nosed forward into the gap provided by the reduced responsibility of the coastal divisions." His hunch was correct, but not proven. A human intelligence extract from the June 4 report stated, "a single soldier from 352 Division is reported to have been making for Arromanches in March." The German strength at Omaha had risen 150% since March and April, but there was no hard evidence. Williams's final report, read on board the *Augusta* the night before the landings, was actually not far from the truth:

> "That the 716 division has followed the pattern of coast read-
> justments is not substantiated; yet it should not be surprising
> if we discovered that it had two regiments in the line and one
> in reserve, while on its left 352 Division had one regiment up
> and two to play."

General Kraiss in fact had two regiments forward and one, the *Kampfgruppe* Meyer's 915 Regiment, as an inland reserve. Bradley could probably appreciate that aspects of the fire plan, weaponry, and the tactics of the Omaha assault may have no longer been relevant to the situation they would face. Conspiracy theories have abounded since, as this potentially explosive conclusion was kept from the lower ranks for fear of jeopardizing morale. Seventy years on and further research suggest a more plausible explanation. When Williams was asked by the official US military historian of *Cross Channel Attack* whether he had deduced that

Kraiss's crack infantry division had been moved forward, he explained he "could not warn the troops in time."

Bradley, generally in agreement with the prevailing view that the first waves were likely a suicide mission, was convinced his men would break through regardless. "You have to crack eggs to make an omelet," was the philosophical deduction. As early as January 1944, he was personally briefed by Royal Engineer Captain Logan Scott-Bowden, who had covertly reconnoitered the beach. "Sir, I hope you don't mind me saying it," he confided during an Omaha briefing, "but this beach is a very formidable proposition indeed and there are bound to be tremendous casualties."

Bradley disingenuously replied, "I know my boy, I know."[31]

THREE

THE STORM BREAKS

2:00 A.M. TO 5:00 A.M.

"Whole World Against Us"

2:00 A.M. to 4:55 A.M.

At 2:10 A.M. Oberstleutnant Karl Meyer inland from Omaha received the call from Chief of Staff Ziegelmann at 352 Division Headquarters. His Kampfgruppe battle group was still the 84th Corps reserve, but it was immediately to march to the Isigny-Carentan area and engage enemy parachute landings. His battalions were based in a five-mile arc southeast of Bayeux, and included some two dozen armored self-propelled guns, the only substantial armor in the area. They had previously rehearsed counterattack moves during training toward Crépon, on the coast to the northeast. Now they were to go in a completely different direction. Moreover, this was not a drill. Meyer had a tricky coordination task to get his units moving in the dead of night. Once they moved they would be off the telephone network and reliant upon radio for communications.

The 1st Battalion Regiment 915 was at Trungy; truck-borne, by unreliable French wood-burning gas vehicles, with suspect French civilian drivers. Over a hundred vehicles had to be gathered and loaded with troops. "As was to be expected," Ziegelmann remembered, "many of the French drivers claimed it was not possible to proceed further, due to engine trouble, and of course this held things up!" Meyer's 2nd Battalion was even farther away from the proposed line of march, as they were at Esquay-sur-Seulles, north of the Bayeux-Caen N13 road. This infantry, as also the 352 Fusilier Battalion at Lingèvres, west of Tilly-sur-Seulles, was mounted on bicycles. Somehow the bicycle-borne units had to move in tandem with truck-borne infantry as well as their own vehicles towing heavy weapons. Movement had also to be coordinated with the heavy self-propelled guns of the anti-tank unit Panzerjäger Abteilung 352. Ziegelmann appreciated Meyer's problems and gave him the order "at all costs to keep his connection with division headquarters." A radio station was allocated to the truck-borne element of the Kampfgruppe to assist.[1]

French villagers to the south of Bayeux awoke to the sounds of trucks starting amid clouds of exhaust and shouted commands and directions. Frenchmen and Germans had lived at peace in Normandy for four years. Nothing happened here apart from the occasional air raid and seasonal German military maneuvers. France was a virtual rest-camp for the Wehrmacht, a privileged posting, a promised land of "milk and honey," girls and champagne, but most importantly, no danger. The local French were anxious and confused, was this *Le Débarquement*? If it was, there would be hardship amid the joy. People hoped it would quickly pass them by, like the occupation in June 1940, and preferably happen somewhere else.

It was also a confusing experience for many of Meyer's green soldiers. Kurt Keller with the Fusilier Battalion near Lingèvres had passed a restless night so far "with never ending droning enemy aircraft passing overhead." They were bivouacked in tents "under hedgerows which endlessly wound their way through the Normandy countryside." The order to move produced chaos, because, "although for weeks we had reckoned daily with an invasion, we still had exercise ammunition in our pouches and various ammunition boxes." They were still configured for peace:

> "The consequence was that in the very moment of an allied landing, when every minute counted for the defense, we had to start handing out live ammunition and filling machine gun belts."

Nor were they helped by the insistence of the weapons NCO, "despite the ordered rush," to record all ammunition issues in his stock book. The transition from peace to war was indeed indefinable.[2]

Meyer had a real problem, and it took more than an hour to get his units moving by 3:20 A.M. His task force was ordered to cross the Vire River over the bridge west of Neuilly and enter the zone farther west, where enemy parachute landings had been reported. "The march is to be made in several columns and small groups," Ziegelmann instructed from Division HQ. They were up against an unknown foe at indeterminate locations, moving with a mix of truck- and bicycle-borne infantry, towing heavy weapons, and setting off from various base locations at different speeds. The HQ staff was completely unsighted, flying blind about where to contain landed parachute units. The numbers and spread of these enemy units were alarming and confusing. German staff officers liked tidy solutions, professionally plotted on operations maps, to which they would then logically respond, but here they had been confronted with a rash of unconfirmed symbols on situation charts.

Two American airborne divisions had dropped north of Caretan, along the Douve River and inland from the 709 German Infantry Division sector defending Utah Beach. The spread was twenty-five miles long by fifteen miles deep. The US 101st Airborne Division, due to secure the Utah Beach exits, could only muster 38% of its strength from its scattered drop. West of them, around Sainte-Mère-Église and the Douve, the US 82nd Airborne Division could only gather 33 percent of its men. Only about one third of the airborne force was anywhere near its designated drop zones. German situation reports could not therefore pinpoint specific troop concentrations or even likely objectives, which confused tidy decision-making. The nearest vulnerable point appeared to be Stützpunkt Vire, between Utah and Omaha, a concentration of German units designed to shield the port of Grandcamp-les-Bains and the entrance to the Vire estuary. This was considered vital ground for the staff of General Marcks's 84th Corps, and as a consequence the only appreciable reserve for Omaha Beach was prematurely committed to protect it, even though the strength and location of the threat was not known.

Meyer's columns were ordered to proceed via the wooded Cerisy-la-Forêt en route to the west. "Once we were finally equipped for live combat," Kurt Keller with the Fusilier Battalion recalled, "we rode off on our 'steel steeds' [bicycles] toward the coast." Reconnaissance vehicles preceded the bicycle troops, who had also to protect their truck-towed or mounted heavy weapons. The elusive enemy lines ahead had yet to be identified. Meyer was more taxed coordinating the move of his diverse columns than he was devising a tactical plan to deal with the enemy. As he watched his soldiers chugging past on French requisitioned gas-propelled lorries and pedaling infantry, he must have thought this was a far cry from the heady Blitzkrieg advances of 1940. Kurt Keller labored along with a machine gun and two ammunition boxes perched precariously on his bicycle. "I was convinced," he nevertheless recalled, "that we would smash the enemy to pieces."[3]

It was not only Meyer's soldiers who had trouble mentally conditioning themselves to the sudden transition from peace to war. Obergefreiter Hans Lücking in Bayeux heard detonations along the coast. "Was this now the invasion or just a heavy air raid?" he considered. "We had no certainty." He climbed an observation platform on the roof of the seminary building near the old cathedral and looked through the long-range scissor binoculars in the growing light of dawn. "It was still very hazy over the sea," he remembered, but he could see ships on the horizon:

> "At least thirty kilometers away, only blurred vision, but it was a fantastic sight. The whole horizon was black, like a wide black band, unbelievable."

Just before sunrise Lieutenant Hans Heinz was also observing from his treetop OP overlooking Colleville. The sea was covered in mist:

> "Then a light breeze came up. First we saw a great number of mastheads, just like asparagus poking out of the thin mist. A few minutes later the wind tore the fog away completely. I will never forget the spine-chilling scene that met our eyes. At first I thought it was a vision, but shortly after I grasped the awful reality of the scenario. There were thousands of ships."

At twenty-one years old, he considered himself mature. He was used to fighting Russians, "often in overwhelming strength, but this was something else, it was as if the whole world was standing against us."[4]

Standing atop the cliff shoulders left and right of Omaha Beach, the view and reactions were the same. "All of the men who had binoculars stood and stared out at this apparition," Unteroffizier Henrik Naube at WN 74 at Vierville remembered. "While the other men demanded to know what we were looking at." Once they had, "reactions varied, ranging from curses to a kind of apprehensive laughter, or just silence." As with Heinz, Naube "had a great sensation that we were on our own in front of this colossal force." No shots were fired from the coastal batteries, and the sea and skies were completely empty of any German presence. Naube saw the invasion fleet "was simply looming out of the sea mist, just getting bigger and bigger, closer and closer, and nothing at all was happening on our side."

Grenadier Karl Wegner at WN 71 on the other side of the Vierville draw had dozed off during the incessant waiting, his head resting on the butt of his machine gun. His number two, Willi Schuster violently shook him awake. "His face was pale," and "I asked him what was wrong?" He pointed to the sea. Wegner was not going to repeat his former embarrassment of being spooked by another fishing boat coming out of the mist:

> "I looked out and saw ships as far as one could see. I'm not ashamed to say that I was never so scared in my life. But the sight was so impressive that no one could help but just stare in amazement."

His section commander Obergefreiter Lang burst into the bunker. Wegner saw "the look on his face was serious, no more games. This was real, some of us will not be here when the sun sets today," he realized. Lang scanned the fleet through the observation slit with his field glasses. He noticed the navy bunker was shooting up recognition flares. "Idiots," he commented, "any fool knew they were not ours."[5]

At the opposite eastern extremity of Omaha Beach Gefreiter Heinrich Severloh had seen five or six large ships' silhouettes standing offshore with visibility "still more dark than light," about ten kilometers away. At 3:00 A.M. Obergefreiter Peter Lützen fired three white and three red Verey pistol flares from the signals bunker, it was the "we are here" recognition signal. No response came from the silent ships. WN 60 to the right across the draw fired off the same pattern of flares, as did the naval artillery at the small fishing port of Port-en-Bessin four miles farther along. All were ignored. Severloh's battery commander Lieutenant Frerking remarked drily that "those out there are definitely from the other Field Post Number."

The regimental commander Major Werner Pluskat, observing to his right from strongpoint WN 59, watched as "the whole fleet began to approach the coast steadily and relentlessly." It was a memory that was to endure. "Never had he seen anything quite so fantastically well organized and disciplined as the approach of this fleet." He excitedly telephoned Major Block at division headquarters, announcing, "there must be 10,000 ships out here. It's unbelievable. It's fantastic." Block was dubious. "The Americans and British together don't have that many ships," he insisted. "For Christ's sake, come and see yourself," bellowed Pluskat, throwing down the receiver. The ships purposefully maneuvered themselves into their bombardment stations. Pluskat was incandescent with frustrated rage; he wanted to open fire but was instructed to delay until the troops themselves were nearing the beaches. "I've known it all along," he complained to his aide Lieutenant Theen. "We're a suicide squad." Terrified, he stared as the turrets slowly turned and elevated. He knew that at any moment they would open fire.[6]

Sergeant Raymond Crouch and Private Leonard Goodgal had been sheltering in a small alcove in the cliff face near Pointe du Hoc, west of Omaha Beach. They had landed in the sea just off the cliffs, part of the off-course parachute insertions by the US 101st Airborne Division. They were soaking wet and shivering, with just one weapon between them and wondering what to do next. The sudden sound of heavy bombers overhead was accompanied by whistling and crashing explosions at the top of the cliff. Bombs began to hit closer and closer to the beach, and Crouch was worried "the whole cliff was going to come down on top of them." Hastily vacating their alcove, they trudged farther west to get away from the explosions. They needed to find a pathway to the top of the cliff so they could rejoin I Company of the 506th Parachute Regiment.[7]

At about 4:45 A.M. the single radar-equipped Pathfinder Mosquito flown by Flight Lieutenant John Gordon from 105 Squadron dropped red illumination flares over the German battery position at Pointe du Hoc ahead of them. Three heavy attacks over the past two days meant the hand-cranked sirens produced an immediate reaction, German crews headed beneath ground. Nobody took any chances. Machine gunner Wilhelm Kirchhoff recalled, "when the bombers came, we thirteen men from the Werfer unit crouched inside our earth built shelter." Three Mosquito aircraft from 109 Squadron dropped green incendiary markers through the five-tenths cloud cover, which cloaked the objective between 30,000 and 18,000 feet. Eight British heavy Lancaster bomber squadrons supported by another four Mosquito marker planes from 5 Group, numbering 115 aircraft, bombed the battery position in successive waves. "There were very many bombers," Kirchhoff recalled, "you couldn't count them." They came in from the sea, approaching from the northwest. Within five to eight minutes bombs were dropping from between 6,500 to 8,500 feet. Watching from the shelter, "you could see the incessant red flashes from the explosions," Kirchhoff observed, "and everything shook." For thirty minutes 634.8 tons of bombs cascaded down in an accurate and concentrated splashing pattern across the battery site, at over twenty tons per acre. The impacts were devastating. "I didn't realize at the time," Kirchhoff remembered, "my hearing was damaged for life."

Nineteen-year-old Gerette Coulmain, living in the village of Saint-Pierre-du-Mont, southeast of the bombing run, saw "that it looked like the whole sky was on fire." The red marker flares lit up the clouds. Every house was spared in the village, where she sheltered with her grandmother, but "every house in the whole area shook." They were cowering in a corner waiting for the bedlam to end, when:

"Suddenly a German soldier appeared in the house covered in a thick layer of white dust. Blood streamed from his head all over his uniform, completely saturated in blood. He spoke only in German, saying over and over again, *Alles Kaputt, alles Kaputt.*"

They managed to calm him sufficiently to learn that "everything on Pointe du Hoc was destroyed, and the commander and all his soldiers killed." Then he was gone.

The small village of Cricqueville was at the end of the bomb run. Louis Le Devin living there remembered, "the night of the 6th of June was the worst of all," and the whole house shook. They hastily fled into their garden bomb-shelter trench, covered in logs and soil. Like Gerette Coulmain could see "the whole sky was on fire." Some overshoots hit Cricqueville, driving the inhabitants out to seek shelter in roadside ditches. The local church was hit, the blast smashing the altar and blowing out all the windows.[8]

The effects of the bombing across the battery positions was devastating. Most Germans in the bunkers survived, but the enormous volume of high explosive smashed everything but the bombproof shelters. Kirchhoff's fifteen-man unit emerged from their bunker to find "the explosions had trashed many trenches and torn away all the camouflage nets." Few trenches or roads escaped destruction and entrances to many personnel and ammunition bunkers were buried. "We did everything we possibly could to restore the position," Kirchhoff recalled. "If only to be able to move about." Many dead and wounded had to be recovered, but the actual number of casualties from the raid was never recorded. Numerous soldiers had burst eardrums or were suffering from concussion. The only working part of the battery was the fire control center located in the command bunker at the head of the cliff promontory, overlooking the sea. Kirchhoff's Werfer Regiment 84 machine gun crews survived intact, as did their trenches at the cliff edge. An antiaircraft bunker on the west side of the battery also escaped serious damage.

The most serious impact was psychological. The surviving machine gunners managed a meal, and as Kirchhoff recalled, "we said to each other, who knows what the day will bring?" Scattered groups of German soldiers were still burrowing their way out of buried bunkers. The fire control team managed to reestablish contact with the gun crews, stationed in the orchard to the south of the battery, but to little purpose. Some of them had found the local farmer's wine cellar and got thoroughly drunk. One veteran recalled years later in an interview that his shell-shocked gun crew simply said, "screw this," and walked off the position. As dawn approached many abandoned the site or were killed or remained buried beneath the rubble.

Kirchhoff, after all these distractions, looked out to sea and was confounded by a view he never forgot. "Suddenly on the horizon we saw the ships." He had never seen the like before:

> "As I looked, an ice-cold shiver went down my spine. I asked myself, what was going to happen to us now, because it was clear that it was about to start."

Their lieutenant strode up and echoed all their thoughts with his terse comment of "Now we're in for it."[9]

"Bacon and Eggs on the Edge of Eternity"
2:30 A.M. to 4:30 A.M.

At sea the contagion of stirring activity spread between decks on transports. Equipment was made ready and piled as soldiers formed queues for breakfast. The motion of the big ships perceptibly changed as they began to heave to in the transport area and drop anchor. When the USS *Ancon*, the 1st Division's command ship, dropped anchor at 2:51 A.M., she was about eleven to twelve miles off the Normandy coast. Weather was still a concern. "The engines had quieted." remembered Captain Charles Cawthon aboard the transport *Thomas Jefferson* with the 116th Regiment, but "even the big liner was registering the waves." With reveille at 2:00 A.M. and assault craft due to be loaded one hour later, many had gone to bed early the night before. Tension meant men dozed fitfully, but any chance of rest could not be ignored. One never knew when the next opportunity might arise. "I dozed, but was awake when the ship's gong sounded reveille," Cawthon recalled.[10]

Officers like Cawthon were often fortunate enough to have their own "lonely cabin," but enlisted men like Technical Sergeant Felix Branham aboard another 116th Regiment transport, the USS *Charles Carroll*, did not. They were tightly crammed inside a bustling forest of canvas hammocks stretched over metal frames. Stacked five feet high, there was barely two feet in between, so "we had to squeeze in and out" of crowded bunks. Stormy conditions the day before had precipitated a postponement of the invasion for at least twenty-four hours. Ships already underway had to be called back. Felix Branham philosophically saw it as yet another "case of hurry up and wait," in army parlance. All the equipment laboriously loaded aboard the landing craft had to be taken back in board. "Overcrowded, tense nerves, being ready to go, and now this damn postponement," Branham complained. "We wanted to go! . . . We were past ready to get the hell off this rocking boat!" Early this morning the heaving ship was giving little indication that stormy conditions had eased.

They were frightened, but as Branham explained, "we wanted to get on with it." "Funny money," the occupation currency, had long since been gambled away. Black humor surfaced to alleviate mounting fear. "We kidded Gino [Ferrari]," whose twenty-first birthday was due in two weeks' time, that "he wouldn't live long enough to become a man," cheerfully predicting that he would be "shot and killed sometime on June 6." Another chum had secreted huge sums of US dollars in his wallet, regarding English pounds a suspect currency. "We jokingly said," Branham recalled, "Smitty, when you hit that beach a bullet will hit you in the head and one of us will be in that wallet. . . . In reality, we were ready to die to save any or all of our buddies."[11]

"Breakfast in the ornately decorated salon" of the *Thomas Jefferson* "was unreal," recalled Charles Cawthon, consisting of "bacon and eggs on the edge of eternity." Sergeant Robert Slaughter with the 116th Infantry Regiment on the *Empire Javelin* was offered "chunks of well-done meat swimming in white gravy, light bread, and coffee. . . . I wasn't hungry," he admitted. But practical soldier realization that this was would be the last good meal for a very long time led him to "force it down." Others simply got Spam sandwiches, franks, beans, and coffee. Cawthon remembered, "we were quiet; each withdrawn into some private inner place; conversation was perfunctory and absentminded." Activity aboard the invasion transports was driven by an automated process designed to deliver troops on the beaches by 6:30 A.M.[12]

Combat photographer Robert Capa aboard the USS *Henrico* was served breakfast at 3:00 A.M.

> "The mess boys of the USS *Henrico* wore immaculate white jackets and served hot cakes, sausages, eggs, and coffee with unusual zest and politeness. But the preinvasion stomachs were preoccupied, and most of the noble effort was left on the plates."

The elegantly dressed staff then went off to change. Their next task was to treat the returning wounded.

At 4:00 A.M. troops encumbered with overweight equipment struggled through narrow, crowded passageways to make their way to boat stations up on deck. The trancelike, automatic process of getting ready in the stuffy, smoke-laden atmosphere between decks was banished on contact with the outside air. "It was pitch dark," Sergeant Bob Slaughter recalled, "windy and unusually cold for June." As they stepped out on deck, "the cold, windblown spray was like a damp slap to the face. . . . We filed out through heavy blackout curtains into the dark of D-Day," remembered Charles Cawthon. "A cold, damp wind was sweeping the deck and fairly whistling through the rigging." The rise and fall of the big ship was more pronounced up top. Landing craft swung out on davits creaking with the rolling motion of the ship. The sea far below looked uninvitingly black, with an occasional dirty-flecked breaker.

Private John Barnes with A Company of the 116th Regiment was asked shortly before embarkation whether he would be prepared to join a flamethrower team. "Did I have any objections to using this weapon?" his boat officer had asked. He tried one out. "I guess I really didn't think of the full consequences," he remembered. Barnes said yes, although, "I didn't even know if I really had a choice." Flame was a fearsome weapon, against which there was no defense. His decision added even more weight to what was an impractical load. Soldiers were issued assault jackets in lieu of normal issue backpacks for the amphibious assault. The vestlike garment had volumous pockets and "pull-strap fasteners to yank off in a hurry." Into the pockets went K rations, a quarter pound of TNT explosive with fuses to blow fox holes, hand grenades, a smoke grenade, a medical kit with syringe and morphine, M-1 rifle clips, and two slung machine gun ammunition belts. An entrenching tool and poncho was affixed to the back, a bayonet, "and whatever else we could stuff in." Barnes had also to carry the flamethrower operator's rifle and regular pack. His name was Russell Pickett from Tennessee, and he "probably weighed a few pounds more than I did—140 more or less." Barnes had also to carry several gallons of the viscous flame fuel in a jerry can fastened to his back on a carrier, over the rest of his equipment.

When he tried to board a truck taking them to the harbor, the unwieldy load pulled him backward off the lorry. It was decided to jettison the extra fuel. "I'm sure we were the two smallest guys in the unit," he recalled, "carrying the heaviest equipment." Lieutenant Robert Garcia with E Company in the regiment discovered that he could not even lift the assault vest onto his back during preinvasion rehearsals. "So much for being a 'foot soldier'," he commented. "We felt more like a pack mule." Charles Cawthon's men registered their displeasure by "loping and braying about the camp." As "long as they were loaded like jackasses" they claimed, "they might as well sound like them."

Climbing into the landing craft was a well-rehearsed procedure, but the weight, weather, and swell were worse than anything they had encountered in training. Sailors hauled away at the davits aboard the USS *Ancon* to gently lower the low-profile Higgins landing craft. These thirty-six-foot-long, ten-foot-six-inch-wide floating "cigar boxes," as they were nicknamed, gently bumped with the ship's motion against the ship's side sufficiently often to make clambering over the rail with seventy pounds of equipment appear hazardous. Riflemen and BAR (machine gun) men were shoved to the front as the platoon load of thirty-six men jostled for space. Heavy bazooka and flamethrower teams were squashed into the rear with the sailor crew of three. The forward ramp was metal, but the rest, sides and square stern, were made of plywood—scant protection against a high-velocity round. Sailors on deck controlled the jerky, uneven descent into the dark, turbulent waters below with ropes. As they did so, men subconsciously pulled up their beltlike life preserver bands over protruding equipment to keep them high above the waist. One of the macabre lessons from the Slapton Sands debacle five weeks before, when German E-boats had got into a landing craft exercise, was that if a man's belt was too low, he was flipped upside down in the water by the center of gravity. The helmet and equipment ensured that he remained so, mute testimony to a design flaw. John Barnes found "it was an awkward assortment around which we buckled a rubber life belt." He found the buckle was defective, but it was too late to do anything. "I didn't bother with it," he recalled, "since it was a last minute addition, and I had no thought of using it."[13]

"My assault team assembled four abreast at our station in complete darkness," Sergeant Donald Wilson on the USS *Henrico* remembered. "One's eyes gradually adjusted so that objects or people close at hand were discernible." They had to descend thirty to forty feet in this gloom grappling their way down rope netting, which "could be an experience":

> "Heavy swells caused our assault craft to rise and fall dramatically and produced alternate slack and tension in the cargo net. Inevitably the time came to climb over the ship's rail, turn, and begin the descent, grasping the vertical ropes to avoid having a hand stepped on, then feeling with each foot for the next lateral rope. The moment of truth came near the bottom—I guessed there was a six to eight foot variance from fall to rise. If you stepped off too soon, you'd be met in midair by the rapidly rising boat. Step off too late and the boat dropped out from under you until you and it reached bottom. Either case produced nasty injuries."[14]

With the tight schedule, the injured might take too long to get back on board, and they would have to accompany the assault.

Scramble nets were universally disliked, and the least favored option to board a bucking landing craft already in the water. Heavy loads had to be manhandled down separately. "The water was very rough," recalled Private Robert Koch with C Company 116th Regiment, and "a lot of the boys got themselves caught up in the nets coming down the side of the ship and we had quite a time getting them loose. . . . Their legs got caught," he remembered, "and they dropped their rifles and dropped their ammunition and the smaller ship was bouncing up and down against the side of the other ship." Three men in the fleet became entangled and squashed to death, battered against the side of transports and landing craft. Loading was the same as for the davit-suspended boats, riflemen to the front and heavy weapons to the stern. Kneeling was too difficult and nobody wanted to sit in the mess slopping about below. The only recourse was to stand, lean on the sides, or crouch on top of equipment for over two hours.[15]

Loading was laboriously time consuming. Men waited patiently on deck for their turn. Sergeant Bob Slaughter remembered "friends mingled on the deck of the *Empire Javelin,* shaking hands and wishing each other good luck, good hunting, and so forth." Captain Walter Schilling, their D Company commander, reminded them, "the German is well trained and will fight like hell to protect his homeland." Twenty-two pillboxes had been identified in their sector, but it was claimed their beach, Dog Green, was not fully manned and then only with "second-rate soldiers; Slovakian, Polish, and Russian conscripts." Slaughter regarded Schilling as a hard taskmaster. "I myself was far from his favorite noncom," he commented, mainly because he was "always getting caught playing stupid pranks." He admitted, "There was no love lost between us, but I had great respect for him. I would have followed him to hell and back."

The Bedford boys in A Company aboard the *Empire Javelin* were also shaking hands on deck. Inseparable twins, sergeant brothers Roy and Ray Stevens were going ashore in separate landing craft. Roy felt unable to shake his brother's hand, declaring "I'm not gonna make it." Ray attempted to defuse the emotion by agreeing they should meet at the crossroads up beyond Vierville-sur-Mer and shake hands there. Of course they would make it, he insisted.

"Guys shouted out to their friends in other boats," John Barnes remembered, but "I didn't." He had only arrived four months before.

Slaughter was impressed with Eisenhower's letter to all the Allied assault troops. "You are about to embark on the Great Crusade," it famously began. Slaughter got his pals to autograph his copy, which he neatly folded, wrapped in plastic inside his wallet. He kept it until his death. Barnes, struggling across the davits overloaded with flamethrower equipment on the other hand, remembered, "we didn't feel like Crusaders." War correspondent Gordon Gaskill heard soldiers singing, parodying the birthday song with, "Happy D-Day, dear Adolf, Happy D-Day to you!" Combat photographer Robert Capa aboard the USS *Henrico* observed the men around him "stood in perfect prayer." Aware of what to expect he remembered, "none of us was at all impatient, and we wouldn't have minded standing in the darkness for a very long time."[16]

Doubts and concerns at what the reception on the beach might be preyed on everyone's mind. Captain Cawthon had a soldier who refused to obey an order just before embarkation. The protest was out of character for the man, who quite rationally disputed the sanity of war. Cawthon tried to reason with him, pointing out he could not be replaced, and that while, "I had a similar sense of its insanity," he did not doubt "it had to be done." This convinced him. It was not always possible to be so accommodating. Lieutenant Robert Garcia with E Company of the 116th, on the *Thomas Jefferson*, had a soldier who refused to board his landing craft at the last minute. "I certainly did not have time to fuss around with that problem," he recalled, and asked the Navy to "preferably throw him in the brig." Fear was infectious and had to be dealt with immediately. "Whatever became of him, I don't know, nor do I care," he recalled. John Barnes with the flamethrower team on the same boat had prayed the night before. "I thought I would make a bargain with God," he confided. "My life spared tomorrow, and I'd become a priest." But now on reflection, "I thought that this was a bad deal" for both parties, "so I said I'd take my chances, but I did promise that I would do everything else He asked of me."[17]

Landing craft engines spluttered into life, raising clouds of diesel exhaust. After a few perfunctory shouts for cable release the craft surged away from the transport sides. Cold spray burst over the ramps and sides of the "Elsies" (as the LC landing craft were collectively called) and immediately soaked everyone. They began to circle, waiting for the various formations to assemble on the water. The command group boat for the 1st Battalion of the 116th Regiment became wedged beneath the ship's "head," or toilet outlet of SS *Empire Windrush*. It remained stuck for thirty minutes, unable to go up and down. "During this half hour, the bowels of the ship's company made the most of an opportunity which Englishmen had sought since 1776," remembered Executive Officer Major Thomas Dallas:

> "Streams, colored everything from canary yellow to sienna brown and olive green, continued to flush into the command group, decorating every man on the boat. We cursed, we cried, and we laughed, but it kept coming. When we started for the shore, we were covered with shit."[18]

Captain Cawthon's boat descended alongside the *Thomas Jefferson* "with a rattle of chains and screech of wire cable." Streams of cryptic, tinny orders came from the ship's address systems while other unintelligible commands were amplified by bullhorns. He remembered:

> "We in the boat were in something of the position of a patient on the operating table listening to a surgical team discuss his condition in a strange jargon."

On reaching the heaving surface of the water, the first wave "slacked the cables and then dropped us with a crash as it rolled on." Thankfully Cawthon realized they would not be slammed into the ship's side because the propeller dug into the water and they were able to follow the shepherding launch that took them out to join the other craft. These were:

> ". . . Circling as in some strange conga line in the dark, with red and green riding lights appearing on the crests and disappearing in the troughs of waves that were four to five feet high."

Everyone was soaked by great spumes of spray plucked by the twenty-mile-per-hour wind from the tops of waves, which dashed over them. Concerned they might swamp, Cawthon passed the word to inflate the life belts.

> "The sudden expansion of perhaps seventy-five belts added to the bulk already crowding the craft, and so we rode, packed like sardines in an open can, feet awash in bilge water and altogether uncomfortable."

Sergeant Bob Slaughter's boat also inflated belts, tightly compressing them, "cold, wet, and miserable" inside the craft. "It seemed," so he thought, "that we were slamming into waves with enough impact to start every rivet ever set."[19]

The US 2nd Bomb Division had meanwhile begun to form up at 10,000 feet northeast of East Anglia, bordering the UK Midlands. At about 4:30 A.M. it swung south. Lieutenant Robert Jacobs was the dead reckoning navigator in the lead Liberator *Liberty Run*, "firing specific flares as the 446th aircraft assembled in formation behind us." Wallace Patterson, a bombardier with the 448th Group over Manchester recalled, "we did lose our leader once in the clouds and then picked him up later on." The four combat wings of the 2nd Division formed four immense aircraft streams as they approached the Channel. Like the ships below, they flew into an ever-narrowing air corridor. John Gibson flying with the 44th Group recalled, "the area kept getting smaller and smaller, so that we were just going through the neck of the funnel." This funnel poured them over the Channel just east of the Isle of Wight as the first pink glow to their right heralded sunrise. Omaha Beach lay directly ahead, thirty minutes flying time.[20]

"It was just getting light as our formation left the English coast," remembered 2nd Lieutenant Ben Isgrig with the 448th Group, "and the clouds broke enough for us to see hundreds of ships in the Channel heading for France." With the cloud thickening ahead, "I began straining my eyes to see some of the invasion fleet our briefing had disclosed," remembered Claude Meconis, copiloting a Liberator with the 446th. "A low overcast in patches obscured most of the water, but whenever open spaces permitted, I could see landing craft and large ships moving south and southeast on a fairly rough sea." Allen Stephens flying alongside was awestruck, as were all the crews at the immensity of the fleet beneath them:

> "I had the surging feeling that I was sitting in on the greatest show ever staged—one that would make world history. As we flew nearer to the target, that feeling increased to exhilaration and excitement, for it was truly a magnificent operation. We saw hundreds upon hundreds of ships below."

Henry Tarcza overhead in a B-17 recalled, "it appeared from our altitude that one could almost step from one vessel to another and walk between England and France."[21] "We could plainly see the heavy warships shelling the coast, which was shrouded in smoke," remembered Ben Isgrig. "And there were more heavy bombers in the air than I thought possible to put up in one area." The bombing approach run became very constricted. Each target was due to be hit by six waves of six aircraft in a thirty-six-aircraft group box. With a standard formation of between 520 to 1,000 yards wide, the approaching armada was almost seven miles wide. The line of targets coming up on Omaha Beach was five miles. Wallace Patterson recalled the complexities facing the 448th Group: "We were number three in the first section," of six aircraft, and each section had separate targets in the same area with bomb loads varying between 500-pound and 100-pound general purpose and fragmentation. "We had 500-pounders and as a target the gun emplacements at Pointe Percée on the coast." Aircraft streams had therefore to compress from seven to five miles in width, a physical challenge for Liberator pilots to fly their notoriously difficult aircraft in close formation. This was before they had even considered the flak that might lie ahead. "We were scared a bit, yes," admitted Liberator copilot Meconis:

> "Because we didn't know exactly what kind of air opposition Jerry would throw at us. Frankly, I expected to see a sky full of fighters and flak, all confusion."

As Wallace Patterson flew in he too noticed the cloud perceptibly thickening ahead. "As we approached the French coast the clouds shut off our vision of the landing itself," he recalled, "but looking obliquely under them we could make out spasmodic flashes of gunfire, though we could not see the source." They were now flying over ten-tenths cloud cover and were completely dependent upon the Pathfinders just ahead. "The coast itself was covered in clouds," Ben Isgrig realized. "We didn't see our target at all; neither did we see flak or fighters." Many pilots like Herman Mitch, flying *Paddy's Wagon*, had cause to remember the Group commander's terse reminder at the briefing that morning:

"There will be a lot of your friends below you today. Be careful you don't drop on them. If you're down there heading for an invasion, you don't want someone to ruin it by dropping a bomb on your boat."[22]

This was the dilemma that Army commander General Bradley had imposed on the Eighth US Air Force. Bomber technology in 1944 required luck to hit the approximate area of a target. Given sufficient lucky strikes, the objective might be destroyed. It was assessed the first assault wave of landing craft would be three miles offshore when the 2nd Bomb Division hit its targets. Three miles represented thirty seconds' flying time. Bomb release delays were calculated from the water line and depending on arrival times for successive waves, release would vary from no delay to 5-, 10-, 15-, or 30-second delays for subsequent serials. This meant as many as fourteen different bomb release times, or even more for lone "independent" bombing runs. The margin of error was further constrained because bombers were emerging directly from the sea, not flying along the coastline. Throw the bombs too early and they would hit their own troops, release too late and they would completely miss. Bradley's strict requirements imposed compromises, which could only dilute the anticipated results.

The four approaching bomber streams were dependent upon H2X radar carried by just twenty Pathfinder aircraft among the 450 approaching the coast. The H2X was a simple revolving antenna emitting high frequency radio pulses, from a dome that replaced the Liberator's belly gun turret. The bounce-back of these radio pulses sketched a radio picture of the terrain below. The greater the number of returning pulses, the brighter the image on the scope. Sharp corners such as on ships and urban areas yielded very bright blips on screens, whereas ocean or flat areas appeared dark. As grim-faced pilots registered the density of the clouds coming up, "Mickey" operators had already picked up an astonishing number of infinite white blips, exposing the extent of the invasion fleet below. It was an awesome technological spectacle they would never see again. "As we approached the coast," Lieutenant Robert Jacobs with the lead aircraft *Liberty Run* remembered, "the radar navigator called me over to look at his PPI scope. It clearly showed the vast armada just off the coast of Normandy—a thrilling sight even on radar."[23]

The huge B-24 streams thundered over the coastline, bomb bays open, totally reliant on the few aircraft technically scanning for the sharp outlines of bluffs and draws on their H2X scopes to reveal targets. Pathfinder Liberator pilots and bombardiers were more transfixed watching second hands ticking away on watches than positively identifying bomb release points. Seconds were counted down for 5-, 10-, 15-, or 30-second pauses. On hitting the bomb release they watched the aircraft trailing behind drop their bombs as soon as they saw their own fall away. Bombers unable to see the leaders flew in on the colored smoke markers dropped to attract the stragglers. For over twenty minutes serial after serial dropped about 13,000 bombs, aiming astride the draws where the German strongpoints were located. It presented an epic spectacle from above, wave after aircraft wave bombing through the cloud layer. Wallace Patterson behind the *Liberty Run* recalled:

> "Just after bombs-away a terrific explosion rocked the entire formation, leaving a dense cloud of brownish-gray smoke. Though it may have been heavy flak, as we were only at 14,500 feet, we are of the opinion that it was a bomb that exploded by some freak accident."

The streams flew on, banking to starboard. "It was daylight, with the sun shining above the clouds in the east," remembered Claude Meconis. "We turned right to head 270 degrees for ninety miles until we were west of the Cherbourg Peninsula." There was intermittent flak.

"A group to our right passed too close to either Cherbourg or the islands west of it," and an intense "ball of flak" came up. The operation turned out to be a "milk run"; just one crew crashed over England. The only negative impact was tired crews and a little airsickness from the constant buffeting, riding mass, and crisscrossing slipstreams. Lieutenant Colonel Philip Ardery in the 2nd Combat Wing immediately checked back with his bombardier for results, because "we could see nothing below us but the deck of clouds into which our bombs disappeared." He wanted reassurance. "I think we dropped them right in the bucket," his bombardier replied.[24]

A week later Brigadier General Leon Johnson, the 14th Combat Wing commander, recalled, "I thought our plan worked out pretty well, personally." Yet when the photographic reconnaissance results came in, Allan Healy with the 467th Bomb Group had to admit, "the D-Day missions were disappointing. No results of our action could be seen." The main impact was probably psychological. The Germans, it was assumed, had been intimidated if not damaged, and Allied troops reassured by the immensity of the air fleets they saw overhead. Healy had, nevertheless, reluctantly to admit, "we had not been able to do what we had in our potentiality to do."

Meanwhile the naval bombardment had begun. "Where are the airplanes?" Lieutenant Robert Lee Smith, the operations officer for Captain Lorenzo Sabin's US Navy Gunfire Support Team pounding Omaha, shouted over the cacophony of noise from naval gunfire. "It was a question no one could answer at the time," Sabin recalled. No one had seen a bomb detonate from the ships as the first wave of landing craft powered on inexorably toward the beach.[25]

"A miss is as good as a mile," it is often said, but the 2nd Bomb Division had erred by as many as up to three. Bomb delays caused virtually all the ordinance to explode at least a mile beyond their intended targets. Apart from grazing the top of some of the Omaha bluffs here and there, there were some 13,000 bomb craters pitting fields and meadows among dead cattle inland. There was not one crater on the beach.

"A Series of Flashes on the Horizon." Bombardment.
5:50 A.M. to 6:20 A.M.

T he reverberating drone of heavy aircraft came out of the sea like an approaching squall. What made it particularly menacing was that nothing could be seen through the clouds. "The noise got louder and louder," Heinrich Severloh at WN 62 on the east Colleville side of Omaha remembered, "and the roar of the motors rose to a hellish thunder as a powerful, ghostly fleet of bombers came directly at us in the gray, cloudy sky." There was virtually no warning, everybody jumped into bunkers, shelters and gun pits. Grenadier Heinz Bongard in WN 60 to Severloh's right recalled, "bombs raining down like being poured from buckets, you could hardly see through them." The "blessing" was the detonations were on the bluffs behind the strongpoints, but the village of Colleville behind "got a severe mauling." "Not a single bomb fell on top of our strongpoint," claimed Gefreiter Ludwig Kwiatkowski manning an antiaircraft post on WN 62. Machine gunner Franz Gockel had no time to leap into the air raid shelter but took immediate cover beneath his heavy machine gun table. "We were covered in filth and smoke, the ground shook and my eyes were full of dust," he recalled. "Then as quickly as they had come, the broad waves of heavy bombers passed over our heads and were gone," remembered Severloh. There was a pause, then:

> "Immediately thereafter, their load came howling whistling and crashing down. The bombs fell like heavy rain, and the first hit barely fifty meters behind our strongpoint."

It was the same for the opposite west side of Omaha Beach at Vierville. Henrik Naube manning WN 73 heard the aircraft approach, a 20mm flak gun fired, "but they were too high in altitude." The first they realized they were under attack was when "bombs came down at an angle, diagonally out of the sky, and the explosions made the whole cliff shake and sway under us." His machine gun crew had pulled a protective metal plate over their concrete trench. They soon appreciated "they were missing us, if we were the target, and the bombs hit inland areas behind us":

> "This was a great relief, and we laughed in a nervous apprehensive manner as the sound of the planes moved away inland too."

Near the center of Omaha, Gefreiter Gustav Winter, sheltering in his "concrete panzer" by WN 66 believed:

> "I think we were bombed by aircraft, but I'm not sure. I couldn't hear properly, but I felt a lot more explosions, which seemed to be some distance away."

A few bombs came close, with shrapnel rattling on the side of the panzer turret, "and a lot of smoke was coming through the air vents." There was a pause and more explosions sounded off inland. "I braced myself and closed my eyes, that was all I could do."[26]

Just inland, there was more chance of bombs hitting the local French than Germans. Lieutenant Hans Heinz viewing from his treetop observation post overlooking Colleville was concerned about his friend Lieutenant Heller. Some of the bomb overshoots had landed around his 6th Kompanie positions. "Later I heard there were no appreciable losses," he recalled. "The whole company had dug in, but Lieutenant Heller's eardrums had burst."

Twelve-year-old Jeanine Dubois had sheltered with her family in an open trench, dug in their garden at Vierville. "Once in the trench we saw some planes flying above us and dad said that we could not stay there." The Germans had mined the area around their house, but had built a large air raid shelter for themselves and their horses. "We told them that we were afraid and they let us in." They were lucky. "The German soldier took me in his lap between the horse's legs," she remembered. Andrée Oxeant shared a ditch covered with a metal plate and logs with some thirty old men, women, and children, "if you could call it a shelter," she commented.

The vast majority of bombs fell into the meadows and pastures beyond the beach. Cattle were flattened by the air pressure and shrapnel from 100-pound fragmentation bombs. Houses were also destroyed. "We could see the black smoke belch out of the fiercely burning village of Tréviers," inland from Omaha, recalled Gefreiter Simeth with Regiment 916. "Where would those pretty girls stay now? I thought to myself. Formigny was just missed. . . . A farmhouse was next to us, and in front of it stood an old woman who bitterly cried that all her cows and horses would be killed." They tried to console her. The Darondel family in Formigny heard the bombing and Monsieur Darondel came out to check his livestock, and "saw two of my horses in a pasture, one mortally wounded and the other resting on its side and copiously bleeding." He led four horses back into the stables; the pastures were becoming too dangerous. "Then my family and I took refuge in a makeshift shelter to await events." Pierre Ferrary and his wife at Grandcamp-les-Bains watched the bombers come out of the sea and fly from left to right across Omaha, "hundreds, thousands," he recalled, "it's a formidable, almost inconceivable swarm." He watched as "one bomb explosion follows another," while "our young servant is sobbing with fear." They had already spent most of the night "between two walls of earth at the bottom of a hole."

At dawn Louise Oxéant had set off with her ten-year-old son Bernard to help milk her neighbor's cows. She sat her son astride a donkey with milk churns tied on at either side. Her husband Aristide watched them go. When they reached the pasture over a mile inland the bombers came and enveloped the whole area in a series of flashing multiple impacts with rising smoke and dust. Aristide frantically set off after them, but they had both been cut down in their neighbor's meadow.[27]

Outside WN 62 on the east edge of Omaha Gefreiter Ludwig Kwiatkowski was amazed to see a group of *Organization Todt* building workers turn up outside. "Our strongpoint was still not completely finished," he recalled. "Dumptrucks were still standing around." The newly arrived and clearly dismayed workers were invited inside the strongpoint, "and had a few rifles quickly pressed into their hands."

Gustav Winter at WN 66 in the center of Omaha was gazing at the fleet when he saw "a series of flashes on the horizon," which he mistook for flares. "Then there was a horrific noise in the air, which was a long crashing sound, and we began to be hit by huge explosions." The eighteen warships of Force "O" standing off the beach began firing at 5:50 A.M. They had thirty-five minutes to engage a spread of sixty targets. Obergefreiter Peter Lützen on the highest point of WN 62 remembered "the whole sea was sparkling, and then this huge thing came flying over." Winter saw "a solid wall of ships," like "a steel curtain across the horizon, that's how many they were." He "had a very bad feeling now." Out at sea, "the warships that were firing on us were lighting up the whole array of ships with the flash of their guns." It may have lasted only thirty-five minutes, but "the intensity of that bombardment was more than anything I had known on the Eastern Front." He likened the experience to a physical and mental buffeting:

> "When one of these naval shells exploded near us, the shock wave came through the ground and traveled through the panzer, which felt like a punch in the stomach. These blows came again and again, every time a kick in the belly, and making my ears ring horribly."

Very soon the ethnic Czech loader was on the floor of the turret, "and began sobbing, the poor idiot." Winter had already discounted him as being not particularly bright.

Henrik Naube's position to his left, perched on the cliff top at WN 73 at Vierville, was engaged by 190 rounds of five-inch armor-piercing and high explosive rounds from the battleship *Texas*. "The intensity was astonishing," he remembered, "heavier and far more accurate than the bomber planes that had just hit us." Naube was an Eastern Front veteran, and had "learned to brace myself against it, both physically and mentally." It was no less terrifying:

> "These shells made a noise similar to a gas blow torch being run at full strength and at first they passed right overhead. We could actually see them as bright shapes flying inland over the beach—huge shapes too, the size of a car engine or similar."

They dragged the steel plate shutters over their trenches again and huddled down, cradling and protecting their machine guns. Much of the naval gunfire was missing. Well-camouflaged bunkers hindered accuracy. The ships were standing four miles off, and low clouds with a light wind meant smoke from the dune grass fires lingered and obscured the beach area. Rising black smoke mixed with the low-level cloud mass above, dimming visibility even further, and making it difficult for the naval fire control teams to identify hazy point objectives from so far out. But even a near miss from a battleship could be demoralizing. Naube was intimidated by the sheer "power of explosions" that "made the concrete of the trench ripple and fracture." Shock waves from the air pressure "punched all the air out of our lungs, and made our eyes bleed." Huge pieces of shrapnel "were flying left and right horizontally, screeching and smashing off the parapet and the steel roof plates."

ROBE

"It went on and on, for salvo after salvo, with absolutely no pause in between the impacts. It was as if a gigantic hammer was falling on the beach, trying to pound it flat."

Naube remembered, "most of us remained calm and disciplined." German veteran accounts at Omaha often dwell on the psychologically stressful impact of the Allied naval bombardment rather than on its destructiveness. It was lethal, however, for anyone caught in the open. "One man near me could not take the stress," Naube recalled, and tried to flee along the exposed zig-zag trench system.

"He was caught by an absolute storm of shrapnel, and his torso was ripped across and broken open. Absolutely ripped open, from front to back. He fell in the open part of the trench, and countless other bits of debris fell on him, mutilating him further."

There were direct hits. Naube watched one concrete Tobruk machine gun shelter thrown into the air about five hundred meters away. "It was terrifying to watch those men flung out, knowing that the same thing could happen to us." They had no option other than brace themselves and stay under cover. Any doubts were negated by the sight of the unfortunate shell-shocked casualty, whose "body produced a lot of steam in the cool air, which filled the trench for a while."[28]

Machine gunner Ludwig Kwiatkowski was alongside Christian Faust in a Tobruk covering the northernmost point of WN 62 overlooking the water filled anti-tank ditch. Not once had they dared raise their heads to look through the vision slit. "That we had not filled our trousers was a wonder," he later recalled. "Not one of us on top of the strongpoint was hit by shells," he explained. "They all went directly overhead." There were some casualties. Obergefreiter Siegfried Kuska's 50mm anti-tank gun position, expertly hidden by a fold in the ground, took a near miss, lightly wounding his loader Franz Heckman. Heinrich Severloh above him recalled, "the naval bombardment was closer, the nearest hitting maybe ten meters behind my machine gun nest. . . . Lots of dirt was being kicked up, but we weren't really in danger. The sky was darkened by dense smoke," punctuated by the "flashes of thundering explosions." The gorse bushes around them caught fire, "but most of the shells of this barrage hit too far above the strongpoint and did little damage." Severloh's hearing would be seriously affected for the rest of his life, but he was not yet aware of it.

Gustav Winter in the center of Omaha at WN 66 summoned up the courage to look outside his panzer turret. Despite considerable surface damage, the defenses all around were still intact:

> "There were huge craters in the sand everywhere around us and in places the sand was on fire from the explosives. The [50mm] PAK gun near us was in one piece, and the crew there signaled to me with a green signal flag that we used. We had no phone or radio of course, and I was deafened anyway."

Heinz Bongard on the east cliff shoulder at Omaha was shaken up by the explosion that destroyed strongpoint WN 60's magazine. It smashed his machine gun position and wiped out the machine gun nest alongside. In essence, however, the fifteen strongpoints defending Omaha Beach were left broadly intact and remained combat effective. "It was our luck that the majority of these huge shells howled over us," recalled Lieutenant Heinz observing from the high ground above Colleville.[29]

Once again, as with the bombing, much of the ordnance that missed the German defense landed amid the seaside resort villages of Vierville, Saint-Laurent, and Colleville. Denise Ygouf had dressed and taken her children to the newly excavated ditch shelter at the bottom of her garden in Vierville. All the noise and shelling overshoots had convinced her this really was *Le Débarquement*:

> "I then realized that I barely brought anything with me and I decided to go back inside the house—desolation! No more windows, the curtains flying in the wind."

Glancing out to sea, "I only saw boats, you could not see the sea anymore." The thirty-six-year-old housewife earnestly attempted to pack a suitcase, but "was forgetting the main things because I was so distressed." She morbidly thought she was either going to die "in that house that was shaking all over the place" or when she got back to the garden, "I was going to find everybody dead in the shelter."

Edmond Scelles lived on a farm at Saint-Laurent-sur-Mer, which took many of the overshoots aimed at Gustav Winter's WN 66 position. Four shells slammed into their house in rapid succession. "Our thick walls were certainly very solid and we believed that they could withstand the shooting," Scelles recalled. "But then a heavy shell directly struck the house and everything heaved and shook." The family decided it was time to leave. On the other side of the street was an abandoned German shelter, constructed with overhead logs. "We decided to hide in there." They agreed they should attempt to flee to Formigny, two miles farther south, but they had to wait for a lull. Edmond Scelles was still not totally convinced this *was* the invasion. There had been landings at Dieppe in 1942 and he thought, "it was another raid they were doing down there" on the beach. Whatever it was, they had to get out of the way.

Fernand Broeckx had woken early that morning in Colleville to find he was in the thick of the activity behind WN 62. "The situation" reflected in the din all around "seemed to me to be worrying." He called to his wife upstairs, "I think it's time you got up," when the shelling descended:

"At this time, I will honestly confess that I was afraid. I had the feeling the house was going to collapse on us. The walls were damaged and the floorboards lifting up. You could hear the tiles falling, one after the other, as well as the crash of breaking glass."

There was black smoke rising above the height of the sand dunes in the direction of the sea. He gathered the family together in their shelter, pressed against the house walls opposite the sea side. "A strong odor of powder caught at our throats," Heinrich Severloh on the other side of the dunes remembered. "It smelled like the remains of a fire, and the air tasted bitter." While Broeckx upstairs collected his belongings a shell came through the kitchen window and struck the inside wall at an angle, ricocheting off against a partition. It "literally spun my wife around, who was hit by a small fragment," he recalled. Neighbors were soon on the scene to pick her up and offer care. Broeckx went back in the house and "calmly turned on the stove to heat up a cup of real coffee, which we had painstakingly saved for the day when we would need a tonic."[30]

D-Day for the inhabitants of the three coastal villages nestled behind Omaha Beach was to be a day of ignorance and anguish. Everybody thought about the welfare of their relatives. It was an emotional day, joy tempered with the harsh realization that if this was truly *Le Débarquement*, life from now on would be hard going. There were no proper shelters. It would have been better if the Allies had landed elsewhere.

Shortly after 5:00 A.M. Oberstleutnant Karl Meyer received the order to halt the westward progress of his columns. The Fusilier battalion from the Kampfgruppe, on bicycles, had started ahead of the 1st Battalion's truck-borne infantry and reached wooded cover at Cerisy-la-Forêt. There had not been any clashes with American paratroopers thus far. It had been difficult for Meyer to launch the *Kampfgruppe*, General Marcks's 84 Corps reserve, with its mix of motorized infantry, bicycle troops, towed anti-tank guns, and tracked armored self-propelled guns. General Kraiss, the division commander, aware now of increasing activity by the coast, was having doubts about the wisdom of committing his only substantial reserve away from the beaches so soon. There was little reliable radio communication with Meyer's units once they had started moving away from the telephone network. Only half of the Fusilier battalion had reached Cerisy Forest and elements of the 1st Battalion 915 Regiment had already passed them in their antiquated requisitioned French trucks. The gas-driven trucks were starting to break down and there were no spare parts. The French drivers were far from concerned, less willing than lazy. General Marcks, the corps commander, had agreed to halt and was considering a change of direction. Both he and Kraiss were being subjected to a torrent of increasingly anxious messages about the level of activity off the coast. Large numbers of landing craft had been observed.

This was the beginning of the nightmare odyssey of the Kampfgruppe Meyer; it was to crisscross the hinterland of Omaha throughout D-Day. Meyer having started the advance westward, seeking enemy contact, only had tenuous contact with his units. It looked as though he might have to turn around and go in the opposite direction. Units were ordered to pause by the roadside and await orders as the increasing light of a gray dawn developed. The self-propelled armor was moving with the 1st Battalion. Gefreiter Peter Simeth, commanding one of the truck-borne infantry sections, was supporting them. "We were to keep the roads clear for them," he remembered, "and help to camouflage them," because with the dawn they expected increased enemy air activity. Kurt Keller with the Fusilier element, struggling with his machine gun and ammunition boxes slung around his bike, had yet to reach the Cerisy-la-Forêt. They could hear the ominous "drumfire" of naval artillery rolling along the coast to their right. "Despite the considerable distance," he recalled, "we could detect the vibration through the ground."

It appeared that the invasion had already started.[31]

FOUR

DEATH RIDE

4:15 A.M. TO 6:30 A.M.

A Wild Death Ride
4:15 A.M. to 6:15 A.M.

Some landing craft had been circling, buffeting through waves for forty-five minutes before the first landing wave formations set off for the beach at about 4:15 A.M. Sub Lieutenant Jimmy Green, on the *Empire Javelin*, carrying several 116th Regiment companies, had previously worked with the US Army Rangers. He regarded them as "a pretty tough group," who "looked as though they could take care of themselves," whereas the 116th he was carrying today was different. "A very pleasant lot, like country boys, they looked like Somerset lads," he observed. "Very pleasant, very open, wanting to be friendly, though we didn't have much chance of speaking to them." His landing craft were carrying the first wave, the so-called "suicide wave among the flotilla." This label was applied with black humor, but now they had to actually deliver. Green noticed, "they were very quiet when they got on board." There were no high spirits. "I think they were realizing that this was it."

Rough swell surging around the transports had caused a few mishaps before they cast off. Green in LCA-910 was giving orders to his coxswain and directing the flotilla when John Barnes's boat, LCA-911, struck his own astern. Unhooking the craft from the mother ship was difficult in turbulent water. Green suspected his boat was holed, which meant the naval signalman would have to keep them afloat using a hand pump. There would be twelve miles to go, over two hours, and much of it in darkness. Troop transports had disembarked their landing craft behind a screen of fighting ships, well out of range of the German coastal batteries.

"Our craft immediately began taking on water as its flat bow slammed into seven-foot swells that sloshed over the front and ended up in our laps," recalled Sergeant Bob Slaughter riding with D Company 116th Regiment. The Higgins boats, designed to work in shallow Louisiana swamplands, were known to bounce and shake even in a moderate swell. For many soldiers, this was to be the longest boat ride of their lives, standing jam-packed and sluiced down with sea water for an average of one and a half to three hours, depending on course, and wind and current conditions. The stench of diesel soon mingled with the sharp tang of vomit. "It wasn't long before all hands were ordered to bail water with battle helmets," Slaughter recalled. Landing craft engines bellowed all around as the ragged assault lines labored toward Omaha Beach.

"The blackness had begun to dissolve into dull gray," recalled Sergeant Donald Wilson with the 16th Regimental Combat Team. "After some time, the control craft broke out of the circle and headed toward shore, followed by our battalion, in a line of assault craft strung out behind."

It was getting lighter still and an epic scene began to unfold. With the increasing visibility Wilson saw that "similar lines could be seen paralleling ours."

The twenty-four landing craft of the 16th Regimental Combat Team (RCT) formed the left forward front of the "Big Red One" 1st Infantry Division. To their right another twenty-four boats carried the 116th RCT, spearheading the "Blue and Gray" 29th Infantry Division. Regimental Combat Teams were so called because of the mix of infantry with specialist demolition and heavy weapons teams that would land 1,450 men in the first wave, supported by sixty-four Sherman DD (Duplex Drive) tanks. They wallowed in on a three-mile front between Vierville to the west and Le Grand Hameau in the east. Behind them would come a further 150 landing craft in successive waves. "It was to be a long miserable ride," Slaughter remembered, and "yes, I actually looked forward to getting ashore. . . . The roar of the engines made it hard to talk or listen," interspersed with sharp banging and slapping reports as boats burst through six-foot waves drenching all on board in a whistling 10- to 18-knot wind.

Captain Charles Cawthon was buffeting along thirty minutes behind with the second wave. "For more of us than we yet realized," he recalled, "it was a wild death ride going in with the tide." Nobody spoke on Cawthon's boat.

> "Talk would have been difficult in any event above the roar of the engine, the wind, slamming of the waves against the ramp, and the laboring of the bilge pump that just managed to keep up with the water washing in over bow and sides. We simply stood together, encased in equipment, inarticulate with the noise and with the enormity toward which we were laboring."[1]

It was still a hazy twilight.

Seasickness was all pervasive. Shutting eyes to close out this misery made balance inside pitching craft all the more difficult. Brains received conflicting signals. Eyes saw a still world, but ear equilibrium sensors were registering the opposite. Such contradictions trigger alarms inside the body and halt digestive tract activity. The only way to harmonize visual and motion stimuli is to fixate on a distant horizon, which was impractical in a rearing and plunging landing craft at night. Men gagged, retched, and vomited, producing the unpleasant sounds and smells that set everyone else off. Dizziness and nausea accompanies this condition. Abdominal muscles contracted until all that was left in the digestive tract, after the onrush of fluid, were "dry heaves," expelling an acidic saliva, which eventually dehydrates the body. Private John Barnes remembered, "one by one the men began to get sick, heaving their last meals." Combat Engineer Captain Robert Stewart had cause to rue "we were fed a dream breakfast, order almost *anything* and get it." This now "went over the side or into their helmets," Barnes observed, "or anywhere." Barnes himself remained impervious, "it didn't bother me," he recalled, "I felt the excitement of being there." In Robert Capa's E Company 16th RCT boat he recalled, "in no time, the men started to puke," caustically observing "little bags had been provided for the purpose," but to little avail. "Soon the puking hit a new low."

Constant drenching by Channel spray added to the gradual physical deterioration of soldiers who had been cooped up for weeks in transit camps during the marshaling process, with little opportunity to exercise. Body resistance was not at its usual peak efficiency. Many were already shivering with the onset of exposure, which creates a carefree lethargy, akin to drunkenness. Corporal Gilbert Murdoch with A Company of the 116th RCT remembered men obsessively popping seasickness pills. "One guy took half a bottle of the durn things and was practically walking in his sleep when he went off the craft."[2]

The tactical decision to offload outside the range of German coastal artillery and subject troops to this exhausting twelve-mile run in to the beach had unintended consequences. The British chose to launch eight miles out. The cumulative physical degradation from seasickness and exposure was countered to some extent by soaring adrenaline levels. Sheer excitement and dread at what lay ahead on the beach distracted some men from seasickness. It cannot be clinically proven, but prolonged retching and exposure may well have blunted some of the combat edge of landing troops. Excessive combat weights would also produce sluggish performances in waist-deep surf. Combat engineer Robert Healey remembers squad members being seasick even before entering the landing craft. Although not retching himself, he remembers how uniforms impregnated with an anti-gas solution "had an awful stench to them." For Lieutenant Robert Garcia, the pervading image of the turbulent ride to the beach was "rough-rough-rough." Seasickness affected many of his men:

> "At one minute we would be on the crest of a swell and see all that surrounded us. The next minute we would be down in a hollow and the scenery was nothing but water, and more water."

"To keep the LCA going and stop it being swamped took your undivided attention," remembered Leading Seaman John Tarbit, coxing his landing craft even, "to steer the thing and keep it afloat."

Low tide on shore was at 5:25 A.M., at which time offshore currents were having a negligible impact on the direction of approach of landing craft. But then the flood tide would rise eight feet inside one and one half hours. Coxswains steering the landing craft were often unaware that the change between ebb and flow would increase the current moving from west to east from 0.2 to 2.7 knots by 7:30 A.M. Overladen craft laboring through high waves at five knots would lose speed in any case, and now they were being pushed right to left by a contrary current going at over half their approach speed. Not only were boats slowing, which would compromise tightly calculated landing schedules, they were coming in at a 35- to 45-degree offset angle. Some of the larger and more powerful boats were creeping up on the earlier waves, and in some instances, overtaking them. If coxswains did not make decisive course alterations, they could land in the wrong place. The first Force "O" assault waves were being irresistibly pushed leftward.

The sky was lightening in the east at about 5:20 A.M. as many of the landing craft plowed their way through the battleship line, seven miles out from the beach. It was a spectacular first light, as US combat photographer Seth Shepard aboard LCI(L)-92 remembered:

> "The blackness changed into a shadowy gray and then into a more distinct but still dull gray until the rays of the sun—still below the horizon—began streaking the heavy clouds with traces of pale pink. This suddenly burst forth into brilliant red for a few minutes and then as suddenly disappeared into the bluish morning skies."[3]

Many veterans on both sides recall the sinister rising dawn was the color of blood that morning.

One hour and ten minutes remained before H-hour. The steel colossus of the battleship *Texas* was dimly visible in the growing light. Second Lieutenant Wesley Ross with the 146th Engineer Battalion glanced up at her massive bow as they wallowed by. "I looked up at the name TEXAS on a huge battleship," he remembered. The Royal Navy cruiser HMS *Glasgow* sailed by her, en route to their battle station. Commander Felix Lloyd-Davis on board recalled they were reciting Lord Nelson's famous pre-Trafalgar prayer over the ship's address system as they sailed past. "All their ship's company took off their helmets," he remembered. "They were at their guns, as they heard us reading the prayer, going in."

At 5:50 A.M., eight minutes before sunrise, the whirring turret mechanisms of the huge fourteen-inch *Texas* guns rotated toward their target
quadrant at Pointe du Hoc to the west of Omaha. Wesley Ross was
completely stunned by the sudden broadside from ten guns:

> "The flame and dark brown smoke was quite a spectacle in
> itself, but the blast was almost unbelievable and would have
> blown off my helmet had my chin-strap not been fastened."

As they sailed on, "we could hear the distinctive *whhuutuu-whhutuu-
whhuutuu* of those fourteen-inch shells." The abrupt effusion of surface
spray that came with the flash and blast from the massive guns smoothed
the surface of the water. This led many eyewitnesses to assume this
outpouring of energy was pushing the huge colossus sideways across
the surface. "The muzzle blast from a salvo was absolutely astounding,"
claimed Lieutenant Robert Garcia, "and believe it or not, I could sometimes see the projectiles flying through the air." Ingenious engineering
absorbed the several-hundred-ton shock of recoil through compressed
air cylinders inside the gun mountings. The apparent sideways wake was
water broiled by the concussive shock of the gun blasts. "Godawful,"
Specialist Sergeant William Lewis with the 116th RCT described gun
reports, "terrible explosions," and an awesome spectacle. "The smoke
ring passed by us and it looked like a funnel of a tornado, growing larger
and larger, finally dissipating." Powerful though they were, the blast
and recoil of the gun systems was not sufficient to propel 57,000 tons of
inertia through the water, but as Sergeant Slaughter recalled, "a mountain
of water came roaring over to toss us around like a cheap cigar box."⁴

The nearest battleship to shore was the converted World War I dread-
naught, the USS *Arkansas*, firing twelve twelve-inch guns. Rod Lewis
with the 146th Combat Engineer Battalion was startled by the impact
of its broadside, which "felt as though it picked us up and shoved us

along." "Let's go, this is it," his platoon commander Lieutenant Keahley exultantly shouted. "There was no mistaking the sound of sixteen-inch projectiles hurtling overhead like so many steam locomotives running at full throttle," Sergeant Donald Wilson recalled. In the growing light, the excitement of the awesome spectacle unfolding around them distracted them from the retching. They were now passing through the destroyer line booming away two to three miles offshore. "One of the men, Peterson," Lewis remembered, "a new man in our platoon was silently crying. 'I am going to die,'" he insisted. Lewis tried to console him, "stick by me and we would make it," he said.[5]

General Omar Bradley, commanding the First US Army aboard the USS *Augusta* had risen at 3:35 A.M., having slept in his clothes. He was on deck at first light and "squinted toward the shore where it was blurred in the morning mist." He had been afflicted by a large boil on his nose, which had been lanced by the infirmary the night before but it "felt ridiculous with that big bandage on my nose." The medic insisted he wear it to prevent infection. Photographers had already been forbidden to take pictures of him on this historic day.

With fifty minutes to go, Bradley knew it was time to launch the 64 DD tanks to provide vital support to the early waves on Omaha Beach. He could see nothing, but understood that marginal conditions were jeopardizing the plan. The navy advice he received was not to launch, but the final decision was in the hands of individual Landing Craft Tank (LCT) commanders. There was immense activity going on around the *Arkansas* but Bradley was powerless to influence events at this late stage. "A faraway roar echoed across the Channel, and off our starboard bow orange fires ignited the sky," he recalled, "as more than 1,300 RAF bombers swarmed over the French coastline from the Seine to Cherbourg."

Lieutenant Robert Spalding with the 16th RCT on the east side of the approaching assault wave spotted men in the water miles out from the shore. "We passed several yellow, rubber boats," he remembered. "They had personnel in them, but we didn't know what they were." Sergeant Robert Slaughter's landing craft came across "three shivering, water soaked survivors from a landing craft or floating tank that had swamped and sunk." Most boats continued on to the beach. "I don't know what outfit they were from or how long they had been in the water," Slaughter commented. Three lucky men were rescued, "but in reality, their ultimate fate just might have been postponed," he admitted. Landing craft were already running low in the water and over capacity. "We left their mates, with Mae Wests inflated, bobbing in the turbulent waves," to an uncertain fate.[6]

The secret development of swimming DD tanks relied on the Archimedean principle of volume displacing water; that a heavy weight can float in a metal bucket if big enough. Their canvas flotation screens were to achieve tactical surprise on the landing beaches. Sixty-four Sherman tank DDs from the 741st and 743rd US Tank Battalions were due to come ashore east and west on Omaha Beach five minutes before H-hour, to engage the bunkers and strongpoints covering the beach exits. General Bradley, observing offshore, had already appreciated that sea conditions were marginal at best. The limit for launch was a maximum Force 3 wind and sea conditions, the waves he was observing verged on Force 4. Even the wash from a passing landing craft was sufficient to swamp the square canvas structures that barely kept the tanks afloat, two feet above water. Lieutenant Edward Sledge with A Company of the 741st recalled, "the complete confidence of the men in our tanks," because "in all our training in England, we had not lost one DD tank." Many tank crews, however, elected to take on an extra 60 to 100 rounds of 75mm ammunition, which was more than a ton extra. Despite the sea being rough, "much rougher than the tanks ever operated in," according to the unit after action report, the 741st launched over three miles out. It was the supreme test of a "wilco" American command philosophy, prepared to risk all to support the mission.

Those launching their vehicles felt—according to later reports—"that the advantage to be gained by the launching of the tanks justified the risk of launching the tanks in the heavy sea."

Two options were open to crews driving off the ramps, awash in the dark, to enter the choppy waters. They could either sit on top and rely on Mae Wests or life rafts in the event of an emergency, or risk staying inside and trust their "Davis Lung" breathing devices. The latter offered protection against shrapnel during the run-in to the beach, the former a quick exit if they did not make it—claustrophobic cover versus naked risk. The Davis Lung was an awkward submariner escape apparatus, which pinched off the nose and gave ten minutes of air from an oxygen bag through a rubber tube. The gadget did not sit easily on the mouth or nose, and tended to snag when exiting a tank hatch. It required a cool head to operate in the chaotic and claustrophobic confines of a rapidly sinking tank. Most tankers considered it overly complex, preferring to rely on familiar life vests and rubber dinghies.

Private First Class Ralph Woodward with the 741st Tank Battalion sat in the assistant driver's seat of C Company Captain Young's tank. When they launched, the water was so choppy "we were lucky we didn't wash back against the ramp," he recalled. As soon as they slipped off, the nightmare began. They had gone about one hundred feet when "pipes started kinking, the struts started snapping back in center," and "the canvas started tearing." Captain Young ordered everyone to bail out. Woodward inflated his life vest, but it got caught in the hatch. In the ensuing panic he dislocated his left arm, which snagged on the tank's .50 caliber turret-mounted machine gun. Before realizing what was happening, he was snatched beneath the surface of the water by the momentum of the sinking tank.

Tanks sank down at depths varying between sixty to one hundred feet. Crewmen involuntarily blew out air at the shock of immersion in cold water and were disoriented by the tumbling gyration of their unwieldy shapes sinking like stones. As Woodward's tank crashed into the sea bed below, "sand came up in my face. . . . The first thing that came to my mind," he recalled, "was my folks will never know where the hell I'm at." There was little wriggle room in the tight crew compartment as a ton of water rushed in, pressing them up against the hull sides. Urgent cries of "clear the hatch," and the sudden overpressure of freezing cold water emptied their lungs, unless cool heads prevailed. Woodward did not even consider fitting his Davis breathing apparatus. "I thought no use setting down there, laying down there, thinking for ten minutes," he remembered, "just that quick, you think of things." Better to end it quickly he thought, "so I started drinking water."

The moment of resigned relaxation at his fate was sufficient to release him from entanglement, and the buoyancy of his life vest propelled him upward. Divers at these depths have to equalize pressure in the middle ear during ascent by pinching their noses shut and blowing. Failure to do this can result in severe pain and ear injury during a rapid rise. Nitrogen bubbles absorbed in body tissue at great depths produce aching joints termed "the bends"; and the excess of nitrogen also affected sensory perception, impairing the judgment of some of the stricken crews. The key was to release air as they rose, but many had none to begin with, and simply lost strength and went limp. Woodward saw lighter water above and popped to the surface. He retched water and blood and spotted Captain Young in the water nearby. They were lucky, a small rocket-bearing landing craft picked them up and reset Woodward's arm in the bottom of the boat. Their driver was still sitting in his seat at the bottom of the sea.

Crews that had clustered on top of their turrets generally fared better. From on top, Staff Sergeant Millard Case with the 741st Battalion heard the ugly ripping sound of the canvas screen of his B Company tank tearing. "I knew damn well the tank was going down," he realized, and immediately yanked the life raft's inflation string. It only half inflated, but he hung onto it, even as the suction from the plunging tank pulled him under the water. He held on until it surfaced, and he and another crew member piled inside the raft. Three of the crew did not make it out. Others like Sergeant Phil Fitts got as far as halfway to the beach when the engine died, flooded by the water intake. "I was the last one to step off the tank rail and into the raft," he recalled. The crew survived, but "the tank disappeared from under my foot into a swirl of water, gone."

There were considerable doubts aboard LCT-549 according to Lieutenant Barry, who thought "the sea at that distance was too choppy for tanks." He tried to get confirmation from "the next senior army officer by visual signal," but it was too late. They had already started to launch. Yellow flags went up and the tankers drove forward to give it a go. Three tanks trundled off the ramp with their crews perched precariously on top. Driver hatches were left open, ready for a quick escape. In no time canvas screens rapidly split and struts buckled under the impact of the waves. Engine compartments flooded, momentum was lost, and within one hundred yards tanks turned sideways, broached, and sank like stones. Sergeant John Sertell, in charge of the fourth and last tank aboard LCT-549, drove over the edge knowing there was an obvious tear in the canvas screen, caused by the earlier buffeting on board. "It was a vain hope," described the astonished Barry. Sertell's body was picked up later in the day by a passing LCT. Twenty-seven of thirty-two tanks from the 741st foundered. Two of them were located thirty years later by French divers nearly nine miles off shore, and at least ten were discovered between four and seven miles out. Ensign R. L. Harkey, aboard LCT-602, launched all his tanks. "I am not proud of the fact," he admitted, "nor will I ever cease regretting that I did not take the tanks all the way to the beach." Lieutenant Colonel Robert Skaggs, commanding the ill-fated 741st, estimated an average of one man per tank was lost by drowning. US Navy Seals were still recovering remains from newly discovered tank hulks in the 1980s.[7]

One of the vagaries of fate was that the 743rd Tank Battalion, ploughing through the same Force 4 conditions, elected not to launch. They were supporting the 116th RCT to the west of the beach. It is conceivable they were influenced by their stormy Channel crossing, which had scattered many landing craft. It was too late to form up in the ordained assembly areas before running to the beach. "We were behind schedule," recalled Captain Lorenzo Sabin, coordinating naval gunfire support, so "all craft proceeded directly toward the beach, bypassing assembly. It would have taken too long for the swimming tanks to labor along at three mph to achieve the overriding imperative of a 6:30 H-hour. The 29th Infantry was depending on them."

The infantry buffeting their way through the drenching spray were oblivious to all this. At the five-mile point, LCA Flotilla Commander Jimmy Green began passing a group of LCTs. He turned to A Company Captain Taylor Fellers with the 116th RCT and asked, "What the hell are these doing here?" "They're supposed to go in ahead of us," the company commander responded. "They were really plowing into the waves," Green recalled, "going as fast as they could, but they were only doing, what, five knots to our eight, and they were shipping water." They would never make the beach by 6:30. "We've got to go in and leave them behind," he told Fellers, "they are not going to make it." There was no choice; they parted company as Green's infantry LCAs overtook, "We've got to get there on time." Only ten of the sixteen 743rd LCTs would reach the shoreline in time to the west of Omaha, and just five swimming tanks—the survivors of the 741st's "forlorn hope"—would make it to the east. The plan was beginning to unravel even before they set foot on the beach.[8]

Sie Kommen!
5:00 A.M. to 6:30 A.M.

Between 4:30 to 5:30 a.m a flurry of telephone reports were received by Oberstleutnant Ziegelmann at 352 Division HQ at Château du Molay-Littry, eleven miles south of Omaha Beach. They gave an observed running commentary of scores of boats approaching the beach. "Sixty to eighty fast landing boats approaching the coast near Colleville," reported Lieutenant Frerking at WN 62. Observers from 916 Regiment, "ahead of Vierville," had detected "forty-five smaller and middle-sized boats," moving toward them. One of Oberstleutnant Ernst Goth's lookouts at WN 74 had counted, "altogether 140 ships assembled in the bay of Vierville." Then at 5:20 A.M. a report was received that "tank landing craft have been clearly observed" among them. This was significant enough for Ziegelmann to warn off Panzerjaeger Battalion 352's self-propelled guns inland. They would have to make ready, as they would likely be called forward soon. Many of them were, however, already committed alongside the Kampfgruppe Meyer, rumbling westward toward the reported enemy parachute landings. Ziegelmann became increasingly concerned. No one anticipated an attack would be made at *low* tide, which was about now. All the landing craft obstacles would be clearly visible to the approaching first wave.[9]

On the west side of Omaha Unteroffizier Henrik Naube gingerly slid away the metal covers protecting his concrete trench. "The cessation of the noise and blast waves comes as a great relief," he recalled, which he took to mean that a landing must be imminent. "My ears were ringing, and I had blood on my face from my eyes." The soldiers around him began to steadily recover and emerged from the bottom of their trenches:

> "One by one, our men put their heads up over the lip of the
> trench they were in, or over the parapet. I lifted the MG 42
> back up and re-sited it in the firing slit."

His father had done just this, he recalled, as a machine gunner at the battle of the Somme in the First World War. "Now here I was doing the same thing." They washed their eyes free of grit and dust, using water from their canteens, and looked out. Just ahead, "the sea was absolutely alive with vessels, which all seemed to be the same design and color. . . . Invasion barges," they called them, landing craft. "There were at least ten directly facing me, coming through the initial swells of the waves off the beach." All around he heard brief stuttering reports of other machine gunners test-firing weapons, survivors from the shelling, ghostly spectres coated in light colored dust.[10]

Across the Vierville draw Grenadier Karl Wegner watched the landing craft. "It seemed like hundreds of them," rocking back and forth in the wake of the larger ships. "Suddenly they all turned and began to come straight in toward the beach." Obergefreiter Lang called out to hold fire until he gave the order.

> "He was on the field phone, but I didn't hear it ring. The sweat rolled down my brow as I watched these boats come closer and closer. My stomach was in knots."

Gefreiter Gustav Winter sealed inside his concreted panzer turret at WN 66 in front of Saint-Laurent-sur-Mer could see very little. "Through my periscopes it was difficult now to see anything because of smoke outside." Grass fires from the burning bluffs were obscuring his vision. "I managed to get my young loader off the floor of the panzer," he recalled, where he had cowered throughout the short fierce bombardment. "We got ourselves into some form of fighting shape, ready for whatever was to be thrown at us." He felt some reassurance from the height his position occupied. Attackers would find it difficult to "climb the cliff that led off the beach onto the dunes," as the low seawall had to be negotiated, "and then a sand cliff of several meters, which was strung with mines." Panzers would never get up it and even men would have difficulty climbing. "At times, the sea wind blew the smoke clear, and I could see large numbers of craft on the sea coming closer." The ramps had "high vertical walls," and "again I had the feeling of a wall of steel coming toward us—an absolute wall."[11]

The Germans had between eight hundred to one thousand troops covering the Omaha Beach area. About 450 of these were manning the WN strongpoints and the rest were dispersed in squads, platoons, and company groups in houses and trenches in the vicinity of the four-mile-wide beach sector. The numbers belied the effectiveness of the men in the strongpoints, because they were all manning or protecting crew-served heavy weapons. WN 62 on the east side of Omaha, for example, with its thirty-nine men was manning two anti-tank guns, two field guns, two mortars, and seven machine guns, as well as providing a forward artillery observation post. These were force multipliers. The approaching American landing craft would soon be enmeshed in a tight web of sixteen anti-tank guns, nine 75mm rapid fire field guns, nineteen mortars, six panzer turrets supported by a total of thirty-six machine guns. The seven or so 50mm pedestal guns used surplus ammunition from obsolete Panzer III tanks, and were potent landing craft killers. Mounted on a concrete ring stand, they could fire twelve to twenty rounds per minute, and were able to penetrate Sherman tanks at close range. Most were sited flush with the ground, with a metal gun shield to the front on a ring mount or inside casemates. Inland were three 105mm artillery batteries with three days combat supply, 2,700 rounds per battery, on standby. Off to the western flank near Grandcamp-les-Bains was a fourth heavy battery of 150mm caliber with 1,800 rounds available. Further beyond were twenty-four of the 32nd Luftwaffe Flak Regiment's much-feared 88mm guns. There was one of these high-velocity guns in bunkers at each end of Omaha Beach, able to intersect in the middle. The resulting "spider's web" of flat-trajectory anti-tank arcs and overhead artillery fire boxes was directed at the killing area, the center of the web, which was the mined obstacle belt on the water line.

Two hundred four-ton "Belgian Gates," so called because they were road obstacles removed from Belgium's former 1940 defenses, were erected along the beach and festooned with mines. They were supplemented by 450 *Hemmenbalk* tripod-shaped ramps, whose sloping edge pointed out to sea, designed to tip over landing craft at high water, aided by mines or with *Stahlmesser* sawtooth devices to rip open boat hulls. Lifted from the previous Czech border were 1,050 "Czech Hedgehogs," jagged railroad sleepers welded into spikey star shapes to snag landing craft or block tanks. A further 2,000 stakes were sunk in the sand using local fire brigade high-pressure hoses, and were tipped with mines. Gustav Winter, peering through his panzer turret at WN 66 could feel reasonably secure that when the approaching wall of landing craft hit the bramble thicket of 3,700 obstacles in their path, the German defenders of Omaha would be presented with a target-rich environment.[12]

Once the enemy had landed, the gun crews and German infantry squads in support would take up fighting. Strict fire control was a priority. Oberstleutnant Goth, commanding the defending 916 Regiment, had ordered no opening fire until the assaulting enemy troops had actually entered the water, inside the obstacle belt, when they would be at their most disorganized and vulnerable. The nine- to ten-man German infantry squads were dependent upon the firepower of the MG 42, so effective that variations are still in use today. It had an impressive cyclic rate of fire of 1,200 rounds per minute, sounding like ripping canvas. Trained operators fired aimed bursts of three to five rounds. *Schütze 1*, the man behind the gun was the "specialist," the most important man in the squad apart from the leader. He was generally an experienced soldier or young Gefreiter, who the company commander had recognized as future squad leader potential. These leaders were either capable young or highly experienced *Unteroffiziere* (NCOs) or Gefreiters (Corporals). The latter would likely be adorned with combat medals (as well as scarred, frostbitten feet) from the Eastern Front. The rest of the squad was youngsters, some so young they were issued candy in lieu of their cigarette ration, and these lads often addressed squad elders as *papa* or *onkle*.

Once the squad leader had sited his machine gun, covering likely enemy approaches, he then selected *Stürmabwehr*, or likely jumping off points for counterattacks by his riflemen. Soldiers were armed with the 1898 rifle, based—according to the standing army joke—on the experience of the wars of 1864 and 1866. In short, an antiquated weapon. Men were trained to withhold fire until the *feuerüberfall*, when the firefight was won, from concealed ambush positions. Thereafter, using signals or radio, it was a question of integrating flat-trajectory-fire—machine guns and anti-tank guns—with high-trajectory overhead fire from mortars and artillery. Everyone was schooled in the urgency of selecting and identifying positions for the storm groups, who were mobile riflemen able to hit the enemy bypassing their locations, covered by the lethal, ubiquitous MG 42. Platoons of thirty to forty men often defended a complete strongpoint, or Stützpunkt, inside company sectors, which would have squads or weak platoons assembled on standby to counter attack.

Many of these young men were experiencing highly intense naval gunfire for the first time. Franz Gockel felt isolated and vulnerable, alone with his Polish machine gun in a one-man bunker at WN 62 at the east end of the beach. "I had no one in the midst of this inferno of naval artillery to speak a single word to," he recalled. At home during allied air attacks, "we called the Mother of God, Saint Joseph, and our patron saints for protection and help." He craved human contact; he knew that Siegfried Kuska the 50mm gunner nearby had his loader wounded, and there was another machine gunner manning a Polish machine gun on his own, forty meters away to his left. "Until then, we had only counted on a landing at high tide," but now at low tide, with "the water about three hundred meters from the shore," here they were. Kuska came crawling across the fifteen-meter divide separating them to warn him, "Watch out Franz," he called out, "*Sie Kommen!* They're coming!"

Gefreiter Heinrich Severloh found the clearly shell-shocked radio operator *Wachtmeister* [technical sergeant] Ewald Fack, cowering at the entrance of Frerking's observation post bunker. "His entire body shivered and trembled," and he had dropped his pistol. When Severloh handed it back, "he looked at me with a face contorted by fear and flickering eyes." Another howling shriek descended and detonated against the zig-zag trench, and Severloh was hurled back when the visor of his helmet was struck by a fragment of shell fuse, which he saw rolling and smoldering at the foot of his trench. Lieutenant Frerking emerged looking concerned and rebuked him for not coming inside to shelter. Severloh was his aide and they were close, "the Lieutenant worried about me," he remembered, "but he appeared to me suddenly to be noticeably transformed." Frerking had been monitoring the approaching boats from the bunker, "as if," Severloh explained, "he didn't believe he would survive that which lay before us."[13]

Lieutenant Hans Heinz could see out to sea beyond WN 62 from his treetop OP in between drifting clouds of smoke. "They had imagined it was going to be a cake walk," he recalled, watching boats entering the obstacle belt:

> "Once their bombers and naval artillery had wiped it over, hardly any resistance would be forthcoming, but then it turned out rather differently."

Ludwig Kwiatkowski manning his machine gun at the north corner of the strongpoint concurred, "the Americans truly believed they had flattened everything." On the western side of the beach Karl Wegner in WN 71 lifted his machine gun into position:

> "I tucked the butt of my MG into my shoulder, resting my cheek on it. I braced myself for the recoil. I checked the view down my sights but, somehow, I just couldn't watch what was happening. I closed my eyes waiting for the order to fire."[14]

It all seemed so unreal. They were waiting for the heavy guns behind to open fire.

France Looked Sordid and Uninviting
6:15 A.M. to 6:30 A.M.

Only at 6:15 A.M., after being underway for an average of two hours or more, did the men in the low-profile Higgins landing craft get their first glimpse of land. "A haze of smoke, barely darker than the dull morning, was the first sign of the shore," recalled Captain Cawthon with the 116th RCT. The coastline came up as a dimly perceived, dirty, chalky wall; cut by *V*-shaped openings to ravines leading up from the beaches. "Then the line of bluffs that lay behind the beach began to loom above the Channel waters," Cawthon observed. An occasional hint of houses and buildings could be seen. Flamethrower assistant operator John Barnes excitedly realized, "we could see the bluffs and above that, the single spire of a church. It was Vierville!" The entire shoreline appeared deluged with dirty red flashes reflecting through clouds of smoke, dust, and spiraling debris. It was one hour after low tide; ebb was being superseded by flood.[15]

They passed the destroyer line at between one and two miles short of the beach. Sergeant William Lewis, an anti-tank gunner with the 116th, saw the sleek destroyers come "within a thousand yards of the shore and let go their five-inch and six-inch guns. . . . The flash of the big guns was blinding and the explosions deafening." They proceeded on through a fire zone that subjected them to a crescendo of sound. Thirty-six M7 Priest 105mm SP Howitzers aboard ten LCTs were deluging the beach with fire from two to five miles out. Sixteen LCTs with two Sherman tanks apiece were firing directly at the beach from under two miles. The battleship *Texas* had switched its fourteen-inch fire from Pointe du Hoc to the village of Vierville, while the *Arkansas* began engaging pillboxes and bunkers that covered the road leading to Saint-Laurent-sur-Mer. "We could actually see the projectiles spiraling as if thrown by a gigantic quarterback," recalled Sergeant Slaughter approaching the eastern side of Omaha. "We plugged our ears with cotton," recalled a still anxious General Bradley aboard the USS *Augusta*. "The ship shuddered," as she engaged her predesignated targets. "The salvo coasted over the armada and we followed the pinpoints of fire as they plunged toward the shore." It was growing steadily lighter, "and because the sun was hidden in a haze overhead, a gray panorama opened about us. . . . I choked down a scalding cup of coffee," he remembered. As he discussed his growing concern with Brigadier General Bill Kean, his chief of staff, the German guns were not replying.[16]

"It was now light enough to start taking pictures," war photographer Robert Capa decided nearing the beach, "and I brought my first Contax camera out of its waterproof oilskin." This was a dawn invasion, not in darkness, like Salerno in Italy. Capa was hopeful he would get good pictures. There was growing excitement around him. Lieutenant George Itzel, a platoon commander with the 147th Engineers felt "overawed" looking around. "As far as you could see from port to starboard it was nothing but ships," he recalled. "You look behind you, it was nothing but ships." "Take a good look!" someone in John Barnes's landing craft called. "This is something you will tell your grandchildren," providing the first distractions after two hours of unremitting misery. Nobody, Barnes remembered, was cynical enough to mutter the obvious rejoinder, "What if we don't live?" At this stage he recalled, "We were excited, and not frightened."[17]

"As we approached the beach we heard a terrific noise," remembered Sub Lieutenant Jimmy Green. There was a pause in the bombardment as nine LCT(R)s each discharged 1,064 five-inch rockets apiece, less than two miles from shore. These whooshing, spiraling rushes went over their heads and landed pointlessly in the water, "a good quarter of a mile off the shoreline." Green was incandescent, "a terrific firework display but absolutely useless and I shook my fist at them." There would be no foxholes on the beach.

The absence of any German return fire was ominous. "I wasn't all that pleased" at the failure of the rocket strike, Green observed, "because I was beginning to make out pillboxes on the beach, and it looked a pretty formidable beach for the troops to take." As they got nearer a fencelike barrier of wooden stakes and metal obstacles could be made out, extending out into the water. Beyond was a dark gold sandy beachline, maybe three hundred to four hundred yards wide to cross, ending at a nine-foot-high bank of sloping shingle. The beach was supposed to be cratered by bombs and rockets to provide cover, but there was no evidence of this, "a virgin beach," Green recalled, and "not a sign of any place where the troops could find shelter." Out of sight beyond the shingle was a waterlogged moat of swampy ground, a virtual anti-tank ditch in front of the grass-covered sandy bluff that rose at a steep angle of 35 to 40 degrees. On the west side of the beach there was a part wood or masonry promenade seawall extending a third of the beach length, topped with concertina wire. Even though it was growing lighter, "it was still a grim, depressing sort of morning," Green remembered, "and the cliffs looked very foreboding and sinister." There was still no effective incoming German fire. "We knew the Germans were there," Green recalled, "because they were popping mortars at us." The lack of a German response was intimidating by its absence.

At the two-mile point Green turned around "to give the order to come into line abreast" for the final touchdown. As the flag signal went up, he saw LCA-911 suddenly slip beneath the waves. A multitude of dots bobbed up in the water, supported by life jackets. Green's orders were explicit: "Don't pick up anybody from the water. Get to the beach on time." He now had a difficult decision. "It went against the grain to leave people in those seas with life jackets and the Americans with all the equipment they had with them," but there was no choice. "It really did hurt to go on," he admitted, "but I had to do it."[18]

"Suddenly, a swirl of water wrapped around my ankles," remembered John Barnes aboard LCA-911, "and the front of the craft dipped down." They had been right on course and even identified the solitary Vierville spire when the disaster happened that everyone dreaded from the start. With water swirling up to his knees, "we shouted to the other boats at our side," but they simply waved back and continued on. There was no warning, no noise or impact, the boat simply "fell away below me." The collision at the transport had holed them and the bilge pumps had finally given up in sight of the beach. When Barnes activated the CO tubes in his life belt, the damaged buckle, which he had noticed at the start, "popped away" from the belt. He "grabbed the back of the man behind me in a panic" to stop himself going under. Luckily their heads remained above water level. At first he clutched at a rifle wrapped in a flotation belt and then their flamethrower supported by two, but his overweight vest continued to drag him down. His platoon commander, reacting to the shouts by people around him to jettison the jacket swam up and released the straps with his bayonet. At last he could float freely. Padley, the radio operator, who had a large SRC 300 strapped to his back, went down like a stone and "no one saw him come up." Boats continued to pass by, but at two thousand yards from the beach, "no one stopped." They were all overloaded, Barnes recalled, well down in the water "on their own mission and their own schedule." It was with sinking hearts they apppreciated that being so low in the water, "we did not see anyone."

Sergeant Roy Stevens had begun to hopelessly bail with his helmet as they went down. He was convinced LCA-911 had struck an obstacle, "just like that. Punched a hole in it." Like everyone else, he recalled, "I was about as scared as I ever was. I could swim, but not real well." His twin brother Ray might wait at the Vierville crossroads for some time, because he would not be there to meet him. They struggled to keep their heads above water.

Still no effective German fire came from the beach. The ragged line of landing craft wallowed through the shallow water of the obstacle belt. The Belgian Gates were 250 yards out from the high-water mark, with fencelike doors festooned with lashed *Teller* ("plate") mines. Beyond was a bramble of assorted wooden stakes, ramps, and metal spikes, all adorned with mines. "France looked sordid and uninviting," remembered Robert Capa observing from his approaching landing craft.[19]

Sergeant Donald Wilson with F Company 16 Regiment had saved eating his apple until they were circling, awaiting the call-forward order for the beach. It was "partly as a bit of bravado," he remembered, "and partly to be doing something to ease the tension," which it did. Some of his men, wide-eyed watching him, "did double-takes and nudged each other." Wilson went through the ritual of passing his little superstitious mojo around, a small wooden carving of the Chinese god of happiness. "My habit was to rub his protruding stomach," which he invited those around him to do, for "a little additional insurance, which could not hurt." At this point his six company landing craft suddenly moved from line astern to line abreast, "throttles opened wide and the race to the shore was on." He recalled:

> "The right and left of my boat, a line of assault craft plunged forward, pushing crests of water ahead of them. I know that the Light Brigade and Pickett's Charge flashed through my mind at that beautiful moment. It was pure excitement. The thrill, the exhilaration of the experience was, and remains to this day, indescribable, yet palpable."

Sergeant David Silva's E Company of the 116th Regiment had meanwhile been pushed from the west to east side of the beach by the current, and was starting to become mixed up with the "Big Red One" assault wave to its left. Everyone ensconced below level in the boats was oblivious to what was going on around them, and the extent to which the assault formation had unraveled. Silva remembered they crouched low in the boat, "to avoid maybe being struck by a stray bullet, or we didn't think they would get through the ramp because it was so thick." Troops felt vulnerable in the wooden Higgins boats; the only metal protection came from the bow ramp. "There was a lot of fear," he admitted, "I think everyone had it a little bit." Senses were assaulted by the noise, which had reached a tangible intensity. "You could see all of this stuff going over our heads and hear it more than you could see it," which was reassuring. "Gee, if anyone survives this," Silva remembered thinking, "we'll walk in!" They were now mixed in with the F and E Company boats from the 16th Regiment. Each boat was an island of itself, with no contact during the run-in with their parent unit:

> "There is nothing you can hear because the sound of the boats is quite a roar and the water around you is hitting the boat. You really didn't hear anything that was going on. You could hear the rockets if they were fired, like whoosh, from the large ships. As far as seeing ahead, you couldn't see much until you got within a mile."

Unbeknown to boat crews, the current was remorselessly diverting the main weight of the first wave away from the Vierville end of the beach, toward the Saint-Laurent in the center and Colleville to the east. Constant corrections in course caused delays and overtaking by larger, more powerful landing craft, which was diluting the symmetry and weight of the attack.

Donald Wilson had only just realized how young the coxswain steering his landing craft was. "He looked about sixteen. A tiny, wide-eyed face peering out from inside his helmet, with his white knuckles gripping the steering wheel. . . . Hardly reassuring!" the grim faced veteran recalled. Up ahead the "low-lying land mass" was becoming more recognizable. The drift was channeling them toward the obstacle-strewn killing area between strongpoints WN 61 and 62. A rocket support LCT "plowing well ahead of our line," released a salvo of rockets, "sort of fluttering as they rose like quail in the air." He watched expectantly as "all I saw was successive rising plumes of whitewater. . . . The son of a bitch had fired them all short," he remembered with some indignation. Firing at fixed range, the captain had not brought the boat in close enough. "A case of lousy range estimation or, more likely, loss of nerve," Wilson concluded.

> "So, no smoke and sand in the air, no holes, no open emplacements or wire taken out, bad news, for which we would pay a terrible price."[20]

Landing craft began to beach at 6:30 A.M., the most vulnerable moment. Jimmy Green dropped the ramp of LCA-910 opposite Vierville. "The Captain went first, followed by the middle rank, followed by the port, left-hand rank, followed by the right-hand rank," just as they had rehearsed countless times before at Slapton Sands in Devon. This time, however, the surf was high and the depth of water undulating. "One minute the surf was around their ankles," Green noticed, "the next minute it was under the armpits." The infantry held their weapons above their heads to keep them dry. "There were a few mortars popping around us but nothing else opened up." There was a palpable feeling of dread but no fire. "It was almost an unearthly silence while the troops got out." The wading troops noticed with dismay that there were no cratered foxholes offering any sanctuary up ahead.[21]

The Germans had been closely monitoring the approaching landing craft, adjusting sights and ranges to suit, awaiting the order to open fire.

Unteroffizier Henrik Naube on his Vierville cliff top position at WN 73 watched Sub Lieutenant Jimmy Green's flotilla disembark A Company into the surf. "They walked slowly and deliberately," he recalled, and "began to advance in this way into shallower water, and the waves came to their chests, then their waists." That was the point, he remembered, "when we opened fire on them."

Karl Wegner in WN 71 down below at beach level was frozen at his gun. "I saw all those men in olive-brown uniforms splashing through the water toward the sand," he remembered. "They looked so unprotected in the wide open space of the beach." The experience was surreal, detached from the scene unfolding before him. The men from LCA-910 went to ground in two long lines, having exited to port and starboard, seemingly unsure what to do next. Wegner became distantly aware of his section commander Lang yelling at him. "*Feur, Wegner, Feuer!*" but he remained motionless until the Obergefreiter brought him to his senses by rapping his helmet with the butt of his pistol. "The metallic clang brought me to life and I pulled the trigger up tight":

"The MG roared, sending hot lead into the men running along the beach. I saw some go down, I knew I hit them. Others dived for whatever cover was out there. The bullets ripped up and down the sand."

He was now killing men, "my mind rationalized it," he recalled, "This was war." He focused on acquiring and eliminating targets. "Now was not the time to think of right or wrong," he decided, "only of survival."[22]

FIVE

FIRST WAVE FLOUNDERED

6:30 A.M. TO 7:30 A.M.

Vierville Cliff Shoulder, Right
6:30 A.M. to 7:20 A.M.

Sub Lieutenant Jimmy Green had landed Captain Taylor Fellers's A Company in virtual isolation at the western end of Omaha Beach, on target, opposite the steep road leading up from the Vierville draw. One of his boats had swamped on the way in. To their left and high up the cliff, a gray bunker was protruding from the light sandstone wall, dominating the road. It looked as if it had been smeared on with a plasterer's knife. On the right cliff face a sinister dark square portended another bunker firing position. Fellers could see maybe one or two Sherman tanks on the shore line to his left, but the nearest troops coming in were F Company, a distant 1,600 yards away beyond them. They were barely discernible, except as indistinct shadows through the forest of wooden obstacles and breaking surf. The dark outline of the massive bluff rampart rising up beyond the beach seemed to hem them in.

Off to his right two landing craft were nosing through the obstacles five hundred yards away, on the other side of the Vierville draw. They belonged to Captain Ralph Goranson's C Company 2nd Rangers, who were to scale the cliffs if the draw was blocked. Their objective was a German position at Pointe Percée. It had two 75mm guns threatening Omaha's right flank. The Rangers would have to run four hundred yards across the flat, obstacle-studded sand to reach the shale beneath the base of the near-vertical cliff.

The first wave coming into Omaha numbered fifty small landing craft, each embarking thirty-one soldiers, carrying the vanguard of a strike force of about 1,550 GIs. They outnumbered the German defenders by more than three to one, but were inferior in firepower. Most of the Germans were securely ensconced in concrete bunkers and well prepared earthen positions, manning crew-served heavy weapons. Thirty-one direct fire anti-tank and field guns, ranging from 50mm to 88mm, could sweep the beach, supported by thirty-six machine guns and nineteen mortars, indirectly supported by four batteries of additional artillery with 105mm to 150mm guns. Nearly every approaching landing craft was theoretically covered by a heavy caliber field artillery piece or anti-tank gun, supplemented by mortars and machine guns able to alternate between two craft. Fellers's A Company soldiers, with typical GI black humor, had already jibed they were the "suicide wave," which with the limitations of the Allied air and naval bombardments, was broadly correct.

Marginal wind, wave, and tidal conditions had shifted the approaching first wave from right to left. Many landing craft had been driven east toward the center of Omaha around Saint-Laurent-sur-Mer and the formidable east cliff shoulder at Colleville. Heavy going meant early landing craft serials were being overtaken by faster craft, breaking up the symmetry of the first wave into clustered landfalls along the four-mile-long beach. This immensely eased German target acquisition because artillery observers could spot and anticipate where the first bunches of landing craft would land. Precisely calculated registration allowed accurate artillery fire to be brought down at a single word of command across the radio and telephone lines between bunkers. The priority of targets was tank landing craft, the largest or nearest vessels. The dispersed nature of the first wave's arrival enabled the maximum concentration of fire upon the few. A Company landed just west of the *Aschersleben* firebox, a designated intersection of 88mm, 50mm anti-tank, and 76mm field gun fire.

A feature of amphibious landings, like a parachute insertion, is an abrupt transition to fighting after a relatively undisturbed run in by landing craft or aircraft. Entry into battle for conventional infantry is more gradual. They can generally see and hear evidence of fighting as they approach the front line, and are emotionally prepared, like the German defenders watching from the bunkers. Men tossed around inside four-sided landing craft boxes, amid spumes of spray, have their horizons limited to a ramp in front, high sides and the raised platform of the coxswain and crew gunners behind. "Our little boat was bobbing around like a cork under a waterfall," remembered Sergeant John Thaxton with F Company the 116th in the first wave, "we were packed like a can of sardines." They endured within these constrained parameters. "Can you imagine standing next to someone when they're upchucking?" he asked. All they wanted to do was get off the boat. "I was not looking forward to being shot at, but my thinking then was I'd rather fight than drown." Cramped and seasick, many had not even bothered looking over the side, possibly intimidated by the noise and what they might see. Most were stoically enduring and retching into the sloshing bilge water at their feet.

There was barely room to see anything. "I was looking forward to getting off the thing," Thaxton recalled. When the ramps went down, adrenaline kicked in, and they poured out. What followed was the equivalent of a cold shower immersion, the sudden transition to intense combat from a standing start. "By this time we were all about deaf from all the noise," remembered Bernard Nider with E Company.[1]

Captain Fellers's A Company, numb to the situation, registered with dismay that there were no bomb crater foxholes on the beach and precious little evidence of any support from either side. There was not a single German in sight but they had clearly landed in the right place. Slapton Sands beach training drills kicked in, and George Roach well remembered the drill. "The Lieutenant would be the first off the boat," followed by the riflemen, who would fan out, immediately followed by the Bangelore torpedo soldiers and wire cutters, who would set about the obstacles. Then the heavier equipment would disembark, the flamethrower with his assistant, machine guns, or mortars:

> "The Bangelore torpedo people would run up to where the
> barbed wire was, throw a pole charge across the barbed wire,
> explode it so that the riflemen could then follow on and fire at
> the pillbox, which was usually situated at a distance from us,
> and then the flamethrower would activate his flamethrower at
> the embrasure, and then the pole charge people would come
> up and lay their TNT packages against the embrasure and
> blow a hole in it."[2]

Fellers's men lay prone on the beach, breathing heavily, having exited the water. They now sought to exercise these drills to clear the Vierville draw. Unfortunately they lay in the confluence of crisscross arcs of fire from three formidable strongpoints, WN 73, 72, and 71, which effectively closed the entrance. A nine-foot-high massive concrete wall sealed the exit, protruding 125 feet from a formidable bunker on the embankment just above the beach. There was a further pillbox sited slightly lower, with apertures enabling it to fire both east and west along the beach. They were difficult to identify, their outline obscured by dimpled concrete bumps and neutral-colored hessian sacking. One bunker still had the original ornamental pillars of the former holiday hotel in place. Not one GI saw the source of the enemy machine gun fire that suddenly spat out.

Unteroffizier Henrik Naube in WN 73 recalled the "troops were about four hundred meters from us":

> "I did not sight on them individually at first, but I began firing and I swept the gun from left to right along the beach. This knocked down the first few men in each line of men; you must remember the MG 42 was so powerful that the bullets would often pass through the human body and hit whatever was behind. So it was that many of these men were hit by a bullet which had already passed through a man in front, or even two men in front. After that, I aimed more selectively, to make the ammunition last as long as possible. I fired short bursts at small groups of men and hit them that way."

A Company was swiftly rendered leaderless and ineffective. PFC Leo Nash remembered Lieutenant Edward Tidrick, bleeding at the throat, rear up and order him to "advance with the wire cutters." It was a futile gesture; Nash had no wire cutters, and in giving the order, Tidrick made himself a target, and Nash saw machine gun bullets "cleave him from head to pelvis." Survivors could not move, because "machine gunners along the cliff directly ahead were now firing straight down into the party." Sergeant Roy Stevens, the twin brother of Ray, who had already sunk in LCA-911, was raked across his midsection by a burst of automatic fire and died on the beach. The MG 42 was very well stabilized when mounted on a tripod and had a rate of fire of twelve hundred rounds per minute; twenty rounds could still be in the air at first strike at distances beyond one thousand yards. On impact it produced a small entry wound, but the shock wave of energy that accompanied the projectile's path through the body caused a visceral explosion of flesh on exit. A Company virtually ceased to exist.[3]

Fellers and every man in his thirty-one-man boat team died. Close to 100 of the 155 A Company soldiers landing on this stretch of beach perished, and nearly all the rest were wounded. Nineteen of the dead came from one small rural community in the town of Bedford, Virginia, including two sets of brothers. Four more would die within the next few days. producing a 90% casualty rate. So few men survived that it is difficult to plot the disintegration of the company.

Company C of the 2nd Ranger Battalion also stormed ashore in isolation five hundred yards to the right of A Company. "They beached us on time in the best place—exactly per our instructions," Captain Ralph Goranson later recalled. "And they paid dearly for it."

"There were two lone landing craft coming in side by side," Lieutenant Sidney Salomon remembered, and, "all of a sudden I hear these 'pings' on the side of the steel hull of the landing craft." Looking over the side there were 'these concentric circles around the landing craft, which was the mortar shells landing in the water around us." They missed, but "it gave an eerie feeling." They landed with sixty-five men beneath cliff top German strongpoint WN 73, which had at least four pillboxes surrounded by two belts of barbed wire.

Goranson's commanding officer Lieutenant Colonel James Rudder had told him, "you have the toughest goddam job on the whole beach." The cliff face rose up before them like a castle battlement. Twinkling muzzle flashes from the machine guns on top of WN 73 kicked up sand and debris around their feet as they ran across the flat beach. Ahead and to their right was a section of collapsed cliff, a cleft in the sheer face, offering the possibility of an ascent from the large stones and shale piled at the base. Within seconds of beaching LCA-418 was hit by mortar and anti-tank rounds, killing twelve men from his first platoon. When the ramp dropped on LCA-1038, machine gun fire splashed up around the second platoon struggling ashore through neck-deep water, hitting a further fifteen men. The volume of fire prevented any chance of reorganizing on the beach. "I told the men to get to the water's edge under the overhang of the cliffs as fast as they could," Goranson remembered. "Right after we landed we took at least four rounds of 88s." As the rounds howled in, "the first was wide, but number two took the landing craft ramp off." (This was more likely the 50mm gun aperture on WN 72, as the 88mm could only fire east along the beach.) "Number three hit in the rear and number four amidships," wrecking the landing craft.

"The Germans had us zeroed in," recalled Ranger Nelson Noyes, they had four hundred yards to go, and "all of us ran across the beach as fast as we could." By the time the men splashed through the shallow water to reach the rocks, Goranson had lost nineteen dead and eighteen wounded, more than half their number. The Vierville draw opening was to their left, with houses visible at the top of the cliff. Squatting amid the stones at the base of the cliff offered only limited cover, and Noyes realized they had run into "enemy crossfire from the right and front." Sidney Salomon was picked up by a mortar blast and flung "face forward" from behind. "I went down in the sand and thought, 'Gee, I must be dead,' because I'd never been in combat before." His platoon sergeant came running by, and as he dipped into his field jacket to pass on his maps, "the sand started kicking in his face." "It was machine gun bullets, and they were shooting up the sand in front of me, and the sand was kicking up in my face." He had to move, "this is not the place to be lying down," he recalled, and he stood up to run the rest of the way.[4]

F Company came ashore 1,600 yards to A Company's left and the cluster of six landing craft immediately attracted a storm of fire from WN 70 and 68. "I went in carrying 60 pounds of 60mm mortar ammo," remembered PFC John Robertson, but his crew was wiped out at the water's edge. "It was a tank coming up behind me as I was lying in the water that got me up and across the beach," he explained. "It looked liked suicide, but better than being run over." Private Rocco Russo had to bail over the side when his landing craft ramp got stuck and reached the seawall where he was considerably shaken up by a close shell burst. "I looked down and saw a big chunk of bloody meat in my lap," he recalled with horror, which "had hit the top of my assault jacket and fallen into my lap." He showed the grisly evidence to his sergeant, Ryan, who "asked if it was part of me." Shocked, Russo replied that he "didn't think so, but I was so scared I wasn't really sure." Company commander Captain William Callahan tried to extricate them by climbing on top of a Sherman tank nearby to direct fire. "I was wounded in both legs and right hip," he remembered, and tried to crawl back onto the shingle but "I was hit in the face and both hands."

G Company, being more dispersed on arrival, attracted less fire, but they were scattered all over the beach. E Company, landing well off the objective further east, "was cut down just as the ramps lowered," remembered 2nd Battalion Commander Lieutenant Colonel Sidney Bingham. The company commander was immediately killed and "chaos reigned." "For some reason," recalled Bingham, "I thought all was well," until, taking cover behind a steel beach obstacle, he saw, "sand kicking up nearby." They were under intense machine gun fire, "there was no doubt in my mind, I was scared and exhausted."[5]

Scarcely thirty minutes after the catastrophic A Company landing, B Company bumped its way through the obstacle belt at the same place, with D Company ten minutes later, to its left. They had all entered the preconfigured German killing area opposite the Vierville draw.

C Company arrived 500 yards along to the east and H Company 750 yards further on. Companies were arriving late at intervals of between ten to twenty minutes, enabling German fire to concentrate and engage them piecemeal. In between were small groups of tanks and tankdozers trying to engage targets from the water's edge, turret down in some cases amid the breaking waves. Feverishly working amid all these dispersed groups were the gap demolition teams from the 146th Engineer Combat Battalion, who beached just before or mixed with the infantry.

The sixteen gap demolition teams were scheduled to land from LCMs three minutes before the infantry, to mark out and blow fifty-yard gaps through the obstacles between the low- and high-water tideline. They were supposed to be preceded by eight support and command teams five minutes earlier, but in essence they would land alongside the men they were due to support. The theoretical plan had not factored in wind, current and tidal conditions, and a well-ensconced enemy within the minutiae of a tightly composed timetable, which was going to unravel.

Team 7 led by Lieutenant Ben Bartholomew came ashore on time, directly in front of strongpoint WN 68, covering the Les Moulins D-3 draw. "The tide was exactly as expected," he remembered, "about 110 feet from the first obstacle at 06:37." Intricate technical tasks had to be speedily completed in the teeth of intense enemy fire. Private First Class Christopher Heil with the 147th Engineer Combat Battalion explained that the plastic explosive they used, "looked and felt like putty or children's Play-Doh. . . . You could wrap it around a tree and cut it right off." It was for cutting through the steel triangles that supported many of the German beach obstacles. Engineer teams trained and operated in groups of six, the capacity of the rubber dinghy they used to float and tow their explosives and equipment between obstacles. Each demolition man carried five or six assembled fuses with cap sticks, which could blow off a man's hand. Theirs was an exceedingly dangerous and demanding job. Each carried forty pounds of compound C-2 (plastic) explosives and tetratol (similar but more powerful than TNT), in a bag over his shoulder, and a rifle carbine. Others carried Bangalore torpedos, which were pipes filled with explosives for blowing wire, and reels of primacord, a form of TNT in ropelike coils. The wooden obstacles and Belgian gates were collapsed by 2–5 "Hagensen Pack" blocks of plastic explosive, while the heavier steel Czech hedgehogs required fifteen-pound tetrytol satchel charges to drop them. With the tide rising by a foot every ten minutes, gaps had to be blown before obstacles were completely submerged. This left barely an hour to complete the mission, impeded by infantry landing around them, and harassed by searching fire from the German defenders, who instinctively realized what they were trying to do. Men weakened by seasickness and with core body temperatures reduced by drenching spray on the run in had to perform intricate tasks with fingers numbed by the cold. At the same time they were distracted by awful sights and sounds all around and constantly buffeted by the surf as they labored in waist–deep, chilly water.

By 6:55 A.M. Bartholomew's team had constructed tetratol charges linked together by primacord ring mains:

> "At that time a vessel loaded with infantry came crashing in, smashing through the timbers and setting off about seven mines on the posts. The boat was followed by other craft with infantry, and it was impossible to fire the charges with the first tide."

The Infantry was pinned behind the very obstacles they needed to blow. Bartholomew's men had to switch instead to dragging wounded men beyond the incoming tide.

When Second Lieutenant Wesley Ross's Team 8 LCM neared the beach opposite WN 68, "small arms fire artillery and mortar fire began kicking up spray among us." Each of his men carried fifty pounds of explosive and, "we had about 400 pounds of backup C2 and tetratol in a rubber raft," which meant a "fingernail-biting time" ahead. His navy gunner "started hosing down the area ahead with twin 50 caliber machine guns," as they came in to beach. Most of the boatload took cover in the only visible bomb crater on the sand. The rubber raft, with its potentially catastrophic cargo of explosives, was pulled and tugged down the ramp and secured to an obstacle post once afloat, while "we were under heavy small arms fire." One demolition engineer remembered:

> "I was just coming out of the water when this guy exploded right in front of me. There just wasn't anything left of him except some of his skin, which splattered all over my arm. I remember dipping my arm in the water to wash it off."[6]

With daring, almost suicidal persistence Ross's team managed to blow a partial gap. He and Sergeant Bill Garland ran a ring main of primacord, reinforced with rope, around several bands of wooden obstacles under heavy German shellfire. One round howled in and struck the sand just sixty feet away, and "ricocheted twenty-five feet into the air and was clearly outlined against the rising sun, before exploding and sending a two-foot fragment cartwheeling through the air in the opposite direction." Three times they returned to blow persistent obstacles still standing. Shortly after 7:10 A.M. they were well into the depth of the belt and had just connected another ring main when another wave of infantry came in among them. "I agonized whether or not to proceed with the demolition, but could not justify killing our own infantry, even though I recognized the importance of adhering to the master plan." Ross achieved one of four partial gaps created between strongpoints WN 70 to 68 near the D-1 draw. "The openings that were cut were badly staggered," remembered Task Force Commander Lieutenant John O'Neill, "because of the irregular landings." Only two breaches of any consequence were opened up in this area and none anywhere near the Vierville draw where A Company landed. When Gap Team 2 arrived an hour late it found most of the obstacles covered by the tide.

The human cost was painfully high. "I didn't notice Smitty until after I got up, for I'd been knocked about and didn't know if I was hit or not," recalled Sergeant "Sol" Evnetsky, working with the 147th Combat Engineer Battalion in front of the Vierville draw. "Smitty was holding my hand, asking me to take him in." Evnetsky only realized he was wounded when he saw the shrapnel wounds all over his face:

> "Every time the waves went out I saw blood coming up the water from Smitty's lower body. He started to cry that he didn't want to drown. I cannot express my feelings, but I'm sure I cried too, for here was my first experience of war. Smitty said, 'Take me in, Sol. I'm losing a lot of blood.' His voice got weaker all the time."

They could barely touch the bottom at that stage, and Evnetsky, half carrying him, could only move very slowly. He was neck deep in water. "Honest," he recalled, "I must have swallowed a quart of his blood." Exhaustion was taking its toll and the further he got in toward the water's edge, "the heavier Smitty was getting." He was tottering on his feet when a Ranger Lieutenant exposed himself to heavy fire and ran down to help him carry his friend, who had passed out. When they reached the stony base of the Vierville cliff, "I started to shake," Evnetsky recalled. "Nothing could stop me." All he could do was cradle Smitty's head in his lap until he died.[7]

B and D companies landed nearby and got into immediate difficulties. Rough seas, strong winds, and the east-flowing current had separated the six D Company LCAs. They gradually identified the large opening in the bluffs. The 88mm at WN 72 fired off to their left with a sharp concussive crack, the flash muted by the blast wall. WN 73 was shooting a 75mm out from its dark square-shaped embrasure, high up on the cliff face to the right of the draw. A storm of red tracers grazed and whipped the sand at knee level to their front. Houses could dimly be seen inside the draw, and beyond was the outline of the church steeple. "Our own boat became even further separated from the rest as we got closer," Sergeant Robert Slaughter explained, "and the coxswain fought to miss obstacles amid the waves and tidal currents of the shoreline." Slaughter peeped over the edge of the ramp, despite repeated warnings to get down. He saw another craft twenty-five yards off to their right and another two hundred yards ahead repeatedly lashed by small arms fire. He got down, realizing it was coming their way, and "fiery tracer bullets skipped and bounced off the ramp and sides as they zeroed in before the ramps fell."

They entered the preregistered fire zone west of *Ashersleben* marked on German artillery maps, their observers had only to give the code word and "left 500." "Then it began to happen," Slaughter recalled:

> "Enemy artillery and mortar shells sent great plumes of water spouting skyward as they exploded in the water. Near misses rained us with seawater."

Slaughter changed from "not the least bit worried," to "very worried about what Jerry could do to us." He was angry. "How in the hell did these sons of bitches survive what we thought was a carpet bombing and shelling of the beach?" The water spouts and explosions jetting up around them was the response:

> "The telltale screech just before the impact and the explosion made the incoming artillery even more terrifying. Even worse, they seemed to land in clusters."[8]

When a shell explodes, the area around the detonation becomes over-pressurized, and millisecond blast waves wreaked havoc among D Company, hemorrhaging and rupturing body tissue and organs in its wake. Flash from an explosion scorches, while metal shrapnel and debris whirling through the air at two to six miles a second dismembers limbs in its path. The human frame quivers like jelly on being subjected to these shock waves, tearing lung tissue and blood vessels. The ability to breathe and move oxygen around the body is dislocated and victims drown or suffocate in their own blood. Men in the open are defenseless against artillery fire. The only preventative measures are to take cover behind mined obstacles, get out of the way, or retreat. Few of these options were available to D Company. Near misses knocked people off their feet, burst ear membranes, causing temporary or permanent deafness. The company was broken and dispersed by this lethal preregistered fire.

Heavy loads, coupled with the incapacitating effects of hypothermia and seasickness from the tortuous spray-drenched approach exacted a physical toll. Veteran accounts frequently allude to the lethargic pace slowed by equipment overloads of an average 68.4 pounds; flamethrowers alone weighed 68 pounds. "Especially if you were hit and going under," explained Sergeant Slaughter. "It was extremely tough to shed the sixty to one hundred pounds of weapons and equipment in time." William Callahan, wounded commanding F Company, remembered, "We suffered heavily crossing the beach, the weakened condition of the men contributing as well as heavy enemy fire." Their uniforms were impregnated with an anti-gas solution and the voluminous pockets on their specially issued assault jackets filled with seawater and sand in the surf. This increased drag weights by as much as one third.

It was "ice cold" claimed Lieutenant Sidney Bingham, commanding the 2nd Battalion in the 116th Regiment with the first wave, and "everyone was soaked to the skin and at least 90% were desperately seasick." His men were in no condition to zig-zag to reduce target exposure and fire and maneuver on landing, like they had often practiced at Slapton Sands. "The fancy assault jacket issued for the operation was waterlogged and weighed a ton." Rifles, he explained, "couldn't shoot" because they "were clogged with sand." Private Robert Lowry with C Company came ashore five hundred yards to the left of Slaughter's D Company. He jumped into water "about level with my mouth," and when he got ashore, "we were so exhausted from being seasick, we just wanted to lie on the sand to recover." Veterans never forgot images of men stumbling to their deaths, moving in slow motion, through storms of red tracers.[9]

Unteroffizier Henrik Naube, shooting up small groups of men from his cliff top machine gun position on WN 73, described attackers below 'staggering forward." Despite the intensity of fire, "they still moved quite slowly, and because of that and the close range, they were easy targets to hit." He had a spectacular view of the curvature of the flat expanse of beach at low tide, hemmed in by the steeply rising bluff escarpment beyond. The golden beach was a dirty bronze color in this light. He saw clusters of landing craft, from A, B, D, and C Companies, hesitantly nosing their way through obstacles, starkly exposed in the surf. Naube was firing over the roof of strongpoint WN 72, built on the remains of the former vacationers' hotel. Its ornamental pillars had been left in place, giving the impression of an innocent seaside façade. The Vierville exit disappearing off to the right was obscured by the cliff face below.

The distinctive flash and resounding crack of the 88mm gun firing below toward the middle of the beach was matched by the flash and report of its sister gun shooting from WN 61 on the other side, four miles away. The splash from the grazing 88mm red tracer base projectiles was clearly visible. "These 88mm gunners were very accurate," he remembered, "and shot into the landing craft straight through the tall vertical bow":

"They fired high explosive, and the shells pierced the bow and exploded inside. [The] ramp was thrown up into the air.

Inside the craft, I could see a large number of troops who had been injured in the explosion, surrounded by men who were still able-bodied. They were clambering and scrabbling over each other, because the craft began to tip forward as the water entered the open bow."

Naube realized from the distinctive helmet shapes that the enemy was American. The 88mm had a perfect defilade shoot along the beach, engaging both tanks and landing craft from the flank. Crippled craft were quickly dispatched. "The 88mm gunners fired another shot into the mass of men," he remembered, "and this threw several of them directly out of the craft into the water." It sank at the bow leaving the propeller whirring in the air, "and this movement tipped the men into the sea immediately," a tangled mass of wounded and able-bodied. The shells shrieked along predetermined arcs at head height, nearly three times the speed of sound. Those at short range never heard them coming, from a mile out there was a split second to react. "As soon as you heard an 88, you hit the ground," recalled Bob Sales in B Company the 116th Regiment:

"If it caught you standing up, it would put shrapnel in you. You knew what it sounded like because you saw so many men die because of it."[10]

Bernard Nider with E Company remembered, "by this time we were all about deaf from all the noise," as their coxswain "gave her full throttle" to beach. "As we hit that sand we got crossfire from the pillboxes with the 88s," he recalled. Men jumped into the water and while waiting to move forward from the rear landing the craft "was hit again by the crossfire in the middle." Nider and his friend Fred Bitsig reached the sand, finding they could only make tortuous progress by ducking into shell holes. They flung themselves into craters even as shells flew through the air. This gave them the idea of throwing and exploding satchel charges ahead to create their own holes, "and by God it worked." They managed to reach the seawall.

The judicious decision by the 743rd Tank battalion not to launch its DD tanks at sea meant that thirty-two of them, with seven waders and three dozers, made it ashore in the first hour, the majority in the first thirty minutes. The LSTs, dubbed "large stationary targets," and their tanks were the immediate priority for German gunners. LCT 591 had offloaded the first DD tanks that A Company had spotted to their left in the surf. They were in the same network of interlocking 88mm, 75mm, and 50mm fire that had decimated the infantry landing craft. American tankers who had trained extensively with Shermans in England thought that after North Africa and the Mediterranean they were the equal of anything the Germans might throw at them. They were taken aback at the powerful muzzle velocities of German guns, and the ease with which Shermans burst into flames when hit. The 88s spat out armor-piercing projectiles at 2,600 feet per second. These struck the outside of the tank with such force that the kinetic energy created sent a jet of molten metal straight through the hull or even beyond. More often than not the metal slug penetrated and ricocheted around inside the hull, eviscerating the crew and sparking off ammunition explosions. "Those German 88s were awful," Pharmacist's Mate Frank Feduik remembered aboard LST-338:

> "Once you heard them bark and you were still alive, you knew they hadn't gotten to you because that shell would be on top of you before the noise got there."[11]

The first DD tank off LCT-591 was hit in the side by a high-velocity shell within five yards of leaving the bow ramp. Two other DD tanks had to maneuver around the fiery conflagration before they could even begin attempting to engage the bunkers. LCT-731, with Captain Charles Ehmka, the B Company tank commander, landed just left of the blazing tank. Intimidated by the fiery eruptions to their right the tank prematurely launched and swamped in the deep water before the wading skirt was completely deployed. Robert Jarvis, a 75mm gun loader in another B company tank was firing the .30 caliber machine gun and recalled seeing very little. "When we first came down the ramp of the LCT," he remembered, "we started firing immediately at whatever pillboxes or targets we could see." He was too preoccupied loading rounds inside the tank to look out of the periscope. "I would get a call for AP [armor piercing] for pill boxes or HE [high explosive] for what looked like trenches or a machine gun nest." Like many tank crews, he fought his own claustrophobic battle in isolation, with no idea of what was going on outside their extremely limited, locked-down vision.

LCT-713 received a crippling blow from the 88mm firing out of strongpoint WN 72, burned, and sank. "You would hear the shells coming at you," remembered Feduik on LST-338:

> "You could hear them whirring by and when you saw them hit the water. . . . well if you were in the wrong place, forget about it."

Seven tanks were soon burning fiercely along the water line, obscuring the Vierville beach exit with thick oily smoke. Captain Ehmka was killed, alongside sixteen of his tankers. Further left, LCT(A)-2307 was repeatedly struck by anti-tank and explosive shells trying to negotiate the uncleared obstacle belt. Only one tank waded ashore, the other two stayed on board, reluctant to exit because of the depth of water. She slowly pulled back and tried again further along, seeking to avoid the intense fire. Eventually the young ensign in command gave it up and turned out to sea, where the holed craft sank offshore, with the two tanks still on board.

"I finally had a few slack moments in firing to look around," recalled Jarvis inside his turret. "I figured by our firing that the beach should be pretty well secured." But when he looked outside, "the surf rolled a body of a sailor alongside of our tank. I recognized the sailor as being one of the crew of our LCT." Focused on the immediate battle, they had not seen the immense damage that had been inflicted on their unit. "It was then," Jarvis recalled, "that I realized everything was not going according to schedule." There was hardly any infantry in sight. Ivy Agee, a beached 29th Division artilleryman, probably explained why. Tanks were "drawing fire all around me," he remembered:

"Wounded soldiers were lying on the beach, they could not move and the tank could not stop. The screams are with me yet."[12]

Grenadier Karl Wegner poured fire into C and D Companies coming ashore from his pillbox at strongpoint WN 71, shooting at beach level. The thunderous echoes of fighting reverberated up and down the cliffsides around the Vierville draw. "I would fire as I had been trained to do," he recalled, "in short bursts fifteen to twenty centimeters above the ground." This had the effect of "splashing" ricochets of tumbling rounds at waist height into the stumbling oncoming Americans, as his bullets grazed the beach surface. "When the gun jammed I would clear it quickly because every second counted." His number two, Willi Schuster, wiped the vibrating chattering belts clean as they moved through the loading pan, as any excessive sand or residue could gum up the mechanism of the MG 42.

"Lang [his section commander] yelled out orders and targets but we really didn't listen to him; we couldn't really hear much anyway. Besides, we knew where to shoot. He was just as scared as we were, but tried not to show it."

They sensed they had the initiative, "I paused for a good look down the beach." They were winning.

"I saw Amis lying everywhere. Some were dead and others quite alive. Landing boats were backing away from the beach. Some of them were burning, hit by our PAK [anti-tank] guns or they had struck mines."[13]

Wegner's optimism was matched by American Sergeant J. Dolan's pessimism. This fire was decimating C Company, he had to leap over the sides of his landing craft to avoid the incoming at the bows. Dolan tried in vain with his officer "to move three or four men laying down in the craft unable to be moved. . . . The shoreline was covered with bodies," he remembered. "I could hear moaning and crying; others I presumed dead." Company command and control was disintegrating, "all was chaos and confusion," he remembered:

"I saw groups of men running up and down the beach and some even went back to the water. I watched in dismay the results."

He reached the seawall and "moved slowly along with the others, none of whom I knew, close to the outside of the seawall to the Vierville pass." Their predicament appeared hopeless.

Offshore, HQ Company commander Captain Charles Cawthon with the 2nd Battalion 116th, was closing on the beach. He noticed that "signs that things were going amiss abounded." The battleship guns had stopped firing, "indicating it was out of touch with the assault and fearful of firing into it." Only a trickle instead of a flow of landing craft were coming back, "which told of craft either destroyed or landed badly off target. . . . Another ill omen was the vacant sky, where we had expected to see fighter-bombers diving and strafing the beach." At thirty minutes into the assault between Saint-Laurent and Vierville, all the indications as he approached suggested it was faltering:

> "The sight was not inspiring or reassuring. Where Channel and shore met was an undulating line of dark objects. Some of the larger ones, recognizable as tanks and landing craft, were erupting black smoke. Higher up the beach was a line of smaller dots, straight as though drawn with a ruler, for they were aligned along a seawall. Scattered black specks were detaching themselves from the surf and laboring toward this line."

It was not clear whether they were advancing or not. Until now Cawthon had felt, "I do not believe individuals in the invasion force were greatly worried." They were preoccupied with the minutiae of the "complex mechanics of the mission and our separate tasks in it." What was happening was completely unexpected for the following waves. "I do not recall any questioning of a frontal assault on prepared defenses from the unstable base of the English Channel," he remembered.[14]

Only twenty-nine of Captain Ralph Goranson's Rangers with C Company reached the base of the cliffs to the right of the Vierville draw. First Lieutenant William Moody recced to the west to find a way up the cliffs to attack the fortified house from the rear that was shooting down at them. Moody was as shocked as the rest of the survivors. He lost his helmet on the way in and picked up another from the beach only to discover that part of the previous owner's brains were still inside. He grabbed another, but this one "came to life," with the owner holding on to it. Company commander Goranson was hit nine times, each time burning or nicking his uniform or scoring his equipment, but he remained unwounded. Benefitting from their climbing training, Moody found a cleft in the cliff, still recognizable today, and scaled the height. Goranson and the rest of the men followed after, using knives and affixed ropes to keep their balance. Lieutenant Salomon's platoon reached the top with only nine of thirty-two men left. Moody was killed by a German sniper.[15]

They infiltrated the rear of Strongpoint WN 73, which had six concrete pillboxes, trenches, and dugouts, linked by tunnels and protected by mines and barbed wire. Goranson led the assault to clear the stone house, which they penetrated from the right flank. They were joined by twenty surviving infantrymen from B Company of the 116th, and began to stealthily fight their way through the strongpoint network, taking out emplacements piecemeal. Unteroffizier Naube fought on, blissfully unaware on the seaward side, overlooking the draw. The German defenders were totally focused on the helpless men they had pinned below and were not looking to the rear. Technical Sergeant Morrow came across one pillbox with Sergeant Belcher, it housed a machine gun shooting up the 116th soldiers at the draw entrance below. Belcher kicked in the door and tossed a "Willy Pete" (white phosphorous) grenade inside. This produced a starburst, white-hot explosion with instant suffocating smoke. Globules of white phosphorous splashed onto their exposed flesh and clothing, and burned to the bone so long as it was exposed to air. The effect in a confined space is catastrophic. "As soon as the phosphorous began to burn on the Jerry skins," Belcher and Morrow recalled, "they abandoned the gun and ran out of the door screaming to the high heavens." After the punishment the Germans had meted out, there was little regard for mercy. "It was just like shooting ducks in a shooting gallery," Belcher remembered.

From the top of WN 73 Goranson could see the full extent of the disaster unfolding on the beach. "I thought we were to be stranded, alone, for some time," he surmised. He and his men resolved to fight on. The German defensive strongpoints on the Vierville cliff shoulder had clearly pinned down the Americans on this west side of Omaha Beach. Goranson nursed his misgivings for hours. "I thought the invasion was a failure," he recalled, "and I wondered if we could make a successful withdrawal and try the invasion some time again in the near future."[16]

Colleville Cliff Shoulder, Left
6:30 A.M. to 7:30 A.M.

At just before 6:30 A.M. on the left side of Omaha Beach, the area of the 1st Division's "Big Red One" assault, clusters of landing craft approached the beach. Some fifteen landing craft, with 450 men consisting of E and F Companies from the 16th Regiment, were jumbled up with two other craft from E of the 116th Regiment from the 29th Division, who were way off target. They bumped and nosed their way through the obstacle belt in threes, fours, and fives, and entered the kill zone of German strongpoints WN 61 and 62, the most formidable on the beach. They were watched closely by the German defenders, with a mix of expectation and trepidation. The landing craft were entering a criss-cross pattern of converging anti-tank gun and machine gun arcs as well as preregistered artillery and mortar fireboxes. They were dispassionate target numerals, to be methodically dispatched by the defenders at will.

Lieutenant Bernhard Frerking's artillery observation bunker on top of the WN 62 hill mass had direct call on four 105mm howitzers from his 1st Battery, located about three miles inland. He stood with his aide, Heinrich Severloh, in the latter's open machine gun position and watched the Americans wading ashore. Until now they had anticipated meeting, "Tommies," but the distinctive shape of the helmets before them suggested otherwise. "Listen Hein," Frerking advised his young aide, "when they get into water up to their knees, then you have to fire, so that they can't spread out." Their 170-foot-high hill strongpoint dominated the beach to their front, easily visible from WN 60 on their right and with a clear line of vision to Vierville four miles away to their left. "It was clear to us that the GIs down there were about to enter into their own slaughterhouse," Severloh recalled. "Poor swine," Frerking simply said softly, and turned into the bunker to begin relaying the coordinates to the artillery. He could be heard outside: *Target Dora, range 4-8-5-0, elevation 20+, proximity fuze—Fire!* "As I turned back to my machine gun position," Severloh remembered, "I also had the feeling that I was ascending a scaffold."[17]

Friedrich Schnüll's 88mm gun flashed out with a resounding crack, sending a red tracer base projectile out into the shallows at 2,600 feet per second. Almost simultaneously it struck the approaching landing craft with a reverberating metallic *clunk.* Artillery came down, raising multiple waterspouts among American infantry wading through the obstacle-strewn shallows.

Machine gunner Ludwig Kwiatkowski had an uninterrupted view of the sands from his concrete Tobruk emplacement, seventy-five yards from the beach. He occupied the northernmost position on WN 62. "We had tracer at every fifth round in our machine gun belts," he recalled. He did not line up iron sights, but "simply steered illuminated lines of tracer into the open ramps of the boats, stitching the area of the ramp from below and then around." He watched forms "somersault out." Bruno Plota, looking out from his 50mm mortar Tobruk position, high up like Severloh, could see "that was a real mess that we had set up, a real mess." Their strongpoint, they believed, was unassailable. "We all stood wonderfully protected in our position," he recalled:

"The poor fellows below had absolutely no cover. Hardly any of the first ones that landed got anywhere near the seawall."

"I could see the waterspouts where my machine gun bursts were hitting," Severloh observed, "and when the little fountains got close to the GIs, they threw themselves down." Panic was breaking out here and there, "and after a little while, all the GIs on the beach had been brought down." Corpses hid a number of men drifting about in the waves on the rising tide, so he "fired further among the many dark forms in the water, which were still three hundred yards from the upper beach.

"We always had a spare barrel for our machine gun," Kwiatkowski remembered. Prolonged bursts with the MG 42 sent the belts flying through, turning the barrel "white hot," and necessitating a rapid barrel change. Further steady bursts meant yet another change, "but the first barrel was still hot, because we had hardly enough time for it to cool down again." There was no other option, so overheated barrels were substituted for hot.[18]

Obergefreiter Heinrich Krieftewirth, at thirty-six years old, was regarded as the "papa" of WN 62. He was the commander of the lower 75mm Skoda gun concrete casemate that fired out west from the strongpoint. His false teeth were still rattling inside the glass where he had left them, on the table next to the bunk block he shared with Franz Gockel. They had been forgotten in the tumult of the sudden alarm, replaced by other considerations. Round after round crashed out from the lower casemate, which had a spectacularly commanding view of the entire curvature of Omaha Beach up to the Vierville cliffs, visible in the far distance. Hans Selbach, loading for Krieftewirth, witnessed the destruction their gun was wreaking in the bay. "We took the landing craft under direct fire with our gun," he recalled, "and could clearly see the damage we were inflicting on the Americans—it was awful." He felt a little regret, "despite the fact they were our enemies." They could hardly miss, "the whole sea was black with ships with no clear spaces to be seen."

Franz Gockel fired his water-cooled Polish machine gun next to Obergefreiter Kuska's 50mm anti-tank gun across the draw toward

WN 61. He saw "the occupants of the first landing craft were shot up, dead, and wounded within a few meters." The first wave was quickly broken up with "assault boats left driving aimlessly about the surface of the water out of control." They were subjected to intense fire from incoming boats, "mainly quick firing guns and very heavy machine guns." Gockel's machine gun became jammed, because the dust from the preceding bombardment had fouled the belt. As he tried to clear the mechanism, it was suddenly shot away from his hands. "Even today," he recalled, "I find it unbelievable I was not injured in the slightest."

The beach was a scene of total devastation, but they still poured in the fire. "From up where I was," Severloh remembered, "I could see the blood flowing into the water; the bodies were piled two meters high in some places." In later years he was to be haunted by these images. "It wasn't my fault I had killed so many people there," he insisted, "I only did what I was supposed to do, and there was no way for me to avoid doing it." In any case, he rationalized, "all of them that had come ashore here, had it in for me, to put an end to me, and I didn't want that to happen." He was alone with no group reassurance. "Suddenly," he recalled, "I had the impression that mine was the only machine gun in our entire sector that had fired." Gockel at least derived some companionship from the battle-hardened Kuska fighting nearby. His 50mm anti-tank gun, cunningly concealed in a natural fold in the ground, was meting out considerable punishment in the ravine separating WN 62 from Strongpoint 61. "Several shot up and burning tanks bore witness," he recalled, "that here, an experienced Russian *Ostfront* fighter had prevented any advance over the seawall."[19]

The young, baby-faced Selbach, loading for "papa" Krieftewirth, could see that "as the tide rose ever higher, boxes and crates flowed in, alongside wrecked parts of landing craft and unbelievably many corpses." Incoming fire from the Americans on both the beach and offshore was increasing. "You only had to shake a bush before you were shot at from all sides," he remembered. Moreover, "there was hardly a meter of ground within the strongpoint that had not been hit by a shell, and we were really scared." Revenge also bolstered them. "We thought of the many bombing victims and destruction in the Fatherland," Gockel remembered, "the same enemy was before us here. . . . Unlike defenseless civilians facing many air raids, we could defend ourselves—and we wanted to survive!" They instinctively realized they were gaining the upper hand, "despite so few defenders left on our feet, we had brought this major landing effort to its knees."[20]

First Sergeant J. Fitzsimmons with E Company the 16th Regiment saw on the way in that the company boats "began stringing out, and finally lost one another." They were supposed to follow the CP [command post] boat, "but that boat too was bearing far left and the others realized it. "You're going left!" they kept shouting at the coxswain, but he ignored them and carried on the same course. As the official combat report later commented:

> "The roughness of the sea, the dense smoke along the beach
> and some mist at sea, all contributed to 'E' coming in at the
> wrong place and becoming dispersed over a wide area."[21]

"E" was mixed up with its cluster of four landing craft with another two off-target from E Company the 116th, as well as two groups of three boats from F Company.

Captain Edward Wozenski came ashore with five of his six boats. "When we hit the bottom," he remembered, "we had approximately four hundred yards to struggle through the water to the beach." This was an immense space cluttered with scores of obstacles. "There was small arms all around so you were up and down, ducking down, as terrified as anyone could be," and totally exhausted, he recalled. This was after a muscle-cramping, several hours long squat in open boats, sluiced down by cold spray and uncontrollably seasick:

"Every time I got up I thought it was pure terror that was making my knees buckle until I finally hit the beach and realized I had about one hundred pounds of sand in the pockets of my [assault] jacket, sand that had accumulated on top of the fifty or sixty pound load we were all carrying in."[22]

David Silva with the 29th Division was mixed up with the same gaggle of landing craft. "The machine gun bullets were everywhere, chipping in the water, and the 'crack' from where the bullets were coming." They heard a distinctive "crack" and "thump." The crack was bullets passing over, having broken the sound barrier, the thump was the report signature of the gun. "The bullet comes and then the crack comes after," Silva explained. "You can't hide from it, no way, because those bullets are firing at about 3,000 feet per second." Cool heads can discern the distance from the gun by counting the seconds between the crack and thump interval, although few did. "When the ramps were dropped" the official 16-E report read, "the automatic fire caught the open ends dead on." The last image many soldiers saw was red flashes from incoming tracer. "Some of them were caught in crossing bands of fire." The command post boat took its heaviest losses at the moment of beaching, only twelve of thity-six men reaching the sand, "the rest got it in the water, as they waded in from a sandbar, or were hit as they returned to drag in the wounded." That day 105 men from E Company perished.[23]

Private Huston "Hu" Riley's F Company landing craft hit a sandbar and lurched to port. The ramp was dropped and "I jumped off the starboard side and went right to the bottom for what seemed like eternity" into a noiseless zone. This was Riley's third experience of a contested amphibious landing, and he kept his head. "As I looked up I could see the small arms bullets striking the water, going a few inches and then just dropping to the bottom. The density of the water had saved him. Bullets do not penetrate water, the projectiles tumble and decelerate on entry. Because the surface area increases up to ten times, they lose their aerodynamic properties and simply sink. "I was not getting anywhere trying to walk along the bottom," Riley decided, so he "squeezed the release on my life belt, and I shot to the surface like a cork." The noise above was deafening, and now he was "bobbing on the water like a big bird, a hell of a target. . . . I removed the life belt and pushed it in front of me," he remembered, hanging on for support. The landing craft he vacated was shattered by one of WN 62's guns, "as all I could see was a bunch of junk and bodies everywhere."[24]

When the ramp dropped on Sergeant Donald Wilson's F Company boat, "two or three people up front appeared to collapse, while one simply held onto the top edge of the hull." They were raked by incoming machine gun fire. Wilson was at the back of the boat with Platoon Sergeant Williams, and they both urgently chorused, "'Move! Move! Move!'" They spread out and headed for the beach, but were soon struggling through increasingly deep water, on leaving the sand bar. "When it finally reached my chin, I inflated the CO_2-charged lifebelt, which popped me above the water, from the waist up." Like Riley he became vulnerable, protruding above the water. "The water surface was being spattered with intense machine gun fire, a number of the team had been hit already," he recalled, "some were killed outright." He punctured the belt with his trench knife and found there was sand beneath his feet. Men around him were hit, "driven backward by some unseen blow," then slipping beneath the water. Glancing back he saw his landing craft had been hit, with smoke billowing from the engine compartment. "The coxswain's body was draped over the wheel," and there were "two bodies on the deck, one of which was semi-erect against the side," he recalled. Macabrely, "he was apparently hung up on something and swayed back and forth as the boat drifted on the swells."

"Several riflemen moved forward, trying to zig ten yards, hit the sand, and then zag for ten yards, but machine guns were on the second stop."

Men he knew intimately, and had trained and campaigned with for years were going down, all around.

"Joe Spechler took off with a twenty-five-pound TNT satchel charge in his hand and another on his back. He ran some thirty yards and exploded, obliterated as little bits of burlap used to strap the TNT blocks together fluttered down and lay smoldering on the sand."

The assault disintegrated in front of his eyes. To his left:

"I picked out Lieutenant Pearre from the adjacent team, moving rapidly forward when he took a direct hit from an anti-tank gun. Most of his torso lay where it happened, but his helmet sailed upward almost in slow motion, finally landing, spinning the vertical white rectangle officer designation still visible on the back."

Stretching ahead of E Company was three hundred yards of sand and then steep bluffs. Sergeant Fitzsimmons recalled, "the seasoned men among them knew that they had to move, but even they felt their strength and will fading." Fire was intense and they were overloaded. "Their natural inclination was to stay there." Fitzsimmons watched as two of his men, Spencer and Walsh, took a few strides forward and flopped down only to be "blown bodily into the air by mines buried on the beach." Both were killed.[25]

Within a few minutes of E Company arriving, the men saw the first engineers land and set to work. Many were late and off course. Their bigger LCVP craft immediately attracted German fire. Ramps splashed down and men waded into water chest deep, tugging and pulling at rubber rafts laden with explosives and demolition equipment. Second Lieutenant Phil Wood with the 299th Engineer Combat Battalion landed with Team 14 ahead of the infantry. "The operation was nothing like what had been expected," recalled Sergeant William Garland with the 146th Engineers. When they landed, "the men thought the infantry would be ahead of them, but the beach was innocent of footprints." Oberfeldwebel Schnüll's 88mm cracked out at WN 61 and Lieutenant Wood:

". . . saw an 88 shell hit squarely in the center of the LCM where the Navy demolition team was trying to launch its rubber boat, filled with explosives. The ammunition in the rubber boat was detonated, and the fire enveloped the LCM. The coxswain was blasted off the vessel."[26]

Team 14 was unable to blow its obstacles because infantry, and struggling wounded, cowered behind them. Lieutenant Frerking at strongpoint WN 62 brought down a salvo of airburst, which caught Team 11 at the critical stage of manhandling their explosive-filled raft off the ramp into the surf. The overhead burst set off a catastrophic explosion that killed seven men. Team 12 was in a similar terrifying predicament, ten men frantically trying to push and pull their preloaded rubber raft off the LCM under intense machine gun fire. It would not budge, so they had to abandon it.

Engineers were climbing up log ramps to set charges amid machine gun fire that "resembled rain drops on a mill pond," recalled Seaman 2nd Class John Talton with Team 9. "Men shinnied up the stakes and stood on each other's shoulders," remembered Lieutenant Commander Joseph Gibbons, "all in the face of heavy enemy gunfire." He saw "enemy fire cut away fuses as rapidly as the engineers could rig them," said one team battle report. "A burst of fragments carried away a fuseman's carefully set mechanism, along with all his fingers." Talton helped his team leader, Warrant Officer William Reymer, and boat chief Mitchner ashore. Reymer had "a triangular hole in his helmet and was bleeding down the front of his face. Mitchner's right eye was hanging from his socket and he was addled."

As Private Chuck Hurlbut's Team 15 neared the beach he felt and heard the distinctive *ping, ping, brrrrr* of machine gun bullets hitting the ramp, preparatory to it dropping. "Jesus," he remembered, "guys started dropping and screaming all around you," yet "somehow the rubber raft got off, and it was right behind me." He grabbed the tow rope and began wading through the surf, pulling the dinghy to the obstacles:

> "All of a sudden I feel it getting heavier. I look around, there's three bodies of guys who were thrown in. Two were face down, I don't know who they were. One was face up. I knew who he was. So I kept pulling."

"There was a sudden boom!" from a mortar strike, and "I was knocked head over heels" and momentarily blacked out, coming to "on my hands and knees spitting blood." He sat down in the surf and pulled the rope in, but all that came toward him was a large section of tattered rubber. "That was the raft," he recalled, "the three guys—gone." Virtually one in three of the combined army/navy team engineers in the first wave became casualties. Of sixteen fifty-yard breaches called for, only six to eight were completed before the rising tide submerged the obstacles. Most of the partial gaps were blown in the more thinly held German sectors between WN 62 to 64 and WN 68 and WN 70.[27]

Press photographer Robert Capa had taken out his first Contax camera from its waterproof oilskin ready to take pictures. He was with

Captain Edward Wozenski's E Company, coming in late because only a small number of landing craft could get through the obstacles at any one time. They were landing in twenty-minute interval wavelets. "The first empty barge, which had already unloaded its troops on the beach, passed us on the way back," he recalled. They were somewhat reassured when "the Negro boatswain gave us a happy grin and the 'V' sign," which was misinterpreted as all going well. More likely the boatswain was relieved at getting out in one piece. Then "the flat bottom of our barge hit the earth of France," Capa remembered. The ramp came down and a curtain drew back revealing "the grotesque designs of steel obstacles sticking out of the water." Ahead "was a thin line of land covered with smoke."

Capa clicked his first image as "the men from my barge waded in the water waist deep." Figures in his photograph can be seen moving rapidly and spreading out, with one man already down in the surf in the middle distance, before he can reach the cover of Czech hedgehogs beyond. His second and third pictures show two wading and one Sherman DD tank with men clustering around the left side, seeking cover from fire from WN 65 to the right. Some of Wozenski's men have already reached the seawall, represented by a ragged line of dots, framed beneath the menacing dark outline of the bluff line beyond. Wozenski "was praying for smoke, any kind of smoke," he recalled, "so that we could get up through the wire" festooned along the seawall. "Heroics have nothing to do with it," he explained, accounting for the stalled advance. "Their automatic weapons were trained on us, and people cannot advance in daylight against automatic small arms."

Capa's Contax was loaded with standard twelve-frame 35mm Kodak Super XX film. He seems to have snapped off five shots from the ramp of the landing craft, recording the men from his craft spreading out even farther as they approach the cover of the three stationary Sherman tanks. One of them is clearly designated number "10," painted on the exhaust funnel of its wader. Injured soldiers can be seen floating in the surf, one face down, while half submerged soldiers hiding behind the metal hedgehogs are pulling others under cover. Capa's coxswain, clearly unimpressed with this reticence at the ramp, "mistook my picture-taking attitude for explicable hesitation and helped me make up my mind with a well aimed kick in the rear." Capa was soon in waist-deep water.

Wozenski described a similar scene to that Capa framed with his Contax. "There were tanks burning, some landing craft had caught fire and the general smoke and haze of a battlefield began to develop. . . . It was still very early and gray for good pictures," Capa remembered:

> "But the gray water and the gray sky made the little men, dodging under the surrealistic designs of Hitler's anti-invasion trust, very effective."[28]

Capa's few surviving photographs of American soldiers pinned down on Omaha Beach are a remarkable document. All that is missing from these in part grainy pictures is the crack and thump of incoming fire, and the clunk of metal striking metal, whirring off steel obstacles. They were taken against a backdrop of disturbing noises, explosions, shouts, and insane screams. There was the throaty throb of landing craft barges, revving as they sought to avoid obstacles, coming and going. The whispering surf juxtaposed against the plaintive sobbing and pleas from the wounded. The stench of cordite, diesel fumes, the tang of sea, vomit, burned grass, and oily smoke cannot be included, but his pictures exude an aura of "I was there," that accurately reflect soldiers' oral accounts.

It took an hour for Wozenski's surviving soldiers to cross the sand to reach the base of the bluffs. Capa appears to have lain prone in the water, among the obstacles, during this time. "I tried to move away from

my steel pole," he recalled, "but the bullets chased me back every time."
He finally made a dash for the half burned amphibious tank stranded
fifty yards ahead, captured on film, and spent a further twenty minutes
cowering in its shadow.

> "Now the Germans played on all their instruments, and I
> could not find any hole between the shells and bullets that
> blocked the last twenty-five yards to the beach. I just stayed
> behind my tank, repeating a little sentence from my Spanish
> Civil War days: *Es una casa muy seria. Es una casa muy seria.*
> This is a very serious business."

Modern terrain analysis of the crest lines and bluff shadows that form
the backdrop to Capa's first pictures reveal his landing place to be just
right of WN 62. The spot is virtually beneath the east side of the present
Normandy American Cemetery and Memorial at Colleville-sur-Mer.
He turned left, taking two pictures from the lee of the tank, of clusters
of infantrymen lying prone in about a foot of water behind a sloping
phalanx array of wooden bench obstacles. They are probably cowering
from fire, possibly aimed at them from Heinrich Severloh and Franz
Gockel at strongpoint WN 62. The men, borne on the tide, are crawling
toward the shoreline like mud-colored amphibians. This angle of the
shot was to provide later inspiration for Steven Spielberg's iconic movie
film depiction of Omaha in *Saving Private Ryan*. "The foreground of
my pictures was filled with wet boots and green faces," Capa later wrote
in his memoir, "shooting from the sardine's angle. . . . Above the boots
and faces, my picture frames were filled with shrapnel, smoke, burnt
tanks, and sinking barges [that] formed my background." It captures
the slurry of wreckage, flotsam, corpses, and frightened soldiers being
pushed toward the shoreline by the rising tide. "The slant of the beach
gave us some protection," Capa remembered:

". . . so long as we lay flat, from the machine gun and rifle
bullets, but the tide pushed us against the barbed wire, where
the guns were enjoying open season."

Capa had his back to the enemy and began to shoot pictures of engineers working on the Czech hedgehogs behind him. One of these men
was subsequently identified from the photographs as William P. Buell, in
the 5th Engineers Brigade attached to the 16th Regiment, distinguishable
also by the half-moon white engineer insignia on his helmet. Wires can be
seen strung between the obstacles he and his men are sheltering behind.
The man prone in the center is lying face down in the water. Landing
craft can be seen in the background of the photograph arriving in flotilla
formation, disgorging men up to their necks in water and leaving in line.
The conveyor belt of reinforcements is still being maintained despite the
heavy fire and wreckage at the water's edge.

"The dead lay all around me," recalled one veteran who landed at
this spot:

"The tide was carrying in corpses, torn off arms and legs, feet
with the boots still on, and even helmets, with decapitated
heads inside. In between, hesitant GIs rose up, and everywhere
there were wounded, but not one medic."[29]

In the midst of the rising tide of viscera and wreckage Capa snapped
the iconic image of Huston "Hu" Riley swimming past. This photograph
has since been used extensively to encapsulate the agony of Omaha Beach
on D-Day.

Riley was paddling to shore amid the bizarre flotsam, "trying," he
recalled, "to keep as low a silhouette as possible." Around him, landing
craft were edging in, "and many were being torn up by the obstacles,
which had Teller land mines attached." German machine gun fire was

skimming the surface of the water, "as I was hit several times in the pack and shoes, but no damage." The photograph shows him trying to keep a low swimming profile, pushing his supporting life jacket just above the surface of the water, looking ahead. Riley estimated it took him at least thirty minutes to cover the one hundred yards or so to reach the shoreline.

> "Since I was very wet, it was a real struggle to try to get up and run. I ran in a half crouch, but I was hit in the shoulder close to the neck with a burst of automatic weapons fire. Two fellows grabbed me by the arms and pulled me to the base of a bluff."

One of the men who helped him was an E Company sergeant, he recalled, "and the other was a photographer with a camera around his neck." Riley's enduring memory of this incident was, "what in the hell is this guy doing here?"[30]

"Some of the men froze on the beach," recalled Sergeant Fitzsimmons with E Company, "wretched with seasickness and fear, refusing to move." Survivors "toiled painfully" to the foot of the bluffs. Fitzsimmons felt "the enemy might well have found and destroyed them" if they had ventured down, "since [the Americans] had no firepower." Elements of L Company, way off course to the east, had landed and were sheltering under the sandstone cliffs directly beneath strongpoint WN 60. They were unable to move. The Germans could not shoot at them because of the perpendicular cliffs. Unable to depress their heavy guns below the cliff edge, they would have to expose themselves to shoot below.[31]

Sergeant Donald Wilson in Riley's F Company knew he also had to rise from the surfline to reach the bluffs. The waves breaking over him were the final spur to act:

"It was time to move and I decided to go for it in one long run; no stopping, no zig-zagging—just go! I got rid of the gas mask, some C rations, the blanket, whatever, then took off running for what seemed to take forever."

There was no general rush to the seawall bank, some "were playing possum and using the incoming tide," while others used it "to sort of sneak ashore." He came across Goldsmith, one of his boat team. "Something had torn a piece out of his helmet and driven it into his cheekbone." He appealed to him to take it out, but Wilson refused, unsure how deep it had penetrated. "By now, the bank was beginning to fill up with mostly wounded," while Wilson "wanted to hook up with somebody—anybody in one piece," but he was surrounded by human wreckage. He saw "a soldier out in the surf thrashing around," floundering to the surface, sinking, and then coming up again. He tried to rescue him only to find "the gaping stomach wound as his jacket slid open." As he tried to unfasten his gear, "he sighed rather loudly and was gone." Then he found one of his officers, Lieutenant Siefert, shot through the throat, just below his Adam's apple. "His chest was covered with blood, which was continuing to pump slowly from the wound." He thought back to when they had walked the beach in West Bay England, firing their .45 pistols at cliff targets in "a sort of can you top this?" game. So it was with some guilt that "on some pretense, I left him, rather hurriedly." He was depressingly unable to find anyone who was not wounded. A glance out to sea confirmed that "obviously, the succeeding wave had been held up—but the amount of shipping and activities offshore were incredible." It was such an irony that none of it was coming into their beach. "It was frustrating," he remembered, "to be in such a jam on the beach with all that power just offshore."[32]

The German defense on this left cliff shoulder of Omaha Beach was repelling the veteran "Big Red One" assault. Colonel B. B. Talley's

US information team, monitoring developments from an amphibious DUKW vehicle offshore, radioed back to Major General Gerow, the US V Corps commander eleven miles out to sea. PC 552's terse message was sent twice, at 6:41 and shortly before 7:00 A.M., and Gerow was informed: "Entire first wave foundered."[33]

Oberfeldwebel Schnüll's 88mm nestled in the side of the bluffs just above the beachline had an angular wall cloaking its seaward muzzle flash. He could see the entire curve of the Omaha bay in between smoke from grass fires that periodically gusted across his line of vision. His powerful gun flashed and cracked out at the rate of two to three rounds per minute. Its flat trajectory was distinguishable from the red tracer base of the shell darting out to the obstacle belt in the distance, and abruptly cascading in a shower of sparks or a fireball against the dark silhouette of a landing craft. The metallic clunk of impact was discernible a second or so after the flash on strike. On the hillside to his left, the 75mm field guns in WN 62 were similarly banging out, dust and vegetation flung away from the concrete apertures with each gun report. Columns of black smoke boiling up in the middle distance bore witness to the destruction they were wreaking on the wide-open beach. The flash from Obergefreiter Siegfried Kuska's 50mm gun could be clearly seen from Schnüll's position, and the satisfying metallic hammer blows heard as he dispatched yet more Sherman tanks milling around the draw entrance between them.

War correspondent and renowned novelist Ernest Hemingway watched offshore. Only sixteen of fifty-six tanks from the 741st Tank Battalion made it to the beach. As he watched, "one of the tanks flared up and started to burn with thick black smoke and yellow flame." Schnüll and Kuska continued to pick them off as "another tank started burning." Hemingway saw little further movement: "Along the line of beaches, they were crouched like big yellow toads along the high water line." Tank mobility was barred by obstacles, crowds of cowering soldiers, and hazy visibility from grass fires among the dunes. They were unable to climb the bluff line, and exposed to remorselessly accurate German anti-tank gunfire as soon as they approached the draw openings the strongpoints were sited to seal. Even more harrowing were the bodies sprawled in their path. Tank men had frequently to expose themselves to climb down and drag them out of the way. Mobility was the only way to survive in action.

Sergeant Leonard Trimpe with the 741st recalled their vulnerable inability to see anything. Wading into seven feet of water off the LCT ramp, his driver called out, "Trimpe I can't see." The water was washing over his scope. "So I stuck my head out of the top of the turret," Trimpe remembered, "to tell him when to drive to miss all kinds of disabled equipment, mine poles and dead bodies, etc., to find a place to enter the beach." They had to move slowly and cautiously; the beach was "a total mess." Hemingway watched as tanks crawled to the beach exit:

"I saw three tanks coming along the beach, barely moving. The Germans let them cross the open space where the valley opened onto the beach, and it was absolutely flat with a perfect field of fire. Then I saw a little fountain of water jet up, just over and beyond the lead tank. Then smoke broke out of the leading tank on the side away from us, and I saw two men dive out of the turret and land on their hands and knees on the stones of the beach. They were close enough so that I could see their faces, but no more men came out as the tank started to blaze up and burn fiercely."[34]

Lung-searing balls of flame erupting inside stricken tanks inca-pacitated crews inside by immediately depriving them of oxygen. They shrieked and shouted in pain and urgency to clear the way out, and in so doing expelled their air. Veterans often tell stories of crewmembers, clambering out of blazing turrets, who would suddenly give up and inexplicably fall back inside.

Only two of twenty-nine DD tanks that launched with the 741st Battalion swam into the beach, twenty-one sank and three more were immediately shot into flames in the kill zone between strongpoints WN 60 to 62. Surviving tanks lurked turret-deep in water like amphibians, hoping not to be spotted as they traded shots with German bunkers. Corporal Jack Boardman, peering through his narrow turret observation slit, engaged the west side of WN 62, but could not see much. His commander, Staff Sergeant Dick Maddock, was constantly thumping his shoulder to open fire, but "it was completely murky," Boardman recalled:

"There was this dust and I guess smoke pall all over the beach. And I'm wondering what to shoot at because all I can see here is this soup."

All he could make out after firing was smoke puffs rising up from the rear of a concrete pillbox he had picked out on the side of the WN 62 hill mass.[35]

The two surviving DD tanks, commanded by Staff Sergeant Turner Sheppard and Sergeant George Geddes started to duel with Schnüll's 88mm at WN 61, and Krieftewirth's 75mm at WN 62. Sheppard recalled a large explosion near WN 61, which "I believe was the ammunition supply for that 88 that was working nearby." He also began to batter the 75mm bunkers at the side of WN 62.

Oberfeldwebel Schnüll had been fighting with his 88mm gun for forty minutes, and had probably fired one hundred or so rounds into the flanks of landing craft and Sherman tanks at the obstacle belt in front of the E3 and E1 gaps. He had a perfect defilade shoot, but the gun barrel was glowing red-hot and the crew was exhausted. No friendly support was visible through his bunker aperture apart from artillery stonks howling in from Frerking's 1st Battery. At 7:10 A.M. Sergeant Geddes's Sherman scored a direct hit on the narrow embrasure of Schnüll's gun, smashing the muzzle brake and putting it out of action. According to one of his loaders, Gefreiter Hermann Götsch, the battle-crazed Schnüll climbed on top of the bunker with his MG 42, and fired from the hip at disembarking GIs from a landing craft nearby. Gedde's next 75mm round tore him apart in a gray-red cloud of smoke that exploded on the bunker roof. The apparent fall of WN 61 was immediately relayed through the 352 Division telephone network.

Götsch and another loader, a Pole, survived the blast and stayed inside the devastated bunker, cowering from intense incoming fire. Götsch felt his bowels involuntarily release and dropped his trousers, and then used his spade to clear the observation slit. Approaching American infantry saw the cover being disturbed at the slit and posted a grenade through the emerging hole, which rolled into a small niche inside the gun chamber and exploded. When the three GIs burst inside to finish them off, they found to their amazement that nobody had been killed or injured. The Pole managed to strike up a conversation, because some of them were US-Polish immigrants. Lucky Strikes were passed around, appropriate to their unexpected survival, and the Germans led off to captivity.[36]

About thirty-five minutes later Sheppard's DD tank put first the lower and then upper 75mm casemates at WN 62 out of action. The explosion inside was so devastating according to Krieftewirth's loader Hans Selbach, that they thought they been hit by a naval destroyer, shrapnel peppered the internal concrete wall. Franz Gockel observed it all, "the gun firing slit was covered in the dust and smoke of the exploding shell." Bruno Plota, bringing up ammunition from outside, was left in shock. Selbach ran out through the smoke and dust into the zig-zag trench network around the bunker to escape to the upper casemate. "Running out below," he recalled, "would have been far too dangerous." He was shot through the lower leg, a flesh wound, but managed to carry on.

Plota telephoned the command bunker and reported Krieftewirth dead, but he did later regain consciousness. There was not a mark on his body, but he was in deep shock.[37]

Shortly before 8:00 A.M., three key bunkers shooting west along Omaha Beach were out of action. As a consequence, fire from the Colleville cliff shoulder perceptibly slackened. A gap in the German defense—an area of rugged bluffs, a few mines, and a coil of barbed wire—was emerging because the 760-yard stretch between WN 62 and WN 64 farther west had no emplacements. Farther along, the sector between WN 64 to 68 was still under construction. A chink in the armor of the German defense had been opened up.

SIX

POINTE DU HOC "THE JIB"

6:40 A.M. TO 11:10 A.M.

═══════════════════════

The Cliff
6:40 A.M. to 7:30 A.M.

Pointe du Hoc was the highest point of land between the American beaches at Omaha and Utah. The conspicuous knife-edged out-crop derived its name from the old French term for "jib," whose foresail shape it resembled. Capturing it had been explained to Lieutenant Colonel James Earl Rudder as a key D-Day objective. The 155mm six-gun battery perched on top could cover the approach to Omaha Beach and even reach Utah. Captain Walter Block with Headquarters Company 2nd Rangers was told, "this bastion could not be permitted to stand by any invading army." The raid, however, did not get off to a very auspicious start.[1]

Not only were the German guns in situ, the executive officer Major Lytle, commanding the Ranger attack force, was found drunk the night before in Weymouth harbor. He was relieved from command, having voiced his opinion the raid was a "suicide mission." Colonel Rudder, summoned from the USS *Ancon* command ship, was obliged to assume command aboard the HMS *Ben Machree*, after Lytle drunkenly insisted the guns had been removed from the cliff top. Only Rudder possessed the overall detail of the plan required to replace him. Major General Huebner the V Corps Commander and General Bradley, the overall army commander, were reluctant to release him because it left no senior Ranger commander at hand to interpret mission progress and any specialist support requirements. This would have unfortunate consequences, because of the many possible permutations to the attack plan.

Rudder commanded a complete Ranger group made up of the 2nd and 5th Ranger battalions. They were under the command of the 116th Regiment, leading the 29th Division assault on the western half of Omaha Beach. The Rangers were due to spearhead and cover the westward inland drive toward Grandcamp and Isigny. The sequence of movement by the Ranger force was entirely dependent upon the outcome of the assault against Pointe du Hoc. Rudder would now command three companies: D, E, and F from the 2nd Ranger Battalion at H-hour. The 5th Ranger Battalion under Lieutenant Colonel Schneider, with A and B from the 2nd attached, were to pause until H+30 minutes to await the outcome of Rudder's attack. If successful, they would follow on and exploit to the west as planned. If not, Schneider's eight companies would go into Omaha Beach with the 116th, one hour later, at Vierville. Company C from the 2nd, under Captain Goranson, was given a separate mission to take out the German emplacement at Pointe Percée, to neutralize German fire on Omaha's right flank. Understandably both

ABOVE LEFT: Michel Hardelay had to assist the Germans with the demolition of his own house at Vierville sur Mer, to make way for German beach defenses. *Courtesy of Lefebvre.* ABOVE RIGHT: Albert Andrés was working on the unfinished German bunkers at WN 66, at the center of Omaha beach the afternoon before the invasion. *Courtesy of Bernage.* BELOW: Edmond Scelles had forty German soldiers billeted at his farm at St Laurent sur Mer. *Courtesy of Bernage.*

THE FRENCH

LEFT: Louise Oxéant and 10 Year old Bernard to the right were caught in the delayed bombing release behind Omaha beach and did not survive. *Courtesy of JM Oxéant/von Keusgen.* BELOW: American soldiers and French civilians were mistrustful of each other at first, Calvados was often mistaken for wine. *Courtesy of Musée Omaha.*

THE FRENCH

ABOVE AND BELOW: The German occupiers did not provide air raid shelters, rudimentary shelters had to be dug by the French themselves. *Both images courtesy of Musée Omaha.*

ABOVE: The danger of sudden arrest for forced labor and other security infringements was a constant civilian hazard in the security belt behind the invasion beaches. BELOW: Jean Marion at Grandcamp overlooking Omaha told his wife when he saw the invasion fleet 'there's no room for the fish.' *Both images courtesy of Musée Omaha.*

ABOVE LEFT: The figures for French civilian casualties at Omaha are not known, the first 48 hours of the invasion possibly resulted in 3,000 French deaths. ABOVE RIGHT: Oberleutnant Bernhard Frerking manned a forward artillery observation post at strongpoint WN 62 at Colleville-sur-Mer. BELOW: Oberleutnant Hans Heinz (seated right) was a Stalingrad veteran, with fellow company commander Hahn to his left. Both would command counter attacks at Omaha beach. *All images from author's collection.*

TOP RIGHT: Generalmajor Dietrich Kraiss, the veteran commander of the 352nd Infantry Division, which unknown to the Americans, occupied a virtually impregnable position on Omaha beach. BOTTOM LEFT: Gefreiter Franz Gockel manned a Polish machine gun at WN 62. BOTTOM RIGHT: Oberstleutnant Fritz Ziegelmann, the 352 Division Chief of Staff, who guessed the invasion had started. *All images from author's collection.*

ABOVE: Wilhelm Kirchhoff manned a cliff edge MG trench at Pointe du Hoc. BELOW LEFT: Kurt Keller was an ardent Nazi, serving with the 352 Fusilier Battalion, mounted on bicycles, part of the Kampfgruppe Meyer. BELOW RIGHT: Oberst Ernst Goth commanded Regiment 916, responsible for the forward sector of Omaha Beach, confident his well trained men would fight well. *All images from author's collection.*

RIGHT: Heinrich Severloh, the so-called 'beast of Omaha', whose machine gun at WN 62, caused so many casualties. *Image from author's collection.* BELOW: Horse drawn German reinforcement column pausing at the roadside inland from Omaha, the Kampfgruppe Meyer was one such mix of truck, bicycle, tracked and horse drawn transport, very vulnerable to allied air attacks. *Courtesy of Musée Omaha.*

ABOVE: One battalion from the Kampfgruppe Meyer was detached to counterattack at Colleville-sur-mer. BELOW: Company level German counterattacks conducted piecemeal just inland from Omaha beach at St Laurent-sur-Mer proved ineffective. *Both images from author's collection.*

THE GERMANS

OPPOSITE TOP: Kurt Keller felt his puny single rifle would have no effect against fresh American waves coming ashore near St Laurent-sur-Mer, at the center of Omaha beach. *Image from author's collection.* OPPOSITE CENTER: Gefreiter Gustav Winter's 'concrete panzer' was located inside strongpoint WN 66 just outside St Laurent-sur-Mer. *Image from author's collection.* OPPOSITE BOTTOM: The Germans could not believe the allies could amass so many ships and approach the beaches undetected. *Image from author's collection.* ABOVE: German bicycle reinforcements on the march, a travesty of the 1940 heady days of mechanized Blitzkrieg. *Courtesy of Musée Omaha.* BELOW: The cliff top shoulders at either end of the beach, like this one near Pointe du Hoc, were key to the successful defense of Omaha. *Image from author's collection.*

TOP LEFT: General Omar Bradley (with glasses) observes the beach over 10 miles away with Admiral Kirk to his left aboard his command ship the cruiser USS *Augusta*. CENTER LEFT: Brigadier General Norman Cota, the unassuming deputy commander of the 29th Division, who provided the necessary inspiration to get men off the beach. BOTTOM LEFT: Captain Joe Dawson, decorated by Eisenhower, commanded G Company the 16th Regiment, the first company group to scale the bluffs at Colleville-sur-Mer. BELOW: Celebrated war photographer Robert Capa, who took the most remarkable photographs of D-Day at Omaha beach. *All images from author's collection.*

ABOVE: Capa's first photograph taken from the ramp of his landing craft, the man at left center has already been shot and is sitting in the water facing the camera. BELOW: Capa is making his way thigh deep in water to tank number 10 in the distance, where men are already taking cover from German fire coming from Strongpoint 65 to their right. He would be pinned down here for over an hour. *Both images from author's collection.*

ABOVE: Capa captures this image of William P. Buell with 5 Engineer Brigade whose distinctive engineer white half moon insignia is clearly visible on his helmet. The demolition wire shows the Czech hedgehog obstacle is ready to blow, the man next to him is face down in the surf. Men are disembarking from landing craft neck deep in water behind. BELOW: Capa turns to his left and captures men pinned down in the obstacles by strongpoint WN 62, only demolition engineers are moving around. *Both images from author's collection.*

THE AMERICANS

ABOVE: Capa's picture of Private Hu Riley, 'the face in the surf' swimming past pushing his lifebelt ahead to keep low in the water, he was seriously wounded shortly after. *Image from author's collection.* BELOW LEFT: Private John Barnes, A Company 116th Regiment, his landing craft swamped and sank off Vierville-sur-Mer. *Courtesy of A. Kershaw.* BELOW RIGHT: David Silva, wounded by machine gun fire before WN 62, possibly fired by Heinrich Severloh. *Image from author's collection.*

ABOVE LEFT: Sergeant John (Robert) Slaughter, A Company 116th Regiment, caught up in the massacre before the Vierville draw. *Image from author's collection.* ABOVE RIGHT: Brigadier General Wyman, (left), the Assistant 1st Division Commander, who took the decisive decision to accelerate infantry reinforcements for Omaha beach. *Image from author's collection.* BELOW LEFT AND RIGHT: Roy and Ray Stevens, the twin brothers who landed with A company the 116th Regiment in front of Vierville. *Courtesy of A. Kershaw.* OPPOSITE TOP: Lt. Col James Rudder, who commanded the Ranger assault on Pointe du Hoc. *Image from author's collection.* OPPOSITE BOTTOM: Lt. John Spalding, E Company 16th Regiment, whose platoon landed alone in a sheltered lee of German fire and were the first Americans to scale the Omaha bluffs. *Image from author's collection.*

THE AMERICANS

ABOVE: Rangers assemble atop Pointe du Hoc, 101 Airborne Division paratrooper Private Sam Goodgal is seated to the right. BELOW: Lt. Coit Hendley's LCI(L)-85 sinks off Omaha. It had briefly rescued photographer Robert Capa from the beach. *Both images from author's collection.*

ABOVE: At 5:50 A.M. and still in poor light, the fleet began to bombard the beaches. BELOW: Heavily laden soldiers from C Company 16th Regiment observe Dawson's G Company landing ahead. A DD floating tank is still laboring towards the beach off their starboard bow. Note the waterproofing on the rifles. *Both images from author's collection.*

ABOVE: The ramp is down and C Company the 16th plunge into waist deep water to the right of Strongpoint WN 62, with Dawson's G Company up ahead. Note the same waterproofing discarded at the ramp. BELOW: Laboring through the water, C Company approaches troops and a wading tank pinned down on the shore line. Demolition engineers are at work on the obstacles, with a number of dinghies off to the left. *Both images from author's collection.*

TOP: Anxious moments offshore waiting to go in. *Image from author's collection.* CENTER: The steep incline of the bluffs is clear in this beach shot later in the afternoon. *Courtesy of Musée Omaha.* BOTTOM: Czech Hedgehogs and the obstacle belt. *Courtesy of Musée Omaha.*

ABOVE, RIGHT, AND BELOW:
The *bocage* hedgerow
terrain, is totally different
from the beaches and
unexpected, as soon as
they traverse the bluffs.
*All images from author's
collection.*

ABOVE: The claustrophobic confines of fighting through the seaside villages. BELOW: Rangers cliff climbing training for Pointe du Hoc. *Both images from author's collection.*

ABOVE: Rocket assisted grappling hooks during training in preparation for the assault on Pointe du Hoc. BELOW: Technical Sergeant Phil Streczyk, John Spalding's veteran platoon second in command, was to become one of the most decorated NCOs in the US army. *Both images from author's collection.*

Huebner and Bradley on the command ships wanted Rudder standing by with them, to advise and coordinate the reactions to these possible contingencies.

Rangers were elite soldiers who were loosely developed from the British commando ethic. James Gabaree with the 5th Ranger Battalion claimed Rangers "were carefully selected individuals who were patriotic, courageous, intelligent, strong, and must have more endurance than the average soldier." They had smaller companies and battalions, and were "trained to act as a team member," Gabaree explained, "but be capable of acting alone in order to complete the mission." This was an especially relevant characteristic this day. "We were an elite group that very seldom took a defensive position, the mindset was to advance."

Colonel Rudder had much on his mind as his three-company contingent with 10 LCAs and 4 DUKWs labored through heavy seas toward the Pointe. They anticipated facing maybe 125 German infantry and 85 artillerymen with their 220-man force. Each LCA carried about 22 men, because they were heavily laden with three pairs of rocket mounts at the bow, center, and stern to fire grappling hooks. There were also assault ladders and hand-held launchers, to power their grappling hooks one hundred feet up the cliffs. Boats were slow, overladen, and plowing low in the water. Captain Walter Block saw the "unbroken line of cliffs, for the most part sheer," he had identified in his briefing photographs. The cliffs were "stretching out on either side of a sharp spear-pointed outcropping. This promontory was the objective, but as they wallowed in toward the coast they noticed many such outcroppings. Wherever they landed, Block appreciated, it was "going to be a pretty hard climb."[2]

The preparatory bombing of Pointe du Hoc had appeared devastating from the ships. "Honestly, it was like the biggest Fourth of July you ever saw, magnified a thousand times," remembered one D Company Ranger. The battleship *Texas* joined in, "hitting the Pointe in a bursting hell of shrapnel and concussion." German machine gunner Wilhelm Kirchhoff with Werfer Regiment 84 cowered in his trench at the edge of the cliff. "I pressed myself into the ground," he recalled, "and although I wanted to get deeper, I couldn't":

> "However, just as before, most of the shot passed over us. A few shells hit the edge of the coast and great masses of rubble fell down and under."

The watching Rangers with D Company saw there was:

> "A direct hit on the cliff's edge; the scene is obscured, and when the debris has settled, a tremendous crater is visible in the sheer outside. The climb at that point has been reduced by at least forty feet."

Yet despite all these signpost indicators and possibly because of the dust and smoke obscuration, the guide boat was swinging inexorably too far to port.[3]

Rudder, convinced they were heading toward the wrong place, began to remonstrate with Lieutenant Colin Beever, guiding them aboard Royal Navy Launch *304*. With one thousand yards to go Rudder could see it was Pointe et Raz de la Percée, which at sea level looks very similar to Pointe du Hoc. Adding to Rudder's sense of dread was the increasingly choppy sea. "All the boys just kept looking at the water and saying, 'Ike has goofed,'" recalled Regis McCloskey with F Company:

> "These boats got tossed around the Channel like corks, and with a full load rode so low in the water that the big waves just rolled over the sides and into the boats. We had to keep bailing with our helmets all the way in, and the boys were so

damn tired or sick by the time we hit the beach, most of them just didn't care too much one way or the other."

Two supply LCAs had already swamped and gone under. Sergeants Lomell and Kuhn had been watching their D Company number three boat with increasing unease, losing speed and slipping back to their left and rear. "Heartsick they watch it, as, overloaded and unseaworthy to begin with, it finally stops altogether," the official report read, "and sinks slowly and reluctantly beneath the waves." Heads bob up in the water, and start to drift rapidly apart. Men in the surviving boats "look at each other, and there is unspoken understanding," they are already twenty-two men down. The Channel was bitterly cold and the choppy waves began to overwhelm the drifting men. It would take two more hours before the exhausted group was recovered. Six of them slipped beneath the surface during that time and the remainder could neither walk nor talk.

Lieutenant James Eikner, Rudder's signals officer, remembered the argument between Rudder and Beever, who was steering them the wrong way. "Colonel Rudder, in our lead craft, literally forced his boat to break ranks and flank west," he recalled:

> "The infuriated British officer doing the navigating thought we were trying to abort the mission, and tried to run Colonel Rudder's craft down; he soon realized his mistake however."[4]

It was 6:40 A.M., too late for H-hour. "The Pointe is visible now, far to the right," remembered the D Company observers. "From this distance, it is a tiny, sharp little wart squarely between the two beaches." The plan had been to land on either side of the promontory to split the German fire—now they would have to head for the nearest spot. Coming in from the east meant there was no time to swing out and divide. As the flotilla turned 160 degrees to starboard, they came within range of German machine guns up on the cliffs, and now faced a slow three-mile gauntlet of fire to run beneath them. Lieutenant Commander Baines, commanding the destroyer HMS *Talybont* and firing in support, thought the slow cliff crawl "suicidal." Corporal Ralph Davis recalled the extent of incoming machine gun fire with fifteen minutes to go, "which ripped along the sides of our boat and sprayed the water like raindrops all around us." Baines could not understand why the boats had gone in the wrong direction, because the massive fall of shot from the *Texas* broadsides at the Pointe "was obvious." At about three hundred yards from the landing, one of the DUKWs carrying power-operated ladders was raked by 20mm cannon fire from the AA mount east of the Pointe, hitting five of nine men, some in the water. Staff Sergeant William Stivison heard the DUKW radio operator saying, "We're sinking, we're sinking, we've sunk."[5]

Private Leonard "Sam" Goodgal and Sergeant Raymond Crouch, the two 101st Airborne Division troopers who had parachuted off course into the sea, next to the cliffs, earlier that night, had spotted boats nearing the shore to their right at about 6:30 A.M. They were picking their way westward along the cliff through the shale, seeking an exit to the top. Crouch frantically waved his arms and Goodgal even found a pair of boxer shorts to attract the craft, moving in parallel offshore. They were ignored by the occupants, now under fire and heading for the spear-shaped promontory sticking out into the sea ahead. The two paratroopers had no idea where they were, but guessed these were Americans. They hurried toward the increasing sound of fighting.

With engines bellowing and revving, Rudder's nine surviving LCAs and three DUKWs turned in a ragged line into the base of the cliff line on the east side of the Pointe du Hoc headland. It was 7:10 A.M., just as Oberfeldwebel Schnüll's 88mm gun was knocked out at WN 61, representing the first reduction of German firepower at Omaha. Rudder was forty minutes late, forty minutes for dazed defenders, after pulverizing naval gunfire, to come to their senses and react. Machine gunner Wilhelm Kirchhoff manning a trench to the right of the artillery observation cupola had only to lean forward to see the beach beneath the cliff face below. "The landing craft came on us from the right," he recalled, "and they were fully laden with soldiers and matériel. The waves were very high as they came in, the small boats pitching violently."

In the boats the Rangers could see Germans silhouetted against the cliff crest, moving around, and starting to fire. Lieutenant Commander Baines aboard the *Talybont* pounded the activity he could see on top with four-inch guns and two-pounder (pom-pom) antiaircraft fire. Beever's motor launch joined in with 20mm Oerlikon fire and twenty rounds of three-pounder cannon. The destroyer USS *Satterlee* also closed, lashing the cliffs with five-inch and 40mm guns which "kept the Germans from being too obnoxious." As the landing craft neared the cratered, pebbled beach the dark outline of the one-hundred-foot sandstone cliff towered above them.[6]

The water-filled craters from bomb and shell bursts prevented the DUKWs carrying the power-operated fire ladders from closing into the cliffside. A series of dry tubular coughs set off hissing banks of grappling hooks, trailing ropes up the cliffs. Some were able to reach 150 yards up and over the cliff edge but many fell short, stymied by the inability of the crews to keep the ropes dry. The rocket-assisted grappling hooks were originally designed for ship to shore rescue work and had been adapted by the Rangers. They shot up in banks of two followed by a tug on the rope below, to dig the hook in the ground or snag on a hard object. Some immediately pulled off. Medic Frank South explained the difficulty of accurately firing the rockets. "Grenades and small arms were hitting against us," he recalled, and "under the circumstances you have a narrow field of vision," so "you did what you had to do." One F Company sergeant unable to fire his tubes unloaded them onto the beach and "hot-wired them and ignited them by hand." They snaked up and snagged at the top. "His face was pockmarked with burnt powder," the Ranger medic remembered, having "just got these things planted and aimed by sight." South couldn't resist the urge to wisecrack "what a terrible complexion he had."[7]

The attack took on the character of a medieval escalade of a castle rampart, with men scrambling up tubular ladders and ropes. The two far right boats got four ropes and toggles up the face, the three center boats managed five ropes and two ladder combinations. The four boats to the left on the east side of the landings managed fifteen ropes and ladders, but many of these were under machine gun fire. In between men free climbed. During the first minutes of the escalade some twenty-five access points were gained. The besieged Germans cut grappling hook ropes and threw down stick grenades to blow men off the cliff face. To shoot and drop grenades required a degree of exposure, immediately punished below by sharp shooting Rangers standing back in the surf and raking the cliff edge above with BAR automatic fire. Leonard Rubin with D Company claimed one German who came bouncing and tumbling down.

Artillery Unteroffizier Rudolf Karl told six of his men to get inside the concrete artillery observation post at the pinnacle of the promontory and went forward to the edge with three men. "We threw hand grenades from the top," he recalled, "until we had no more." These had a one-pound TNT charge in a fragmentation sleeve, attached to the throwing stick. Tossed over with a four to five second delay, they exploded with a blast radius of fourteen yards. "They had no cover down there," Karl recalled, "and the effect in between the Americans on the beach was devastating."

"Our signals and telephone operators were also forward in the trenches and fired down below with rifles," machine gunner Kirchhoff remembered, "we were really galvanized at that moment":

"As soon as they landed beneath, the ramps came down and the soldiers jumped out. We didn't need an order to open fire, we started shooting as soon as the ramps were down."

The Rangers were well in range and "had absolutely no cover." Kirchhoff did not aim, but rather sprayed fire across the ramps. "The first soldiers that emerged fell over, because of the pressure from those at the back," he recalled. Very soon, "dead were floating in the water with wounded in between—I could hear the shrieks and howls." The main incoming fire was from the destroyers offshore. Fighting from the trench next to him was Karl Jagla—a young rifleman—shooting as fast as he was able. It was his twentieth birthday.[8]

"As I ran off the LCA I went into water above my head," remembered Lieutenant George Kerchner with D Company. With all the excitement he didn't inflate his life jacket, and swam to shore. "My radio wouldn't work, so I threw it onto the beach." Both his superior officers had already been shot down. "I found a rifle and tried to locate the machine gun, but I couldn't." He has snapshot memories of the assault. Rudder shouted at him to get up the cliff, and "I remember that some of my men were hit—Pacyga, Cruz, and Harris." He joined the frenzied storming of the cliff face, with men pulling and scrambling themselves up the score of ropes that twisted and snaked down from the top. "We could see Jerries running around the top of the cliffs and they were shooting at us and tossing grenades," Kirchner recalled, but "I was too wet and miserable to mind."

The soaking they had received on the run-in and landing made it difficult to rope climb. Corporal Ralph Davis jumped into water, "up to my neck, and half ran and half swam to the protection of the cliff's edge." Climbing was laborious, "the bank was wet and slippery," he remembered. Cold wet hands and muddy boots added to the weight of soaked uniforms and equipment made it exceedingly difficult to get a grip. Upward movement was only possible by pulling and straining arm work on the ropes, while kicking and scrabbling at the crumbling sandstone cliff face to gain egress. Soldiers in effect walked up the sheer face, while hauling at the rope with their arms, somehow retaining a grip on weapons. Lieutenant Wintz who landed last on LCA-883 afterward explained, "he was never so tired in his life." Davis recalled:

> "My legs were a dead weight, my body was numb and cold,
> and my hands were chilled blue, so that I could hardly grab
> the rope to climb the cliff."

Handholds were gouged out with knives as pulling on ropes and toggles, ladders and free climbing, men sought to scale the equivalent of a nine-story building. Wild yells above often signified the triumphant cutting of a rope and a Ranger would hurtle back down the cliff. "As I climbed the rope," Davis recalled, "bullets were hitting either side of me, and potato-masher grenades exploded beneath me."[9]

Kirchhoff remembered German soldiers congregating at the cliff edge and firing and tossing hand grenades down. A mortar was brought forward and set up almost perpendicularly, "and fired directly from me, below onto the beach." He was in a daze, standing up in the trench with an MG 42 cradled in his arms, trying to shoot down over the edge. "I can't remember how many shots I fired and who brought up the ammunition belts," he recalled. There had been five box loads of belted ammunition stacked in the trench at the start of the assault. "One fired a burst at one of the boats," he explained, "a short pause, and then again." A grappling hook landed nearby, "and one of the artillerymen crept up to it and cut the rope." They stood their ground, "the Americans tried to get to us, but they couldn't, and remained on the beach," he recalled, "trying again and again."

Sergeant Bill "L-Rod" Petty was on his third climb, frustrated by cut lines and ropes slippery with mud. He watched Germans lean out and try to machine gun Rangers from above as they climbed. The man next to him was hit and swung out from the cliff and slid down, gathering momentum as he bounced off ledges and rock outcroppings taking, "a lifetime before his body hit the beach." Petty froze momentarily before being galvanized upward by another close spray of ricocheting automatic fire. Bombarded by crumbling rock debris raining down and pulling frantically at grass tufts near the top, elements of the mass infiltration trickled over the escarpment. About twenty-five small groups spilled over the edge at multiple points. Emerging from small clefts, they scrambled the last few yards and desperately rolled over and flung themselves into shell holes beyond.

They were aided by some bizarre fire support. The DUKWs alongside were fitted with powered, extendable London Fire Brigade ladders. These had been customized with twin Vickers K guns mounted on top. "The fire brigade ladders were spectacular," medic Frank South recalled. "The guy on the ladder couldn't get close to the cliff face," because of the craters below. The movement of the surf corkscrewed the ladders through 45 degrees at ninety feet in the air, an amazing sight for friend and foe alike. "He was up on the top with a Vickers gun trying to fire at the Germans," South explained. He barely managed suppressive fire, but at least, "he was a moving target for the Germans."[10]

The two 101st Division paratroopers Crouch and Goodgal ran up in the midst of the action on the beach. One Ranger sergeant remembered his surprise at seeing two paratroopers running toward him, gesticulating at airborne patches while yelling, *"We're Americans! We're Americans!"* Singularly unimpressed, he pointed at the ropes and told them to get up the cliff. Without realizing who he was they came across Colonel Rudder, who said, "stick with me," and led the way up the rope. Crouch's first view at the top was to look into the staring eyes of a dead German soldier. "He was just a young boy," he remembered, "and he had a knife in his back." Being an eighteen-year-old himself, he thought, "Oh lord, what have I gotten into?" Crouch picked up a rifle and Goodgal a machine gun when they reached the plateau. Medic Frank South remembered their appearance and how they "pitched right in." They became part of Rudder's headquarters group defense.[11]

Sergeant Len Lomell was wounded "through the fleshy part over my right hip," as he waded through the water on landing, remembering "it just burned like hell." He was exhausted nearing the top of the cliff, while "the Germans were firing down at us, trying to drive us back into the sea, trying to kill us, knock us off the ropes." A speedy ascent was their only survival chance. His radio operator Bob Fruhling pleaded, "Hey Len, can you help me I am exhausted, my strength is going I am going to fall." Lomell was also at the end of his strength, "and didn't know if I could continue." He called across to Leonard Rubin, who came "and grabbed Bob and tossed him over onto the top of the cliff." They made it as Lomell covered them with his machine gun, "Lenny saved both of us that day," he admitted.

Individual boat post-combat reports suggest the right, or west, side of the assault was up the cliffside in five minutes, some individuals getting to the top in thirty to forty seconds. The main problem was machine gun fire from Kirchhoff's Werfer Regiment 84, firing from the left outside casemate 3. It took fifteen minutes for the boat crews in the center to get up and longer for those on their left. All the Rangers were up within thirty minutes, against sporadic opposition. The cliff face was so badly knocked around that First Lieutenant Amos Potts claimed "naval shells had completely changed the appearance," which assisted the ascent. "I would guess that 30% to 40% of it was gone." Frank South agreed. "I would say," claimed Sergeant Lomell, that "my platoon, the 2nd in D Company, were up those cliffs in five to ten minutes, no more." Fifteen men were dead.

"The Americans eventually managed to climb up, and paused just below the cliff edge," remembered Kirchhoff.

"They were in dead ground, so we couldn't see to shoot them. I believe they just glued themselves to the cliff face."

They waited for an opportune moment to spring over the top. He could see "dead Americans rolling about in the surf for a long time," but once again "the warships fired a number of shells against our position, directly on the edge of the cliff." Their position now became untenable, so Kirchhoff and his men pulled back into the battery interior.[12]

The Plateau
7:30 A.M. to 11:10 A.M.

R angers emerging at some twenty different points began immedi- ately to fan out in all directions from the cliff edge. The landscape, painstakingly memorized and analyzed from detailed maps and air photographs, had fundamentally changed. Transformed by bombing and naval gunfire, it was difficult for them to orient themselves to terrain that now resembled the surface of the moon. Speedy infiltration resulted in scores of fast-moving actions by small groups, heading toward their casemate objectives. The German defenders, unable to follow the various lines of attack, could not concentrate to meet them. "It led to a totally confused muddle," remembered Kirchhoff, "there was no more order":

"Up until then I had fired something like 10,000 rounds. I had to change both machine gun barrels several times. The muzzles were sometimes red-hot."

Sergeant Lomell came across Captain Baugh of E Company as soon as he got to the top. "He had been shot and had his hand practically blown off, and wasn't in such good shape." They would send a medic they assured him, because, "my platoon couldn't wait for nothing," they had to spike the guns and "went ahead in a rush":

> "We didn't stop; we played it just like a football game, charging hard and low. We went into the shell craters for protection because there were snipers around and machine guns firing at us."

The Germans were unable to exploit the innate superiority of their MG 42s because of the cover provided by the cratered landscape, nor were they able to pinpoint the direction of advance of nine different groups heading for their assigned bunkers. "We'd wait for a moment and if the fire lifted," Lomell recalled, "we were out of that crater and into the next one."[13]

Every individual Ranger knew his mission and broadly where to go, despite the altered landscape. The primary objectives were the gun emplacements and the observation cupola (OP) at the head of the Pointe. Company E had been assigned the OP and casemate 3, D company the western three guns: 4, 5, and 6, and F Company casemates 1 and 2 and the antiaircraft position east of the fortified battery. After sweeping through the bunkers there was to be a consolidation and reorganization on a line just south of the complex, then a forward exploitation to cut the east-west road between Vierville on Omaha Beach to Grandcamp-Maisy and Isigny.

The various Ranger groups swiftly closed in on the concrete gun emplacements. "When we got there, we found there were no guns," Lomell recalled, "the big emplacements had telegraph poles looking like a big gun from the air." This caused universal dismay. "It startled and disappointed us," Lomell complained, "because we were psyched to do it, and we meant to do it, even if it killed every one of us." There was no alternative except to continue with the plan. As Lomell described it, with "our platoon being the first in, we decided to go for broke and go inland." There was still a lot of incoming fire:

> "There was an antiaircraft position off to our right several hundred yards and a machine gun off to the left. There was another machine gun that we had gotten on the way in. The antiaircraft gun was firing flat trajectory at us and by the time we got to the road I only had about a dozen men left."[14]

Unteroffizier Rudolf Karl was spotted by a group of Rangers who came over the lip of the cliff northeast of the large undamaged observation bunker. Led by Lieutenant Leaggins and Staff Sergeant Cleaves, they threw grenades at the solitary German soldier, who disappeared inside the bunker. In the confusion of the fighting it was assaulted from both sides, with neither side aware of the presence of the other. Radio operator Benno Müller with the 369th Signals Company inside recognized that they were cut off. "*Ja,* we were now attacked from the front and rear," he remembered. Müller was still in radio contact with the guns, which had been relocated to an apple orchard in the rear, after the devastating April air attacks. The contact was of limited value because, "they couldn't shoot any more, they were all blind drunk." They heard the ribald behavior across the radio net:

> "That night some of the gunners had already foraged a great deal of alcohol and taken it back to their rear position. Later they went back and picked up the rest of the drinks supply, everything down to the champagne, that was still available."[15]

The conversation ended when Private Thompson came up and heard enemy radio traffic, he looked around for an aerial and shot one off the top of the OP. He then threw a grenade into the entrance and the rear group sat back to wait. Private Aguzzi was left on watch, while Lieutenant Leaggins took the rest of the group off to their inland mission.

There were nine Germans pinned inside the bunker. Its steel armored doors opened in two sections, to ensure the entrance was not permanently jammed by debris. The cupola was the command post nerve center, working the target coordinates for the guns to the rear. Inside was an operations room, complete with a large table and bunks for nine men. Three inset machine gun ports covered the entrances. When the first Rangers came over the cliff edge to their front, machine gun and rifle fire spat out of the ground level embrasure, the hollow gun reports amplified by the concrete chamber within. Sergeant Denbo and Private Roberts rolled into a trench five feet from the OP and posted four grenades through the firing aperture, of which three fell inside. The machine gun fire stopped but Denbo was wounded in the head.

Four more Rangers joined this frontal attack group led by Lieutenant Lapres. One of them, Sergeant Yardley, had climbed the cliff with a bazooka. His first round cracked out and struck the edge of the embrasure, flinging back the occupants from the concussion and peppering them with concrete shards. The second round flew straight inside and produced a satisfying bell-like report, accompanied by black smoke. Only when Lapres's group went around the back did they find Private Aguzzi still on watch. The grenade damage and shrapnel gouges on the walls inside are still visible today. The Germans retreated farther back and secured themselves behind the armored plate door. Intermittent fire still rang out from the besieged bunker, but the Rangers could not get inside. A watch was maintained, but very much distracted by the sporadic sniping and skirmishes that were going on all around the complex, as Germans suddenly emerged from holes and tunnels they had dug free.

Rangers from D and E companies formed the nucleus of the advance to cut the road, thirty-six men reaching it with seven killed and eight wounded on the way. Lomell described the advance as "leap-frogging," protecting each other until they reached the road and crossed it. "When it came my turn to sprint forward," he explained, "I looked over the hedgerow, and my God, there were five of those 155mm howitzers neatly camouflaged in a little apple orchard and completely covered." The guns appeared to be facing Utah Beach, at the ready, with ammunition stacked for firing, "a text-book scene," Lomell remembered.

It was shortly after 8:00 A.M. and the Rangers had been on Pointe du Hoc for almost an hour. He saw "the Germans were putting on jackets and assembling in the corner of a pasture, a hundred or maybe less yards away." The lack of over watch was probably attributable to the constant air and sea bombardments that had unnerved the artillerymen. One of the gun crewmen, Karl Jäger from number six-gun, claimed he was not the only one to disappear during the hellish invasion night at three o'clock in the morning. They had a jaundiced view of any authority, "they could lick my ass," he allegedly remarked to Emil Kaufmann, another surviving gunner in the battery. Lomell did not hesitate to approach the unguarded guns, accompanied by Sergeant Jack Kuhn.[16]

They had two 2½ pound thermite grenades, which they placed in the traversing mechanisms of two of the Puteaux 1917 vintage 155mm guns. "These are special things," Lomell explained, "which make no noise but for a silent 'pop,'" ideally suited to the stealthy sabotage they were engaged in, with German troops close by. Thermite burns in air producing intense heat from the oxide mix, which creates oxygen for heat. This massive infusion of white-hot energy welded metal together with very little sound apart from the fizzing melt, which gummed the moving parts of the traversing mechanism together. The sights were clubbed with rifle butts, to ensure the guns were totally inoperable. "It might look as though there is nothing wrong with it," Lomell explained, "but it cannot be used."

As Lomell and Kuhn fell back to get more grenades, an E Company patrol under Sergeant Frank Rupinski also came across the guns from the east side of the hedgerow. They had enough thermite grenades to post one in each gun tube to spike all the guns. The coup de grâce was administered by blowing up the main cache of propellant charges, which made the destruction obvious. Runners were sent back to Rudder's HQ with the inspiring message that the costly mission had been accomplished after all. This was transmitted by radio at 11:10 A.M.; neither V Corps nor any other unit received it.

Rudder set up his headquarters near the eastern flak bunker, in a huge crater, near a section of collapsed cliff that gave easier access to ropes and ladders. The plateau atop Pointe du Hoc was, however, far from secure. Many of the remnants of the German garrison were consolidating around the very active 20mm flak gun bunker to the west. There was also an effective German machine gun harassing Rudder's HQ about 1,500 yards to the east of the strongpoint. A Ranger attempt to capture the western flak bunker was rebuffed in a costly storm of fire. Some forty German prisoners had been rounded up in the mop-up of the battery positions, but resistance from tunnels and holes was still sporadic. Rudder had about a hundred Rangers defending a tenuous perimeter to the south of the blocked road, but an ominous number of Germans had already been observed moving toward Saint-Pierre-du-Mont to the east. Rudder's determined leadership and warships offshore were keeping counterattacks at bay, but Ranger casualties were inexorably mounting, beyond the thirty to forty already lost.

Force C consisting of the eight companies of the 2nd and 5th Rangers commanded by Lieutenant Colonel Max Schneider were offshore at 7:08 A.M. waiting for the order to "go." Captain John Raaen remembered lying off Pointe du Hoc and Pointe Percée for about forty-five minutes. "We circled and circled," he recalled, "praying for the message from Force A that they had landed successfully." Raaen, with HQ Company 5th Rangers, had set off that morning from the HMS *Prince Baudouin*, with the Captain's stirring "Goodbye Rangers and

God bless you" played over the intercom. After this inspirational start "the boat began to reek of vomit." Their tiny LCA craft were buffeted by waves six to eight feet high. "We were crammed into three rows, no shoulder room," Raaen recalled, "no knee room and the sea was rough." Max Coleman in the same battalion remembered heaving about "in a sea choppy enough to turn the stomach of Sinbad the Sailor." The waiting was interminable. "I know that our thoughts and words were that we were expendable troops," recalled a concerned Lieutenant Robert Edlin with A Company 2nd Rangers. "We felt reconciled to a lot of casualties."

The code word *crowbar* came through, indicating Rudder's force had actually landed at Pointe du Hoc. The next signal, indicating the successful storming of the cliffs, never came. Raaen heard two indistinct messages:

> "One was a beach master on Dog white [Omaha] saying the troops were landing without resistance. Another one had the word 'Charlie' in it, but we couldn't make it out. We weren't sure what it meant, but it didn't mean success."

At 7:45 A.M. Rudder radioed "*Praise the Lord*," which meant, "all men up cliff," but the forty-minute delay in achieving the landfall cost him his reinforcements. As Raaen remembered, "if we had received no signal, meaning success by H+30 minutes, it was over the beach instead of the cliffs." Commander Stratford H. Dennis on the command ship HMS *Prince Charles* had not spotted the agreed alternative; flare signals from the Pointe, so the eight remaining Ranger companies were ordered to proceed to Beach Dog Green on Omaha.[17]

This was to have fateful implications for the rest of the day. Rudder's subsequent *need ammunition and reinforcements* signal and another, *many casualties*, did not get through. By then there was a rapidly escalating crisis distracting all attention on the command ships, trying to discern what was happening on Omaha. There was no senior Ranger presence to advise Generals Huebner or Bradley about what support might be needed, or what may have happened in the event of no news. The scale of the disaster unfolding on Omaha was dwarfing any concerns about Rudder's isolated hundred or so Rangers, the fate of thousands now became the issue.

Colonel Schneider waited until 7:10 A.M., just when Rudder landed and decided to divert. They were already ten minutes over the deadline; it was time to get moving.

SEVEN

WIN OR LOSE?

6:45 A.M. TO 8:30 A.M.

═══════════════════════

The Center. Saint-Laurent-sur-Mer
6:45 A.M. to 8:00 A.M.

S econd Lieutenant John Spalding watched the obstacles coming up, with the sinister outlines of Teller mines attached as they bobbed through the shallows. "No path had been cleared through them, so we followed a zig-zag course in," he recalled. He was with a lone landing craft from Company E, the 2nd Battalion 16th Regiment, part of the 1st Division. Despite the thunderous noise coming from the beach, the shoreline had only come in sight fifteen minutes before. Bizarrely, the surface of the sea had been covered by thousands of fish, killed or stunned by the rocket bombardment. It was 6:45 A.M., an eerie land-fall, they were completely alone. Away to their left numerous landing craft were coming into the lee of the German strongpoint WN 62 hill mass. To their right, toward Saint-Laurent-sur-Mer, there were none at all. Desultory machine gun fire was leveled at them, "about eight hundred to one hundred yards out," he remembered, "but it was not effective." Spalding, originally a lawyer from Owensboro, Kentucky, had an ethnic Pole, veteran Technical Sergeant Philip Streczyk, as his second-in-command. His thirty soldiers landed in isolation four hundred to five hundred yards from the nearest German emplacements. Like so many others, they were way off course and late. The lone LCVP attracted some fire, but with such a rich target environment to their left, German gunners paid them little attention.

The main problem was circumventing deep underwater runnels as they waded ashore in V-shaped formation. Spalding pulled the valve on his life belt and lost his carbine when the strong current swept him out of his depth. Many of the others were soon in trouble, shedding heavy weapons and equipment. Spalding "swallowed half the ocean," with water up to his mouth as he made a grab for the assault ladder Streczyk was trying to drag through the water. "Lieutenant, we don't need your help," the sergeant called out, but Spalding recalled, "Hell, I was busy trying to get help, not to give it." They reached the beach without loss, but lost the boat's flamethrower, mortar, bazookas, and much ammunition, as well as the ladder designed to get them over anti-tank ditches. Up ahead was the ruined house they had expected to see, their objective, but Spalding did not appreciate that it was the wrong house. They were fifteen hundred yards off course to the east. Two of his men were hit and wounded on shore, which were surprisingly light casualties relative to the carnage inflicted to their left. His men "were too waterlogged to run," he recalled, "but they went as fast as they could." That was a form of slow motion, "as if they were walking in the face of a real strong wind."

They urgently sought to clear the beach, and according to Spalding, "walked on across, because nobody stopped them," thereby minimizing exposure time:

> "We had bypassed a pillbox, from which machine gun fire was coming and mowing down F Company people a few hundred yards to our left. There was nothing we could do to help them."

They were alone. "We could still see no one to the right and there was no one up to us on the left," he remembered. There was no sign of the rest of E Company, and "back in the water, boats were in flames," a dispiriting scene. "After a couple of looks back, we decided we wouldn't look back any more."

Although they had landed in a relatively quiet backwater, they were under continuous small arms fire. To get off the beach they had to cut a hole in the wire with a Bangalore torpedo, pass through a swamp, and then negotiate a minefield to get to the top of the bluffs. Sergeant Streczyk was sent off with Private Richard Gallagher to find a way through. They found a narrow, indistinct path, probably used by German security patrols from WN 62 when the tide was in.

Streczyk and Gallagher cleared light opposition on the trail ahead and were soon supported by the rest of Spalding's platoon as they moved up the defile. They infiltrated their way through an undefended sector of grass-covered bluffs with "pretty heavy brush," seemingly a defense vacuum between WN 62 and the next strongpoint along, WN 64 to the west. Spalding lost two men pushing his platoon up the heights, a far safer option than staying on the beach. Sergeant Bisco kept warning, "Lieutenant watch out for the damn mines" Spalding remembered. "They were a little box type mine and it seems the place was infested with them, but I didn't see them."

The so-called *Holzmine* [wood mine] housed in a small, rudimentary wooden box, had sufficient explosive power to blow off a foot. The whole point of mines was to maim and demoralize rather than kill. The visceral image of shattered leg stumps and agonized screams not only warned the enemy, but reduced attacking strength, because men had to be diverted to carry casualties away. There were various types infesting the defiles and gaps around the German positions. The *stockmine* was a concrete cylinder filled with metal splinters, attached to wooden stakes; *Glassmine M43s* were explosive charges inside cheap glass jam jars. The "Bouncing Betty" *schutzenmine* was especially feared because stepping on the mechanism bounced a mine three to five feet in the air, which exploded at crotch or abdomen height, scattering 350 steel balls over one hundred yards. Courage and determination was needed to traverse these mine-infested areas, sited to be covered by enemy fire. Spalding recalled, "we lost no men coming through them," although the next company coming through hours later lost several men.

Sergeant Francis Murray with the 1st Division came up the bluffs later:

> "The guys would go single file and there were about four men laying there with their foot blown off from mines. We could not walk on either side, just step over them. There were mines either side of ya, more or less. They would go as far as they could, they would step on a mine and another guy would take over, marking them. He would step on one, and there were three or four of them laying there."

Spalding's men escaped scot-free: "The Lord was with us and we had an angel on each shoulder on that trip," he remarked.[1]

The path Spalding took follows the same paved route that can be walked today from Omaha Beach to the Normandy American Cemetery and Memorial high on the bluff plateau. His platoon overwhelmed two enemy machine guns at the summit, one of which was manned by an ethnic Pole from one of 726 Regiment's *Ost* battalions. Sergeant Bruce Buck recalled an incensed Streczyk punching the prisoner and discovering sixteen other Germans who surrendered. Streczyk was "kicking them in the ass and talking to them in Polack, wanting to know why they fought so hard." Spalding reached the top of the bluffs at this thinly defended escarpment by about 8:00 A.M. His group of about twenty soldiers could exploit left or right. The steep climb up was in partial dead ground to the machine guns at WN 62 and obscured from the top by undulations in the thick brush and grass-covered dunes. On their right, four hundred to five hundred yards away, were the weapon-chattering emplacements and concrete embrasures of WN 64, still under construction. When Sergeant Murray made it to the top he later recalled the dominance of the feature they had captured:

> "Now you think of it, its rather awesome when I look down
> from here, of the German view of us. I don't think I would
> want to do it again."[2]

Thirty minutes later, at about 7:00 to 7:15 A.M., G Company, commanded by Captain Joseph Dawson, landed in the same spot as Spalding. They too saw "thousands of dead fish" offshore and mistook surviving tank crews floating by on rafts as guides to direct the infantry. Dawson's force of six boats attracted the heavy German fire that Spalding's men had opted not to look back at. "Bullets were dropping around us like rain but the good Lord seemed to be with us," Dawson recalled. They were still well away from the nearest German strongpoints, which were bracketing the landings with armor-piercing and explosive shells, but as Technical Sergeant V. J. Miceli remembered, "the nearest did not fall closer than fifty to sixty yards away."[3]

Any delays at the waterline invited swift retribution. One of the boats, "taking in too much water," Dawson remembered, came in slowly behind the main cluster; the men "couldn't bail fast enough." With water up to their knees, the weight and volume shipped had fouled the craft's ramp mechanism. "So the men had to climb over the sides," all the time lashed by German machine gun fire, "a broadside target" that cost them fifteen men. Some boats were nearly dissuaded from landing due to the height of the surf, because the tide had risen considerably since Spalding landed. Most GI casualties were inflicted between the boats and the shingle; mortar and machine gun fire meant "we lost sixty-three men all told," Dawson estimated.

The extent of the physical drain from the turbulent passage, with men tightly crammed into the flat-bottomed Higgins craft, became all too apparent on beaching. Lieutenant Martin Stine remembered on his boat:

> "When the ramps went down, some of the men couldn't move ashore. They stumbled and fell in the water. They had become so cramped because of crowding that their muscles would not respond. They lay in the water for a few minutes, rubbing their legs. Finally, when the circulation was restored, then they crossed ashore."

This stumbling slow motion advance ashore exacted a price. "It was the feeling of the men," Technical Sergeant Miceli commented, "that our losses would have been cut in half if the loads had been lighter." Unlike any other company at this stage, Dawson's reached the shingle at the base of the bluff, with most of his company intact with their light machine guns and mortars. But they could not distinguish a single German target.[4]

"The scene along the shingle as 'G' landed was one of complete confusion," Dawson remembered. Looking around he saw, "the assault wave had become pinned down, mentally if not physically." Three tanks were already knocked out, blazing on the waterline. They were mixed up with men from the 116th Regiment's E Company, way off course and "demoralized in part" by the error of landing in the wrong place. Men were landing in sectors where engineers were blowing Belgian Gates, and were taking cover behind obstacles prepared for demolition. "Unfortunately they were in the wrong place at the wrong time," and both Dawson and Miceli watched in horror as "they died when our own explosives took out the obstacles." "There was no coordinated fire from the Americans ashore," Dawson observed, and all around them:

> "'G' could see a line of men along the shingle, frozen to earth and taking no steps against the enemy. They were bunched shoulder to shoulder and were huddling on patches of ground which gave them partial cover from fire."

Dawson started to organize his soldiers and set up fire support teams with his mortars and machine guns. His was the only combat-cohesive infantry company group on the east sector of the landings. Several hundred yards from the water's edge he saw, "a sergeant laying there and two men and seemingly refusing to advance." He remonstrated with them, "I exhorted them strongly to follow me," and even briefly returned a few steps to shout at them again, "when I suddenly realized that they would never move again." Dawson instinctively appreciated they had to get off the beach, and if not through the draws then over the bluffs.[5]

Meanwhile, the Germans, distracted by more LCVPs coming through the obstacle belt, switched fire from "G" Company to engage the new arrivals. Now "G" could pinpoint German targets from winking muzzle flash signatures, coming from cunningly concealed bluff positions. Dawson got his men moving, blowing gaps in the wire, and came across two dead American soldiers, the result of Spalding's earlier advance on the same path half an hour before. The entire company group went up the same hill and were briefly held in place by a crossfire from two machine guns. Dawson destroyed one of them, lobbing two grenades into the emplacement.

The destruction of the west-firing 88mm and 75mm guns at WN 61 and 62 resulted in a perceptible slackening of attacks from that direction. Even more boats were managing to land reinforcements at the relatively sheltered base of the bluffs. The situation on the fire-swept beach remained critical, but Spalding and Dawson eventually met up. They assessed the situation and opted to attack the Germans from the rear. Spalding turned right with his platoon of twenty to twenty-two men and began to traverse the undulating brush layers and wooded area toward the flank and rear of Strongpoint WN 64. Dawson collected all the men he could and moved off with a weakened company toward the village of Colleville inland. Sergeant Streczyk released a yellow flare to signal the beach below that a breakthrough had been achieved.

Captain Edward Wozenski, pinned down with E Company the 2nd Battalion 16th, saw the yellow smoke signature through the battle haze to his right. "I had said the first son of a gun that gets up on top of that bluff will set off a smoke flare," he recalled. Assembling as many men as he could grab, he set off in the direction of the flare, "because I couldn't get up where I was." Getting soldiers to move was not as straightforward as he thought. "I remember distinctly taking my trench knife and pressing it into people's backs to see if they were alive." Those that responded were rolled or kicked into movement with a "Let's Go!"

> "I picked up half a dozen people this way, but I didn't realize that terror could be so great in a man that he would not turn round to see who was sticking a knife in him. Later on it dawned on me that two or three were alive but just wouldn't turn round because of absolute terror."

Wozenski climbed the path where he saw the yellow smoke as Streczyk from Spalding's platoon came down, driving the Polish prisoners before him, "with a big grin on his face." Then to his horror, Streczyk "right in front of my nose" stepped on a teller mine. "My God," Wozenski spluttered, "how stupid can you be?" The unperturbed sergeant responded, "Oh, don't let it worry you, it didn't go off when I stepped on it going up." With his nerves in tatters Wozenski continued on to the top, where, "I had a head count." He had landed with eight officers and 180 men, and "I counted thirteen men and one officer beside myself." After nearly three hours the first chink in the German defense of Omaha had opened, left of center, and it would be prized further apart.[6]

A disappointed Lieutenant Colonel Max Schneider, having diverted Ranger Force C off Pointe du Hoc toward Omaha, was in a hurry. He received no word from Rudder and set off late, which meant it was almost 7:30 A.M. before he started his approach toward Dog Green, at the Vierville side of Omaha Beach. His British Royal Navy coxswains served him well. Three flotillas totaling nineteen LCAs turned 90 degrees right and headed toward the beach in three waves, five LCAs with A and B Companies from the 2nd Rangers leading, followed by two waves of seven craft each carrying the 5th Rangers.

Schneider was an experienced veteran of the North Africa, Sicily, Salerno, and Anzio landings. He knew what to do, with an instinctive feel for German defensive capabilities. His lead wave saw the wreckage and bodies opposite the Vierville draw and slipped left, but not far enough. Their landing craft began to weave in among mostly submerged obstacles, festooned with mines. One Company B craft erupted three hundred yards offshore, its back broken by an underwater obstacle. Men spilled into the water and came under machine gun fire. Captain Edgar Arnold, commanding B Company was abruptly knocked onto the sand, "by some unknown force" on landing, his carbine smashed from his hands. "The thing that struck me was the total chaos on the beach," he remembered. "Dead men seemed to be everywhere." Lieutenant Robert Edlin was shown pictures of the wife of Sergeant Klause, one of his section commanders, on the run in, to relieve tension. He next found Klause wounded at the water's edge, "and about to give up to the tide," amid all the destruction, "when I reminded him of our conversation, it brought him back." Arnold, dismayed at the intensity of fire, admitted, "I began to get visions of being pushed back into the sea." Schneider, viewing the debacle ahead through binoculars, is alleged to have blurted out "I'm not going to waste my battalion on that beach!"[7]

Lieutenant Heinz Fuehr, manning strongpoint WN 68 with the 8th Kompanie Regiment 916, recalled many of the landing craft "struck mines and sank":

> "We could see the American soldiers who had survived the mines waiting for the boats to flood, so they could begin their swim to the beach."

Off to his right Gefreiter Gustav Winter was manning his modified Panzer III turret mounting a 75mm gun, set back from the houses facing the beach. "I was determined to hold this resistance point," he remembered, but still felt vulnerable. "We were there, just me and this scared boy, in our concrete panzer as this great army came slowly toward us." Winter's position was in depth and he could not see the lower beach directly in front, but he did have a sight picture of the obstacle belt, now partly submerged by the rising tide. "I saw several explosions when a craft hit a Belgian Gate with a mine.":

> "The detonation blew big pieces of steel from the hull. I saw one craft in which the front ramp was blown off completely, and inside were a large number of men, all of them scrambling

around as the craft tipped over and sank. Several of these craft were on fire in one place or another."[8]

"I was shoulder to shoulder with Colonel Schneider in the lead boat," remembered Technical Sergeant Herbert Epstein, "and clearly saw what was happening to Companies A and B near the Vierville draw." Schneider conferred with the British flotilla leader and both agreed they should turn east and try again about half a mile down. Lieutenant Jack Snyder reckoned the change of direction: "Violating orders from above saved the battalion. We landed without a casualty due to this," because "another unit continued on to be almost annihilated." With impressive seamanship, the remaining two waves with 14 LCAs carrying five hundred men executed a right angled turn and wallowed along a course parallel to the beach, seeking a better landing spot. Epstein was effusive in his praise of the Colonel's quick decision in a tight spot:

> "I have always felt that Schneider was the unsung hero of Omaha Beach. He was certainly my hero, and I credit him with saving my life and countless others by his savvy and decisiveness."[9]

At about 7:50 A.M. the 9th Ranger Battalion came ashore as a cohesive unit, within an area of fifteen wooden breakwaters. These were fifty-five feet long, sticking out to sea and a similar distance apart. The locals had erected the posts, reinforced with boulders at the base, to reduce beach erosion. "Waves lashed at us, throwing the boat right and left, pitching, tossing, and smashing into German obstacles" Captain John Raaen recalled:

> "At one point we were crashing down on a pole-type obstacle with a Teller mine attached to it. Too bad—this is it! But

another wave grabbed us, throwing us to the left, and we were past the mine and a few minutes later, the rest of the obstacles."

"Our coxswain had done well by us," Raaen recalled, dashing off the ramp in only ankle-deep water. They sprinted through ten yards of shallows, "amid the damnedest racket in the world," to reach the seawall. "You could hear the bullets screaming by," he recalled. The breakwater alcoves provided ready cover, lying prone, from enemy automatic fire coming in from the flanks. "Artillery was falling at the water's edge, but only small arms from our right was hitting the seawall." They could see bodies from the hapless earlier waves strewn all over the beach. "I think the only reason that we survived was that there were so many targets for the Germans to shoot at," remembered Charlie Klein with the 5th Rangers. "They were shooting around us and not spending enough time to take an aim," he explained. "So at that point I said we were pretty lucky."[10]

Cecil Gray with E Company remembered, "watching tidal pools with machine gun bullets kicking across them and then they stopped." This was the signal to get up and move. "They were reloading ready to fire again so I kept running." Jack Burke with A Company the 5th Rangers was to be forever haunted by the sounds. "I can still hear them to this day, as well as the odor of exploding shells, the engine sounds from landing crafts, and people yelling orders," as the ramps went down. He remembered people being hit in front of him on the ramp, whereas bizarrely off to the right, there was a British naval officer standing waist deep in water wishing them "Good luck, Yank," as they left the boat. "I heard a lot of screaming," and those lying in the water "yelling for help.":

"Artillery shells have a whistling sound, you only hear it maybe two seconds before it explodes. It is a definite sound that everyone in combat recognizes, and the general effect is to yell 'Get down!' or something similar. Incoming mortar shells have a 'whooshing' and you don't have much time to hit the dirt, possibly a second. If the mortar is firing close you can hear a 'thump' as the shell is dropped down the tube, but that is rare. The Screaming Mimi is a different animal, because it screams like a bunch of cats all screaming at the same time. It is not accurate, but it can unnerve some people."

Lee Brown, who landed with Schneider, remembered "the zip-zip-zip" of machine gun fire, which "had us ducking back down quickly". His canny chief Schneider did not immediately exit the ramp just as, "a machine gun strafed right in front of the LCA," Brown recalled, "and would have cut down many of us coming right off." Brown had been about fifth or seventh in line. Schneider paused to take off his encumbering Mae West life belt before tossing it on the beach, "the delay likely saved my life," Brown concluded.[11]

John Raaen looked back and watched the last man exit the boat, Ranger Chaplain Father Lacy. He was fairly old, short, and fat, "at least thirty pounds overweight," Raaen recalled, wearing "thick glasses"; a most unlikely looking Ranger. He got no more than ten feet clear of the ramp when a German shell hit the fantail of the LCA. Raaen looked away in dismay and did not see him again. He later discovered Lacy had survived. He "didn't cross the beach like we heroes did," he explained:

> "He stayed down there at the water's edge, pulling the wounded forward ahead of the advancing tide. He comforted the dying; calmly said prayers for the dead . . . Father Lacy stayed behind at the water's edge, doing the work for which God had chosen him."

The breakwater fences provided excellent cover for the Rangers as they sought to consolidate and decide the next move. "We were virtually untouched in the landing on Dog White by virtue of Schneider's decision." Lieutenant Charles Parker with A Company recalled, "smoke was covering the whole area, that meant the Germans couldn't put too much direct fire on us."[12]

They were also out of sight from Gustav Winter to their left at WN 66:

> "There was a long, long period of time where there was just smoke, explosions, and firing from the beach direction. . . . I could see flashes and clouds of smoke coming again and again. I was in a state of real anxiety, not knowing what was happening."

Nor did the Rangers, who had landed expecting to immediately march west and relieve Rudder at Pointe du Hoc. They saw that the 116th Regiment had been cut to pieces and had not even established a beachhead, essential before the Rangers could continue with their mission. In fact, nobody was moving. Cecil Gray with E Company was cowering behind the four-foot-high wooden seawall. "We hunkered there for a while," he recalled, "I was one scared cookie . . . I guess we all were." Ranger Victor Miller was lying on substantial four- to six-inch-diameter pebbles on this stretch of beach with company clerk John Spurlock:

> "I remember that John was carefully reaching under him and lifting a rock at a time, and moving it to make his body get lower and lower, which wasn't a bad idea after all."[13]

At 8:00 A.M. a complete Ranger battalion with about five hundred men had established itself on the beach between Saint-Laurent-sur-Mer and Vierville, between German strongpoints WN 68 and 70. "We didn't lose a single boat," recalled Captain John Raaen, "We didn't get mixed up, and as we came in to touch down we had perfect formation." On the east side of Saint-Laurent there was G Company, plus Lieutenant John Spalding's platoon from the 1st Division. The only toehold on the westernmost part of Omaha was Ranger Goranson's C Company elements, embedded inside WN 73, still fighting on the heights at the right of the Vierville draw.

The two major landing concentrations either side of Saint-Laurent had profited from the unfinished state of the bunker at the center of Omaha Beach. This stymied the ability of the Germans to mutually support their strongpoints on either side of Saint-Laurent. These sectors of beach were relative backwaters compared to the intense fire received from the two cliff shoulders, east at Colleville and west from Vierville. Fire from WN 61 and 62 had slackened, enabling G Company with the 16th Regiment to get up the bluffs. The Achilles' heel of the German defense was in the center. The quick-firing 50mm gun at WN 65 was tenuously holding the two chinks in the defense together.

These weaknesses were only visible with hindsight. At 8:30 A.M. reporting by both sides suggested the two-division front attack mounted by General Gerow's V Corps was turning into a debacle. The Germans suspected they had already won. The balance between the success or failure of this assault was visibly teetering. Both sides would call for inspired leadership.

Leaders
7:00 A.M. to 8:30 A.M.

Nineteen-year-old Marcel Leveel living at Moon-sur-Elle ten miles north of Saint-Lô had woken with a start that morning to "sounds like the clicking of castanets." The whole house was shaking, "rattling the badly joined windows and doors." Neighbor Léon Barey burst in, claiming the explosions were coming from along the coast. Leveel was not sure, "at first, I try to figure out from what direction it is coming." Sounds he had never heard before, "a tremendous, faraway noise overwhelms us." He went outside where it was cool with overcast skies, but "easier to figure out the location of the bombing," which clearly "is coming from the direction of the sea, no doubt along the coast, several kilometers away." There was the constant sound of distant thumping impacts. "I am not able to distinguish between the detonations," he recalled, "for a long time they came regularly and with the same intensity."

He joined a group of newly arrived refugees, staring out from the north side of the road, "to try to figure out what is going on." There were some World War I Verdun veterans among them who suggested, "it was definitely naval artillery from what had to be very large guns." Just like what they had heard at Verdun, "except for the fact that airplanes are also attacking." They heard bombers overhead, "flying low, hidden by clouds so we can't see them," but 'in the general din, we can barely hear them.'"[14]

Luftwaffe Lieutenant Thomas Beike had been sitting in the cockpit of his Messerschmitt Bf 109 on standby since 6:30 A.M. that morning. The airstrip was located seventy miles east of Omaha, on a plain belonging to a country estate in the Lisieux-Evreux sector of the fighter wing *Jagdabschnittführer 5*. He was comfortable enough with his "polished boots" existence in the locally requisitioned chateau, but like many a Luftwaffe pilot, "was under the surface a somewhat tormented individual." There were women, drink, and good life aplenty, but no aircraft parts, fuel, and fresh pilots to be "an effective fighting force." Many a time he had been unable to take off in a fully armed and fueled aircraft because there was no coolant for the engine. They were outclassed by the big Allied air formations and "we simply did not have enough good quality fresh pilots to replace those lost in the air." Repeated Allied bombing had led to the wide dispersal coastal squadrons.

They sat in three aircraft, after driving to the airstrip "as the gray light came up," passing a solitary, abandoned Allied glider on the way. This was alarming, and troops were already combing the area for the occupants. The Germans' dispersal points were concealed under false trees and they had thick camouflage nets over their cockpits. A runner turned up periodically to report on the latest situation, "but still there were no orders!" Massive overflights by Allied aircraft magnified the feeling of total inferiority. "It was a rather gray, damp morning that day," Beike remembered, "and the enemy planes' exhausts stood out very bright in the murky light." Finally the runner came up to announce they were "to intercept enemy aircraft over the coastal area." The priority was to down troop transports and bombers. At 9:00 A.M. engines burst into life and the order was rescinded and they switched off. "To do justice to our commanders," Beike admitted, "it must have been very difficult to make sense of the situation, and to take a decision on where to allocate the fighters." Retaining straps were loosened, and they settled back down into their cockpits to wait. No sign of action yet.[15]

Eleven miles inland from Omaha Oberstleutnant Karl Meyer's Kampfgruppe had taken nearly an hour to grind to a halt. Shortly after 7:00 A.M. the bicycle-borne Fusilier Battalion 352 was stopped, but the lorries of Grenadier Regiment 915 were not halted until 7:45. The tracked assault guns from the panzerjäger [anti-tank] companies had to be dispersed and heavily camouflaged beneath the trees in the Cerisy Forest. Enemy air activity was ominously increasing in tandem with the growing light.

Jacques Duchien near Grandcamp had been in a trench all night with about a dozen people. They also saw signs of increasing air activity. Planes flew by so low they sounded "exactly like the lowering of an anchor chain." The local French Underground sector chief of Grandcamp, Jean Marion, remembered seeing only about twenty navy men with a couple of light guns manning a line of trenches outside the town at first light.

People were curious: What was going on? Were the Allies winning or losing? Where were they? Families became increasingly concerned at the safety of their relatives and their whereabouts. They saw a massive armada, thick with ships, standing off the harbor. "People gradually came out until everybody stood looking at the fleet. . . . There's so many ships there's no room for the fish," Marion told his wife. The Germans began to blockade the streets, and "tried to hold them back," he recalled, "but they couldn't—they too were watching."[16]

General Dietrich Kraiss, eleven miles south of the coast at his chateau headquarters at Le Molay-Littry, faced a dilemma. He regularly conferred with his chief of staff, Fritz Ziegelmann, and was overwhelmed by the volume of confusing telephone and radio reports from coastal strongpoints. Much of the information was calm and lucid, some critical, some positively bizarre. Enemy forces had apparently scaled the sheer cliffs at Pointe du Hoc, aided "by rope ladders that were released from detonating shells," according to one 916 Regiment telephone report. A frustrating picture was emerging at 8:00 A.M. His own division was holding its ground and giving a very good account of itself, but the enemy appeared to be turning the 716 Division to his right. Thirty-five Allied tanks had broken through fifteen miles to his east [at the British Gold Beach] and were already bearing down on Meuvaines south of the coast.[17]

Kraiss's own cliff shoulder bastion to the east of the beach near Colleville was under pressure, the nearest point to the tank breakthrough. WN 61 housing the 88mm gun was surrounded, according to latest reports, and up to one or two companies of enemy infantry had infiltrated between WN 60 and 62, despite losing men in the minefields. It was estimated that maybe two battalions were ashore in the central sector between WN 64 and WN 70. Kraiss had already dispatched the Kampfgruppe Meyer, the division reserve, in the opposite direction to the crisis unfolding to his right. Meyer's group was halted with difficulty and ought to be recommitted, but the dilemma was where? Kraiss, a veteran of countless similar crises on the Eastern Front, instinctively knew he was winning at Omaha. He needed to shore up his crumbling neighbor to the right, where the city of Bayeux was clearly the enemy objective. The spur to action was a report from Major Block from his own staff. One of the faintly unreliable *Ost* battalions had informed him that Allied tanks had broken through in their sector, but he could not reach his 716 division commander to tell him. He recognized that 352 Division's flank would be vulnerable. The battalion was instructed to hold in place until Meyer could arrive.

Ziegelmann made a hurried telephone call to General Marcks's HQ at 84 Corps. "I described the situation and requested emphatically the return and subordination of [Meyer's] reinforced Grenadier Regiment 915. . . . It no longer appeared necessary to send it into action against American paratroopers behind Utah," Ziegelmann argued, it was needed, "for the protection of the right division flank and a counterattack toward Crépon and Meuvaines." Marcks agreed to the request.

Meyer waited two hours around Cerisy Forest before receiving an oral order directly from General Kraiss. His mix of bicycle and motorized infantry with towed heavy weapons and tracked self-propelled guns was turned around yet again and ordered to proceed, this time, in two different directions. The bulk of the Kampfgruppe was ordered back the way they had come, to the east side of Bayeux, to attack the British breakout. The start line would be outside Crépon. His II Battalion 915 was detached and ordered to march north through Blay to Colleville, to attack the reported incursion between strongpoints WN 60 to 62, "and throw the enemy penetration back into the sea."[18]

Meyer's men had already covered about thirty-four miles, many on bicycles without any rest or rations. The change of direction meant backtracking another fifteen miles to Crépon, covering nearly fifty miles in all. Inefficient wood-burning, gas driven trucks were starting to break down. French drivers were not too enthusiastic with their support, and their lives had become dangerous with the start of low-level Allied fighter-bomber attacks. Vehicle convoys were stretched out on dangerous roads where progress was becoming increasingly marked by burning trucks. Meyer's contact with his parent 352 Division was intermittent; away from the telephone network, they were dependent on inefficient radios. "Sometime later, we bicycled in the direction of the coast," recalled Kurt Keller, with the 3rd *Kompanie* of the Fusilier battalion. By the time they had got as far as Formigny, they had to abandon their bikes and proceed on foot, "because machine gunning and rocket firing *Jabos* [fighter-bombers] made it practically impossible to move." Part of his unit, including the company commander, had to remain sheltering in the Cerisy Forest. "The rest of the company was scattered by several Jabo attacks and virtually decimated." Only the vanguard of the column, about sixty men, reached the coast.[19]

Albert André at Saint-Laurent-sur-Mer had been warned off to continue with the construction work at WN 66. It seemed unlikely they would unload the tank turret perched on the back of the truck stuck in a pothole since the previous afternoon. Albert, living nearby, recalled there was a German soldier shot in the head, he thought ambushed by American paratroopers. "There was a little dog that followed him," he remembered, "he stayed beside him for eight days." French casualties and damage to property steadily increased; Madame Raymonde Hue in Vierville remembered a shell that hit the local bakery killed the baker's nine-month-old boy and his cousin Pauline. Michel Hardelay's house was also struck by "a tremendous explosion that deafened my mother and myself"; it "was followed by a powerful blast mixed with dust and a strong smell of gunpowder." The shell burst on the garden wall, where a number of rabbit pens were standing. "I could see some of them panicking and running all over the place," he recalled. They were in the midst of the fighting. "I saw two German soldiers passing by with their heads bent, carrying a Mauser in one hand and a box of bullets in the other." The bombardment "above our heads" was so intense, "it was forming an arch of projectiles between the allied fleet and the German artillery."

Edmond Scelles was in a similar predicament in Saint-Laurent. Shells whistled and shrieked overhead from the interior toward the beach. "They [the Germans] were in Formigny," he remembered, "in a farm that belonged to Monsieur Nowichet's son, where there were four guns." Prieuré Farm, where they lived, doubled as a garrison location and ammunition dump for the Germans. Vehicles drove in and out to replenish supplies. "We did not go out," Scelles recalled, because like the majority of the locals, "we did not have a trench!" After two shells hit the main house the family decided they would get out during the next lull. Meanwhile they moved into a German shelter and at the first opportunity, "we took the road to Formigny, to friends." As they fled they met a German officer on the road, who told them, "you are doing well to leave, but it's only going to last for a few hours." Scelles saw the Germans were confident, and "had the impression that they were going to push them back in the water; they were probably expecting reinforcements coming back from Trévières." The local French had been watching the practice of these coastal maneuvers for years.[20]

The Germans had good reason to feel confident. Oberstleutnant Ziegelmann talked by phone to the commander of WN 76 at Pointe et Raz de la Percée. From there he could see WN 74 and the Vierville draw just under a mile away. The report suggested the crisis might already be over:

> "At the water's edge at low tide near Saint-Laurent and Vierville the enemy is in search of cover behind the coastal zone obstacles. A great many motor vehicles—and among these ten tanks—stand burning on the beach. The obstacle demolition squads have given up their activity. Debarkation from the landing boats has ceased; the boats keep further seaward.

The fire of our battle positions and artillery was well placed and has inflicted considerable casualties upon the enemy. A great many wounded and dead lie on the beach. Some of our battle positions have ceased firing; they do not answer any longer when called on the telephone."

Oberstleutnant Ernst Goth, commanding Regiment 916 and responsible for this sector, was part of the conversation. They had beaten off the attacks, he reported, but needed reinforcements. General Kraiss and Ziegelmann had however, already taken the key reinforcement decisions, which depended on Goth holding firmly in place. The Americans they could see appeared on the point of giving up.

Machine gunner Ludwig Kwiatkowski at WN 62, the threatened east end of Omaha, was exuberant. "We truly believed the invasion appeared almost at an end," he remembered. "We all believed we would get the Iron Cross 1st Class pinned to our chests and be sent on vacation." Lieutenant Hans Heinz could see from his Colleville vantage point that the young men pinned down on the beach in front were leaderless and paralyzed with fear. He knew the signs, having experienced the same at Stalingrad. Command and control was not functioning among the Americans, only small groups seemed to be actively pressing on to objectives. He rubbed his tired face and realized he had yet to shave. He would indulge that little luxury, he mentally promised himself, when the Americans had been driven back into the sea.[21]

At the Vierville end of the beach, at 8:30 A.M. Grenadier Karl Wegner could see from WN 71 that "landing boats were backing away from the beach":

> "Some of them were burning, hit by our PAK guns or they had struck mines. I saw one of the boats hit by a mine while it backed away from us, sending shrapnel into the sea and a group of men who had just landed from it."

Unteroffizier Henrik Naube observing from WN 73 above noticed a rising tide of viscera, with "bodies rolling and swaying with the movement of the water, and there were such things as helmets, rifles, and equipment floating and rolling with them." Hein Severloh at WN 62 saw it as:

> "A roughly three hundred meter long and meter wide ribbon of body slime; there were hundreds and hundreds of lifeless bodies of American soldiers—in places piled on top of each other."

Inside the band of sludge, "wounded men moved around in the bloody, watery slime, mostly creeping." They sought to gain access to the upper beach and seawall. Occasionally, from about fifty to sixty GIs left at the water's edge, one "would occasionally run around in a crouch." The Germans began to feel some empathy for the destruction they were visiting on men deposited at their mercy with the clinical persistence of a conveyor belt. "My loader was moved by this," Naube recalled, "and he shook his head, saying that the Americans should not sacrifice their men in this way."

They began to notice that landing craft were increasingly deterred from making a final approach. Naube watched one turn away, "making a maneuver as if it were trying to turn around and leave the scene." When it presented its flank broadside an 88mm shot tore through it below the waterline. "The explosions tore off large pieces of its side, and the craft began to capsize rapidly." The hull rose up, exposing the interior, jeeps, trucks, and "vehicles were falling onto the troops as the floor became almost vertical, crushing many men." Men jumped off the sides into the water, leading Naube to consider:

> "If many more try to turn away like that, there won't be enough Americans to replace the dead ones on the beach, and so we will win this dreadful fight."

Wegner shared his view. "What I saw convinced me that, for the moment, it was worse there than where we were," he remembered, "although we had taken—and still were getting—a pounding." The battle had reached a tipping point, willpower was making an impression on material mass. Hans Heinz remembered his veteran Feldwebel who had insisted they might have sufficient ammunition to settle many assault waves, but what then? Oberstleutnant Ocker's Artillery Regiment 352 had three days' worth of first-line ammunition on hand that morning. He was already broadly hinting to Ziegelmann the chief of staff, "that the ammunition stock was already considerably down."[22]

Hans Heinz was correct about his assumption of an American command vacuum on the beach. More than one in two of the company commanders and junior boat section leaders had been killed or wounded during the piecemeal destruction of the early waves. Heavy casualties had been expected in the first wave, virtually written off, akin to 1914–18 expectations of the consequences of a direct frontal attack. It was anticipated that successive waves would swamp the defense and make headway. Invasion maps displayed obstacles, wire, and minefields in incredible detail, including the clusters of strongpoints covering the beach exits. Few surviving pre-landing accounts make any mention of bypass and maneuver schemes to eliminate these bunkers, other than by sequential head-on attacks. There appears no expectation of scaling bluffs to take them in the rear or flanks. Instead the tactical plan was subordinate to an operational imperative to quickly get as many support weapons and heavy artillery ashore as soon as possible, to counter anticipated panzer counterattacks. Detailed D-Day landing charts read like an unloading exercise at Slapton Sands. "Timings should have been trebled," wrote one later 1st infantry Division post combat report. The assistant G-3 of the Division, Major Kenneth Lord recalled, "every vehicle and gun had to be measured and a template drawn to make sure that when we loaded, the vehicles would go where we planned." Just this one item "took days of planning," Lord remembered. More cerebral effort went into logistic support planning than tactical deductions of the likely enemy reaction to the landings.[23]

The deaths of so many commanders meant there was little cohesive American leadership on Omaha Beach for the first ninety minutes. The very nature of the initial clash along the beach was a so-called "meeting engagement." Landings late and in the wrong place meant the newly arrived troops did not know where the Germans were. Moreover, the conventional structure of infantry platoons and companies was superseded by boat section groups of thirty-two men. These had first to assault specific objectives on landing before reorganizing into conventional company groups. This tactical scheme was compromised by the confusion and shock of landing under withering fire. "I couldn't make radio contact," remembered Lieutenant Colonel Sidney Bingham, whose 2nd Battalion of the 116th lost most of its company commanders and junior officers within the first few minutes of landing. "I had no control," he admitted, "and might as well have been in the States for all the good I did that day." Leadership was "by small groups led by the true heroes," he claimed, "most of whom were killed," and, "sad to say, very few decorated because there were no eyewitnesses." Leadership as a consequence of manifold radio failures had to be by voice in the din of battle. This was akin to battle conditions in the American Civil War.[24]

Shock and dismay following a physically degrading boat trip in marginal sea conditions, and then withering fire, played a role. It became immediately apparent to landing American soldiers that this battle was not going well. "As ranking noncom, I tried to get my men off the boat and make it somehow under the cliff," recalled Sergeant Harry Bare in Bingham's battalion. "I saw men frozen in the sand unable to move." The impact of the carnage around them was both intimidating and dismaying. "My radio man had his head blown off three yards from me," Bare remembered. "The beach was covered with bodies, men with no legs, no arms—God it was awful. It was absolutely terrible." Another soldier passing a smoldering LCI saw bodies, "sprawled on the ramps" at either side, "two and three deep, those on the bottom oblivious to the weight of those on top." He ran "through an instep-deep pool of blood that seeped from the head wound of a dead sailor." The shocking sights induced a mental paralysis that could only be overcome by robust direction and inspirational leadership:

> "As I came around the end of a stalled tank I found myself staring, horrified, into the chest cavity of a mutilated corpse. It was cut diagonally in two from the left armpit to the bottom of the right rib cage. The upper part, along with the viscera, was nowhere to be seen; the lower part, all too visible, was lying prone before me, naked except for brown GI shoes that identified it as being recently a part of a US soldier. The bowel contents streaked out on the sand behind, demonstrating progressive states of digestion."

Radio operator John Hamilton remembered his company commander carried in with no legs. He heard the conversation with the doctor. "I want to ask you a question and I want you to tell the truth," the officer said. "If I've got a chance, I'll stay awake. I'll fight. If I haven't, I'll go to sleep." Hamilton recalled, "I often wondered if he made it." When Edgar LeRoy Arnold came ashore with the 5th Rangers, he saw "complete chaos on the beach." With dead men everywhere, he could not distinguish whether they were winning or losing. "I began to get visions of being pushed back into the sea," he admitted:

> "One thing that did appear stupid, although I didn't give it much thought at the time, was a white flag waving on a rifle in the water about twenty feet from the edge."[25]

The operational plan required command and control to be exercised by the 1st Division until the beachhead was secured. The advance command post (CP), with Lieutenant Colonel John Matthews, the 16th's Executive Officer in charge coming from the USS *Henrico*, was due to land at 7:20 A.M. Command would then switch to Colonel Taylor, the regimental commander, who was to come in with the rear CP from the USS *Samuel Chase* an hour later. Matthews was to prepare the headquarters for Taylor's arrival. Lieutenant John Bentz Carroll came in with the advance group between the second and third waves. When they arrived a shell hit the rear of their landing craft and the ensign and helmsman "disappeared along with the controls." He remembered:

> "It was shooting *rat-tat-tat* on the front of the boat. Somehow or other, the ramp opened up, probably due to the loss of the controls, and the men in front were being struck by machine gun fire. They were being hit as they jumped."

"This is it!" Matthews shouted, "This is it! Good luck!" before being hit in the head by a machine gun bullet and killed. The advance CP suffered thirty-five casualties just moving from boat to beach. Carroll found himself pinned down among the obstacles with "machine gun bullets hitting all around us and killing a lot of men in the water." A strong tidal surge and surf impeded progress, "we would have to grab out" at the mined posts "and hang on" before making a dash through the surf for the next fifty feet beyond:

> "The men would line up behind those poles. They'd say, 'You go—you go—you go,' and then it got so bad that everybody had to go anyway, because the waves were hitting with such intensity on these things."

Carroll was knocked briefly unconscious, but someone pulled him beyond the water line. As he came to, "I felt somebody tapping me on the leg," and on looking found, "here was a GI who was 100% naked." All his clothes had been blown off and he was wounded in the neck.[26]

The advance CP was completely ineffective. The Air Force communications officer was felled running about thirty-five to forty feet behind Carroll. "I was looking back over my shoulder at him," he recalled, "when he was hit by a shell; he had a hole right through him." Much of the heavy radio equipment, taken ashore in waterproof bags, was abandoned in the rush to get to the shelter of the seawall. Technical Grade-5 John Pinder, a radio operator in Matthew's group, went back into the surf to retrieve it, despite the horrific facial injuries he had suffered from a mortar blast on the landing craft ramp. "The side of his face was left hanging and he could only see from one eye,'" remembered Sergeant Robert Michaud. "He held his hanging flesh with one hand and gripped the radio and dragged it to shore." This was some achievement; the ungainly SCR-284s were awkward, forty-five-pound sets, roughly the weight, size, and shape of a modern air conditioner.

Pinder, to general astonishment, continued to wade around in the surf in the worst of the fire to salvage even more radio equipment jettisoned by wounded soldiers. Three times he went back, hauling out yet another heavy SCR-284 before being struck in both legs by machine gun fire. He kept going, "although by this time he was greatly weakened by loss of blood," remembered witness Sergeant Leeward Stockwell, and helped to set up the equipment on the beach. The sets "were the only means of communication that the regimental CP had at the time," he recalled. Pinder refused all medical attention, doggedly helping until he was hit yet again and died.[27]

With no headquarters, the command coherence of the 16th Regiment was seriously compromised. Companies were totally intermingled. "You'd find an E Company man in 'I' or something like that, or an 'F' in 'C' and so forth," Carroll remembered. At this point the veteran core in the 1st Division began to assert itself. Men who had seen action before realized they needed to take out the objectives pinning them down, if only to survive. "What really got us going," Carroll explained, "was the hard core of young lieutenants who had experienced Sicily and Africa, and the old Regular Army noncoms they had with them." The best that could be achieved was a sort of "gang leadership," whereby "officers and NCOs just gathered men by bodies, maybe twenty-five to fifty together."[28]

Stop the Boats
8:30 A.M.

There was a disconnect between the tactical need to assault and take the bunkers on the beach with infantry, and the operational imperative to land artillery and heavy weapons to support them against panzer counterattacks from the hinterland. This resulted in too many unproductive vehicles piling up on a beach ever narrowed by the rising tide. Despite the failure of the tactical plan, the conveyor-belt arrival of follow-up support units continued. Two field artillery battalions with a compliment of twelve 105mm howitzers were launched into the heavy seas aboard DUKWs. Not one single DUKW carrying the 11th Field Artillery made it ashore and only six from the 7th Field Artillery Battalion were not swamped. Master Sergeant John Heckman watched the 111th's DUKWs line up in the hold of the LST and saw them all sink shortly after launch. "I can still hear those men calling for help over the noise," he remembered. Heavy mortars belonging to the 81st Chemical Mortar Battalion weighed 330 pounds each. They could only be brought ashore by breaking them down into three parts, which were carried onto the beach on two wheeled handcarts.

Many were carried away in the heavy seas. An antiaircraft battalion was brought in aboard 18 LCVPs. Their guns had to be towed up to the high tide line with vehicles. "The toll of life was appalling," the after-action report of the 397th recorded, "men bleeding and drowning everywhere." They landed just after 7:00 A.M. in the same fearful conditions of withering fire that the hapless infantry had endured before them. "The enemy would force a group of us down prone in the water," one gunner recalled, "and then spray the cluster with machine guns." They were followed at 8:30 A.M. by eighteen more LCTs carrying two antiaircraft battalions, and not one single Luftwaffe aircraft was seen anywhere in the sky.

Major General Huebner's 1st Division had seen some anxious moments fighting off German panzers during the previous year's invasion of Sicily. Two anti-tank companies were therefore included within the loading tables for this assault, one each for the 16th and 116th Regiments. Each company had nine truck-towed 57mm guns at each flank, soon stuck in the sand. Pinned down by enemy fire, they were submerged by the tide and created fresh underwater obstacles. All the crews ended up fighting as infantry. Squad leader Sergeant William Lewis in the 116th Regiment's anti-tank platoon remembered, "we lost half of the DUKWs in the rough seas while awaiting the signal" to go in. "They just shipped water, turned over sideways, and sunk." The remainder came in 110 minutes after the first wave and were immediately pinned down. "We were huddled there just trying to stay alive," Lewis admitted, "there was nothing we could do except keep our butts down." He recalled the total paralysis of command. "We were disorganized because everyone was in the wrong place," and three out of four company commanders due to support the 116th were dead. "Many officers and noncoms were casualties so we became disorganized." They mixed in with the 1st Division men in their area "and they helped a lot." One of the 1st Division sergeants "taught us how to fire at the Germans," and "got things going with four or five of our men." An incoherent mess of mixed supporting units and vehicles was left stranded on the beach. "It took a week to find our units and get organized," Lewis remembered.[29]

The wind, tidal current, and fierce German fire to the west of the beach drove the mass of approaching landing craft east, toward the center of Omaha. This was the area where Schneider's fourteen landing craft brought in the 5th Rangers as an integrated battalion. It was the Achilles' heel of the German defense of Omaha, a sector of half-constructed bunkers WN 64, 66, and 68. This central sector, apart from the wide draw in front of Saint-Laurent, was characterized by a series of near perpendicular bluff lines. This made it technically difficult for German gunners to shoot defilade and plunging fire from its slopes. Grass fires from the naval bombardment intermittently obscured visibility with dense smoke. At 7:30 A.M., LCVP-71 approached the beach alone, ready to disgorge twelve officers and fourteen enlisted men, eleven of whom carried heavy backpack radios. This was a good place to land.

LCVP-71 had still to negotiate a gauntlet of mined obstacles protruding above the surf. It was one of the key craft to beach at Omaha that morning. On board was Colonel Charles Canham, the commander of the 29th Division's 116th Regiment, leading the assault against the west Vierville side of the beach, and Brigadier General Norman Cota, the Deputy Division commander. Driven by wind and tide their boat repeatedly smacked into a post adorned with a Teller mine, once, twice, and then with the third blow dislodging the mine, which splashed into the surf. "Kiss everything goodbye!" blurted out someone in the boat, but the mine did not explode, which at that distance would have been calamitous. A screen of DD tanks in front offered some protection from small arms fire coming in from the flanks, which impelled a rush to the seawall. The two commanders, accompanied by a number of junior and staff officers, made it. One staff officer, Major Sous, was killed, and an enlisted man wounded.

The tall, lean "Stoneface" Canham was the notorious, uncom-promising "ball-buster" of the regiment. He had been accepted into West Point in 1921 as a lowly sergeant. "War is not child's play," he had reminded his regiment before disembarking, "and requires hatred of the enemy"; he said to his green un-blooded volunteer ex–national guardsmen. "At this time we don't have it," he emphasized, "I hope you will get it when you see your friends wounded and killed." On landing he immediately set about identifying and organizing leaders amid the wreckage of his regiment. He had few illusions of what was at stake. "Remember, the Hun is a crafty, intelligent fighter and will not have mercy on you" he had reminded them. "Don't have it on him."

They beached in the area of wooden breakwaters that was to benefit the subsequent 5th Ranger landing. Cota could tell at a glance that the GIs lying prone in heaps along the breakwater shingle and four-foot timber seawall dared not move. Even more disturbing was the reluctance to do so. Cota was already prowling the seawall pushing soldiers forward when the 5th Rangers arrived. Both he and Canham recognized that the enemy was aware of this growing concentration of numbers behind the seawall, and would be soon dropping mortar and artillery fire upon them. Cota quickly met with Colonel Schneider and ordered him to scale the bluffs from where they were. Cota's unflinching yet affable authority in the face of withering fire impressed the men, contrasting with and supplementing Canham's steely determination. "You men are Rangers! I know you won't let me down," Captain John Raaen heard him say. "Colonel, you are going to have to lead the way," Cota announced to Schneider. "We are bogged down. We've got to get these men off this goddamned beach."[30]

"I was in awe of Cota's bravery in standing upright over them," Ranger Lee Brown recalled, "all hunkered down behind the wall and being impervious to fire." Bangelore torpedos cracked and blew gaps in the wire and the Rangers started to scale the bluffs. Jack Burke with the

5th Rangers, "heard the Bangelore men yell, '*Fire in the hole!*' then the explosions . . . and we took off." "The guys I saw were Rangers," Francis Coughlin with the 5th's HQ remembered:

> "We all got together a gang of us. I remember going up the back of a path into a house and it was through a minefield."

From the beach, it looked like the only dent in the bluff line. "That was the way the Germans got up the cliffs and the fields," Coughlin recalled, "and that's how the Rangers did it."[31]

Forty minutes later and two miles farther east Colonel George Taylor came into Easy Red between WN 61 and 62, with the 16th Regiment rear headquarters aboard two landing craft. John Thompson, an accompanying correspondent from the *Chicago Tribune*, remembers Taylor admonishing the coxswain, who backed away to avoid the heavy fire. "Coxswain!" he roared above the din of battle, "take us in! Regardless! My men are in there! Take us in!" They disembarked in water up to their necks, Taylor recalling, "it was a helpless feeling wading while shot at." He was a robust no-nonsense officer who did not suffer fools gladly. Private Pete Lypka, who had served with him since Sicily, recalled he had "a habit of saying what was on his mind in as few words as possible." He had probably not been appointed a general yet because, "he was no apple polisher." "There was a state of confusion," the 1st Division after-action interview with Taylor recorded, "the troops were lined up on the beach like cans in a store room." Very little shooting back was happening. "All were interested in holing up and keeping out of the fire." Taylor exposed himself, striding up and down the beach, looking for officers. He gathered groups of men for them to lead, and gave them objectives to take. His Distinguished Service Cross citation read "he converted a bewildered mob into a coordinated fighting force." Captain William Friedman with the headquarters remembered his, "great stentorian voice" ringing out, "Get the hell off the beach! If you stay on, you're dead or about to die!"[32]

Movement by small groups had already started, gripped by veterans who understood their parlous situation and were taking action. Once Oberfeldwebel Schnüll's 88mm gun was knocked out by 7:20 A.M., small bands of men infiltrated either side of the damaged bunker and tried to work their way through the minefield in the Cabourg draw at exit F-1, to outflank strongpoint WN 60. Movement was starting at the center and east of Omaha Beach, but none of this was visible from offshore.

The V Corps's decision to land large vulnerable LCI [landing craft infantry] within an hour of the first wave landings was a considerable risk. There were very few marked channels, enemy machine gun fire was still intense, and the underwater obstacles had now been largely submerged by the tide. Landing the 380-ton 160-foot LCIs popularly dubbed, "Lousy Civilian Ideas," across an open beach in strong tidal currents would have been difficult in any case. The craft could beach up to two hundred men in chest-deep water, with a mix of vehicles at a specific place, and significantly in a compact mass. Between 7:35 and 8:30 A.M. nine of these large craft came edging into a congested beach. Seven of them driven by current and the desire to avoid the powerful strongpoints at Vierville and Colleville, came in between strongpoints WN 68 and 64. Some of their guns were in open emplacements because the casemates were under construction. The LCIs on the west side sailed into the killing area of the 88mm bunker at WN 72.

LCI-91, tentatively landing troops down ramps at either side of the bow was damaged by a mine. With the tide pushing her against more obstacles she disengaged to move one hundred yards along to try again. At the second beaching, "an 88mm shell struck the center of the well deck," according to the commander Lieutenant Arend Vyn, "and exploded in the fuel tanks below." This set off a massive fireball, "and within seconds the entire well deck was a mass of flames." Captain Robert Walker, with elements of the 116th Regiment headquarters aboard, "heard a blast and saw that a man wearing a flamethrower had been hit and his fuel tank was on fire." The men around him had already been scorched:

> "The man with the flamethrower was screaming in agony. He went over the starboard side and dived into the sea. I could see that even the soles of his boots were on fire."[33]

Seth Shepard the combat photographer aboard LCI-92 had watched the approaching beach transition from "a smoky haze" to "plainly visible," with mounting trepidation. He could clearly see, "that we were in for a tough time." When LCI-91 off the starboard bow was "enveloped in flames and smoke, my heartbeat multiplied." She had been the first to beach and they were scheduled to land just after. With just a few hundred yards to go, "we felt nearby explosions from shells and could see funnels of water shoot up in the air." Braced against the port side of the ship with his camera, he tried to take photographs.

"Then it came! A terrifying blast lifted the whole ship upward with a sudden lurch from the bow." A mine had set fire to the main fuel tanks, "and blew a hole in the starboard side big enough to drive a Higgins boat through." "A sheet of flame and steel shot out from the forward hold," which had contained forty-one soldiers. "The ship quivered as if it were pulling apart," he recalled, and he and three companions were thrown to the deck by the concussion. Two soldiers forward had been blown out of the hatch in a sheet of flame and the rest incinerated by heat, "like the midst of a blast furnace." They were stunned, and "our ears were ringing with the deafening vibrations." One of the firemen nearby was blown backward, "his hair was blazing," which another crewman with a badly singed face slapped out, badly burning his own hands. The 88mm tracking the catastrophe fired an airburst over the soldiers crowding the stern trying to escape the blaze forward. Round after round slammed into LCI-92, snapping the ramps, the center of the craft, and destroying the conn tower, the nerve center of the vessel, "in a blinding flash and explosion." The LCI was systematically battered apart. The order to "abandon ship" was lost amid the howling whoosh and metallic impacts of successive incoming 88mm shells. Shepard realized she was in her death throes:

> "Some soldiers were jumping overboard and others slid or let
> themselves down a chain up forward of the damaged ramp.
> The cries of some of the soldiers in the deep water was pitiful.
> All the while the terrific explosions, fire, and heavy smoke
> filled the air and the littered decks heaved under the impact
> of still other shells as they ripped through the steel plates."

Shepard and a few of the crew struggled ashore through the hellish fire. "Once up on the beach we sank exhaustedly on the pebbles," he remembered, "reaching the lowest point of human existence."[34]

Hardly anyone ever saw a German soldier on the beach. At the Colleville end Technical Sergeant Calvin Ellis briefly spotted four enemy riflemen fire at his men from the top of the bluffs, then run and drop out of sight into an emplacement. Harassing fire from both flanks drummed home the hopelessness of their predicament. War photographer Robert Capa, having made his way ashore and near Ellis, focused his telescopic camera lens on a German officer on the bluff above them, probably at WN 62. He "stood with his hands on his hips, boldly barking out orders to soldiers behind him," a depressing image he thought. "The sight of that cocky Nazi officer, so sure of himself, was heart stopping," Capa recalled.[35]

At 8:39 A.M. Brigadier General Willard Wyman, the second-in-command of the 1st Division, came ashore between the Saint-Laurent and Coleville draws. With him was Associated Press reporter Don

Whitehead, who had already established a reputation covering the inva-sion of Italy. Like Capa, he strived to see the action firsthand. They were shelled as soon as they landed. Whitehead was genuinely shocked; he had no comprehension of what had already transpired that morning:

> "I lay on the beach wanting to burrow into the gravel. And I thought: 'This time we have failed! God, we have failed! Nothing has moved on this beach and soon, over that bluff will come the Germans. They'll come swarming down on us . . .'"

About nine minutes before, two hours after H-hour, realization dawned that the conveyor belt of men and matériel being uninterruptedly tipped into the maw of this unequal battle needed to pause. There was no more room on the narrow ribbon of beach left un-submerged by high tide. The commander of the 7th Naval Beach Battalion, managing the flow, gave the order to stop all landing craft approaching until further notice. Those inbound were ordered to wait outside the obstacle belt, if megaphones on the guide boats could hail them.

Drifting offshore was Colonel Benjamin Talley's command DUKW. He radioed back what he could see to the command ship. As deputy divi-sion chief of staff, he was the eyes and ears for Major General Huebner's 1st Division. He later recalled:

> "Hundreds of men were in the water, mostly clinging to the obstacles, which had not been breached; and hundreds of helmets appeared to be floating in the water alongside the obstacles. Actually they were the heads of men clinging to the obstacles for protection . . . [Four tanks] were moving in a single file parallel to the beach. Suddenly one of them burst into flames. An instant later, a second, and then a third

was afire. The fourth one backed up and returned to the water's edge . . ."

General Eisenhower's worst preinvasion fears were being realized. He had written a press release to account for just such a potential failure; the note secreted in his wallet. He saw none of this. There might be between six thousand to eight thousand fighting men ashore, and they had just had their umbilical chord to the invasion fleet severed. They were on their own.

EIGHT

THE CRISIS

8:30 A.M. TO MIDDAY

Dilemmas

8:30 A.M. to 11:00 A.M.

P harmacist's Mate Roger Shoemaker aboard the USS *Henrico* remembered, "we were too far away to really see what was happening on the beach." They could make out nothing, and now three hours after disembarkation, "everybody on board was becoming very tense and worried about our landing boats." None had returned. When one finally did get back the coxswain reported that, "the men he carried in had been badly shot up trying to reach the shore," and "he didn't think any of his men made the beach." Shoemaker's heart sank because the coxswain "looked like he was about to cry."

General Omar Bradley, commanding the 1st US Army aboard the USS *Augusta,* was the leader farthest removed from the action on Omaha Beach. "As the morning lengthened," he recalled, "my worries deepened over the alarming and fragmentary reports we picked up on the Navy net." He had no control over the battle on the beaches, like his corps and division subordinate commanders, Major Generals Gerow and Huebner, "who clung to their radios as helplessly as I." Training binoculars on the shoreline nine to ten miles distant gave no clues, "though we could see it dimly through the haze and hear the echo of its guns." Bradley was under pressure. There were reports of progress on the British beaches and Utah, but the news seeping back from the smoky horizon to his front was all bad:

> "From these messages we could piece together only an incoherent account of sinkings, swampings, heavy enemy fire, and chaos on the beaches."

At 8:30 A.M. the two leading V Corps assault regiments were due to have reached the east-west coast road a mile beyond the beaches. Frustratingly, V Corps had not even confirmed they had landed. Optimists were attributing the delays to poor communications.[1]

Coast Guard Lieutenant Coit Hendley commanding LCI (L)-85 wondered whether his girlfriend Sylvia Grashoff, a WREN (Womens Royal Naval Service) back at Dartmouth, knew the invasion had started. Hendley's boat arrived just as the beachmaster ordered a halt to further landings. "As we approached there was no immediate sign of trouble," he remembered. Flashes from warships bombarding offshore appeared to be the only activity, "plus a few puffs of shellfire at the water's edge." This was as it should be, two hours into the landings. Hendley anticipated landing on a secured beachhead. "Closer to the beach we saw signs that the landing was not going to be easy," he recalled. The sector ahead appeared blocked by sunken LCIs and "a confused mess of small craft which were abandoned, broached, or hung up on obstacles covered with mines." Even so, the control vessel hailed them ten minutes out from the beach and directed them to go in. It was shortly after 8:30 A.M.

Hendley's 160-foot-long craft snagged on an obstacle and reversed engines. As it backed away a shell struck amidships, bursting inside number 3 troop compartment. "We could hear the screams of the men through the voice tube," Hendley's quartermaster recalled. The ship moved along the beach for a hundred yards and attempted to beach again in a clear space, but they exploded a mine just under the bow. They had eighty-nine men from the 1st Medical Battalion on board, and about one hundred combat troops, who began to disembark from the port forward ramp. "Shells had been bursting near the ship the whole time," on the way in, Hendley remembered. Machine gun fire spraying the water to starboard prevented that ramp from being used.

Robert Capa was intently following the action onshore. "Wet shaking hands" had spoiled many attempts to reload his camera. "I had it bad," he admitted; the courage bank was running out. "It was a new kind of fear shaking my body from toe to hair and twisting my face." LCI (L)-85 was a savior; it represented the chance of life as medics with red crosses painted on their helmets poured from it. "I did not think and I didn't decide it," he remembered acting on reflex, "I just stood up and ran toward the boat." Wherever he looked along the beach, his veteran's eye saw only defeat and failure. He needed to get his pictures back to London, a difficult moment to explain in his subsequent memoir:

> "I knew I was running away. I tried to turn but couldn't face the beach, and told myself, "I am just going to dry my hands on that boat."

Sergeant Donald Wilson also watched LCI(L)-85's approach toward the shore. She had large red crosses painted in white circles on the hull and superstructure. "Medics were badly needed on Easy Red!" he recalled. The captain, Coit Hendley, remembered a number of troops had disembarked before shells started smashing into the ship. Capa recalled the moment the last medics were just exiting as he climbed on board, at which point he felt "a shock on deck," and suddenly was all covered with feathers. Looking up he saw the part of the superstructure had been blown away and, "the feathers were the stuffing from the Kapok jackets of the men that had been blown up." Wilson watched as round after round began to dismember the ship:

> "An anti-tank shell struck the hull next to the port gangplank, blowing it away so that it just dangled in the water. The Jerry gunner then raised his barrel and put one right down the deck, followed by a couple more."

He too spotted the white fragments hanging in the air, afterward:

> "The explosion sent medics and their gear flying in all directions. I vividly recall seeing a cloud of white bandages floating down into the smoke on deck."

Hendley thought maybe two-thirds of the medics made it to the beach before the ramp was snapped off. "It went over the side, taking all the men with it." The ship backed off into deeper water and began a ponderous turn that presented the German gunner with a broadside-on target. Wilson saw "the first round was low but ricocheted off the water, striking high on the hull." The next two exploded on the water line and LCI (L)-85 was momentarily dead, listing heavily in the water. "We had fifteen dead and thirty wounded on board," Hendley recalled. The radio man Gordon

Ameberg was engulfed in the radio shack explosion which blew off his leg. The horrified Hendley "found his leg lying on the deck and kept walking around it," until "finally one of the crew with more guts than I kicked it over the side." LCVPs maneuvered alongside his stricken craft to ferry any uninjured men back to the beach, and included shaken cameraman Capa. Hendley took the wounded and dead to the USS *Chase* and cut away when his ship started to settle at the bow. Soon just her stern was visible above the water line until she was scuttled with a demolition charge.[2]

Capa tried his luck again, this time wading out toward LCI (L)-94, a similar vessel to Hendley's. Coast Guard motor machinist Charles Jarreau saw this "poor fellow" approaching "in the water, holding his cameras up to keep them dry, trying to catch his breath." They helped him aboard, and as the craft moved back out to sea Capa took his final pictures of the receding beach. The obstacles had been virtually submerged by the tide, and a thin black line of soldiers can be seen silhouetted on the beach. Hazy smoke obscured all but an outline of the bluffs towering over the beach behind. Landing craft can be seen making their heavy, foamy passage through choppy waters beneath heavy dark clouds. He took photographs, subsequently published, of the crew giving transfusions to badly wounded men laid out on the open deck.

Aboard the *Henrico*, Pharmacist's Mate Roger Shoemaker sensed the growing feeling of unease as many more landing craft came back alongside "with similar disturbing reports about what was happening." Soldiers were still embarking for subsequent waves. "May God protect them," he thought, because, "as far as the eye could see, boats were headed toward the beach." Shoemaker was almost reduced to tears by the fearful state of some of the returning wounded. "Never have I seen such suffering," he recalled:

> "The wounds were terrible. One man lay quietly on a litter smoking a cigarette, with five machine gun wounds in his

chest. Another had one of his buttocks shot off, exposing six inches of the huge sciatic nerve."

Capa was brought to the USS *Chase*, where "the last wave of the 16th Infantry was just being lowered, but the decks were already full with returning wounded and dead." Not good for morale. Despite being utterly tired he took more pictures of American soldiers stepping across the davits to board their LCVPs. It had been too dark to get the same pictures that morning. At this point in the day, having barely survived his two hours on the beach and experienced a sinking, he probably assumed his pictures were chronicling a defeat. "The mess boys who had served our coffee in white jackets and with white gloves at three in the morning were covered with blood," he remembered, "and were sewing the dead in white sacks."

Lieutenant Coit Hendley and his surviving crewmembers were huddled together on the deck of the salvage tug that had scuttled LCI (L)-85. Hendley, wracked with guilt, sat apart and wept. His girlfriend Sylvia, who worked with a naval communications unit in Dartmouth had tracked his ship and discovered it was sunk with "all hands lost." His father in South Carolina later saw the sinking craft on a newsreel, which said the same. He was to spend a week trying to get further information from US Coast Guard headquarters.[3]

Lieutenant Colonel Schneider's 5th Ranger Battalion meanwhile moved up the bluffs at an angle between Saint-Laurent and Vierville, a steep eighty- to ninety-feet climb. They followed narrow tracks with Achtung Minen! signs beside them. "There were signs all over the area," recalled Senior Sergeant Victor Miller. "It was very possible that these were mined and we would blow ourselves up if we proceeded. Yet we had to go!" The paths were likely worn by German security patrols. Just ahead of them and climbing vertically to the left was a mixed force spearheaded by Lieutenant Robert Bedell's C Company of the 116th, with other soldiers who had tagged along. They reached the crest first, pushed along by Brigadier General Norman Cota, the deputy commander of the 29th division. He was accompanied by his aide, Lieutenant Jack Shea, who watched the wire blown by a Bangalore torpedo. Shea recalled the first man through the gap was cut down by a burst of heavy machine gun fire:

> "'Medico!' he yelled when hit. 'Medico! I'm hit! Help me!' he moaned and cried for a few minutes. He finally died after sobbing 'Mama' several times."

The main factor slowing the upward pace was the fear of stepping on anti-personnel mines, each man scanning the ground ahead with trepidation. Long dune grass and thickets of bushes near the summit provided cover from German fire. Shea was knocked back down the slope by a mortar bomb that left him unscathed but killed two men next to General Cota and seriously wounded his radio operator. Farther to their right, over a score of Rangers from A Company of the 5th under Lieutenant Charles Parker quickly gained the top and crossed the fields to bypass Vierville, pushing on independently toward Pointe du Hoc.

When they reached the summit the Rangers were enveloped by thick smoke from grass fires. "A shell hit close that set the brush afire," recalled Albert Nyland:

> "They told us to use a gas mask, which was no good, it just pooled that smoke into our faces. The ones that put it on, and I didn't, and I saw these guys suffering and coughing and everything. I thought, Jesus, what are they using against us now?"

Captain John Raaen remembered it "was so bad that we found ourselves gasping for breath, gulping in smoke. . . . I couldn't see ahead through the tears." He fumbled for the gas mask, something most soldiers thought they would never use. When he pulled it out, his maps and ration bars stowed around it were dropped and scattered, then he lost his helmet when he bent to retrieve them. He wasted time fumbling around, straightened himself out, and almost immediately stepped back into fresh air; he was furious with himself.

At 9:00 A.M. the joint force crested the top of the bluffs. Ranger Sergeant Victor Miller recalled, "We suddenly hear this *whoosh! whoosh! whoosh!*" at the top, "and one, two, three, four rockets fly over us," heading for the beach below. Looking down he realized, "it was far more dangerous there than it was on top." Far below, LCI (L)-91 was disembarking men from her forward ramps when "suddenly these men were engulfed in flames." A flamethrower pack exploded, smothering the ship's bow in a slurry of fire. "With that terrible image in our minds we turned our backs to the beach and moved inland," he remembered. They came across the road running parallel to the beach and turned right for Vierville–sur-Mer.[4]

On the other side of the flat field plateau the terrain changed; it was an abrupt transition. Behind them lay flat sandy beach, amphibious terrain, which they had trained over countless times at Slapton Sands in England. Beyond was an alien wilderness of crisscross hedgerows, small copses, and labyrinthine sunken lanes. The villages of medieval-looking houses with massively thick stone walls were strongpoints in all but name. This was the Normandy bocage and the "hedgerow" war they would fight in it would be more akin to jungle than conventional warfare.

At 9:07 A.M. Brigadier General Willard Wyman, the second-in-command of the 1st Division, sent his first message to Major General Huebner: "Beach slow," he reported. This was a gross understatement of the shocking scene Wyman saw on arrival. Only small groups of men had ascended the bluffs in his sector. More than one hundred vehicles were piled up on the narrow shingle belt, hemmed in by the tide and unable to move inland, and the amorphous mass of bulldozers, tractors, half-tracks, DUKWs and tanks was being repeatedly hit by German artillery fire that could hardly miss. Wyman quickly perceived the problem, "the beach has too many vehicles," he radioed at 9:50 A.M., "send combat troops." Huebner, aboard the command ship *Ancon*, sharing the headquarters with his V Corps superior Major General Gerow, understood, "I had no control," and moreover, "didn't expect any control." As he indicated, "a division commander exercises his command functions through the training, deployment, and launching of his troops for combat." Division and Corps command was about timely marshaling resources their subordinate commanders needed to physically fight the battle. Wyman, his deputy on shore, was acutely aware of this, and at 10:10 A.M. took the decision Huebner would have been looking for. "Reinforce 2nd battalion at once," his next message read. This was a decision, not a request, and would have a decisive impact on the outcome of the battle.

Before Wyman's intervention, Huebner recalled:

> "I had not had very many good reports. Most of these reports were rather fragmentary in character but they informed me that the fighting was heavy and we were still confined to the beach itself."

Huebner could at last direct energy and activity at his level of command to see this key decision implemented. Gerow, his corps commander, was similarly bereft of workable information. His chief of staff Colonel Stanhope Mason was frustrated with the quality of the "eyes and ears" reportage that Colonel Benjamin Talley was providing from his DUKW offshore. Much of it was "so much useless 'bafflegab,'" Mason complained, pointless descriptions of the obvious, which was blocking more relevant radio traffic from the beach. Talley was one of Gerow's favored acolytes, typical of the trusted men senior commanders surround themselves with, exchanging loyalty for career preferment. Mason's view of "the wizard of Attu," his contemptuous nickname for Talley was that he was, "fluent, ambitious, glib, and opinionated." They needed actionable reports and were not getting them.[5]

Sitting at the top of the command pyramid and ultimately responsible for success or failure at Omaha was General Bradley, the 1st US Army commander. He sent his aide Major Chester Hansen ashore with Admiral Kirk's gunnery officer to find out what was happening, coming back "with a discouraging report of conditions on the beach." Brigadier General William Kean, Bradley's chief of staff, was according to Hansen's diary, "afraid first day that [the enemy] might kick us off." The landing was hours behind schedule and Bradley could see a crisis inexorably developing. A force of 25,000 troops and 4,400 more vehicles was due at noon, but only a portion of the initial assault force of 34,000 and 3,300 vehicles had made it ashore. With the situation still critical Bradley admitted, "I reluctantly contemplated the diversion of Omaha follow-up forces to Utah and the British beaches."

Admission of failure is not a part of the US Army's collective psychology; it could have unfortunate personal career as well as operational implications, well understood at all levels of command. "Unofficial" signals allegedly changed hands. General Dempsey the 2nd British Army commander further east would not be able to take the US V Corps across its beaches, "because it is too crowded to go in together." Flooded beach exits at Utah would be prone to vulnerable traffic jams. Failure at Omaha would isolate Utah to the west and slow the British momentum already achieved exiting Gold beach farther east. The Americans could not be seen to be the cause of this in the midst of their first attempt to penetrate the Nazi-held European heartland. The looming disparity in casualty figures relative to the other beaches was bad enough for Bradley. Like many of his senior American contemporaries, he was sensitive to condescending British comments about US performance in a war that by any interpretation had not gone especially well for the British so far. Scanty reports suggested the British landings had gone broadly according to plan. Bradley was not in a happy place, "I was shaken to find," he later admitted, "that we had gone against Omaha with so thin a margin of safety." He was also starting to hear that, "instead of the ragtag static troops we had expected to find there, the assault had run head-on into one of Rommel's tough field divisions." The impasse needed to end.⁶

By about 8:00 A.M. destroyers off Omaha, having failed to establish communications with their fire teams on the beaches, closed to look for targets of opportunity. At 9:00 A.M. Captain Harry Sanders, the commander of destroyer Squadron 18, ordered his eight destroyers "to close the beach as far as possible and support the assault troops." The tide was high and in their favor but many craft were milling about beyond the obstacle belt, checked by beach masters from going in. Very little information was coming out of the beaches and much of it was contradictory. On board the destroyer USS *Harding* Admiral Charles Cooke felt he was viewing "a complete disaster," whereas the ship's executive officer Lieutenant Gentry thought "everything was proceeding according to the book." Rear Admiral Carleton Bryant, leading the Omaha Beach Bombardment Force, had few doubts the operation was unraveling. "Get on them, men get on them," he urgently ordered Sanders's ships and three British destroyers over radio:

> "We must knock out those guns. They are raising hell with
> the men on the beach, and we can't have any more of that.
> We must stop it."⁷

The unused potential that Sergeant Donald Wilson had seen doing little offshore closed in, demonstrating impressive seamanship. Destroyers were about 350 to 400 feet long, and at 1,500 tons had an underwater draught of about ten to fifteen feet with five-inch main guns. Their close approach to the beach inspired awe and raised morale all around. "Suddenly as I looked on, a destroyer came down from the right," recalled Wilson, "running parallel to the beach, really traveling, with seeming every gun on board blazing." She sped by, peppering strongpoint WN 62 with shells. Wilson instinctively, "tried to sink deeper into the bank as it passed because they were firing so low and I wasn't sure everything they were throwing would clear the bank." It inspired all that watched as she, "went down the beach some distance and then turned out to sea in a huge circle."

Obergefreiter Peter Lützen, manning his emplacement high up on WN 62, recalled, "when the ships started shooting at us again, they were more accurate than the first time." Gun loader Bruno Plota was in the lower 75mm casemate. "We could see outside through the aperture," he recalled, "but everything heaved and shook horribly." Machine gunners Friedrich Faust and Ludwig Kwiatkowski took cover in their Tobruks as the second dose of naval gunfire came in. "The stuff flew just over us, we had the luck, because our concrete shelter was at the base of the hill, to avoid it again." Heinrich Severloh, higher up the hill mass, remembered, "after every heavy impact thick debris and an amazing amount of soil came raining down on me." Earlier that morning his machine gun position had a step down into the trench, "after the second naval barrage, I could only kneel in a flat depression in the ground."[8]

At 9:33 A.M. Lieutenant Commander Ralph Ramsey took the USS *McCook* just 1,300 yards off the beach at Vierville-sur–Mer, and according to the log, "commenced firing on two guns, which were set into cliff and were enfilading beach." The action took just thirteen minutes, "one gun emplacement plunged from cliff, other flew into the air." With no direction from shore, it was difficult to see what they were firing at, despite narrowing the distance to hundreds of yards. Commander Robert Beer came in with the *Carmick*, also off Vierville and picked out what the pinned infantry seemed to be shooting at, and then fired for half an hour at "every possible mound or emplacement and everything that looked like a hole in the cliff." They could not be certain whether they hit, but saw that soldiers on the beach started moving again. "We followed what seemed to us the only reasonable course of action," explained Commander Clarence Boyd on the *Doyle,* standing off the E1 Saint-Laurent draw:

> "Picking out spots that seemed to be machine gun emplacements or likely positions, ascertaining as best we could that our own troops were clear."

Such locations were saturated with fire. Boyd had the satisfaction of observing, "that after about an hour the troops advanced to the top of the ridge and the boats resumed landing." Taking in destroyers so close was extremely risky and keels virtually scraped the bottom. Grounding on shoals would have made them easy prey for German artillery batteries inland. Boyd on the *Doyle* actually halted eight hundred yards off Easy Red Beach to engage the casemates on top of WN 62. This meant "maneuvering ship to stay in position against current, which is running west at 2–8 knots" at flood tide.

War correspondent Gordon Gaskill witnessed the intimidating passes, which often went along the entire beach. "Two destroyers moved in incredibly close," he remembered:

> "So close we could almost yell to the crews, so close Germans were hitting them with rifle bullets. They fired broadsides directly at us, it seemed, and while their shells were just above our heads, plus the thunderclaps of their five-inch guns, it was almost as terrifying as the German artillery. Their gunfire was amazingly accurate."

Not one of the sleek destroyers was hit by heavy caliber guns during these forays because the beach bunker arcs of fire were constrained by the thick concrete walls that cloaked their muzzle flash from the sea. Consequently the guns could not take on their most dangerous adversaries. Some came as close as five hundred yards, point-blank range in naval terms. Lieutenant John Carroll, with the 1st Division advance CP, saw ships firing flat trajectory from six hundred yards offshore at German gun emplacements. "Chunks of cement as big as a foot square were falling all around us and on us," he recalled. "The shells were coming in no higher than one hundred feet over our heads."[9]

One came in so close that Technical Sergeant Jim Knight, a Gap Team engineer pinned down in the E1 Saint-Laurent draw, thought the ship gliding inexorably toward shore, "was being beached. . . . She wasn't listing or smoking, my first thought was that she had either struck a mine or taken a torpedo." Lieutenant Owen Keeler was the gunnery officer aboard the USS *Frankford*, and recalled how her Captain Commander Semmes took her to within three hundred to four hundred yards of the beach. "The tide was in our favor at the moment," and Semmes, "navigating by fathometer and seaman's eye, took us in close enough to put our optical rangefinder . . . on the bluff above the beach." Keeler, watching a Sherman tank firing, was able to calibrate the optics to "examine the spots where his shells hit." Knight recalled, "being just lifted up when some of these shells went over us, and kind of slammed back down in the ground after the shell had gone by and exploded." Sergeant Allan Anderson, commanding a half-track nearby, recalled the "awful experience," and "the concussion was beyond belief." Showered by sand and debris, he was not to regain his hearing for several days.[10]

The distinctive conical-shaped concrete bunker housing the 50mm German pedestal gun at strongpoint WN 65 had caused a lot of damage. Nestled at the foot of the wide Saint-Laurent E1 draw, it was the key to unlock the beach exit. Sergeant Hyman Haas, commanding a pair of half-tracks from A Battery of the 467th Antiaircraft Battalion, was stalking it from amid cluttered wreckage at the waterline. It was hit by a combination of flat trajectory .50 caliber and 37mm cannon AA fire. Ten 37mm rounds went directly through the porthole of the pillbox, Haas recalled, "we fired one full clip and part of a second clip directly into the pillbox. Platoon commander Lieutenant Wallace Gibbs with the same battery saw "thirty to forty" rounds pummel the aperture and enter the opening, amid puffs of smoke sending concrete shards flying in all directions. The scarred façade is still visible today. Concrete muzzle flash deflectors on either side facing the sea accentuated the conical shape of the pillbox, and with the gun barrel so close to the ground, she was a difficult target to effectively engage. A five-inch shell from the *Frankford* smashed open a substantial hole through the gunner's protective metal shield on the right and took out a chunk of concrete at the back of the bunker shelter wall, spraying viscera throughout the interior as it howled through. WN 65 had proved a tough nut to crack. When dazed German survivors staggered out, one of the AA medics remarked, "I hope to hell none of these sons-of-bitches are wounded, because I'll have to work on them!"[11]

Gustav Winter was on the other side of the draw, manning his "concrete panzer" turret at strongpoint WN 66 when he saw "big flashes that threw sand a great distance into the air." The naval destroyer fire was neutralizing the open emplacements in the unfinished area of the strongpoint. "The noise during all this time was unbearable," he recalled, "with huge impacts coming again and again." He was virtually blind, only able to view activity through the gun sight. German soldiers running back from the water's edge were "caught by a shell blast and thrown in pieces across the sand, which was a horrible sight."

Winter observed a rippling explosion at the edge of the dunes that "ran left and right in a line," probably explosive cord blowing barbed wire. This produced a cloud of sand, which to his surprise suddenly unveiled "an

American panzer," which "came up over the top of it, onto the dunes." Winter fired at the white star painted on the front and heard the ringing ricochet of his shell bouncing off the frontal armor and going over the beach beyond. Almost immediately the Sherman returned fire, striking his gun mantle, dislocating the sight, and dazing him. Other Shermans crawled into view, dueling with the 50mm open pedestal mount to his left. One of the tanks hit a mine and began "burning like one of those flame torches that metal welders use." The oxyacetylene flame produced by flaring propellant from the shells stored in the turret and hull sent up "a very tall, blue flame, going up many meters in the air." Winter attempted to shoot again, but the gun sight was completely askew. The next incoming Sherman round penetrated his own turret and struck the young Czech loader:

> "It shattered his whole chest at once, and passed straight through him, and ricocheted around on the floor of the hull without hitting me. The bulk of his body had slowed the shell down, just enough to stop it bouncing off the walls and hitting me, I think."

Winter slid out of the turret side hatch, reeling with shock and crouched behind the turret. The PAK gun off to his left continued the fight, despite incoming rounds clanging and bouncing off its metal gun shield. When it finally stopped firing the crew continued to shoot back with a machine gun. Winter watched, detached and semi comatose, as American infantry closed in and hosed the emplacement down with a flamethrower. "The flames were enormous," he remembered. The whole emplacement was smothered in fire, "burning stuff was dripping off it and making a pool of fire on the sand." American infantry ran past him, until one noticed him and "hit me in the face with his rifle stock." Grenades were posted inside the concrete panzer and incinerated the boy's remains, left inside with all the ammunition. "I remember that these soldiers were dripping wet from the sea, and steam was coming off their limbs." One of them gesticulated toward the beach and sent him running with a kick in the pants. With German resistance virtually expunged from exit E-1 and strongpoints WN 65, 66, and 68 overrun, space opened up in the center of Omaha Beach providing room for Wyman's reinforcing infantry to land.[12]

General Kraiss was more preoccupied with the major Allied break-through on his right, threatening Bayeux. There was, however, some concern about the situation at Colleville, at the east side of Omaha, because that was the nearest point to the breakthrough he intended blocking with the Kampfgruppe Meyer. Fritz Ziegelmann, his chief of staff, had received an unsettling enemy radio intercept at 10:35 A.M., at around the time Brigadier General Wyman sent his information back, stating, "everything is going OK, only a bit too late." Precise timings for the intercept and its translation may have been obscured during its reception and onward transmission through the German chain of command. Ninety minutes later Ziegelmann was trying to chart the progress of Meyer's eastward redeployment. "When are you going to start?" Division headquarters asked, and "In what direction?" There was no response. Kraiss felt able to focus beyond Omaha, because he felt the invasion had been seriously blunted in his own sector.[13]

At the same time General Bradley aboard the USS *Augusta* was contemplating defeat, considering whether to divert V Corps to Utah or across the British beaches. He was focused at the operational, not the tactical beach level. "Whatever the improvisation, our buildup would have to be maintained if we were to withstand an enemy counterof-fensive," he surmised later in his memoirs. His aide Major Hansen felt the tension in the command group. "Situation on the Omaha Beach is critical," he wrote in his diary. Brigadier General Kean, Bradley's chief of staff had told him:

"We've got to get our stuff ashore, get V Corps in across the lateral road and establish ourselves on the high ground before he [the enemy] gets ready to hit us."

Bradley, like Kraiss, was acting on information two hours old. The GIs on Omaha had penetrated the German coastal defenses in at least seven places and neutralized five of twelve beach strongpoints. Kraiss was convinced he had repelled the invasion at Omaha, but actually the center and east side of his defense was visibly crumbling. Events were running faster than the senior commanders could assimilate. The troops fighting on the beach had already determined the outcome.[14]

More Infantry
9:30 A.M. to 1:00 P.M.

Luftwaffe Lieutenant Thomas Beike, sitting at readiness in the cockpit of his Messerschmitt Bf 109 fighter aircraft near Évreux was ordered at mid morning to conduct an armed reconnaissance patrol over the coast near Caen. The 109 was not suited to such a mission. "Visibility was very limited forward," Beike complained, "because the engine cowling was right under your chin." He had to dive to observe, and the absence of a bubble canopy meant he could not see behind, while his wings obstructed the view to either side. "So we were to be reconnaissance pilots!" he cryptically thought, "hardly a promotion but it finally got me into the air." He was determined to do what he could, accepting, "you must improvise in such times." Improvise was the byword, the three Messerschmitts had no radio communication with their base, only with each other in the air. The mission was observe, fly back, and report. His commander stepped up the cockpit ladder and passed over his own Leica aviation camera to take pictures, emphasizing the importance of gaining information. Beike pushed it inside his seat harness, "the chances of using a hand camera in such a situation are almost zero," he admitted.

The only Luftwaffe activity over the beaches that morning had been by a squadron of *Jagdgeschwader 2* [Fighter Wing 2], a dozen Focke-Wulf 190s under Hauptmann Wurmheller. It flew the eastern extremity of Omaha and the neighboring British beach at Gold with indeterminate and hardly reported results. This was late morning. Medic T/5 Cecil Breeden, patching up a wounded man on the beach from the 29th Division, recalled him pointing to a distant dogfight. They watched a German plane being shot down:

> "The pilot bailed out but his parachute caught on the wing. The plane rolled wing over wing all the way down. Every time the wing came up and down, the chute opened and then folded under as the plane rolled. We heard the pilot's screams all the way down."

The most dramatic overflight came at 9:40 A.M., a strafing run by Oberstleutnant Josef "Pips" Priller and his wing-man Feldwebel Wodarczyk. These two Focke-Wulf 190s from *Jagdgeschwader 26* swooped over the British beaches at Sword, Juno, and Gold, bordering Omaha, at 10 to 150 feet, all cannons blazing. Lieutenant William Eisemann with the US Navy gawped at the two silhouettes, guns chattering "at less than fifty feet" which "dodged through the barrage balloons." On HMS *Dunbar,* Leading Stoker Robert Dowie watched both planes streak through the combined antiaircraft fire of the whole fleet, before zooming up into the cloud and turning inland for Paris. "Jerry or not," Dowie conceded, "the best of luck to you. You've got guts."[15]

Lieutenant Beike and the trio of Messerschmitts took off and climbed away in staggered formation before leveling out and turning northwest to Caen. Almost immediately, they were jumped from behind by two

American Mustangs. "They tore right through us before we got our wits together," Beike recalled. "I blush with shame when I remember that, to be attacked so quickly and in such a basic fashion." The aircraft scattered, "I wasn't hit, but one of my comrades was, and he began to make a lot of gray smoke as he turned away." The priority was to take evasive action, "because the air was full of these damned Mustangs," but he saw an ominous orange glow spread rearward from his comrade's stricken aircraft. When the cowling broke off in pieces he inwardly groaned when the flames shot back over the open cockpit. "I remember seeing him with his arms over his face like this," he demonstrated, "and then he was simply lost in all the flames." They had celebrated his twenty-fifth birthday the night before.

The two surviving aircraft gained height and accelerated to the coast, evading the Mustangs and German flak. "Those flak gunners were in a panic, shooting at anything, it seemed." He crossed rail lines near Caen and the river inlet with its docks at over 370 mph, and "the coast itself just leapt up at me at that speed." In front an astonishing vista of a massive line of ships opened up, under two miles offshore. "This just happened like that, in the blink of an eye," he recalled, no time to take pictures. "My canopy glass was just full of these ships." He had never witnessed such a fleet, "the sea was absolutely solid with metal."

He wheeled westward along the coast, banking wings to get a better view of the shoreline, while crossing Juno and Gold beaches. The water's edge was crammed with vehicles and there were boats and vehicles below on fire. Momentary glares from flamethrowers were visible inland, and the impact of shells in the flooded areas beyond the coast, "sent out a concentric shock wave through the water that was very noticeable. . . . So this is the big invasion, this is it," he recalled thinking, "no other explanation was possible." His presence in the sky overhead stirred a veritable hornet's nest of protective fighters below, who came up after him. He dived down to minimum height and maximum speed, hardly registering

Omaha beyond Arromanches to his right. "I used a huge amount of fuel accelerating to the southwest," as far as Saint-Lô to elude his pursuers, before turning east to Évreux.

The mission was over and, "I tried in my mind to estimate the number of ships on the sea, but I couldn't do it," he recalled, "it was thousands, surely." Panzer columns were moving on the roads below and many more were dispersed in fields, but fortunately "nobody fired at me." When his airstrip came in sight, "I saw on the runway the burning outline of our third Messerschmitt." He had come back with his engine on fire and exploded as he came in to land. "I was the only one to survive, you see." The rising column of smoke was a beacon for American fighter planes, "who came back just like a pack of wolves," after realizing they had been bombing a decoy airfield. As Beike landed the airstrip was strafed and he had to run to the main shelter to report amid bomb bursts. They were pinned down at the airstrip for several hours and grounded by a stream of contradictory orders:

> "They ordered us to strafe the beaches, and then no, leave
> the base and take the planes inland, and then no, wait for
> orders . . . each time our heads spun a little more."

They were not able to take off again until the following day.[16] Lieutenant Erwin Hentschel's 6th Company with the 1st Battalion Regiment 915 was laboring with French wood-burning trucks toward Colleville. "I briefly saw one German fighter," he recalled, "just a glimpse." Having been diverted from the Kampfgruppe Meyer to relieve the pressure on Colleville, he would not arrive until late morning. His was one of two German counterattacks directed by General Kraiss against Omaha Beach. The first to arrive was *Oberst* Goth's II/916 elements, the local reserve, directed to move against Saint-Laurent-sur-Mer in the center at 10:30 A.M. Lieutenant Hans Heinz recalled they did not get there before about 2:00 P.M. Companies arrived piecemeal and suffered for it. Heinz's close friend Lieutenant "Hahn and *Stabsfeldwebel* [warrant officer] Pennigsdorfe's 3rd platoon caught it," he remembered, "when they ran into an American engineer ambush, and the whole platoon was wiped out." The next in line was Lieutenant Berthier's men arriving from Surrain three miles away, and, "practically all the 7th Company men were killed or wounded," Heinz remembered. Heinz was extracted from Goth's staff and ordered to take over from the severely wounded Hahn. After a brief orientation he was ordered to continue forward with the two surviving platoons, "and throw the enemy penetration back into the sea!"[17]

Kurt Keller's 3rd Company from Fusilier Battalion 352 finally reached the coast at Saint-Laurent in the late morning with just sixty men. Their column was strung out and inserted into a confusing situation. "There were no clear orders from our platoon commander, who did not know where we were supposed to go," he remembered. Immediately they were "nailed to the ground," by a storm of naval gunfire amid "awful cries from wounded comrades" and "heavy pressure waves from explosives that shook everything about." His previously anticipated heroic baptism of fire, so often discussed in training, was reduced instead to him, "holding his hands over his ears and wishing he could burrow and hide in the ground like a mouse." He noticed the soldier sheltering in the crater alongside him "endlessly flicking the on/off safety catch switch of his rifle with feverish nervous tension." They endured the barrage for twenty minutes, then "out of the crater with our whole bodies shaking, we ran to the coast on doddery legs heavy as lead." Fighter-bombers swooped down. "The Jabos hunted us from shell hole to shell hole," and "the decimated company was even further reduced."

When they got to Les Moulins, Gustav Winter's previous WN 66 strongpoint, Keller found, "motionless corpses of dead German soldiers everywhere." The shore was reached at about 10:00 A.M., where there was, "an astonishing assembly of ships, an uninterrupted black wall of ships," a fearful impression. An hour later Lieutenant Erwin Hentschel's group reached the coast at Colleville, where, "at a stroke the din started," he recalled. "We attacked through the village and beyond, until we could see the barrels of the battleships." General Kraiss was still confident he could restore the situation at Omaha Beach.[18]

Within twenty minutes of Wyman's reinforcement call, the 2nd Battalion of the 18th Regiment landed comparatively intact across a wide front, to the west of the Saint-Laurent exit. LCI-489 and 18 LCVPs disembarked 750 men at high tide; most of the boats scraped or hit underwater obstacles, but none were damaged. Lieutenant Colonel John Williamson, the battalion commander, ordered his E Company to advance on the right flank and finish off strongpoint WN 65 by attacking from the west, while the rest of the battalion moved left with three companies to clear the high ground of opposition.

There was some consternation aboard LCI-489 when, "suddenly all hell broke out," according to Pharmacist's Mate James Argo. The LCI captain yelled, "Get off the bridge!" which was promptly abandoned as "fire started coming from everywhere. . . . The German bunkers that were supposed to have been blasted out in an air raid weren't," remembered Argo. They had already been discomfited by the appearance of "a couple of dead men draped over obstacles in the shallow water," as they came in.

Over the next ninety minutes, more than three thousand fresh infantrymen came ashore just east of the Saint-Laurent draw. The original plan assumed the 16th and 116th Regiments would secure the beach, while three reserve regiments totaling over 10,000 men would wait offshore and land unimpeded to push on to the next phase objectives five miles inland. This feature of the plan was accelerated to overcome the crisis, but seizing the inland objectives would have to come later. Wyman coordinated the reception of 2,500 reinforcements from the 29th Division 115th Infantry in his sector. Major General Huebner, at last able to grasp the nettle, radioed Cota, the deputy commander of the 29th Division to use the 115th to clear the high ground southwest of Saint-Laurent, in the 1st Division sector. The momentary embargo imposed by the beach master on craft landing at Omaha was revised. At 11:46 A.M. Huebner directed all control vessels to "rush all infantry elements to beach." The first wave of eight LCIs carrying the 1st and 2nd Battalions of the 115th started to land at 11:00 A.M., followed by the 3rd Battalion an hour later. The bulky LCIs could land a complete company at a time from their port and starboard ramps at the bow. When LCI-554 came in, Ensign J. Terranella remembered shells dropping around and mines exploding. "The sight of so many dead bodies and damaged craft made us feel as if we were lucky so far."

As the 115th post-combat report later made clear, "it came as quite a shock to many when, just prior to going ashore, the men . . . heard that they might have to land fighting." Previous briefings had stressed they would disembark onto a secure beach, "troops would merely walk ashore, make for the high ground, and then walk until the objective was reached." Second Lieutenant Richard Ford with K Company was assured, "this was not to be too difficult a job," because "there were only labor troops in the area. . . . Famous last words," he recalled, because, "they weren't throwing shovels at us when we landed." This was the beginning of a massive infantry insertion. At 12:23 P.M. four LCIs brought in the 1st Battalion of the 18th Regiment from 1st Division, and the 3rd Battalion landed just over an hour later.[19]

Landings were opposed, but with nothing like the venom experienced by earlier waves. Private Lewis Smith with the 18th was in action for the first time. Taking cover at the shingle, he glanced at the men either side, seeking human contact and shared direction. The man "on my left had a hole blown out of his back," he recalled, "it looked like he had taken a direct hit from a mortar or shell." The one on his right had lost the top of his head, shot off by machine gun fire. Senior Sergeant Donald Parker came across a dying young soldier. "Get a chaplain," the soldier whispered, but Parker had to say, "I won't be able to find one now, our line will move any second." "*Do something*," the soldier appealed, grasping his arm, and after a pause, "I'm dying." Parker was crestfallen. "Let's repeat the Lord's Prayer together," he offered. They began with, "Our Father, which art in Heaven, hallowed be thy name," but were interrupted by a screaming shell detonating nearby. Parker flattened himself next to the praying soldier but found, "when I raised up again, the war had ended for him."

Kurt Keller, shooting at the renewed landings, felt "naked before these enormous odds." The buildup of troops on the beach ahead was remorseless, "a mass of packed landing craft approached the beach already overflowing with troops." What could he achieve with just a rifle? With eight to ten boats approaching, he took aim at the ramps, with "my hands shaking" as he gripped his rifle. He fired round after round until all his ammunition was gone, and shook the shoulder of the man next to him to appeal for more, but "dipped into a gaping wound full of viscous blood." A huge shell splinter had opened up his shoulder and penetrated his body. "Shocked, I turned him over on his side to get at his ammunition pouch; he would not need any more ammunition." He felt sensitive handling the body because, "I still had the feeling that turning him over must have caused some pain." He loaded another ten rounds, with hands covered in congealed blood, and carried on shooting.

As the Americans closed in, he was suddenly confronted by a GI coming directly at him. With trembling hands he quickly aimed at his chest and fired:

> "The American was left standing, let his rifle drop, and sank to his knees. Slowly taking his helmet off he laid it on the rifle and looking up to the sky, he crossed himself and fell over on his face."

The image was to haunt Keller forever. "How could a man be so devout and believe in God at that moment?" he recalled thinking. "Hitler was my god, until then."[20]

The 1st Division engineers were sweeping mines and bulldozing lanes through the shingle under fire. As the intensity of fire around the Saint-Laurent draw eased, a bulldozer managed to fill the anti-tank ditch. Work began to open up a road and construct a transit area for vehicles jam-packed on the beach. No unit the size of the landed 115th Regiment had yet managed to scale the bluffs. Getting 2,500 men up these slopes was going to take time and considerable coordination to disentangle units mixed up on landing. Second Lieutenant Richard Ford called to his men, "follow me," thinking, "how corny, I sound like John Wayne." But "it was certain death to stand or wait on that beach," and they filed off toward the bluffs. "I never looked back to see what the rest of the company was doing," he recalled, "or where they were." The plan had clearly changed, but nobody in authority seemed to know what the new one was. The soldiers did not need to be told the current one was not working. "I was shocked to see the number of bodies and the amount of matériel that was littering the beach" Ford remembered. "At this point, I didn't think I would ever see England again, let alone the United States."

Streams of soldiers began to climb the sand dune bluffs. What they were meant to do when they reached the top was not specified. Colonel Eugene Slappey, the regimental commander, was one of the last to reach the beach. His landing craft was hung up on an underwater beach obstacle. His 1st and 2nd Battalions had, nevertheless, started to press inland. Only a chance encounter on the beach with Brigadier General Wyman offered clarification. The village of Saint-Laurent, firmly held by the Germans, was to be the 115th's first objective. The snakelike columns moved ponderously. "We were overloaded," Ford recalled, "the men had close to 60 lbs. on their backs." The trail they followed was littered with dead and dismembered men:

"I speculated that they had set off personnel mines as their bodies were quite mutilated and mangled and reminded one to be cautious. Walking, in a crouch position, along their bodies it was quite safe, but the goriness was very sobering to say the least. I passed one fellow who had been blown in half. You could see the organs hanging out of the upper half of his body."

Private Huston "Hu" Riley, Robert Capa's famous "Face in the Surf" photo subject, climbed the bluffs later in the afternoon. Wounded in the shoulder and neck, "an aid man poured a bunch of sulfa on the wound." He had carried on with two holes in his body, "one stayed in my back until I got home, and one is still in my shoulder." Command of F Company had gone to the 1st Sergeant, who, when he saw the blood on his back, sent him back down to the beach and off to England.[21]

At 11:00 A.M. Colonel Talley radioed the V Corps HQ aboard the USS *Ancon* from his DUKW offshore that he could see, "men advancing up slope behind Easy Red." This was the first positive news that had been heard all morning. "Men, believed ours on skyline," he reported, around the Saint-Laurent draw, "things look better." Unknown to senior commanders, the immediate crisis was over. General Bradley agonized over whether the Omaha landings were salvageable; he did not receive this positive input from V Corps until two and a half hours later. The immediate crisis was over in that the deadlock on the beaches *appeared* to be broken. Major General Gerow was hedging his bets. Some of the German defenses had been overwhelmed but it was an uncomfortably narrow margin of beach. The three villages inland were still firmly held by the Germans. Substantial numbers of infantry were ashore, but they had yet to traverse the bluffs. The invasion in the Omaha sector was hanging by a thread. "When we got on top of the bluff," 2nd Lieutenant Ford remembered, "we rounded up as many of our men as possible." His unit was not yet conducting a preplanned or coordinated advance. "I had no idea where the company was," the platoon commander admitted.[22]

German machine gunner Heinrich Severloh at strongpoint WN 62 frequently glanced uneasily over his left shoulder. Since about midday, "I had been able to see many US soldiers in dark columns climbing the slopes between Saint-Laurent and Vierville, almost five kilometers from my position." The serpentine lines creeping up the dunes appeared menacing. He was aware that "more and more Americans had landed in all of Omaha bay." Tanks were increasingly visible ashore. As disconcerting as these signs were, the Russian Front veteran knew the purpose of strongpoints was to fragment attacks and dissipate momentum. This would set the conditions for the counterattacks they had frequently rehearsed, to come in from the rear. The panzers would then advance and drive the Americans back into the sea.[23]

NINE

VILLAGE FIGHTING

11:30 A.M. TO DUSK

Colleville, East

11:30 A.M. to 7:00 P.M.

Off the Rue Principale winding through the few dozen stone houses at Colleville village, was the Rue de la Mer. The entrance lay a few dozen yards from the town hall and around the corner from the church. This narrow lane led down to the sea, about a mile to German strongpoints WN 61 and 62. Approximately seventy yards from the northern edge of the village, along this lane, was an innocuous metal armored door, set in a concrete frame at the side of the valley wall. Inside was a three-room underground bunker, with an escape hatch leading up some steps at the far end to the plateau above. This was strongpoint WN 63, the command post (CP) for Lieutenant Edmond Bauch's 3rd Company 726 Regiment. It also doubled as the 915 Regiment CP and telephone exchange connected to WN 69, the primary Omaha Beach German telephone exchange at Saint-Laurent. Bauch had just replaced Ernst Ottoeier, the former First World War veteran company commander, and had recently arrived from the Russian front.

Bauch had monitored the battle on his telephone all morning, in the increasingly fetid bunker conditions. Comings and goings had done little to dissipate the rank odor of sweat, cordite, antiseptics, and blood coming from groaning wounded soldiers spread across the floor and tables. Since 9:00 A.M. the tenor of terse telephone messages coming through the 352 Division exchange had transitioned from satisfaction to increasing alarm. No information was forthcoming from the Vierville strongpoints and it was unclear whether strongpoints WN 65 to 67 had been captured by the enemy or not. Bauch was at least relieved to hear at 10:30 A.M. that the II Battalion 916 Regiment was to be committed to Saint-Laurent nearby, at the center of Omaha Beach. His primary unease was the sector to his front. Enemy soldiers were infiltrating between the strongpoints at the end of the Rue de la Mer, at WN 61 and 62, suggesting they might be heading toward his own command post. Thirty minutes before, just one machine gun was still firing from WN 62, but apparently WN 60 was still holding out to its right.

News reached them about Vierville after midday. WN 71 and 73 were giving a good account of themselves, and were being reinforced, while WN 66 and 68 still held the center of the beach. Fourteen minutes later Bauch relayed alarming news that "the situation on the left wing"—his sector—was critical, as "the enemy has already advanced up to the church in Colleville." His men could hear firing around the corner in the village and there were sharp exchanges of fire down the Rue de la Mer. WN 62 reported masses of tanks "congregated in front of the anti-tank ditch."

The situation was not good. Bauch could not be certain about WN 60, he knew WN 61 had fallen, but WN 62 according to the telephone log was still holding out.[1]

Lieutenant Bauch felt increasingly exposed. He knew a battalion from the Kampfgruppe Meyer had been detached to restore the situation at Colleville, but it could not be determined over the din of battle whether they had arrived. Oberstleutnant Ziegelmann at 352 Division headquarters shared his concern. "At about 11:00 hours, the weather conditions changed," he recalled, "and the sun broke through the clouds." With the sun came Jabos:

> "The first enemy fighter-bombers appeared before long and started to paste the widely spaced groups of the reinforced 915th Infantry Regiment. The movements ceased, since more and more fighter-bombers appeared."

All German movement on the Normandy roads became increasingly ponderous. Edmond Scelles, who fled to Formigny by road, remembered:

> "The Germans went by bike, columns of bicycles! With trolleys with four wheels, no vehicles, there was no petrol."[2]

German artillery support from the Houteville battery supporting the Colleville sector slackened after midday. Oberleutnant Frerking was becoming increasingly frustrated in his observation bunker at WN 62. He ordered a salvo to straddle LCIs approaching the beach, only to be told by the battery chief, "only single shots possible Herr Lieutenant," he was told, "because of a shortage of ammunition." Oberstleutnant Ocker, commanding Artillery Regiment 352, had personally promised him a truckload in support, but it was strafed by Jabos less than a mile from the battery, vaporized in a succession of ear-splitting explosions. Half the ammunition supply had been relocated inland several weeks before, to spread the vulnerability of the dumps.

Major Werner Pluskat, Frerking's artillery group commander, did not get back to his chateau headquarters until 2:00 P.M. He had spent eight hours dodging in and out of ditches to get back, constantly harassed by air attacks. Shivering with shock, and with his uniform filthy and in tatters, he was also informed the guns were out of ammunition. He remonstrated with Ocker at regimental headquarters until he was promised a resupply. The entire convoy was obliterated in a chance raid that was deflected from hitting a train. "Pluskat, I can't help you any more," Ocker phoned back, "its up to you to do what you can now."

At 1:30 P.M. German machine gunners Christian Faust and Ludwig Kwiatkowski, manning the northernmost Tobruk emplacement at WN 62, realized the two strongpoints to their right at WN 61 and 60 had probably fallen. Trucks and tanks were gathering unmolested in front of the emplacements. Kwiatkowski was anxious. "We needed to disappear before the Americans get too near with their flame throwers," he recalled. They moved back, Faust cradling their hot MG 42 in his arms. When they approached the side of the hill one of the metal side entrances to WN 62 fell open and they were motioned inside by Unteroffizier Schulte. They read fear in his face and heard Polish voices inside, preferring not to confront the flame throwers following up behind. Soldiers were thinning out and moving back to the reserve position in Colleville. Obergefreite Peter Lützen was also moving back, observing that, "practically the whole area between WN 62 and WN 61 opposite was teeming with hundreds of Americans and many vehicles."[3]

Heinrich Severloh continued to shoot out from his position after Faust and Kwiatkowski withdrew. His machine gun had overheated several times. "From where I was, I could see who was moving and stayed above water," he recalled. He picked up his rifle, "with fifty rounds, I only missed five times at the most," he claimed. "You could see where the shot landed in the water, over the top to the side." He allegedly fired 12,500 rounds from the MG 42 with a modified special Boehler Antinit steel barrel, an experimental model capable of firing 20,000 rounds. In the 1990s, exaggerated TV documentary accounts claimed he inflicted 2,500 casualties, well over half the accepted total losses at that time. One American veteran recalled, "half way up the heights," of WN 62, "there was a machine gun," that was especially effective, and "was the last that carried on shooting in this sector, and did so with tracer." The tracer attracted fire from the destroyer USS *Frankford*. American accounts claimed its fire was so accurate that no one dared climb over the seawall. "The GIs lying there when I arrived," the veteran remembered, "were already speaking about that damn beast up there, and this beast fired on until the afternoon."

Severloh was labeled the "Beast of Omaha" by the postwar media, promoting an exaggerated myth that he found dismaying. There is little doubt that his resistance was very effective, but he was haunted rather than proud of the achievement. He had recurring nightmares, which included a persistent snapshot of what happened:

> "There were two high concrete slabs and a really tall American soldier, who I shot in the head. His steel helmet came off and went wobbling through the sand as his jaw dropped to his chest, and he fell over forward. I can still see him to this day. Whenever I would close my eyes, this man would fall over. Horrible. It tormented me badly."

His primary allegiance was to his artillery chief, Lieutenant Frerking. "It was my duty to serve my first lieutenant," he claimed, "if I had run away before, I would have felt terribly guilty." Despite the obvious buildup on the beach, he carried on firing until about 3:00 P.M. "Stupid, but I wasn't going to let him down," he emphasized. Frerking was reduced by this time to calling in single shots only.[4]

Captain Joe Dawson's G Company from the 16th Regiment had been the first to ascend the bluffs between Colleville and Saint-Laurent that morning. It was still an integrated company group with machine guns and mortars despite having lost sixty men on the beach. He approached his earmarked objective, Colleville village, from the northwest, astride a meandering dirt road along which they were hailed by a French woman farmer, *"Bienvenu à France!"* she called, "Welcome to France!" This was an incongruous prelude to a bloody battle. Major William Washington recalled Dawson talking to another farmer outside the village, who told him there were two hundred German soldiers inside. "That guy's putting you on," Washington, the executive officer of the 2nd Battalion claimed. "He was sent out here to feed you a bunch of crap." The Americans were generally mistrustful of the French; they were unfamiliar with the language and had been briefed that all civilians had been cleared from the coastal belt. Any left behind were likely to be collaborators. "Just take your company and go on in there and clean 'em out," Dawson was directed. He pushed on, thinking he would be attacking thirty to forty men, not the hundred or more already ensconced in the village.[5]

The German tactical concept for village defense was to establish forward strongpoints to break up attacks, while holding an irregular front line inside the core of the village, angled to create defilade fire and cul-de-sac killing zones. Colleville was a linear conglomeration of two dozen buildings and outbuildings stretching 650 yards from end to end. The ancient church with its towering steeple occupied a nose of high ground at its western edge, which offered a spectacular view of the sea and beach. Houses were walled-in farms, sturdy stone constructions that were fortresses in all but name, requiring minimum preparation for defense. Civilians were still in residence. The dilemma for French refugees was should they stay and risk the uncertainties of fighting, or take their chances on the open roads? The experience of the Luftwaffe strafing in 1940 suggested stay at home, and Allied fighter-bombers were very much in evidence. No one could tell whether this was truly the *débarquement* or a raid like Dieppe. Indeed, the intensity of the fighting on the beach made it debatable whether it would even succeed. Liberation would come at a price.

Fernand Broeckx remembered, "we took refuge across the street at our neighbor's house, which seemed more solid than our own." There were no shelters for civilians other than homemade. It was a risk to remain among the increasingly desperate German soldiers, who were turning ugly. Broeckx barred two German soldiers from his house who demanded entry to procure blankets. They were clearly angered by his reluctance to hand any over, so Broeckx took them to his cellar entrance to show them, "Here we are twenty-three in number; there are women and children among us, including a mother with a two-month-old baby in her arms. . . . They didn't look convinced," he remembered, and vented their spite by setting fire to a farm twenty yards away. "They could do nothing to confine the fire, because the machine gun fire had already started." Civilians were acutely vulnerable.[6]

Dawson's company hit a number of buildings at the western perimeter of the village they described as the "bivouac area," probably an outer strongpoint. This vicious house-to-house clearance fought with rifles and grenades cost twelve men before the company was able to converge either side of the main street leading into the village at 1:00 P.M. They barely progressed beyond the village church before being engulfed in a storm of fire on the Rue Principale. Further along was the Café Violard, next to the Pommier family's grocery where German soldiers had enjoyed a coffee or wine during more congenial times.

At about the same time Lieutenant Erwin Hentschel's 6th Company 915 Regiment, the promised reinforcement from the Kampfgruppe Meyer, renewed its counterattack. "We went forward with a Hurrah!" he recalled, and "in a short time we had more American prisoners with us than German soldiers." Lieutenant Bauch around the corner was able to send a reassuring telephone message to 352 Division Headquarters that, "Colleville has been reconquered from the enemy." Ziegelmann lost no time relaying this apparent success to General Marcks's 84th Corps. Hentschel recalled that, "within a quarter of an hour we had hauled lots of Amis out of the hedgerows." As he pushed farther into the village his vanguard became separated from the rest of the II Battalion 915 following behind.

"Suddenly we came under fire from all sides," he remembered, but they continued to move forward with about 110 men. He called for artillery support but his forward artillery observer reported, "they had no more ammunition." The advance lost momentum and degenerated into a myriad of separate firefights in a maze of bushes and buildings. "Although we had dragged so many Americans out of the hedgerows, there were so many more sitting within," he recalled. The attack was petering out. "It was totally pointless conducting such a counterattack," he remembered with frustration. "What should I be directing it against?" When he reported back to his battalion commander he was told, "Then hold the line as long as you can." The German tactical dilemma was whether to continue the attack across such difficult terrain, or go over to the defensive? Compromise solutions thus far had produced indeterminate results. Hentschel was running short of men so he gave the order to dig in around the coast road, effectively blocking it. "I hoped that a panzer division would come some time soon," he remembered, "and then the American attack would be settled."[7]

The whole defensive fabric of strongpoint WN 62 was coming apart. Russian veteran Obergefreite Siegfried Kuska recognized, "further resistance was useless," and decided, "to pull back and try and break through to company headquarters." He took his wounded loader Heckmann with him. Gefreiter Franz Gockel had already gone back to their bunker to scavenge for food, having not eaten for eight hours. He rummaged through his sentimental possessions, taking the rosary his mother had given him and his father's Lourdes medal, which he was convinced kept him alive during the First World War. Standing incongruously on the bunk table was Obergefreiter Krieftewirth's false teeth, swimming in a glass of water covered in a film of dust. *What on earth would the finder of these teeth think?* Gockel thought as he hastily departed. Unknown to him, Krieftewirth had survived and was being led back to the rear, in a state of abject shock, with the other walking wounded. When Gockel climbed the embankment to get back to his position he was shot through his outstretched left hand. Looking down, "I saw three fingers hanging loose by torn tendons." His comrades congratulated him, this was the celebrated *Heimatschuss* [home shot], guaranteeing evacuation back home. "Be pleased you can still run," they said, waving him back to the rear for treatment. Gockel set off along the Rue de la Mer, heading for WN 63 just over a mile away, mindful of his mother's letters, which always ended with, "May God protect you."[8]

Faust and Kwiatkowski made good progress to the rear, following the path previously worn by signalers laying telephone cable to the command post across the minefields. At the edge of Colleville they were strafed by a low flying Jabo. "He came so low," Kwiatkowski recalled, "I could clearly see the pilot in the cockpit." They jumped to the left, with Faust carrying the MG 42 marginally slower. "The burst went through Faust's shoulder and disemboweled him from top to bottom," he remembered:

> "I swiveled around to help my friend, lying at the edge of the ditch, completely split open. I immediately turned him over smothering my hands with blood and muck, his intestines had fallen out. He simply said, 'Ludwig,' and his head fell sideways."[9]

Peter Lützen was in the same ditch with the WN 62 walking wounded. "There is nothing we can do, we have to leave him," he advised.

They split up and made their way back through the network of ditches and trenches.

Company runner Michael Schnichels was lying in a Colleville street. A shell exploding in a livestock stall had impacted on a horse and knocked him over, showering him with viscera. Schnichels was seriously wounded, his left arm, ribs, and spine lacerated with shrapnel. He dragged himself beneath the horse carcass when he heard Americans approach and played dead, an appalling spectacle, lying in a large pool of his own blood, liberally splattered with chunks of horseflesh. The American soldiers closely examined him and saw an eye flicker open. One of them knelt and gently placed a burning cigarette between his lips. Medics carefully attempted to recover him but he passed out again.

"I hoped to meet our company reserve in Colleville," remembered Ludwig Kwiatkowski, "but they were long gone." The sounds of battle grew in intensity as he approached the village. "Over there, something was really going on as I got near," he recalled, "an absolute din underway."[10] Joseph Dawson's G Company had bitten off more than it could chew. Three men were killed and two seriously wounded occupying the church and houses nearby. Having penetrated Colleville, they were enveloped by Hentschel's counterattack from all sides and penned into an oval-shaped perimeter inside the village. As the G Company after-action report described it, "no front could be fixed." At 2:30 P.M. Dawson sent word to his battalion commander that he did not have the strength to take Coleville against this opposition. Two of his sections were separated from the main group on high ground one thousand yards beyond, covering his flank. He could not make progress into the village with his remaining three sections. Captain Edward Wozenski was pinned in buildings on the southwest edge of the village perimeter, with E Company survivors. Dawson was deafened by the point-blank fire that erupted when he entered the church, amplified by the enclosed stone nave. One of his men pitched forward, shot by a German sniper concealed in the lofty steeple belfry above. The sniper and three others hiding below were shot down when they revealed their positions, but Dawson was wounded in the knee. Two Germans fled around the corner to WN 63 and told Lieutenant Bauch that there were Americans in the church belfry, virtually on their doorstep.

Bauch sent three men to join the two survivors and retrace their steps to sort out the situation in the church two hundred yards away. When they failed to secure an entry the frustrated company commander went to see for himself. Lieutenant Hentschel's men had also reached the church, and he dispatched a *panzerschreck* [bazooka] team to blow the Americans out of the steeple. Bauch arrived and looked through the metal gateway of the gap that provided the eastern entrance through the surrounding stone wall. He had little idea of the situation and did not know the steeple tower was probably occupied. When he turned to issue orders he was hit in the back of the helmet by a sniper's bullet, which blew out his face. There was now no chance of coordinating the defense of the village with Hentschel's reinforcing counterattack. The *panzerschreck* team surmounted the wall and put two rockets into the steeple roof.

Meanwhile the newly landed 1st and 2nd Battalions of the 18th Regiment were steadily but slowly moving up behind, toward the sound of battle during the afternoon. Dawson was unaware of these reinforcements approaching. There was a slackening of fire as they moved around the south side of the village, but it picked up again once they had gone. The advance off the beaches lacked urgent momentum. Having witnessed the awful punishment on the beach, there was scant enthusiasm to hurry for more of the same. The 16th up ahead had demonstrably suffered heavy casualties, and men were still being lost crossing gates and hedgerows well zeroed-in by German machine guns and mortars. They had never encountered the maze of hedgerows, sunken roads, and tree-lined embankments they came across in training, completely unlike the beaches. Opposition was at close range and difficult to detect with an inexperienced eye. Sheer weight of numbers impelled a form of momentum but it was not characterized by any élan with fast rushes and swift consolidation.

Staff Sergeant Donald Wilson with F Company had scaled the bluffs with a small group of men and was approaching Colleville village by the afternoon. For the first time he encountered, "whole units, not little groups like ours," moving past. A major told him:

> "The tide turned when little groups started to move inland.
> First in ones and twos, then in groups of fives and sixes, penetrating and hitting key German positions."

Further waves had been released for landing on the beaches, "and now we saw them," Wilson remembered, "vehicles and even some armor." The major told him "the intent was to push on until stopped, because there was much concern about the possibility of a counterattack."[11]

By 3:00 p.m. Heinrich Severloh was observing more and more ominous dark columns of enemy snaking up the bluffs to his left. The barrel of his machine gun was "shot out," having lost the rifling, "and had become so hot that dry grass caught fire on its muzzle." His two rifles overheated after four hundred rounds. "I knew the time had come," he recognized, "when all was lost." American infantry was closing in on the strongpoint. "I didn't want to kill anyone else—it was enough," he later reflected. He found Lieutenant Frerking with two radio operators and a distraught 726th infantryman already waiting to leave outside the observation bunker, all covered in a fine film of dust. They decided to dodge through the trenches to the rear, with the infantryman going first. As soon as he set off, "a regular hail storm of bullets rained down on the mound immediately." They were the last to leave at about 3:30 p.m. and needed to be quick, as the Americans coming in from the west had identified urgent activity. "You go next, Hein—take care," Frerking said to him:

"He had addressed me with the familiar *du* for the first time. We didn't have time to say much more. These last seconds of our parting were full of sad misgivings."

They briefly shook hands, leaving much unsaid, but expressing mutual affection. Severloh moved at a crouching run from hole to hole, bullet impacts bursting around, marking his progress. Kurt Warnecke, one of the radio operators caught up with him when they reached the lane that led to Saint-Laurent, four hundred yards beyond the strongpoint. He was considerably shaken and breathless. The others had not made it, he told him. Frerking had been shot through the head. Severloh never forgot his battery chief, "the only one who had kept human feeling awake within him, during an inhuman war."[12]

Franz Gockel reached Colleville, "running and crawling," nursing his Heimatschuss shattered left hand. He was surprised to discover the Americans were already in the village, "with rifle and machine gun fire sounding out all over." There was little relief on reaching WN 63, at the head of the Rue de la Mer. Bauch, his company commander, had been killed with another officer and fourteen men from his unit. Outside the bunker entrance was a poignant scene with, "corpses of German soldiers stretched out and covered with tarpaulins, with just their boots or shoes visible." Fighting was still raging with crackling small arms fire and the dull thump of grenades around the corner at the church, just sixty yards away.

Gockel climbed aboard a truck with the other wounded, his hand throbbing with pain. One of his friends, Franz Wilden, who had done basic training with him in Holland, passed him a piece of dry sausage. The truck drove off down the road toward Sainte-Honorine-des-Pertes, heading for the division hospital at Bayeux. Suddenly they emerged onto a stretch of vulnerable open road, "with no trees or hedges bordering the route, with a clear view of the sea, crawling with ships," he recalled,

"many of them huge." Barrage balloons were suspended over the fleet
to deter low-flying aircraft. As they approached Sainte-Honorine ruined
houses were seen, blocking the road. Unknown to them, elements of the
American 3rd Battalion 16th Regiment had moved beyond strongpoint
WN 60 and were already in Le Grand Hameau, on the outskirts of
Sainte-Honorine. American patrols were also nearing Cabourg, along
their same road; no German traffic could get through. The driver decided
to go back to Colleville and try his luck on another road to Bayeux.
Gockel and the walking wounded did not want to risk that open stretch
of road again, under the pitiless gaze of battleship guns. They climbed off
and began walking to the village of Étréham, farther inland to the east.

By late afternoon US Navy and Army officers became convinced that
the Colleville church steeple housed German artillery observers directing
fire at the beach. The destroyer USS *Harding* closed to within 3,500
yards to settle the issue, firing sixty rounds, which collapsed the church
tower and swept the village from end to end. This represented the nadir
of the G Company D-Day experience. Although they were one of the
first companies to get off the beach, they had left some sixty men in the
shallows and at the foot of the bluffs. They had skirmished all day with
the enemy, negotiated minefields under fire, and lost another twelve men
in the fierce firefight to gain entry to the village. The howling storm
of naval gunfire, "leveled the town, absolutely leveled it," recalled an
inconsolable Dawson, "and in so doing we suffered the worst casualties
we had the whole day—not from the enemy, but from our own navy."
Ten men were killed or wounded fighting into the village and another
eight lost to the naval bombardment. "I was angered by it, angered
beyond all measure," Dawson complained, "it was totally disgraceful."
Despite releasing orange marker smoke, the bombardment continued.
"The cordite fumes became so intense," company veterans remembered,
"that all of 'G,' including the aid men attending to the wounded, had to
carry on in gas masks." Dawson saw, "the enemy in Colleville did not

waver during the fire," and according to later prisoners, "the German side did not lose a single man."[13]

There was a growing appreciation of the fighting capabilities of the German troops facing them. "German soldiers, mostly very young boys," assessed Colonel Stanhope Mason, the 1st Division Chief of Staff. "Heinies have to be rooted out of every strongpoint," and "they stick tight, still dogged and bitter fighters." Progress beyond the beaches was equally laborious. "We kill snipers within one hundred yards of CPs when we set them up," Mason reported two days later. "They hide in hedgerows and carefully pot-shoot." By early morning realization dawned that they were up against a "crack" 352 Division, not the second-rate troops originally predicted. Lieutenant John Carroll with the 16th Regiment CP described them as "seasoned rough men." Mason commented, "they are falling back little by little."

Sergeant Robert Slaughter was visibly impressed by a, "rather small and frail looking" German prisoner being roughly interrogated by a regimental intelligence officer on the beach at Vierville. "The prisoner was on his knees with his hands behind his head," he remembered, menaced by the officer's carbine. As the policy was not to take prisoners for the first two or three days, "I expected the officer to eventually shoot the prisoner." The German was totally uncompromising, refusing to give away minefields, simply repeating his name, rank, and serial number:

> "The lieutenant's carbine barked, but the bullet was aimed at the ground between the prisoner's knees. The arrogant German looked straight at the officer with a smirk, *Nicht hier*—he pointed between his knees *Hier!*—he pointed to his head. This told me something about our adversary."[14]

Second Lieutenant John Spalding's platoon was also caught up in the fighting along the western extremity of Colleville. They were momentarily surrounded but managed to crawl out past a German machine gun, with two dead and one live German manning it. "Without saying a word, we exchanged the German's life for our own safety," Spalding remembered. "I'm sure that I saw a twinkle in the German's eye as I crawled past him." Dawson clung to the west side of Colleville while the Germans remained in occupation of the east. But for the fact that by mid afternoon the 16th Infantry's 3rd Battalion managed to cut the road leading to Colleville from the east, necessitating the Germans to face two directions, Dawson might well have been ejected from the village. The remnants of Captain Edward Wozenski's E Company of the 116th, who had landed with cameraman Robert Capa, were holding ground to Dawson's right. They too were exhausted and dismayed by dusk on the most traumatic day of their lives thus far. Private Walter Bieder recalled his company commander's poignant emotion, "Wozenski broke down hollering, 'Where's my men?'" They had landed early that morning with two hundred men, and now there were "sixty of us left."[15]

Vierville West
10:00 A.M. to 1:30 P.M.

After turning right at the top of the bluffs east of Vierville, Lieutenant Robert Bedell's C Company force from the 116th followed the dirt road to the village. Fragmentary resistance along the line of bluffs was easily rolled up or bypassed. They reached the eastern outskirts of the village at 10:00 A.M. and filed through the buildings and along the street with hardly a shot fired. Minutes later they were at the junction of the coastal highway and where the road led down to the Vierville cliff draw, still echoing with the sounds of gunfire. With that, the German defenders at WN 73 to 71, dominating the sea entrance to the draw, were cut off from any possibility of escape or reinforcement. The core of the

German Vierville defense was the line of bunkers along the promenade and cliffsides. There was no apparent reserve or counterattack force in depth at the village, and the many German infantry packs found piled at the top of the road suggested that if there was, they had abruptly departed. The local Norman civilians were as surprised as the Germans with the sudden appearance of American soldiers to their rear.

Half an hour before Albert André, living in the village, had been warned off by a German lieutenant to, "be careful, Tommies in the sea, maybe behind, one hundred yards away." He watched in hope. Victorine Houyvet, a thirty-one-year-old teacher in the village remembered, "I was putting on a skirt when an American showed up at the door!" She was absolutely shocked at the sudden appearance of the very tall soldier, having had no idea about the progress or extent of the landings. "I was so bewildered," she recalled, "that I put my hands in the air, thinking, *What is this beanpole doing here?*"

> "There had been plenty of talk about the landing, but we didn't think it would be at our doorstep. He took his revolver and fired, thinking I was a German. Luckily, I was in front of the bedroom door and was able to get out of the way, otherwise he would have killed me!"

The bullet went through the window, but the cautious soldier remained outside. "I can't say it was a very pleasant first encounter," Madame Houyvet complained.[16]

Twelve-year-old Suzanne Hardelay's first view of Americans entering Vierville was walking legs. "We saw only the legs because we were a few steps down the basement," she remembered. Her father was convinced they could not be Germans. Row after row of legs strode by until they were suddenly distracted by the noise of their small pig, scuffling about in a small hut. The soldiers dropped to the ground and stealthily stalked the hut "on all fours with rifles," until the pig appeared and the tension dissolved into guffaws and laughter. The majority of the Americans passing through were in a hurry and simply said, "American," as they passed the inquisitive locals.

Emotion in the village transitioned from tension and alarm to elation when they grasped what the hurrying columns of Americans signified. It had happened so quickly. Farm worker Michel Levoir remembered a German soldier suddenly bursting into their washroom to shoot at the Americans outside. "My father seized the German, making him realize we had ten kids in there," he recalled. "He immediately understood and was gone." Within twenty seconds of departure, "an American came in to ask if we had any Germans—*Boche*—in there. We were still afraid."[17]

Many American soldiers seemed tall and intimidating. Civilians remaining inside the five-kilometer prohibited coastal zone were assumed to be collaborators and regarded with mistrust. Women were moreover not necessarily noncombatants. Lieutenant Brown with B Company with the 18th Regiment had shot a female sniper in Colleville, dressed in a German officer's uniform, allegedly acting as an artillery observer. Lieutenant William Fulk, the Battalion S3 recalled, "he didn't know it was a woman until her helmet fell off. . . . Brown and his men stripped the upper portion of the body to confirm the fact it was a woman."

American soldiers preferred locals to first taste any food and wine they offered to ensure it was safe. Janine Chambrin in Vierville remembered, "The Americans did not know Calvados [a strong apple brandy] and swallowed their glasses like it was wine and they almost choked!" Americans padded silently through the village on leather soles, unlike the clatter of steel-capped German jackboots. They were strange. "Yeah" sounded suspiciously like the German *Ja*. *Le débarquement* was not always the signal for a spontaneous display of elation for the long-awaited Liberation. The civilian dilemma was whether it was actual, or would it be contested with an awful toll in devastated property and lives? Suzanne

Hardelay remembered an American officer later shooting down into their Vierville basement shelter.

> "My mother came up like a madwoman and asked him, 'Had they come to deliver us or kill us!' The officer could speak French and explained to my mother that every time they were passing by, they had some soldiers killed or wounded."

Madame Hardelay showed him where the Germans were hiding, and three Germans emerging from the Ruisseau basement nearby were shot.

Civilians in Verville were caught up in the fighting. The enormous fleet lying offshore convinced them this was the Liberation, but it was to come at considerable cost. When a shell exploded in fourteen-year-old Simone Jeanne's garden, "I began to lose it," she remembered. "That's not possible any more, we can't stay here any longer, we are going to get killed." The family emerged upstairs one after the other: the grandparents, her mother, sister, and then herself, which completely startled the American soldier shooting from their window. "The poor guy dropped his arms when he saw there were some civilians," Simone recalled. The family went outside to occupy a shelter trench.

> "He yelled at me, but we did not care because we could not understand a thing. He wanted us to go further away, there was shooting everywhere."

When they got out they saw the Ygouf family farm was on fire.[18]

Lieutenant Colonel Schneider's group of four hundred Rangers reached the crest of the bluffs to the left of Brigadier General Cota's 116th Regiment party. The enemy was not contesting the advance on Vierville to their right. Schneider's larger group, milling about in confusion, needed to be reorganized. Runners were dispatched and officers summoned for hasty orders. Schneider was focused on his primary mission to relieve Colonel Rudder's force four miles to the west, isolated at Pointe du Hoc. Vierville could be an obstacle to a speedy advance, so the Ranger force moved inland to bypass the village to the south. They were immediately confronted by elements from the III Battalion 726 Regiment and the 7th Company of the 916 Regiment local reserve, as well as reinforcements from the 352 Division Pioneer Company, all seeking to reach Vierville and the coast. Two hours of fruitless hedgerow skirmishing followed, before Schneider recognized the best option was to wheel right and push through Vierville in order to pick up the coastal road leading west.

Ahead of him, Lieutenant Bedell's C Company had become bogged down on the western outskirts of Vierville, having advanced beyond the key coastal road junction leading down to the beach. Terrain west of the village changed from open fields to hedgerow bocage. Every time a German machine gun opened up and was attacked from the flank, another hidden gun would pin down the movement. The C Company men found it difficult to pick out the enemy positions by muzzle blast or smoke, because the Germans were using smokeless powder. The 726 Regiment blocked any further westward movement, while another battalion from Regiment 914 was being brought up to eliminate the Ranger enclave at Pointe du Hoc.

German defenders on the beach had no idea the Americans were behind them. The deftly sited 88mm gun at WN 71 continued to bark out defiance. No landings of any substance had broken the stalemate in front of the Vierville draw and the stark wreckage of vehicles and landing craft seemed to signify an American defeat. Red tracer-backed 88mm shells spat out intermittently from the well-concealed bunker on the promenade, grazing the waterline with a flat trajectory. The burning hulks of LCI-91 and 92 obscured much of its killing area, from where many craft had been redirected to the center of Omaha opposite the

Saint-Laurent draw. Very little is known about the gun commander and crew of this intrepid strongpoint, which wreaked so much havoc on the western half of the beach. Neither is it clear who destroyed it at about midday or early afternoon. Sergeant Robert Slaughter with the 116th Regiment claims to have been part of a .30 caliber machine gun group that engaged the aperture. "I watched," he recalled, "as a string of fiery tracers ricocheted around the opening of the gun emplacement." The German crew fought it to destruction. There are 75mm tank shell and machine gun bullet scars on the metal gun shield inside, still visible today. The killing shot seems to be marked by the huge gouge on the right side of the concrete wall inside, probably a five-inch shell from the USS *McCook*, which went through the embrasure. Her log records that at 12:17 P.M. she, "destroyed six houses, (one three-story) and stone wall housing snipers and beach guns." This might be the false porch façade of the prewar Hotel Legallois, on whose site the bunker was located. The damage strongly suggests the trajectory of an incoming naval shell angled from offshore.[19]

Unteroffizier Henrik Naube, manning his cliff top trench at WN 73, being fought through by Goranson's C Company 2nd Rangers, "saw flashes and gunfire for the first time on top of the cliffs on the other side of the ravine that we were close to." This was the first intimation something was amiss, suggesting the Americans had somehow scaled the cliff position. He was even more fearful when he saw, "long, very bright orange spurts of flame visible through the smoke," with a strong smell of gasoline. "I had a terror of flamethrowers," he admitted, against which there was no defense. They were priority targets and he had already machine-gunned one American below carrying the distinctive fuel canister strapped to his back:

> "There was a very large explosion, and he disappeared com-
> pletely in a fireball which went up into the air in a mushroom

cloud. Both sides stopped firing for a moment, perhaps because we all saw what happened to this soldier."

The strongpoint opposite the draw at WN 71 was crumbling. Grenadier Karl Wegner at beach level was confused and despondent; the death of Lang their section commander, cut in half by a machine gun burst, produced a "very grim" mood. The situation was unclear. "We could see smoke belching from some of our strongpoints, while others had fallen silent," he recalled. "The field telephone was cut off and we were three scared kids in a bunker," feeling "quite alone." Ammunition was desperately short, "we kept up our fire at the Amis on the beach, but only to keep them away from us," he remembered. Wegner was now the senior officer with Lang's death, and found the responsibility in a collapsing situation overwhelming. When he called for another ammunition belt, only fifty instead of the regulation two hundred was slapped onto the feed tray. There was no more. He looked at his companions in disbelief, standing amid a pile of empty ammunition cans, belts, and spent cartridges; they had got through some 15,000 rounds.

It was time to depart, so they cannibalized all the rifle rounds left in their pouches to assemble a 68-round belt. Wegner resolved, "to use the firepower of their MG 42 to get us out of here." They were uneasy about the implications of the *Führerbefehl* on their proposed withdrawal. The dead Lang, a Russian veteran, had regaled them with stories about getting shot by the *Kettenhund* [military police], for doing the same. (The word kettenhund means *chain dog*, and refers to the metal insignia German Military Police wore around the neck.) They hoped this was not true. Tossing their last two grenades either side of the bunker entrance, they burst out the door and ran for it, with the machine gun and five rounds apiece in their two rifles.

Naube across the Vierville draw in WN 73 saw a nightmarish image of hand-to-hand fighting among the cliffs directly opposite. He was unable to fire his gun into the melée to support his friends, because both sides were so mixed up together:

> "The ferocity of the fighting astonished me. Men were lunging at each other with fixed bayonets, and with their rifle stocks, and even with entrenching tools or shovels. The Americans were charging upon our German gunners in the barbed wire entanglements up there. Some men were in flames, and other men were shooting or stabbing them as they staggered on fire."

Naube "accepted that I was going to die," after the misery they had inflicted on the beach. "I knew that we had enraged the attackers by killing so many of their comrades." A tank shell hit the parapet next to his firing slit, which struck his helmet and shoulder, blowing the machine gun out of his hands. The loader fell dead beside him, a piece of shrapnel the size of a knife protruding from his body. "What chance was there of the Americans showing us any mercy now?" he felt, stunned and cowering at the foot of his trench. A series of multiple crackling detonations went off all around him. "I recall that many pieces of concrete were tumbling around, and some of these fell on top of me," and he passed out.[20]

C Company of the 116th was unable to break through the German defensive block west of Vierville and had to dig in. More and more 29th Division men were now making their way up from the beach, where they had been pinned all morning. "Later that afternoon, we still hadn't gotten further than the top of the hill," Sergeant Robert Slaughter with D Company remembered. "A few German bicycle troops appeared, riding down the road parallel to the beach as if on a Sunday outing." Piecemeal German reinforcements were constantly arriving. "We surely ruined their picnic," Slaughter recalled, "with a few rounds of well placed rifle fire that separated many of them from their vehicles. . . . After that, we began to think about defending against the expected counterattack that we were told would take place in less than twenty-four hours." Men slipped back to the beach to bring up more automatic weapons, ammunition, and supplies to bolster their position, which was beginning to look very tenuous.[21]

The Regimental commander, Colonel Charles Canham, with his arm in a sling, was gathering and organizing men for the defense of Vierville, waving a pistol in his left hand. By the time the 5th Rangers had disengaged themselves from their abortive attempt to go around Vierville, they found the German defenses too strong to push west, out of the village. The testy Canham appropriated Schneider's Rangers, and despite their indignant protests, pressed them into digging a defensive blocking position around the west side of Vierville. Rudder's command was expendable, the need to maintain the 116th Regiment beachhead at Omaha greater. They needed time to recover and reconstitute.

Brigadier General Cota was meanwhile starting to walk down to the Vierville draw entrance with a small command group. He sought to energize the movement of tanks and vehicles from the beach and move inland, to bolster the C Company and Ranger screen around Vierville. Ferocious naval gunfire detonating around the entrance to the draw suggested the beach defenses ahead were still being contested.

The 28,000-ton behemoth the USS *Texas*, a prewar Dreadnought battleship, slipped in to within three thousand yards of the Vierville draw. At 12:23 P.M. she opened up at point-blank range with her fourteen-inch guns firing on flat trajectory. Each shell weighed 1,125 lbs, standing as tall as a man, and could blow a tennis court–sized crater. The red flash, spume of spray from the broadside blast wave, and rolling smoke turned all heads her way. "The concussion from the bursts of these guns had seemed to make the pavement of the street in Vierville actually raise beneath our feet in a bucking sensation," remembered Cota's aide, Lieutenant Jack Shea, "and had knocked several of the regimental group off their feet." Cota's command group paused just beyond the crossroads above the beach exit. "That firing probably made them duck back into their holes," Cota surmised.

Fearful though it appeared to American observers, this was the point at which many Germans sheltering in the remaining bunkers around the draw began to give up. About thirty or more Germans emerged stunned from emplacements at the end of the draw, and several dozen stumbled out from caves lining the cliff draw road. Cota's group walked on down to the anti-tank wall, blocking the gap, and edged through the small man-sized passageway to emerge onto the beach promenade. Shea and Cota had come virtually full circle to the place where they had landed five hours before. Shea recalled:

> "Bodies of riflemen, obviously of the 116th Infantry by the insignia they wore, were spread along the base of the concrete, inclined seawall. The first body lay about forty yards east of the exit, and in any 100-yard sector from there down to Dog White beach, there could be thirty-five to fifty bodies."[22]

The next step would be to demolish the concrete wall blocking the draw.

Vierville, the first village to fall on Omaha Beach, was liberated at 1:00 P.M. General Kraiss reported to General Marcks at 84 Corps Headquarters that with the exception of Colleville-sur-Mer, "the 352nd coastal defense sector is firmly in the hands of our coast defense forces." The precisely composed German reports reaching Kraiss were not reflecting the seriousness of their situation on the beach. General Bradley recalled that thirty minutes later, "V Corps relieved our fears with the terse message":

"Troops formerly pinned down on beaches Easy Red, Easy Green, Fox Red advancing up heights behind beaches."

Both opposing generals had claimed incongruously to have mastered the crisis at Omaha Beach at the same time.[23]

Saint-Laurent Center
11:30 A.M. to Dusk

Retaining Colleville was vitally important for General Kraiss, because it represented the nearest vulnerable point to the major breakthrough that had occurred to his east. British armored units were streaming inland toward Bayeux from Gold Beach. Although Kraiss was complacent about holding the Omaha sector, his subordinate regimental commander, Oberst-leutnant Ernst Goth, responsible for its tactical forward defense, was having misgivings about the situation at Saint-Laurent-sur-Mer. The Americans controlled two of the three roads that led inland from Omaha Beach. The third, with its junction at Saint-Laurent, connected to his headquarters at Formigny. It was the only way out for any withdrawing German forces and the only road in for reinforcements and resupply. If it was lost, any remaining men manning the beach defenses would be trapped.

The village, located three quarters of a mile inland, was of typical strong Norman stone construction, with hedged orchards, pastures, and barns. Goth had been feeding in reinforcements to the infantry platoons of the 8th and 10th companies of Regiment 726 all day with engineers from Landesbau Pioneer Battalion 17, a construction unit. Goth's local reserve, the 5th and 7th Companies from 916 Regiment, had been badly mauled during piecemeal counterattacks that had started at 11:00 A.M. Lieutenant Hans Heinz, who had taken over the remnants of this force, just two platoons strong, put in a counterattack on the east side of Saint-Laurent at 2:00 P.M.

"Now began the jump from hedge to hedge," he recalled. The attack struck disoriented groups of American soldiers, who had been pushing inland from the bluffs. "On the way a number of exhausted GIs fell into our hands," Heinz recalled, "all the fight gone out of them." His attack made slow progress through ditches filled with rainwater, "and with a lot of bellowing and a few hand grenades we jumped a few hundred meters further onto the coastal plateau." This brought them to the site of the present-day Normandy American Cemetery and Memorial. "The terrified enemy rushed back toward the bluffs in great numbers and then down below." However, it was not long before, "we came under heavy fire," because "the enemy had better communications than we did." Naval gunfire descended and Heinz ordered the withdrawal through the same water-filled ditches they had used to advance.

Kurt Keller remembered, "at about 2:00 P.M. a huge explosion sounded out above the noise of battle along the four-mile-wide bay." The Americans had blown the huge anti-tank wall that blocked the Saint-Laurent draw at Les Moulins. "Soon after the explosion the situation changed," he remembered. "The Americans pressed up the shallow valley and reached the road that led inland." The remnants of his Fusilier Company could still hear German machine gun and rifle fire to their front, but it was growing weaker. "Then small groups of GIs began to climb over the sloping edge of the bluffs":

> "We few surviving soldiers fixed bayonets and ran against the Americans with loud cries. During our training we were told that screaming at the enemy would instill fear—so I shrieked like a wild animal. Then in the middle of this awful carnage someone called out, 'Back to the coast road!'"

Only about four dozen men got back.[24]

The surge of infantry ordered in by Brigadier General Wyman led to a considerable intermingling of units on top of the bluffs opposite Saint-Laurent. Units from the 29th Division's 115th Regiment heading southwest to the village crossed the paths of 1st Division 18th Regiment units moving southeast toward Colleville. "I was with the 1st Division in all the confusion," remembered Corporal Herbert Krieger with C Company of the 115th. "At about that time we were all separated and were in complete chaos." An officer told them:

> "Make sure you step in the same footsteps as the man in front of you, because of the mines. If you didn't you would end up like the people lying around you."

They were unprepared for the hedgerow terrain. "Don't do that," the soldier next to Krieger advised, when he exposed himself to fire over the hedge line. "Look at these dead guys around you." His companion simply poked his gun over the top and fired, without seeing the enemy, "stupid but safe." American infantry firepower at company level was inferior to that of the Germans, although numerically superior at 190 or so men compared to the enemy's 142. A German company carried fifteen MG 42s against two US machine guns. The American BAR light machine gun at section level was a good automatic but limited by a twenty-round magazine, whereas the fast-firing MG 42 was generally belt-fed with two hundred rounds. American progress was often, as a consequence, dependent upon artillery support; which had yet to arrive on the beach in numbers.

Inexperience stymied progress. Private Don van Roosen in the same unit remembered that, "progress slowed while a few people tried to deal with the local situation":

> "It was to happen many times in the future as we learned to fight. We had all the firepower but were slow to use it. The

trial-and-error learning began at once. We were very conscious of being alone."

All the tanks were on the beach; they had no artillery and only poor communications with the naval guns, "so we had to cope by ourselves." During a pause van Roosen looked back at the breathtaking scene at the beaches. "I had never seen so many ships," he recalled, I began estimating and stopped at a thousand, as a guess." All that latent power, still not being used.

The 2nd Battalion of the 115th disentangled itself from the confusion and managed to bypass the German resistance nests fighting in the D-3 Les Moulins draw, screened by the 1st Battalion penetrating farther south covering their left flank. They turned and penetrated into the eastern edge of Saint-Laurent village. *Achtung Minen!* signs bedeviled progress, as did sudden local German counterattacks. Van Roosen remembered:

> "We went through densely shaded paths and passed small groups of 1st Division men headed in the other direction, toward their own objectives."

Behind and to the right, the 3rd Battalion 116th Regiment began to assault the high ground at strongpoint WN 67, which housed the notorious "Moaning Minnie" German Nebelwerfer rocket battery. It was hit by concentrated machine gun fire and straddled by naval artillery until "all of a sudden there was a terrific explosion and a big ball of fire," recalled Lieutenant Robert Garcia with the 116th. They had hit the ammunition or rocket propellant dump.[25]

The frontal attack mounted against Saint-Laurent was not what the 2nd Battalion 115th had anticipated. As a reserve unit, their D-Day task had been to "mop up" and be prepared to repulse the inevitable German counterattack when it came, not house-to-house fighting. E and

F Companies cautiously advanced astride the main village street, six or seven houses leading up to a squat Romanesque church surrounded by a solid stone wall with an ornate wrought iron fence. The village pattern was a cluster of six or seven hamlets with connecting dirt roads. Less like Colleville and Vierville, it was an in-depth strongpoint forming part of the beach defense. It was positioned three-quarters of a mile from the central part of the Omaha's defense sector, the weakest point, because many of the bunkers were still under construction. Tunneled emplacements linked defended localities within the village to bunkers overlooking the beach.

Private William Wilch with E Company of the 115th scouted ahead of the main advance. "Some French civilians showed us where the Krauts were," he remembered. They held the church and a big stone barn on the line of approach. "The Krauts had machine guns in the steeple, and they sprayed everything that moved." Locating the Germans was difficult, especially for combat-green troops. Snipers fired from one spot and then scrambled through tunnels to emerge a hundred yards away. "We had a long firefight with the people in the steeple, Wilch remembered, "but they were killing us."[26]

Norman civilians were again caught up the intense fighting. Madame Poree Renée recalled the initial mistrust and surprise by the first American soldiers to enter the village. "They thought there were no civilians, so those who remained in the Commune were spies!" Her husband and mother were taken hostage by them, she claimed, and the Americans, "wanted to shoot them." The official history of the 115th acknowledged that, "fighting during the first few hours was rough, with few of the rules of warfare observed. . . . German snipers targeted red-cross medic armbands while few prisoners taken by our troops reached the collecting cages." The civilians in Madame Andree Oxeant's shelter panicked when a German soldier entered. "The men with us wanted to throw him in a well," in the courtyard. Retribution would inevitably follow if the

Germans came back, and "the German soldier was shaking because he was so upset. . . . He was just a kid," Oxeant saw. They "managed to explain he should go and hide somewhere else." Three other Germans were fighting from a ditch nearby.

Thirty-three-year-old Mathilde Andre married to a Saint-Laurent farmer remembered, "the Germans closed the curtains so that we could not see the light." Building entrances were blocked, windows opened, and rooms darkened as part of the German defensive measures. Fire was then aimed outside from inside darkened interiors. Tiles were removed from roofs to create sniper firing ports and machine guns positioned in basements to produce ground-level grazing fire, which increased the hit rate from ricocheting rounds. The Andre family was confined to a room alone. "All of a sudden," during the fighting, "we heard them climb the stairs, and we counted them." Six German soldiers occupied the house, but "there are only five! So where is the other?" The Americans had got him, "and killed the other Germans who were with us." Private William Wilch remembered, "we killed almost every Kraut that was in there."[27]

Naval gunfire deluged the village, becoming as difficult to dodge as German snipers. The USS *Thompson* brought down the church steeple. Tanks eventually made their way up from the beach and entered the village. Two 105mm M-7 "Priest" self-propelled howitzers were led in to provide close fire support, and "they fired direct shots at the enemy-occupied houses from a couple of hundred yards away," their battery commander Lieutenant Colonel John Cooper recalled. "The Germans began flying out of the windows right and left. . . . We ended up capturing the buildings due to this devastating direct fire."[28]

The 115th Infantry Regiment suffered more than one hundred casualties on D-Day, the vast majority during the fight for Saint-Laurent. Half the officers with the two first companies that entered the village, E and F, were wounded. By nightfall the Germans had been encircled and reduced to a few buildings covering the junction to the west of the village, the road leading to Formigny, the last remaining retreat artery. The Germans clung on tenaciously to these last houses. Darkness came with the realization that no substantial German reinforcement would be able to break through the coastal villages to reach the beach. General Bradley had a tenuous bridgehead of sorts, but American engineers desperately needed to open all five draws, if they were going to get sufficient heavy vehicles off the beach to resume the advance at daybreak.

TEN

TENUOUS FOOTHOLD

4:00 P.M. TO MIDNIGHT

Kampfgruppe Meyer

4:00 P.M. to 11:55 P.M.

General Kraiss was optimistic enough at 1:00 P.M. to send a message to General Marcks at 84 Corps Headquarters that he had the situation in hand along his coastal sector. His primary reserve, Oberstleutnant Meyer's force of a thousand or more truck- and bicycle-borne infantry with ten *Sturmgeschütz III* self-propelled assault guns would very soon hit the enemy penetration streaming out of Gold Beach on his right flank. He had already committed fourteen Marder 75mm assault guns to support the II Battalion 916 Regiment's counterattack at Omaha.

The situation was tight, but containable. He had not, however, heard any reports from Meyer since early morning, which was disturbing. The sun had begun to burn off the low clouds around the coast at midday and swarms of Jabo enemy fighter-bombers had risen like vengeful insects. Oberstleutnant Fritz Ziegelmann reacted to the concern by sending a liaison officer along Meyer's route to find out what was happening.

Every time a truck or vehicle was hit on the roads the smoke provided a beacon for even more strafing runs by the allied air forces. Second Lieutenant Quentin Aanenson, flying a P-47 Thunderbolt on successive sorties since first light, was looking for vehicle columns just like Meyer's. "We caught a group of Germans in an open area where there were no trees, and so there was no place to hide," he recalled:

> "And we caught them before they could really get off the roads and run toward the ditches. And I remember the impact it had on me when I could see my bullets just tearing into them. We had so much firepower that the bodies would fly some yards."

Fighters hunted the Germans off the roads. Aanenson's .50 machine guns could dismember a human body in much the same way it demolished thin-skinned trucks. Armored vehicles often had their optics damaged or worse. Aanenson could also carry up to two thousand pounds of bombs beneath his wings. "As I was doing this I was doing it knowing I had to do it," the pilot admitted, and "I got sick." After landing, "I had to think about what I had done," but his resolve was unaltered. The next day, "I went out and did it again. And again and again and again."[1] Ziegelmann's liaison officer reported back at 3:30 P.M. that:

> "Ceaseless fighter-bomber attacks meant the *Kampfgruppe* Meyer could only move forward slowly through streets and along roads, and had losses in men and matériel."

Even so Ziegelmann was encouraged that, "an attack starting at 16:00 was considered achievable." Meyer's mixed force of truck- and bicycle-borne infantry had taken about eight hours to cover twenty miles, which amounted to walking pace. Little is known about Meyer's route or casualties. His columns had to be broken down into smaller packets and move dispersed in rushes, accelerating from cover to cover to avoid detection. They then had to rendezvous at nominated checkpoints to reorganize. Surveys of similar German formations seeking to move forward to the coast forty-eight hours after D-Day reveal losses averaging about 10% of vehicles to air attacks. Most were soft-skinned trucks but also included armored vehicles with scores of men killed and wounded. Meyer may well have lost a hundred casualties and half as many vehicles.[2]

Evidence from surviving radio and telephone traffic suggests that when Meyer arrived at his concentration area between Bazenville and Villiers-le-Sec, seven miles east of Bayeux, the unit needed time to reorganize. He did not reestablish radio communications with 352 Division until 4:50 P.M., and had only just linked with the 1st Battalion 916 Regiment to his left. His carefully husbanded assault guns had barely rolled up and were immediately gathered to join an attack he had promised for 5:00 o'clock. Two minutes after the proposed H-hour for Meyer's counterattack, Ziegelmann received an intelligence radio intercept from division headquarters. This assessed, "enemy forces in the Meuvaines area," Meyer's proposed objective, "have to be estimated as one full division." He would stand little chance against such odds, but contact was lost with Meyer again. The ensuing radio silence would last another ninety minutes.

At this time Meyer's infantry were disembarking from trucks and dropping bicycles as they shook out into attack formation. The men had to be quickly briefed on the situation and attack objectives confirmed, as well as to confer with the freshly arrived self-propelled guns. This was a vulnerable moment, the 1st 915 infantry were moving to occupy their jump-off positions left and 352 Fusilier Battalion right, constantly harassed and delayed by air attacks. Virtually as soon as Meyer took off his radio head set, having spoken with division headquarters, two British infantry battalions burst into Villiers-le-Sec amid a storm of gunfire and occupied the hill to its south. Chaos ensued on the German start line.

The Fusilier battalion was overwhelmed and Company 1352's self-propelled guns were not ready to deal with the sudden appearance of Shermans from C and D Squadrons of the British 4/7th Dragoon Guards. The sudden British envelopment outnumbered them by three to one, and a frantic running battle developed to the south, all the way to Saint-Gabriel. The Sturmgeschütze desperately sought to hold the surge and knocked out two Shermans and damaged two others, but lost four of their own as they were bypassed. The 1st Battalion 915 was badly mauled as elements from three British battalions attacked through their area. Meyer's Kampfgruppe was wrong-footed along its hastily set up start line by the unexpected appearance of two brigades, the 69th and 151st, which drove into them just as they were about to attack. They belonged to the British 50th Northumbrian Division, bearing down on Bayeux, its first day D-Day objective.

Since Kraiss's last optimistic signal to Corps HQ at 1:00 P.M., events were giving cause for concern. The fourteen Marders from the 1st *Panzerjäger* Company supporting the 916 Regiment's counterattacks between Vierville and St. Laurent were demolished by naval gunfire, five to six being knocked out south of Vierville alone. The vulnerable crews were simply swept off the open gun decks of the self propelled guns by a storm of shrapnel from air and ground bursts. The surviving 352 Division telephone log reports following Meyer's 5:00 P.M. H-hour went from bad to worse. The first suggested his two battalions would actually confront a division and likely be swallowed up. Eight minutes later it was reported Saint-Laurent had fallen into enemy hands. Fifteen minutes after that Corps advised Kraiss that a breakout was occurring at

Utah Beach to his left. Then at 6:10 P.M. he heard that the II battalion 915 Regiment counterattack into Colleville was surrounded and that, "the wounded cannot be brought back any longer."[3]

At 6:30 contact was at last reestablished with the Kampfgruppe Meyer. Another disaster appeared to be unfolding, there was no word from his 1st Battalion 915 near Bazenville and the Fusilier Battalion had fallen back three and a half miles to Saint-Gabriel. The situation was unclear. Meyer, it seemed, "was presumably wounded and taken prisoner," according to his headquarter survivors. Ziegelmann learned later they had been overrun by a major enemy spoiling attack on the start line, and hit by naval gunfire and air attacks even as the battalions formed up. Meyer tried to disengage by using the "rolling pocket" stratagem, often used in extremis in Russia. The east side of the pocket was tenaciously defended while the west side pressed home attacks to break out. Meyer's headquarters was overrun and he was killed together with the Fusilier Battalion commander and the *Panzerjäger* company commander. This meant Kraiss had lost three division senior commanders and his primary reserve force all in the space of ninety minutes with no result.

At 8:40 P.M. the surviving assault guns and the remnants of the Fusilier battalion were reported moving west, and two hours later they were pushed out of Saint-Gabriel by the 5th East Yorkshire battalion. There was no reserve now left to contest an American consolidation of their Omaha beachhead. The 56th Brigade from the British Northumbrian Division got to within one mile of Bayeux after dark, while the 151st Brigade had gone through Meyer's force to cut the Caen-Bayeux road. The division's 69th Brigade advanced eight miles inland and linked up with the Canadians coming ashore at Juno Beach. At five minutes to midnight Meyer's Fusilier battalion announced it had escaped the pocket with six assault guns and forty men with a further fifty men from the 1st Battalion 915. Kraiss had inflicted catastrophic losses on the early waves at Omaha, but in so doing had fought his division to a standstill. 352 Division could not afford to hemorrhage even more forces attacking the beaches, it must go over to defense and seek to stabilize a line inland.

Major Stanley Bach, the 1st Division liaison officer attached to the 29th Division remembered how heavy artillery and mortar fire descended intermittently on Omaha Beach all afternoon. At 3:20 P.M. a direct hit on a gasolene truck exploded another nearby, the fireball enveloping one hundred square yards of beach in a nightmare slurry of flame. Soldiers frantically rolled men in the sand to extinguish the fire from their clothes. Those rendered immobile by shrapnel wounds burned to death. Bach climbed the bluffs forty minutes later bypassing horrific mine casualties en route, one man with, "no body from the waist down, just entrails and chest organs." When he reached a wood five hundred yards beyond, they found a man kneeling, who, "we think is praying or scared," he later recalled. They turned him over to discover, "he is dead—died on his knees praying." From late morning to early afternoon the situation on the beach was as Bach described:

> "Men being killed like flies from unseen gun positions: Navy can't hit 'em; Air cover can't see 'em; so infantry had to dig 'em out."[4]

According to Lieutenant John Carroll at the 1st Division Command Post, "some semblance of regimental control" did not occur "until around 4:00 to 5:00 P.M." The priority was to get the engineers to open the five draws leading off the beach by nightfall. A start had been made on the Saint-Laurent E-1 exit, but it was still going nowhere, because the Germans still held the vital junction in the village that was their escape route to Formigny. At about 3:00 P.M. a resounding crack sounded in the Vierville draw, when the 121st Engineer battalion of the 29th Division blew up the massive anti-tank wall blocking the valley entrance. "I was astonished by how completely the wall was destroyed," recalled their commander Lieutenant Colonel Robert Plager. "It turned out that the Germans had not reinforced the wall with steel rods—that was a fatal mistake." By midafternoon the Saint-Laurent draw road was opened, enabling men and some vehicles to come up the road, despite the western extremity of the village being held by Germans. Traffic moved through the sniper and preregistered mortar and artillery fire sporadically descending on the main road junctions. Another unlikely road was created from the narrow dirt tracks leading up from the Cabourg F-1 draw. At 4:30 P.M. the Colleville draw on the east side of the beach inland from WN 61 and 62 was finally secured, and thirty minutes later tanks were moving through the Saint-Laurent draw in the center. The Vierville road was cleared of rubble and operating by 6:00 P.M. and thirteen lanes cleared through the tidal obstacle belt. Two hours later the D-3 Les Moulins draw was open and the Colleville draw finally drivable one hour after midnight.[5]

At dusk only one hundred tons of the planned 2,400 tons of stores and supplies had been landed on Omaha Beach. Much of this had been damaged or destroyed by German artillery. The beachhead was only about 1.4 miles deep at the farthest penetration, a tenuous foothold, and by far the smallest of the five landing beaches achieved on D-Day. Technical Sergeant Felix Branham who landed with K Company the 116th, recalled retracing steps to the beach. "It was shocking to see how many men were washing in the surf and many of them K Company," he remembered. These were men who had served with him in the territorial National Guard:

> "Men I grew up with, caddied with, double-dated together, puffed off the same cigarette, drank out of the same bottle, lying there dead. Stark faces with eyes and mouths open, stone cold dead. It went through my mind that we were brothers, always would be. They died so we might live."[6]

Pointe du Hoc. The Angle.
Midday to Midnight

Sergeant Raymond Crouch and Private Leonard "Sam" Goodgal were involuntary 101st Airborne Division attachments fighting with Rudder's beleaguered Rangers at Pointe du Hoc. They had not slept for thirty-six hours or eaten for twenty-four. Fitful sleep during the night of June 4, after the temporary postponement of the invasion, was followed by the physical and psychological trauma of jumping from a burning Dakota aircraft, being shot at from the ground, and splashing into the sea next to the cliffs off Pointe du Hoc. They reached the beach only to dodge and endure air and naval near misses as they picked their way along the treacherous shale at the foot of the cliffs. They had no equipment and one weapon between them, and were caught up in the early morning Ranger assault on the German battery above the cliffs. The Rangers themselves climbed light, with only personal weapons and two grenades per man. They had just one chocolate D-Ration bar each, after having sprayed the contents of their stomachs into the landing craft bilges during the wave-tossed approach. Only fear and adrenaline kept hunger pangs at bay.

Fighting at Pointe du Hoc developed into two main groups. Lieutenant Colonel Rudder's headquarters group was established in and around a shell crater carved out by fire east of the headland, at the edge of the cliff, in the midst of the battery position. Another second group, with over one hundred Rangers, was defending an *L*-shaped perimeter on the other side of the Vierville to Grandcamp road, which they blocked. The loose line had the remnants from D Company securing the vertical section of the *L*, facing west, and E and F Rangers holding the horizontal line facing south.

Goodgal and Crouch were incorporated into the headquarters command group and fought all day. During the morning a hasty German counterattack came out of the village of Saint-Pierre-du-Mont, which was broken up by intense rifle fire. By midday a "lull" developed, but Rudder's men continued to be shot at from across the flat fields stretching to the village, and regularly harassed by sniper and artillery fire. They were also regularly engaged by the 20mm cannon from the surviving German flak outpost to the west, a rallying point for the Germans. Rudder was shot in the thigh at about 10:00 A.M. Four destroyers rotating on station offshore prevented any substantial German counterattacks forming up and blew away the troublesome machine gun to the east, which had caused considerable grief during and after the landing. A section of the cliff face was dropped into the sea, and with it, the gun.

Morning and afternoon fighting cost the perimeter group ten killed, twenty-four seriously wounded, and ten missing, so that by late afternoon it was down to about sixty-five men. Pressure on the beleaguered force increased. Goodgal and Crouch were frequently called upon to foray out from the headquarters to pry out snipers, who frequently resurfaced from concealed tunnels and half buried bunker entrances. Some were captured. "The Germans knew how to surrender,: Goodgal remembered. "They'd take their helmets off, unbutton their coats, throw away their rifles, and shout 'Kamerad, Kamerad!'" Surrender was a vulnerable moment. "I never took a prisoner who had a helmet on," Goodgal admitted. There was still a group of surviving Germans cut off and besieged inside the observation bunker at the head of the Pointe. They were hermetically sealed behind its massive internal armored doors, preventing the Rangers from getting at them.[7]

The Germans were scratch-building a counterattack force to smother the Ranger enclave, which had become a distraction to concentrating decisive force against the right flank of the 116th Regiment, exposed and pinned down at the Vierville draw. The Rangers blocked the German reinforcement road from Grandcamp. The nearest German unit was a thirty-five-strong platoon from the 9th Company 726 Regiment, which was the company reserve in the neighboring village of Saint-Pierre-du-Mont. But 726 Regiment was too thinly stretched to effectively respond, because its 3rd Battalion was spread from Omaha to the Vire estuary bordering Utah Beach. Goth's 916 Regiment was completely committed defending Omaha Beach, so 352 Division rationalized the situation by adjusting regimental boundaries. Oberstleutnant Ernst Heyna's 914 Regiment took over the Grandcamp and Pointe du Hoc sectors, previously held by Goth's 916 men. This retracing of lines on maps provided a neat war game staff solution, but posed practical difficulties for the troops on the ground. Heyna's 914 Regiment had been skirmishing with landed American paratroopers around Isigny and Carentan all night. He also had the unfolding Utah breakout crisis hovering over his western shoulder to contend with. Now he was required to dispatch two companies of infantry from the 1st Battalion 914 headquartered at Osmanville to the fight, six miles away from Pointe du Hoc. With some difficulty the 3rd and 4th companies were pulled out of the line facing the American paratroopers. They became vulnerable to air attack as soon as they started moving. The first units able to reach the Ranger enclave were the 12th Company from 726 Regiment and Heyna's 3rd Company, withdrawn from Isigny. They began to form up for an attack at about 4:00 P.M.

A measure of the confusion affecting German troop movements around Pointe du Hoc is reflected by Werfer Regiment 84's decision to withdraw its machine gunners. They had seriously impeded the Ranger cliff climb and on the plateau. Possibly affected by the adjustment of the regimental boundaries or the apparent lull in fighting, they independently opted to pull out. Wilhelm Kirchhoff recalled his *Oberwachtmeister* radioing his artillery headquarters that there was no threatening activity where they were, on the east side of the plateau. "Not a single American had appeared," he recalled, "if I had only seen a head show itself over the cliff edge, I would have shot at him." Their five *Kubelwagen* VW jeeps were called forward and they drove off at 2:00 P.M.

"Because of the Jabos," Kirchhoff remembered, "we stuck to the tracks and covered roads, not the coast road." It took two nights traveling to rejoin their unit in Caen, lying up in farm houses and barns en route.

Grenadier Karl Wegner and his two surviving crew, Willi and Helmut, managed to evade the Americans in Vierville after escaping their bunker at WN 71. "We didn't know then that the Amis were already in the village," but they managed to move southwest by keeping to the ditches. Clusters of dead Germans sprawled across the road made "it look as though a Jabo had caught them in the open." Eventually they encountered a feldwebel who directed them to a command post nearby. Assembling remnants forming up exuded failure, he remembered, "some were wounded" and "all were dirty and tired." "Be wary of the Kettenhunde," (military police), the feldwebel warned, "because they might accuse you of cowardice and desertion." Wegner spoke up defending his group, and despite the sergeant assuring him, "that I did do the right thing," he was reminded, "they might not see it that way." He was told, "to keep my mouth shut and he would do all the talking." A petulant officer closely questioned Wegner and wanted to know what he was doing here, because his parent unit was farther west. It was explained that elements of 914 Regiment were attached to Goth's 916 Regiment to beef up the coastal defenses on the eve of the landings. Wegner and his two companions made up a complete machine gun group, so they were sent to the 4th Company as replacements at Saint-Pierre-du-Mont, where the unit was already in action against the Rangers.

Wegner remembered being handed over five hundred rounds of wood-tipped blanks with a mix of one thousand live and tracer. He protested to the feldwebel and was told, "now listen up! The Amis are not like the Ivans because they value lives." Save the live rounds for when he needed to retreat, he was advised, "and fire a belt or two of this stuff [blanks] at them, because they will always take cover and give you time to get away." American soldiers generally assumed the wooden rounds were meant to poison, as they could be painful and caused infections when fired at short range. Wegner came away suspecting, "I had just learned a valuable lesson."

Units were constantly supplemented by such ad hoc replacements and immediately fed into the line. Wegner and his gun group had escaped their bunker forward on Omaha Beach only to be sent three miles west to join the German perimeter intent on reducing the isolated Ranger pocket at Pointe du Hoc. On arrival they found the fierce and aggressive Ranger defense had already unnerved the attackers. "They were far better soldiers than us," Wegner admitted:

> "We couldn't make any headway against them and they were too few in number to make a big attack against us. If they did it would be bad for us. For now it was just another game of waiting to see who moved first."

It was the Germans. At 4:00 P.M. a mix of platoons from the two reinforcement companies put in an attack that seemed to come from the German flak battery. They moved in from the west, heading straight for Rudder's headquarters group.[8]

Sergeant Elder who controlled the two sole 60mm mortars the Rangers had brought up the cliffs opened fire at very short range. He lobbed bombs from almost vertically sited tubes to accurately straddle the German line, which quickly went to earth amid the cratered landscape. His bombs were on target and thereafter Elder accurately walloped concentrations of German soldiers, who were thinned by BAR automatic fire as soon as they broke cover. Chased by this well-placed mortar fire, the Germans pulled back. Elder had extinguished the closest move the Germans ever made to reach the Pointe, with his steady deluge of 75 rounds.

Across the Grandcamp road, the advance group killed about fifty Germans and captured forty during the afternoon's skirmishing among the myriad of hedge lines around the *L*-shaped perimeter. General Kraiss became impatient, and at 7:35 P.M. he conferred directly with Goth at 916 Headquarters in Formigny. Ziegelmann was directed to order the 1st Battalion 914 Regiment "to clear up the situation at the Pointe du Hoc strongpoint with a counterattack." He knew the Rangers were contained, but they were a distraction to his rear, and he wanted them out, because the situation at Omaha suggested he would have to establish a new in-depth defense line that night.

Rudder meanwhile had lost over one third of his men. But as it grew dark a party of twenty-three men from A Company 5th Rangers emerged from the gloom. They had been led by Lieutenant Charles Parker, around Vierville and across the fields through the German line to the east of the perimeter. "We ran like hell, fighting and dodging battles through the fields," remembered James Gabaree, "until we heard that sweet sound of an English speaking voice that demanded the password." "Ace" Parker responded with "Tally-Ho!" and the perimeter was reinforced by over half a platoon, dispersed in pickets around the perimeter. More importantly, Parker's arrival signified that the 5th Rangers were on their way.[9]

The sun went down at 10:10 P.M. and twilight lasted thirty-five more minutes. When darkness descended the whole terrain perspective on the plateau at Pointe du Hoc was transformed, and with it the tactical situation. The *L*-shaped position, with its apex facing southwest with the Parker reinforcement, was manned by about eighty-five Rangers. Rudder's dilemma was whether he should pull his force back beyond the road to thicken up his loose defense of the Pointe. The arrival of the 5th Rangers was regarded as imminent, so it was decided to maintain the tactical block on the Grandcamp road. Darkness degraded previously good observation, despite the rise of a three-quarter moon. Until now the tri-company perimeter had operated on an informal basis, with D, E, and F Company men spontaneously adjusting the line according to the threat. This loose arrangement worked less well in the dark. Ammunition was low and boxes of captured German potato-masher grenades were distributed as a standby for the night defense. Many Americans were using German weapons they had picked up, having run out of ammunition or lost their own. D and E companies had three Schmeisser machine pistols [Tommy guns] each, and E was using three German MG 42s. This was a recipe for future confusion in the gloom. Previously good fields of fire to the south fell away in the poor visibility, further degraded by pitch-black shade beneath orchards and hedgerows.

The dark ground sloped downward to the south, and the first intimation to the Rangers that something was amiss was whistle blasts, shouting in German, and a deafening outbreak of flashing fire reports to the front and around them. "The enemy attacked with vengeance and enormous firepower," James Gabaree recalled, "at one point they were within fifty yards of us." All along the south-facing E Company front, the Rangers fired back. In places, the first they knew of the German attack were black shapes blundering through the undergrowth into their positions, which the Rangers shot at from point-blank range. "To our men in the foxholes it was practically hand-to-hand combat; we were in a survival mode," Gabaree recalled. Salva Maimone with E Company remembered, "we were shooting at their tracers." The Ranger outposts missed the stealthy German approach through the orchard. BARs were firing through whole twenty-round magazines at sustained fire rates. "Every time we'd shoot, they'd come back with more fire," explained Maimone. "They had lots of mortar shells going into the position where they thought we were; but we weren't there." Much of the mortar barrage was detonating behind the perimeter.

"When we attacked," recalled Grenadier Karl Wegner, "we learned that they were good fighters all around." The Ranger use of captured German weapons was disorienting in the dark, and the Germans constantly called out their personal names to establish positions. "Once we heard the familiar rattle of our MG 42s off to our right," Wegner recalled, "I thought one of our groups had broken through their lines." His section commander Kalb reined him back, "Wegner, the Amis are using MGs they captured from us, so keep your foolish head down." Chastened, Wegner realized, "he was right."

Within a few minutes an immense sheet of flame lit the sky to the west, the spot where the German 155mm guns had been disabled that morning. An ambient, slow ammunition burn probably ignited more propellant in the ammunition dump. The whole area was bathed in light, silhouetting many of the German attackers in the glare, immediately dampening down the intensity of the firefight. Shooting petered out, either the attack was simply a probe in strength or the effort was distracted by the enormous conflagration to the rear. Germans caught by the light in the open were shot down. Maimone remembered the fire dying down, the glare compromised night vision, "we started to slack and tried to feel our way—what a way to shoot," he recalled.[10]

The Rangers started to shift around in their positions in the darkness. Their loose command organization precluded an immediate counterattack, it was too dark and ammunition was low. Men walked past their fellows who did not call out from foxholes. Adjustments were made between some trenches, but nobody checked overall. There was confusion, two men had moved back to the command post saying they had been told to withdraw, but nobody gave the order. On the east flank of the perimeter, all had remained quiet.

Back at Rudder's headquarters Medic Frank South remembered, "they kept bringing in the wounded and they kept coming." One of his friends, Sergeant Thomas, was brought in from F Company, having been shot in the stomach. "It's okay, I can make it," he claimed, but "he started getting a bit woozy—we made him lie down," South recalled. "He started getting contractions and huge pains and he had peritonitis, so we filled him with as much morphine as we dared." They were cut off from any further medical assistance; all the anxious South could do was administer care. He felt totally helpless, "he died aboard ship—he was a friend," and "that happened time after time," he remembered. The medics had also to defend. "Then at one point there was supposed to be a breakthrough," South remembered, "and there were Germans, so I went into the line with a captured Schmeisser and then back into the bunker."[11]

The Germans pulled back, but the casualties among E Company holding the vital angle of the *L* had been weakened at the critical point. Rangers yearned for daybreak and better visibility. Communication between the dispersed Ranger lines was difficult. There was no reserve and they could hear intermittent activity in the low ground to the south, enveloped in blackness. Outposts beyond the angle were withdrawn to fill gaps in other parts of the line. No commanders were checking out the foxholes in the vulnerable angle to confirm the situation, it was desperate for everyone. Priority was given to pass around ammunition and get the wounded out. The Germans now knew the location of the main defensive line. They planned to hit the identified weak spot, the corner holding the perimeter together. H-hour was set to one hour past midnight.

Dusk to Darkness
5:00 P.M. to Beyond Midnight

Coast Guard photographer Seth Shepard and the survivors of LCI (L)-92 had dug into the beach near their smoldering, stranded landing craft and watched the chaos on the beach unfold. He noticed the wounded were uncomplaining. "They lay there still, waiting with haunted eyes," he recalled, "but not asking for help because they knew that every able soldier with a gun was needed forward in the lines." Shepard's companions scavenged the wreck to salvage canned self-heating pea soup and blankets. They were soaking wet and exposed to the cold

Channel wind. "I never realized a human being could vibrate as much as I did then," he remembered. They did not get off the beach until shortly before midnight when LCMs came in a quarter mile away to evacuate the wounded and stranded crews. "The full moon rising back of us gave a hideous light to the dead bodies lying along the beach road." As they made their way to the boats, "we saw bodies stacked up like a lumber pile down further." They stayed drifting offshore until their LST was filled with wounded before returning Saturday night to England. "I'll never forget those peaceful English hills and how good they looked to us after the French coast under fire." Back at the beach, forty-one dead American soldiers remained stuck inside the charred forward troop compartment.[12]

John Barnes's landing craft with A Company the 116th had swamped two thousand yards out from Vierville, during the H-hour run in to Omaha Beach. As they drifted in the freezing water they heard the sounds of continuous firing from the beach. By the time they were picked up men were succumbing to exposure. They were taken back to their point of disembarkation on the troopship the *Empire Javelin*, "the very same one we had left at 4:00 A.M. in the morning."

> "How long had it been? It seemed like just a few minutes. When I thought to ask, it was one in the afternoon. We had been gone nine hours, over four in the water."

As darkness fell, "the shock wore off. What could we do?" Looking around, "the ship seemed vacant," populated with departed ghosts. "We had no weapons, no equipment whatsoever, no helmets, nothing but wet clothing." They arrived at Plymouth the following day and "were told not to say where we had been nor what had happened." It was to take four days to rejoin their unit, but for the moment it was, "as if [we were] on a secret mission to a foreign land." News of the invasion was all over the English newspapers, but "we never spoke of anything military to the English people we encountered."[13]

The plan for the Omaha Beach landings had not gone well. Major General Huebner departed the USS *Ancon* at 5:15 P.M. to establish his headquarters on the beach. "It seemed that all the elements were in a great mixup," Lieutenant Colonel Robert Pratt with the staff of V Corps reflected:

> "We had selected one beach for a regiment [the 16th] of the 1st Division, and another for a regiment [the 116th] of the 29th Division, so that as they became reinforced, these would become divisional sectors."

Huebner was still in overall charge of the two regiments until the beachhead was secure. The assault, however, had not followed the neatly traced outline of the staff plan. Unexpected fierce German resistance at the two cliff shoulders either side of the beach and the drift caused by wind and tide had brought only partial success in the center around Saint-Laurent. An aggressive response by the 1st Division's 16th Regiment had at least knocked out sufficient long-range German guns at WN 61 and 62 to offer some respite in the center. Wind and tide coincidentally deposited many landing craft in the center, opposite the unfinished German bunkers around the Saint-Laurent E-1 draw. It was no coincidence that the first sizable successful insertions by Dawson's G Company and the 5th Rangers with Cota's C Company the 116th occurred here, a very tenuous foothold.

Command at division and corps level had done little to facilitate this success. The clockwork nature of the logistic buildup, continuing despite the failure of the infantry assault, led to a traffic jam of useless vehicles on the beach. Brigadier General Wyman took the first productive command decision of the day when he accelerated landings by more infantry.

The sheltered enclave created in the center by hard fighting infiltrations between strongpoints, led by junior officers and NCOs, achieved far more than the designated division and corps plans. Inspirational example provided by Brigadier General Cota and the regimental commanders was more about low-level platoon and company leadership and shouted oral orders than heady decision-making at higher formation level.

Troops came ashore carrying too much weight. They were equipped to fight anticipated panzer counterattacks—the next phase—not engage in the flexible mobility required of an amphibious assault, the here and now. Intelligence had failed to identify the whereabouts of the missing formidable 352 Division. Unlike the other defending German coastal divisions elsewhere, it was not a second-rate, "static" division, it was equipped and capable of both attack and defense. The inflexible landing plan imposed by higher formation produced a confusing blurring of the distinction between the assault and buildup phase. Pratt's assessment of a "mixup" on the beaches was the consequence of battalions from the two different divisions obliged, because of wind and tide and the severity of resistance, to land in each other's areas. The only relatively safe place to land that morning was in the center of the beach.

Major General Huebner instinctively sensed this need for coordination on arrival and began to energetically disentangle the mess. Major General Charles Gerhardt, commanding the 29th Division, was already ashore at Vierville, but powerless in command terms to do anything other than plan for future offensive action until the beachhead was secure and the chain of command reaffirmed. Twelve LCIs had started to disembark the last of the five US Army infantry regiments scheduled to land on D-Day. These nearly 2,500 fresh troops would enable Huebner's 1st Division to continue its offensive the next day without pause. V Corps also felt obliged to land its reserve, the 743rd Tank Battalion, which began to land in the early evening. Only three tanks were still in action with the 741st, which had been squandered in the choppy waters off

Colleville. Two were under repair but forty-eight had been lost or disabled during the day's fighting. On their right the 743rd was exiting the Vierville draw from 10:30 P.M., with thirty-one DD and eight wading tanks. At the end of the day the US V Corps had managed to pack the equivalent of nearly two divisions, about 34,200 troops, into its ragged beach enclave, four miles wide by about one deep.

Lieutenant Hans Heinz was beginning to recall the disturbing Feldwebel's advice during an inspection days before the invasion. They might hold off the first, second, third, fourth, maybe even fifth waves on an invasion he said, until the ammunition gave out. Then, "they're going to kick in the door on top of us and then all is lost." Heinz's counterattack between Saint-Laurent and Colleville was hit by such a concentration of naval gunfire that, "I ordered the men to try to get out through the shelling by themselves, not in groups." It seemed to be the only way out, "through that terrible fire." They would rally and regroup at the battalion command post. Despite his best efforts, he found on reporting to Oberst Goth, the 916 Regiment commander, that "he was not pleased with me at all." The testy Goth, "yelled at me that I couldn't fight and should be shot." Heinz was not present for the final failed counterattacks. The stony faced lieutenant responded, "let me go back to my men and I will show you how well I can fight." Insulted and disappointed at the dressing-down, he later appreciated on reflection, "he was only giving me a shove in the right direction, because now I had renewed spirit."[14]

General Kraiss, like the senior Allied commanders coming ashore at Omaha, also had not, despite his best efforts, had a satisfactory day. He had prematurely dispatched his primary reserve, the Kampfgruppe Meyer, in opposing directions, to no effect. His beach defenses had fought two of Major General Gerow's lead V Corps divisions to a complete standstill, but he fragmented his beach reserves and dissipated them in fruitless local counterattacks. Manpower might have been better employed defending rather than attacking. He did not have the resources to plug the infantry infiltrations that came through gaps and unfinished sections of the bunker line and had run out of artillery ammunition. Ceaseless Jabo fighter-bomber attacks swarmed over every attempt at reinforcement or resupply. In any case, the British at Gold Beach, and the Americans across the Vire estuary at Utah outflanked Kraiss on both sides. He went over to the defensive on a line announced at 8:40 P.M., stretching from the east end of Colleville village about a mile inland to WN 74 west of Vierville, at Pointe et Raz de la Percée.

"The beach was a terrible sight that evening," remembered Unteroffizier Henrik Naube, captured semiconscious and wounded at WN 73. He could see medics from his stretcher trying to retrieve bodies still floating in the water. "The edge of the water was a red color from the blood, I could see that distinctly." Naube was amazed he was spared. An American had stood over him with a Thompson machine gun, looking at him as he lay motionless, feigning death. "I don't know whether he was considering killing me or what else was in his mind," he remembered, but eventually they took him down to the beach on a stretcher. It was clear from the volume of men and matériel being brought ashore that, "the Americans were secure in this beach and were moving inland now."

Franz Gockel, fleeing with the walking wounded, was fortunate enough to be picked up from the road after dark by a German ambulance, and passed many burned-out and smoldering vehicles en route. He saw they were handing out apple juice at an aid station in Balleroy south of Bayeux, as captured American paratroopers with Mohawk haircuts looked on. "Not for the Amis!" they all exclaimed, "because we hadn't seen apple juice in Germany since the beginning of the war." They asked the Americans why they had such bizarre plume haircuts and they explained, "for bonding and good luck." "So much for the good luck," the Germans teased, but the Americans simply said, "we're still alive."

Vire was on fire as they passed through, with "food still standing on the tables, where the inhabitants had fled the bombing." They managed to get through the side streets, where at one point Gockel, confronted by French civilians, was fearful for his safety because of the bombing. "One had a dagger under his smock and said, 'For the Americans,' to me in French. They were angry and disappointed with their 'liberators,'" and in contrast, asked how his wound was and the situation on the coast. Gockel was shocked at the destruction he encountered at Vire. "Dead and wounded French civilians lying in the streets and no one reacting to calls for help, apart from a few dazed and shaken survivors." He eventually reached Paris in a few days, transported in a Wehrmacht truck that traveled only by night.

Heinrich Severloh was pinned inside Colleville village by the fighting that night, guarding a small group of American prisoners. He tried to break out to reach his battery location at Houteville, but as it grew light at dawn, he turned himself over to his American captives. He was taken away by soldiers from the 2nd Battalion 16th Infantry and searched. The Germans were advised not to try to escape, because as one officer explained, "we would have good grounds to shoot you, on account of the losses you inflicted on us." Severloh maintained a judicious silence and did not say a word to his captors or any of the other German prisoners. "I hoped, silently, that there were no longer any witnesses to my actions yesterday." Eleven days later the so-called "Beast of Omaha" was aboard the converted passenger liner *Queen Mary*, heading for detention in the United States.[15]

GIs still coming ashore after dusk discovered to their amazement that enemy soldiers were just as likely to be in their rear as in front. Sergeant Robert Slaughter with D Company the 116th fell into a deep sleep in a shallow foxhole scooped out of the hard shale, "because we did not have enough energy to dig deeper." Although German forces still contained the tenuous foothold carved out by the beachhead, they were outnumbered by about thirty to one; annihilation the next day was assured. Slaughter and his squad slept soundly even though, "we found out later that German soldiers were dug in less than twenty-five yards away."

Shortly before midnight twenty-two twin-engine JU-88 dive-bombers attacked the fleet in Omaha bay. Joseph Graham, who commanded LCT-638, remembered, they "were met with the most tremendous antiaircraft barrage imaginable":

> "You could not see anything anyway. Everyone was just throwing up ammunition hoping to hit something. Quite a few of our own barrage balloons were shot down"

Robert Slaughter looked at what he believed to be a Me 109 fighter plane, traversing the entire fleet from right to left, just above the level of the ship's barrage balloons. "Every ship in the English Channel opened fire on that single airplane," he remembered, "illuminating the sky with millions of tracer bullets." Thousands of onlookers paused to watch his progress, "somehow, he flew over the fleet and circled back unscathed."[16]

It was a vulnerable moment for those still onboard the ships. Corporal Herbert Krieger with the 115th Regiment was waiting to be ferried ashore. "Those on shore were wishing they were on board," he remembered, "and those on board were wishing they were on shore." His LST was hit during the air raid, and "it sounded like you were in a metal bathtub and a bunch of large rocks were hitting it." Graham's LCT anchored with its bow pointing toward the beach, and from the wheelhouse he watched one of the German aircraft hit, running the line of the beach "and astern of us":

> "I turned in time to see a section of the wing fall off and the plane was on fire as it hit the water about one hundred yards off our stern. The pilot had bailed out and landed about twenty-five yards off our starboard side. The gasoline fire from the crash was spreading toward our stern."

Engines were started to maneuver the boat out of the path of the flames. "Several of the crew members wanted to try to rescue the pilot, but I wouldn't agree," Graham admitted. The water was too choppy for a dinghy launch and the German pilot he suspected would be armed if he had survived. The issue was settled by the appearance of an LCM, "and someone in the LCM killed the pilot with a Thompson submachine gun." Graham spent the rest of the night trying to keep his men awake, threatening court-martial if they dozed off again. Corporal Krieger saw, "a ball of fire exploded above us and cheers went up to no avail," he remembered, because "the antiaircraft were hitting balloons." Three aircraft were shot down.[17]

Fourteen-year-old Simone Jeanne in Vierville was suddenly startled when, "a German guy broke the window and asked my grandmother to open it." It was a tense moment, "he was absolutely crazy, and his eyes were bulging out of their sockets." He came in and scrambled about searching beneath the bed and in the wardrobe. The family was terrified. "He was by himself and I did not know if there were some more Germans outside.":

> "He was shouting and my grandmother told him quietly that there were no Tommies. We were scared stiff. My sister went up in the attic with him but there was nothing, so he left and we never saw him again."

Michel Hardelay remembered, "the night went pretty quiet" in Vierville. He was awestruck at the epic sight of huge numbers of ship silhouettes in the bay. In the morning he decided he would take photographs to record this historical moment, he had two pictures left on a roll of film. Thirteen-year-old André Renard saw his first Americans in the village that night. "We were then in the kitchen, sleeping under the table with two or three mattresses on top of it." The window had been left half open to release the stifling heat, "and we saw somebody's head passing by the window and looking inside." The American signaled for them to bend down, "I never forgot that image," Renard later recalled.

The positions of the American and German soldiers facing each other at Vierville were more sharply defined than the more fluid situation at Colleville. Fernand Broeckx was still in the village. German soldiers had entered the house to steal bedding for the night. "The majority of the Germans seemed absolutely exhausted." He could see, "young men of sixteen to eighteen years. 'What are you waiting for in order to surrender?'" Broeckx asked a French-speaking officer. He responded, "with a desolate air," saying, "what can you do? These are our orders." The German survivors at Colleville were contained within a three-sided box, some would be there to fight at dawn, others had already begun to break out south through the tangled bocage, to reconstitute in the rear. Short running firefights erupted through the night as small groups sought to escape.[18]

Kurt Keller's company from Fusilier Battalion 352 escaped the collapse of German resistance in the Saint-Laurent draw with just over forty men. "From now on fighting in the sunken hollowed out tracks of the Normandy bocage began," he remembered, "and my first prayers to God." Normandy, a pastoral land of fields, cows, and farmhouses that produced milk, butter, and Camembert cheese was transformed overnight. Picturesque church steeples were turned into sniper outposts, ammunition was stockpiled in barns, and hedgerows concealed artillery. Keller remembered how:

> "The earthen banks with thick hedges lined with ivy-covered trees and high natural stone walls gave some protection against Jabos, but hindered visibility. In this country one never knew whether danger lurked behind the next bush, a state of affairs that kept us constantly tense. Survival was only possible by day if you hid beneath thick camouflage."

"The hedgerows were new to us," recalled Private Thomas Lasater, who had landed with M Company of the 116th. "We had never had any training in this kind of terrain." This was the typical experience around the beachhead perimeter that first night. "There was always an entrance through each hedgerow but the enemy always had it covered with fire-power." Nobody knew where the front line was, so the sensible solution was to locate a safe place, dig a foxhole, and wait for daylight. Lieutenant Jack Shea, Brigadier General Cota's aide, remembered:

> "During the hours of darkness between D-Day and D+1, it became apparent that many of the units of both the 1st and 29th Divisions engaged in minor firefights between themselves due to the promiscuous shooting of the troops concerned."

Ranger John Perry nearby was told on the night of D-Day, "to stay in our holes because the Germans were close by." The standing instruction was to throw grenades rather than open fire, "so as not to give our position away." Movement at night attracted hand grenades tossed over hedgerows, and in the morning men were surprised to see the corpses of the few horses and cows that had been grazing nearby. "The night of D-Day we were scattered all over the place," remembered Marion Wheeler a 29th Division combat engineer. "I don't know what the others thought, but I figured the situation called for each of us to take care of ourselves until we get some orders to do otherwise."[19]

"We could send out a recon party at night," recalled Kurt Keller, "or an assault raiding group," because that was the only time they were not afflicted by swarms of low-flying fighter-bombers. "The night was our strength," he recalled, "and the Americans knew it." German soldiers had trained across this very terrain for months prior to the invasion. Keller felt insignificant armed with just a rifle, "against the overwhelming might of matériel" the Americans were applying. Each time they fired their 5cm mortars, which had to be dragged through the undergrowth every time, they had to quickly change position. "After every second bomb we had to move," he recalled, "to avoid the certainty of enemy return fire."

"These hedgerows were made of dirt and rock and they were six feet tall," complained Thomas Lasater:

> "One of the machine gunners from one of the rifle companies in our regiment had set his air-cooled machine gun on a hedgerow and a German on the other side grabbed the barrel and tried to pull it away from the gunner. The gunner pulled the trigger and held it, causing the barrel to become so hot the German couldn't hold it any longer."

Keller complained, "we couldn't even send a forward observer up before, at the latest, he would be made a prisoner behind the next earth bank. . . . The enemy could be just over the hedgerow," Lasater stressed, "and we found that to be the case many times."[20]

Close-in hedgerow fighting was as terrifying as it was intimidating. Combat engineer Marian Wheeler passed out with exhaustion after propping himself up against a sloping bank inside a field on the perimeter. He was awoken at first light by the sound of incoming machine gun fire:

> "When I opened my eyes I saw tracer bullets coming from across that small field and they all looked as if they were going into my forehead, then they would raise up into the bushes and small trees on top of the hedgerow. I froze. I doubt that I was even breathing. Then another burst would come and the same thing would happen."

It became obvious that he would have to break cover and expose himself to change position, otherwise the methodical searching fire would get him. At the next pause between bursts he grabbed his pack and rifle and somersaulted over the hedge to the safe side. Not a single shot was fired when he appeared; he was not seen. "When I quit shaking a little," he picked up the backpack, "and found it riddled with bullet holes." He realized the German machine gun was firing on preregistered, fixed predictive lines. The enemy gunner simply sat behind the earth bank after laying the machine gun on an arc up top, "and was just firing to let us know he was there."[21]

The Germans were tenaciously clinging onto the fringes of the tenuous four square miles of beachhead the US V Corps had carved out of Omaha bay. Both division headquarters, the 1st and 29th, were up and running by 8:00 P.M., and General Gerow, the V Corps commander, came ashore half an hour later. With 34,000 men and two battalions of tanks at his disposal, the offensive could begin at first light with an American superiority of 30 to 1.

There would be a lot of emotional and psychological trauma to overcome. The two assault regiments had been fought to a virtual standstill. Captain Charles Cawthon reported to his battalion commander Major Bingham, who only had ninety men left, that on the beach, "I had found nothing except the dead, wounded, and emotionally crippled":

> "Sorrow was a presence in the command post that night, but it was still a dim presence. Weariness was there also, for twenty-four hours of intense physical and emotional strain had elapsed since reveille on the *Jefferson*, but neither weariness nor sorrow was dominant. Overriding both was what I can identify only as life forced to a hard, bright flame to survive."

Charles Cawthon described the "intensified life force," as being, "dread and exhilaration from the same source at the same time." Dread of possible death or mutilation in battle alongside exhilaration that life—despite all this—would persist. Cawthon wrapped himself in a waterproof poncho and slipped away into a light and troubled sleep that night. Sergeant Robert Slaughter in Clay's regiment, sheltering in his shallow foxhole, was likewise deeply troubled. "We would eventually get through all this," he rationalized, but there was so little information in the narrow beachhead:

> "We had no communication or news of other sectors. I was confused, totally exhausted, and still in shock at the terrible carnage that had been inflicted on us."[22]

Gefreiter Georg Seidl rode through the darkness at the end of D-Day on a bicycle carrying a peculiar burden, a wounded Ranger Sergeant balanced on his handlebars. "I was ordered to bring a prisoner to the command bunker, where the aid station was," he remembered. The 914 Regiment was setting up for the final attack on Pointe du Hoc; H-hour was set to one hour after midnight. Seidl pedaled awkwardly along the dark road, with the sounds of fighting receding behind him. "He had a bandage on his head and was very tall," he remembered:

> "His feet almost dragged on the ground and because he had a head wound, he lost balance many times, wobbling back and forth. It was dark and I couldn't see very well with him sitting in front of me."

Seidl, dwarfed by his ungainly passenger, threatened to roll into the roadside ditch at every turn. "I eventually had to hold on to him with one hand and steer with the other," he recalled. Both men wore vastly dissimilar uniforms and would not have hesitated to kill each other if they had met an hour before. "I thought to myself that this was the end of his last day of fighting, but only the first for me."

The battle for the heartland of northwest Europe had begun. Yesterday France had been at relative peace, a state of hostile tension that had lasted four long years. As the odd couple wobbled on through the darkness, Seidl found himself thinking that "strange things happen in war."[23]

BEYOND 24 HOURS

The second major German counterattack came into Pointe du Hoc at 1:00 A.M. with whistles and shouting from the south and southwest. E Company did not detect the moving shadows until shapes had closed to within fifty yards and suddenly overran the vulnerable base angle of the *L*-shaped position. With activity masked by darkness and broken by disorienting flashing explosions nobody in the Ranger line understood the seriousness of the penetration when a quiet descended. There was no reserve available to react and too few leaders able to move about and check what had happened. The next German thrust two hours later collapsed the fragile line. Most of the mortar fire rained down off-target but this time German machine gun fire opened up in enfilade, lashing the inside of the Range-occupied hedgerow from both sides. Men running urgently by heading toward the Pointe were the first intimation that something was amiss. Sergeant Hathaway with the 5th Rangers yelled at passing shadows, "Hey! What's up?" A rifle was thrust into his face by way of response and the password demanded. He was so rattled he could not even form the words. "The Germans are right behind us," he was told, "get out quick to the Pointe!" The vulnerable extended Ranger position covering the Grandcamp road collapsed, and only about forty-eight men had got back to Rudder's outpost on the Pointe by 4:00 A.M.

Salva Maimone was with a group E Company survivors left behind. "My buddy was shot through the shoulder, and the bullet ran all the way through and left a hole as big as my fist." He pushed sulfa into the cavity. His sergeant waved a surrender flag when the Germans closed in with bayonets. "Who's all's alive stand up," they demanded, "otherwise we're going to stick bayonets in them." Maimone tried to get his wounded friend to stand up and walk. About twenty Rangers were led away. E Company lost about twenty of its thirty men, while the others had two killed, one missing, and five captured. The night action dramatically reduced the Ranger perimeter to about two hundred yards deep around the Pointe, leaving about ninety to one hundred walking defenders, many of whom were walking wounded. Fifty-one seriously wounded men were waiting for evacuation. Rudder by now had lost some 43% of his strength.[1]

At daybreak Rudder ordered Lieutenant Elmer "Dutch" Vermeer, the battalion demolitions officer, to settle the stubborn occupied German observation bunker at the head of the promontory once and for all. A twenty-pound sack of C-2 explosive was wedged against the rear door of the bunker and detonated. The explosion ripped it off and radio operator Benno Müller with the 369th Signals Company finally came out. They had been trapped inside the fetid, foul bunker with a dead body for over twenty-four hours and were out of ammunition. "We opened the armored door at about midday and held out a white sheet. . . . We were just six left," he remembered, "and came out with our hands up." To their relief, "the Americans treated us well and were friendly." They were taken aboard one of the resupply landing craft and out to "one of the big ships." The Rangers were not finally relieved until June 8, when a relief force from the 116th Regiment with Rangers reached the village of Saint-Pierre-du-Mont, spearheaded by tanks from the 743rd Tank Battalion.

The move beyond the beachhead the next day did not begin well. Major General Gerhardt was irritated when the 175th Regiment scheduled to land opposite Vierville, at the west side of Omaha Beach to move on Isigny, was instead landed in the center, at the Les Moulins D-3 draw. This meant the entire regiment landing late at midday, had to march in loose formation, 1½ miles across sand harassed by sniper fire. It was a sluggish start, what made it "even worse," according to James Milnor Roberts, the V Corps commander's aide, was:

> "They were skipping over the bodies of the guys who had been killed the day before, and these guys were wearing that 29th Division patch; the other fellows, brand new, were walking over the dead bodies. By the time they got down where they were to go inland they were really spooked."[2]

The US V Corps gradually expanded the Omaha beachhead reaching the Aure River and its D-Day objectives two days late. The 116th pushed west and took Grandcamp on June 8 when the 175th Regiment entered Isigny. The German 352nd Division continued to offer stiff resistance, but the massive strength of the American buildup shifted the advantage to the advance. The following day V Corps launched its first concerted three-division attack, pushing twelve miles inland and seizing the dominating terrain at the Cerisy Forest. Carentan fell on June 12, which linked the Omaha and Utah beachheads and on the 13th the "Big Red One" pushed twenty miles out, joining up with the neighboring British beaches at Gold. General J. Lawton Collins's VII Corps advanced from Utah across the peninsula to Cherbourg on June 20—a hollow victory, because the Germans had destroyed the harbor facilities. For the next seven weeks the Allies were bogged down in bitter fighting for the tangled bocage hedgerows around Saint-Lô and Caen, not breaking out until Operation Cobra in the last week of July.

Montgomery's preinvasion assessment that the campaign would be a race to dominate the invasion foreshore proved correct. The carrying capacity of the allied invasion fleet was infinitely superior to that of the French road and rail network, under the eye of the allied air forces. Allied reinforcement divisions could be fed from southern England into the Normandy bridgehead at the rate of one in less than twenty-four hours, while for the Germans under unremitting air attack, it might take a week or more.

General Omar Bradley never faced a more vulnerable moment in his military career than the morning off Omaha Beach. His headquarters and staff were ashore four days later. He planned the Cobra breakout from Normandy, which put him in charge of the 12th Army Group. Eventually he would command four field armies, over 900,000 men, the largest number of American soldiers ever to serve under one commander, and lead them to the Elbe River in mid-April 1945. After the war Bradley became the US Army chief of staff and the first chairman of the Joint Chiefs of Staff. In 1953 he retired from active duty but remained in public life until his death in 1981.

Sergeant Raymond Crouch and Leonard Goodgal accompanied the Ranger advance with the 116th as far as Grandcamp. This took them closer to their parent 101st Airborne Division, and Colonel Rudder provided them with a jeep to get back. Goodgal wisely requested a letter of explanation from Rudder about what had happened, "otherwise I knew the guys would think I had been goofing off." Rudder even recommended consideration for a Distinguished Service Cross, but when the pair rejoined the 506th Regiment nobody believed them. "When I showed my Lieutenant Colonel Rudder's letter," Goodgal recalled, "he just ripped it up and told me to rejoin the company, which we did. . . .

The company had been hit pretty hard," he remembered, "and nobody seemed too interested in hearing our crazy story."[3]

Ten years later James Rudder took his son Bud back to Pointe du Hoc, sponsored by an anniversary article for *Collier's* magazine. He found himself surrounded by ghosts: 78 men had been killed with 131 wounded and 24 missing, out of a total of 233 Rangers. They found a frayed, weather-beaten rope ladder still suspended on the cliff edge. He showed his son a bunker where, "the artillery captain, a nice-looking, black haired boy—I wish I could remember his name—was killed right here." Rudder was knocked over by the same shell, which ironically came from an American vessel. He rolled up his sleeve to expose a red welt on his forearm. "Right under that is a piece of the concrete from right here," he said to his son and the reporter. "You carry it around with you for ten years, and you bring it back where it came from." Then he showed them his leg wound scar, "a clean penetration" through one side, with an exit scar on the other. The bunker exploration occurred on a depressingly bleak, rainy day. Even at the heady moment of relief, Rudder had lost more men. The two lead US tanks opened fire when they met, killing four men and wounding six.[4]

Many of the survivors of the first wave landings at Omaha remained in shock for some time, unable to comprehend what had happened. The first two regiments suffered six times more casualties on landing than subsequent waves. The figures are still contentious today. Joseph Balkoski's detailed assessment of infantry, corps, and army unit losses, as well as navy and air force, conclude a total of 4,720 casualties, or 13% from a landed force of 35,000. Most previous estimates had averaged around the 2,000 to 2,500 mark, with 1,465 dead. Can this be judged a defeat or victory? When war photographer Robert Capa left the beach after 8:30 A.M., he suspected his pictures recorded a defeat. The surviving eleven images could be interpreted in editorial terms as hard fought success, or alternatively, failure.

Stars and Stripes Army newspaper correspondent Private Andrew Rooney interviewed survivors shortly after, and "most of them thought it had been a disaster." This did not reflect the official view:

> "All they saw was dead friends. Guys drowning in the water, and dead people all around them. And back in London headquarters they were calling it a great victory, a great success. It didn't look like a success to the guys who were there fighting it. But it turned out it was in fact a success, and the guys who were up close and saw it first hand were wrong, and the people who had the grand view of it were right."[5]

By the time Capa awoke from an exhausted sleep, his ship the USS *Chase* was on its way back to England. At Weymouth the next morning Capa handed over his film to an army public relations officer, for onward transmission by courier to London, taking the next available boat back to France. He now appreciated that the invasion had been an overall success. John Morris at the Time, Inc. London office anxiously awaited the arrival of the pictures, agonizing over whether they would meet a tight New York publication of June 19. The pictures were seen to be potentially "fabulous," but an accident in the dark room, shortcutting the negative drying process, melted the emulsion. Only eleven images survived the disaster, of which ten originals exist today. The pictures published in *Life* magazine on June 19 were perhaps the best of the invasion. In 1999 Capa's D-Day coverage was ranked 27th among New York University's top one hundred examples of twentieth century journalism. Capa went on to record the rest of the war's milestones: the fall of Paris, the Rhine crossing, and defeat in Germany. On May 25, 1954 he was killed stepping on a mine while covering French operations in Indochina, the first American reporter to die in what would become the Vietnam War.

Sergeant Ray Stevens's boat LCA-911 had swamped off Vierville-sur-Mer, and he spent four hours in the water alongside John Barnes, also with A Company the 116th. They were recovered back to England and were back within five days as battle replacements. The sinking meant Ray Stevens never got the chance to greet his twin brother Roy on D-Day night at the Vierville crossroads. Before rejoining A Company, he and Clyde Powers, another Bedford man, checked out several rows of crosses they found at a makeshift graveyard set up at Colleville. Each cross had a poignantly draped dog tag hanging from it. Stevens went to the "S" area, and on scraping the mud from one of the tags, discovered it belonged to his brother Roy. With increasing dread he and Powers checked the other crosses and found all but six of the Bedford men who had landed on D-Day, including Clyde Powers's own brother Jack. When they reached A Company, in the line, they asked about their company commander Captain Fellers. "Killed" was the bleak response; only one of nine officers who landed were still fighting;, all the others were new. Stevens asked Sergeant Jack Newcombe about his brother; he could not comprehend he was dead. "Don't know," he replied, "we haven't had much information. Haven't been able to keep up, it's a mess."[6]

For the French, *Le débarquement* transitioned from a vague threatening approaching phenomenon to the reality of a nightmare. Nobody knows the precise figures from the villages around Omaha, but it is believed the first forty-eight hours of the invasion cost three thousand French lives. The preliminary Allied bombing of the road and rail network in the months preceding killed 15,000 and injured 19,000. Some three hundred died at Saint-Lô after 8:00 P.M. when Allied bombing sought to block the major road junctions that could reinforce the German beach defenses. So many French civilians had been killed and injured on the roads in 1940 fleeing the German *Blitzkrieg* that many decided the safest course of action for families would be to remain in place and await liberation. The intensity of fighting, however, precluded this. The day after D-Day thirteen-year old André Renard was narrowly missed by a sniper's bullet that smacked into the wall between himself and his elder sister. "I spent one month without being able to talk," he recalled.

There was uncertainty about what would happen and mutual suspicion of the invaders. Henry Leroutier recalled in Saint-Laurent that, "the first Americans brought us nothing, but the latter gave us sweets, chocolate, and cigarettes." He was relieved they had come, but "I gave them nothing because they would not have accepted, they were suspicious of us." Michel Hardelay remembered how tense the situation was in Vierville the day after the landings. They had been summoned to evacuate the village, and he heard rumors, "that the Americans had started to re-embark and that they were taking us with them." Others thought they might be moved to a safer area at Saint-Laurent. Edmond Scelles in Saint-Laurent recalled three Germans fighting their own isolated stand in a ditch behind the Lemiere family home until June 9. German corpses tended to be left face up, robbed of boots and other valuables by French civilians. They might lie there for days or weeks, whereas the Allied dead were always covered, face down, often with a bouquet of flowers placed over them.

French civilians were also caught up in the grim battles among the hedgerows. Désiré Pottier remembered a German ambush, when amid the sounds of gunfire, "it was painful to listen to the war cries of the soldiers charging with their bayonets." When silence resumed the severely wounded were brought out and laid on blankets between the houses. Young children looked curiously on:

> "Some were still taking drags from a cigarette despite it all. Severed arms, bits of lung sticking out of rib cages . . . It was almost unbearable."

It has been estimated that 19,890 civilians were killed during the liberation of Normandy.[7]

The 29th Division lost 1,272 men on D-Day, 1007 from the 116th Regiment alone. "D-Day was the Longest Day, there's no doubt about that," recalled Private Robert Sales in B Company, "but for those who survived, it was just one day, I had 180 to go":

"I couldn't begin to tell you how many men right beside me got killed. The average infantryman survived a week, if he was lucky."

Sergeant Stevens recalled the cumulative effect of these casualties: he had five self-inflicted wounds in his company on one day alone. Before D-Day the 29th Division numbered around 14,000, and more men and replacements poured in as more men were killed and wounded. "By the time we took Saint-Lô six weeks later," Sergeant Robert Slaughter recalled:

"It was said that the 29th was really three divisions: one in the field, another in hospital, and yet a third in the cemetery."

Sales emphasized D-Day was just twenty-four hours, acceptable in casualty terms because it was huge, and expected in any case to be highly dangerous. It was also recognized to be a likely turning point in the war, "yet we couldn't fathom the terrible odds of surviving just one day fighting in the hedgerows of Normandy," Slaughter recalled.[8]

There was still much to endure for the 29th Division by war's end: Saint-Lô was captured on July 18, 1944; Brest between August 25 and September 18; the Ruhr encircled in February 1945; and the Elbe River reached on May 4. The division suffered 20,620 casualties, of which 3,887 died. When they eventually returned to the United States, the men attempted to lead normal lives. Robert Slaughter was twenty at the end of the war and married and settled in Roanoke, Virginia, working for the *Roanoke Times* until 1987. He actively participated in veteran affairs until his death in May 2012. Charles Cawthon served as a battalion commander in Korea and retired from the US Army Reserve in 1967 with the rank of colonel, dying in July 1996. Brigadier General Norman Cota received the US Distinguished Service Cross and British DSO for his actions on Omaha Beach and was appointed to command the 28th Infantry Division. He took part in its iconic march down the Champs-Élysées after the liberation of Paris in August 1944, and fought in the Hürtgen Forest. He retired from the army as a major general and became a civil defense director for Montgomery County, Pennsylvania in the late 1950s. He died in October 1971, and is buried at West Point.

The haunting specter of post-combat stress disorder never really left them. Ray Stevens, who lost his twin brother, stopped drinking heavily in 1948, when the bad dreams started to fade, but for many 29th Division veterans they did not. "They were hurt, not so much physically, but in the brain," Stevens explained. "They'd start talking and you'd get to crying." Friends like Clyde Powers, who also lost his brother, "got torn up inside; the drinking—it got to them in the end."

Ray Nance, the last surviving officer of nine in A Company the 116th, passed away in April 2009, aged 94. At the sixtieth anniversary of the D-Day landings he admitted he was still plagued by survivor's guilt and the occasional episode of post-traumatic stress disorder. After a long period in the hospital he farmed after the war before becoming a rural letter courier. Even this offered little respite from the anguish because some of the families on his route had lost sons on D-Day. "I never was very good at reading hearts," he admitted, and felt, "there was a little twinge of guilt that I was allowed to come back."[9]

Oberstleutnant Fritz Ziegelmann, the chief of staff of the German 352 Division, believes they lost two hundred killed, five hundred wounded, and another five hundred missing on D-Day. This represented one fifth of the division's effective infantry strength of six thousand. General Kraiss reported to his superior General Marcks shortly after midnight on D-Day that, "tomorrow the division will be able with all available forces to offer the same kind of hard resistance to the supreme enemy, as was the case today." He was as good as his word. The 352 Division fought a tough, determined battle around Saint-Lô, forestalling its capture by the Allies for forty-three days. It suffered a further 5,407 casualties between June 6 and June 24, and was pronounced *abgekampft*, or burned-out by July 30. This meant it was no longer combat effective as a division with battalions numbering less than one hundred men. There were just four heavy anti-tank guns and two Sturmgeschütz III self-propelled guns left. The seven other units that had been incorporated into the division were also fought out. On August 6 Kraiss was mortally wounded by artillery fire in the rubble of Saint-Lô and died hours later. He was posthumously awarded the oak leaves to the Knight's Cross. Oberst Ernst Goth, the 916 Regiment commander covering Omaha Beach recalled later that in the Normandy bocage, "every day an attack by fresh American regiments was beaten back." The pressure was unremitting:

> "Every day heavy artillery fire, then every two or three days permission given to withdraw one or two kilometers, because of danger to our flanks. Every day losses, no Luftwaffe over-head, no panzers left."

The remnants of the Regiments 914 and 915 that disintegrated either side of him were placed under his command and incorporated into a renamed *Kampfgruppe Goth*. Division 352 had temporarily ceased to exist. "By the end of my period of command on July 20," he remembered, "I had men from 175 different units under me."

"The smell became unbelievable," Sergeant Robert Slaughter, opposing them, recalled, "Bodies would blow up into a purple balloon, and the smell would stay with you, always with you." His experience echoed that of Goth:

> "I was out there forty-two days without changing socks, without changing underwear. It was hell every day. You get up at 3:00 A.M., go after the next hedgerow, fight for that hedgerow, then get knocked back a hedgerow, lose half your company, and then get men straight from the States who couldn't fire a rifle. It just got worse."[10]

On September 21 the remnants of the 352 Division merged with the survivors of the 581 *Volksgrenadier* Division to form the 352 *Volksgrenadier* Division. The unit fought at Arnhem and the Battle of the Bulge before surrendering as a weak Kampfgruppe at Darmstadt in mid April 1945. Oberst Ernst Goth, who had originally wanted to be a teacher, went home, finally passing away in Munich in 1986 aged 89.

Lieutenant Hans Heinz was severely wounded at Saint-Lô and was returned to convalesce in Germany until the end of the war. Grenadier Karl Wegner, who escaped WN 71 at Vierville, survived the fighting at Pointe du Hoc and was taken prisoner at Saint-Lô and lived to see the end of the war. Franz Gockel lost the three fingers of his left hand at WN 62, as well as his sense of smell. After a short recovery in the Reich he was taken prisoner in November 1944, fighting northwest of Colmar near the German border. Repatriated in March 1946, he returned to working in his father's roofing business in the Ruhr. In 1958 he returned to Normandy with his wife, and renewed his friendship with the Renard family, who had looked after him at Colleville during the occupation. He died in 2005 aged 79.

Fusilier Karl Keller won the Iron Cross first class in Normandy, but became disillusioned with the Nazi regime as a consequence of the nightmare retreat to the Rhine in September. He was increasing outspoken and deserted, handed back by locals at home and sentenced to death. This was commuted for service with Penal Battalion 500, which was dispatched to the Russian Front. His unit was encircled and overrun in April 1945 and he was taken prisoner by the Soviets. After being forced to participate in the cleanup of the Auschwitz concentration camp he entrained with 1,500 other German captives, forty-four to a wagon, and was sent eight thousand kilometers east to Siberia. He later escaped by rail and journeyed 3,500 kilometers westward, stowing away on the wrong train, which took him to yet another labor camp. He was not repatriated until November 7, 1949, when he found his hopeful mother waiting for him at the railway station.

Gefreiter Heinrich Severloh kept very quiet about his role on Omaha Beach when he was transported to Boston in the United States. He picked cotton, harvested potatoes, and even worked in a Miami kitchen, meticulously avoiding attention. In December 1946 he arrived in Bedfordshire England, working as a laborer on road construction. He was sent back home in March 1947 after his father had written to the British military authorities that he was needed on the family farm. He married and had four children.

Severloh later made contact with the Legrand family at Houteville in Normandy, his former battery location, and the wife of Lieutenant Frerking, his chief, who was killed at WN 62. Severloh had recurring nightmares about the running American soldier he had shot in the head, with his helmet wobbling in the sand. In 1963 he contacted David Silva, a 29th Division veteran, whom he found after reading his personal account in Cornelius Ryan's book *The Longest Day*. Silva had landed near strongpoint WN 62 and was wounded by machine gun fire. Severloh convinced himself that he was likely one of his victims. Silva had become a Catholic chaplain after the war and believed, "forgiveness is the way to eternal life." Severloh had contacted him, he believed, because "maybe he felt he just wanted to speak to a soldier, he did not know he had become a priest." Silva recalled when they met:

"He was hurting a lot and had tears in his eyes. It was a wonderful thing to see him again and he must have wanted that very badly, because he was the one that instituted the process we went through."

Severloh sought to exorcise his demons. "He didn't say, 'Will you forgive me,'" Silva explained, "I had a friendship with him." The point was you could apologize to "a unique person," not those in the cemetery. Severloh had attracted a lot of dramatic TV documentary coverage alleging he had probably shot two thousand American soldiers, which was over half the total casualty toll. Like many of the surviving veterans, Severloh's bad dreams probably continued until his death at Celle in Germany in January 2006.[11]

Staff Sergeant Donald Wilson with the "Big Red One" Division had fallen into a comatose sleep in a shallow roadside ditch outside Colleville on the evening of D-Day. He and his small group were sprawled about and looked as though they had been killed trying to seize a farm building nearby. "Hell they're not dead, they're just sleeping," concluded a group of lingering bystanders marching by. "This is as close as I've come to knowing how Lazarus felt," explained Wilson. Among the 1st Infantry Division, 107 never did get to wake up; 1,346 casualties fell on D-Day, 971 in Wilson's 16th Regiment alone. He received the Silver Star for his actions on that day, and prospered more than most on return to the United States after the war. He worked in sales and marketing enjoying fifty-eight years of marriage with eight grandchildren before he died in February 2004 aged 82.[12]

Further agonies lay ahead for the 1st Division: the breakthrough at Saint-Lô in July, and then continuous fighting up to the German border at Aachen, which was reached in October. The division subsequently fought in the hellish subzero conditions of the winter Bulge battle and reached the Ruhr in February 1945, crossing the Rhine at Remagen the following month. The war ended in Czechoslovakia, by which time the 1st Division had lost 20,659 men, of which 3,616 were killed. Few of the men who had originally stormed the D-Day beaches were left.

Captain Edward Wozenski, whose E Company was badly mauled at the Colleville draw when he took photographer Robert Capa ashore, survived the war. He enjoyed a successful postwar army career, retiring as brigadier general. Colonel George Taylor's inspirational leadership at Omaha earned him a Distinguished Service Cross and promotion to brigadier general. He retired from the army in 1946 and suffered a stroke fourteen years later, succumbing to its effects in 1969. Captain Joe Dawson, who led the first company over the Omaha bluffs served on with his beloved G Company for a further five months before becoming physically and mentally burned out. He was sent back to the States where he retrained as an officer in the Office of Strategic Services, remaining with them until the end of the war. Dawson managed to control his demons and enjoyed a lucrative career as the owner of Dawson Oil, building upon prewar training as a geologist. His marriage lasted over half a century and he raised two daughters before passing away in 1998.

Low tide at Omaha Beach today on a summer's day offers a breath-taking vista of golden sands with runnels of sparkling water twinkling in the sunlight. Popular with campers, beach walkers, and wind sailors, horses are often seen striding sedately by, being gently exercised by relaxed riders. Popular with Parisian holidaymakers again, it remains a delightful tourist pearl along the Normandy coastline. A small vacation village has overgrown Oberfeldwebel Friedrich Schnüll's 88mm bunker at WN 61, still intact, but tucked away behind holiday accommodation. About 850 yards to the west is the small entrance, virtually hidden by dune grass, of the path that leads up to the American cemetery. The going is quite steep, climbing ninety to one hundred feet to the top, where it emerges onto a plateau of 9,386 snow-white crosses and Stars of David, immaculately set out as immortalized by Steven Spielberg's film *Saving Private Ryan*. The dead quite literally stand here on parade, and they include 307 unknowns and three Medal of Honor winners. The Garden of the Missing nearby displays the names of 1,557 men with no known graves. The 172-acre site was dedicated on July 18, 1956, and was donated without charge or tax by the people of France.

This is the same path that was trod by Lieutenant John Spalding and Sergeant Philip Streczyk's platoon; the first successful penetration of the German defenses at Omaha Beach. Edward Wozenski always thought Streczyk should have been a Medal of Honor recipient for what he did that day. He eventually became one of the most decorated NCOs of the Second World War with four Silver and six Bronze Stars. For his actions on D-Day he received the Distinguished Service Cross and British Military Medal. In all he was to log 440 days of frontline combat duty, which ended under intense bombardment in the Hürtgen Forest, where, shaking and babbling incoherently, he was taken out of the line. He survived countless near misses and many wounds, including a severe pistol wound to the neck, for which he refused evacuation. His combat fatigue was so severe that he was sent back to a convalescent hospital in the United States, feeling guilty he had left his men. On discharge he became a builder in Florida and married Sophie Karanewsky, with whom he had four children. In persistent pain from lingering wounds and wracked with nightmarish battle dreams, he took his own life in 1957.

John Spalding, the commander of the platoon that emerged at the top of the bluffs also encapsulated the emotional damage that the lines of iconic crosses and memorials do not tell us about. Spalding was awarded the Distinguished Service Cross for his accomplishment. During the weeks and months of intense combat that followed, Spalding, according to one medical evaluator, "started to worry, apprehensive that he would make poor decisions which would be costly to his men." Professional dedication and an overwhelming sense of responsibility kept him going. He was wounded near Aachen in September 1944 only to return to his platoon in time for the terrible winter fighting of the battle of the Bulge, which finally broke him. He was transferred back to the United States with combat fatigue and wracked with fever, anxiety, and depression. His confidence had gone and he blamed himself for the deaths and injuries in the platoon, which he ascribed to his own poor leadership. "I didn't have any unusual experiences," he claimed to a reporter during a brief leave prior to discharge. "I didn't do a thing. My men did it all. Don't give me credit."

He soon divorced his wife Perdetta, with whom he had a son shortly after the war. He remarried Mary Christine Love in 1946 and they had a daughter and two sons. Spalding was much respected by the local community and was elected to the Kentucky State Legislature the following year, and served two terms. He had a good job at the local department store and seemed to have turned a corner, but in November 1959 he was shot dead by his wife Mary Christine. She was unable, either through shock or denial, to explain why she did it, stating simply, "something happened, I don't know what it was." Spalding was forty-four when he died. Perhaps his personal demons had never left him. Although charged with murder, his wife was committed to a mental institution and released several years later, before expiring in 1991.[13]

Walter Ehlers and his brother Roland both served in different companies with the 18th Regiment of the "Big Red One." They had agreed a pact on D-Day that if one of them was hit on the beach, "we'd leave it up to the medics, and that's what we did." Roland went missing after the landings and Walter did not find out officially what had happened until weeks later:

> "He got killed as he was coming down the ramp on his LCI. His whole squad got wounded or killed. I cried like a baby when I heard. I would have rather come back without my arms and legs than to come back without my brother. That's what

it meant to me. I never saw him die. That stayed with me for over fifty years. I had nightmares about that. He'd come back every night. And he'd be all neatly dressed, and smiling like he usually does, and we'd have a conversation. First thing, he'd disappear. Or I'd go to do something and he"s gone."[14]

Much of the cost of Omaha went beyond the tangible certainties of casualty lists alone.

BIBLIOGRAPHY

GENERAL PUBLISHED SOURCES

Badsey, Stephen and Tim Bean, *Omaha Beach* (Stroud, England: The History Press, 2011)

Bailey, Roderick, *Forgotten Voices of D-Day* (London: Ebury, 2009)

Balkoski, Joseph, *Omaha Beach: D-Day, June 6, 1944* (Mechanicsburg, Penn.: Stackpole Books, 2004)

Bernage, Georges, *Omaha Beach* (Havertown, Penn.: Heimdal, 2002)

Bowman, M. W., *Air War D-Day: Assaults From the Sky*, vol. 2 (Barnsley, England: Pen and Sword, 2013)

——, *Air War D-Day: Bloody Beaches*, vol. 4 (Barnsley, England: Pen and Sword, 2013)

——, *Remembering D-Day* (New York: HarperCollins, 2004)

Harrison, Gordon, *Cross Channel Attack* (Washington DC: Center of Military History, 1951)

Henkin, Y., *Uneasy Red: A Self-Guided Journey Around Omaha Beach, Following in the Footsteps of Those Who Fought There on D-Day* (self-published, 2014)

Kershaw, Alex, *The Bedford Boys* (New York: Simon and Schuster, 2003)

——, *Blood and Champagne* (New York: Macmillan, 2002)

Kershaw, Robert J., *D-Day: Piercing the Atlantic Wall* (Shepperton, England: Ian Allan, 1993)

Kluger, Steve, *Yank: The Army Weekly: World War II from the Guys Who Brought You Victory* (London: Arms and Armour, 1991)

McManus, John C., *The Dead and Those About to Die: D-Day and the Big Red One at Omaha Beach* (New York: Penguin, 2014)

Miller, Russell, *Nothing Less Than Victory* (New York: Willliam Morrow, 1994)

Neitzel, Sönke and Harald Welzer, *Soldaten: On Fighting, Killing and Dying. The Secret WWII Transcripts of German POWs* (New York: Simon and Schuster, 2012)

Prime C., *Omaha Beach* Tue 6 Jun 44, Orep 2016.

Ramsey, Winston G., *D-Day Then and Now*, vols 1–2 (London: After the Battle, 1995)

Ryan, Cornelius, *The Longest Day* (New York: Simon & Schuster, 1959)

Sterne, Gary, *The Cover Up at Omaha Beach: D-Day, the US Rangers, and the Untold Story of Maisy Battery* (Barnsley, England: Pen and Sword, 2013)

U.S. Army Center of Military History, *American Forces in Action: Omaha Beachhead* (Washington DC: U.S. Army Center of Military History, 1945)

Whelan, Richard, *This Is War! Robert Capa at Work* (Göttingen, Germany: Steidl, 2009)

Zaloga, Steven, *The Devil's Garden: Rommel's Desperate Defense of Omaha Beach on D-Day* (Mechanicsburg, Penn.: Stackpole Books, 2013)

———, *Rangers Lead the Way: Pointe-du-Hoc D-Day 1944* (Oxford, England: Osprey, 2009)

———, *D-Day 1944. Omaha Beach* (Oxford, England: Osprey, 2003)

PERSONAL ACCOUNTS

American

Barnes, J. J., *Fragments of My Life* (privately published, 2000)

Bradley, Omar, *A Soldier's Story* (New York: Henry Holt, 1951)

Capa, Robert, *Slightly Out of Focus* (New York: Henry Holt, 1947)

———, *Images of War*, (New York, Grossman, 1964)

Cawthon, Charles R., *Other Clay* (Lincoln, Nebraska: University of Nebraska Press, 2004)

Metcalf, George Reuben, *With Cross and Shovel* (Riverside Press, 1960)

Shepherd, Seth, *The Story of the LCI(L) 92 in the Invasion of Normandy on June 6 1944* (public domain; US Coast Guard account)

Slaughter, John Robert, *Omaha Beach and Beyond: The Long March of Sergeant Bob Slaughter* (Minneapolis: Zenith Press, 2007)

29th Division, *Diverse Eye Witness Accounts* (courtesy Dr. Simon Trew)

German

Eckhertz, H., *D-Day Through German Eyes: The Hidden Story of June 6, 1944*, books 1 and 2 (DTZ History Publications, 2015/16)

Gockel, Franz, *Das Tor Zur Hölle* (Verlag Hirlé,2003)

Keller, Kurt, *Vom Omaha Beach Bis Sibirien* (Garbsen, Germany: HEK Creativ Verlag, 2010)

Keusgen, H. K. von, *Omaha Beach* (Garbsen, Germany: HEK Creativ Verlag, 2015)

———, *Stützpunkt WN 62. Normandie 1942–1944* (Garbsen, Germany: HEK Creativ Verlag, 2004)

———, *Pointe du Hoc. Rätsel um einen deutschen Stützpunkt* (Garbsen, Germany: HEK Creativ Verlag, 2011)

Milano, Vince, and Bruce Conner, *Normandiefront* (Staplehurst, England: Spellmount, 2011)

Pluskat, Werner, C. Ryan papers interview.

Severloh, Hein, *WN 62* (Garbsen, Germany: HEK Creativ Verlag, 2011)

French

Lefebvre, Laurent, *They Were on Omaha Beach* (privately published, 2003); includes US accounts.

Marion, Jean, C. Ryan papers interview, July 30, 1958.

BIBLIOGRAPHY

"Norman Witnesses," Omaha Beach Memoirs website

Roberts, Mary Louise, *D-Day Through French Eyes* (Chicago: University of Chicago Press, 2014)

UNIT ACCOUNTS

Balkoski, Joseph, *Beyond the Beachhead, The 29th Infantry Division in Normandy* (Mechanicsburg, Penn.: Stackpole Books, 1989)

Bass, Richard T., *The Brigades of Neptune* (Lee Publishing, 1994)

——, *Clear The Way!* (Lee Publishing, 1996)

Baer Jr., Alfred E., *D For Dog. The Story of a Ranger Company*

Berger, Sid, *Breaching Fortress Europe* (Dubuque, Iowa: Kendall Hunt, 1994)

Ewing, Joseph H., *29 Let's Go!: A History of the 29th Infantry Division in World War II* (Nashville, Tenn.: Battery Press, 1986)

Sorvisto, E. M., *Roughing It With Charlie* (Novy Vštisk, Plzeň, Czechoslovakia)

US Army Military History Institute, *2nd Ranger Battalion, Narrative History of HQ Company April 43–May 45.*

ARCHIVE SOURCES

Published

Isby, David C., *The German Army at D-Day* (London: Greenhill Books, 2004)

Boberach, Heinz, ed., *Meldungen Aus Dem Reich* (Band 17, Manfred Pawlak, 1984)

Winter, Paul, *D-Day Documents* (London: Bloomsbury, 2014)

US Unpublished

G Company 16th Infantry, June 17, 1944, group interview 16-G conducted Aug. 22, 1944.

16 E on D-Day, NND735017 US National Archives.

F Company 16th Infantry, July 4, 1944, US National Archives.

A Company 1st Medical Battalion, and *1st Battalion 16th Infantry*, NND735017, US National Archives.

HQ 1st Infantry Division *G-3 Journal*, 02.30-11.46 June 6, 1944.

Pointe du Hoc, combat interviews 337, 2/5th Ranger Battalions, Record Gp 407. Normandy Landings June 6–8, 1944. US National Archives.

Report Kenneth Lord Asst G3 1st (US) Infantry Division titled "*Omaha*," in letter to U.S. Military History Institute Jan. 9, 1988.

Spalding, Lt. J., interview, 1st Division Rear CP Belgium, Feb. 9, 1945.

German Unpublished

Auszug aus dem Fernsrech-Meldebuch (Ia) der 352. I.D. Küstenverteidigungsabschnitt "Bayeux" June 6, 1944.

Gefechtsbericht über die Kampfe im Abschnitt der 352. Inf Division am June 6, 1944.

Gefechtsbericht der Heeresküsten Artl. Abt. 1255 fur die zeit v. June 6–9, 1944.

Gefechtsbericht des Ost-Btl s.642.

Kriegstagebuch Heeresgruppe B. June 1–15, 1944.

Kriegstagebuch der Führungsabteilung AOK 7 [Seventh Army] für die zeit vom Jan. 1–June 30, 1944.

Ziegelmann Fritz, Oberstleutnant, MS B-021; questionnaire, History Division HQ US Army Europe, 1945.

BIBLIOGRAPHY

ARTICLES AND PERIODICALS

Anderson, C. J., "Screaming Eagles at Pointe du Hoc," *World War II*; July 2001.

Fortuna, David, "Bedford Boys," *World War II*; June 2004.

Getz, L. L., "The Face in the Surf," *World War II*; June 2004.

Hendley, Coit, "D-Day: A Special Report," *Washington Times*; June 6 1984.

Pohanka, B. C., "Beach With No Cover," interview with Lieutenant John Bentz Carroll, *Military History*; Feb. 1992.

Shoemaker, Roger, "Lasting Impressions of the Longest Day," *World War II*; June 2004.

Sterne, G., "Timewatch Credits the Rangers with Leading the Way," *The Armourer*; Issue 86, March/April 2008.

Thompson, John H., "D-Day's Cauldron. Beach Called Easy Red Soaked in Blood," *Chicago Tribune*; May 29, 1994.

Zaloga, Steven, "Tanks on Bloody Omaha," article courtesy S. Trew.

FILM AND TV

Carey, C., *Bloody Battlefield. Omaha Beach*, LWT UK Channel 5.

Cavaness, T., *The Pointe du Hoc Bunker Story*, YouTube.

Czogalla, A., *Invasion in der Normandie*, German Spiegel TV 2003.

Freeston, J., *Battlefield Detectives. The Guns of Pointe du Hoc*, History Channel 2005.

Kirk, R., *D-Day. H-Hour*, Greystone Communications Inc., History Channel 1994.

Max, R., *America's Secret D-Day Disaster*, SNI/SI Networks Co Ltd 2014.

Morrissey, D., *The True Story: Saving Private Ryan*, Discovery History Channel.

Swift, G., *D-Day 360*, Windfall Films 2014.

UK ITN, *D-Day Plus Forty*, Channel ITN TV 1984.

Wooding, P., *World War II's Greatest Raids. Rangers Lead the Way*, Impossible Pictures 2014.

ENDNOTES

INTRODUCTION
1   Cawthon, in *Other Clay*, p. 37.
2   Presidential quotes from *USA Today*, June 6, 2014.

PROLOGUE: 1:00 A.M. JUNE 6, 1944
1   Goodgal and Crouch, C. J. Anderson, in "Screaming Eagles at Pointe du Hoc," *World War II*, July 2008, p. 36.
2   Kirchhoff and Karl, H. K. von Keusgen, in *Pointe du Hoc*. Various. Raid 0921, S. J. Zaloga, *Rangers Lead the Way*, pp. 17 and 19.
3   Naube, H. Eckhertz, in *D-Day Through German Eyes*, pp. 45–6.
4   Ziegelmann, interview, *352 Infantry Division—Special Questions*. MSB-021. Historical Division HQ US Army Europe. Reports, 352 Div Tel Log. US "Oberleutnant," *352 Infanteriedivision, (1. Invasionstag)*, Doc (RH 19IX/2).
5   Armagnac and description, in Roberts, *D-Day Through French Eyes*, p. 13.
6   Destorses, ibid, p. 71.
7   Broeckx, ibid, pp. 72–3. Hardelay, L. Lefbvre, in *They Were on Omaha Beach*, pp. 121–2.
8   Hardelay, ibid, pp. 119 and 124; Scelles, p. 120.
9   Goodgal and Crouch, *World War II* July 2008, p. 38.

ONE: THE FAR SHORE: 1:00 A.M. TO 4:30 A.M.
The Plage d'Or. 1:00 A.M. to 4:00 A.M.
1   Severloh, interview, from A. Czogalla 2003, Spiegel German TV and *WN 62*, p. 22.

2 Pluskat, interview, from C. Ryan, Ryan Collection Ohio Archive, pp. 2–4.

3 Gockel, in *Das Tor Zur Hölle*, p. 77.

4 Comparison figures, taken from R. J. Kershaw, *D-Day: Piercing the Atlantic Wall*, p. 28.

5 Hardelay, L. Lefebvre, in *They Were on Omaha Beach*, pp. 1 and 4; Scelles, p. 7.

6 Winter, H. Eckhertz, *D-Day Through German Eyes*, pp. 150–151; Severloh, *WN 62*, p. 26.

7 Gockel, p. 54.

8 Selbach, taken from H. K. von Keusgen, *Stützpunkt WN 62*, pp. 65–66.

9 André, Lefbvre, p. 3. Dogs incident; in von Keusgen, pp. 73–4; Severloh, interview, German Spiegel TV.

10 André, G. in Bernage, *Omaha Beach*, p. 76.

11 Gockel, p. 40, Brass; in V. Milano and B. Conner, *Normandiefront*, p. 46.

12 Lemière, in Lefebvre, p. 6; von Keusgen, *Omaha Beach*, pp. 58–59 and *Stützpunkt WN 62*, pp. 68–9.

13 Scelles and Hardelay, in Lefebvre, pp. 4 and 7–8.

14 Gockel, pp. 46–47, and 72.

15 Keller, *Vom Omaha Beach Bis Sibirien*, p. 18; Winter, in Eckhertz, p. 153; Severloh, *WN 62*, pp. 46–7.

16 Gockel, pp. 41, 45, and 50–51.

17 Sexual cases, taken from von Keusgen, *Stützpunkt WN 62*. Keller, pp. 18–20.

18 Scelles, in Lefebvre, pp. 6–7; Legallois, in von Keusgen, *Omaha Beach*, p. 52.

"Where the German Soldier Stands Nobody Gets In!" **3:00** A.M. **to 4:30** A.M.

19 Winter and Naube, in Eckhertz, pp. 152 and 42–43. Pioneer soldier, taken from *Pi Bn. 352. Befehl Nr 32/44*; dated April 18, 1944. Doc. RH 26-352/3. [Trew]

20 Rumors, taken from ed. H. Boberach, *Meldungen aus dem Reich*, Band 17 4 May 44–Mar 45, 18 May; p. 6536, 4 May p. 6510, and 11 May p. 6523. Goebbels, Diary, 19.4.43. Letters, in ed. O. Buchbender and R. Sterz, *Das Andere Gesicht Des Krieges. Deutche Feldpostbriefe 1939–45*. Hauptmann, Jan. 2, 1944, p. 129. V1 Oberleutnant, Jan. 20, 1944, p. 130. NCO Lyon, Feb. 23, 1944, p. 130. Cpl 90th Pz Gren, April 27, 1944, p. 131. POW survey, in S. Neitzel and H. Welzer, *Soldaten*, p. 205.

21 Gockel, p. 34. SS Reports, Meldungen, May 11, p. 6526. Winter, in Eckhertz, p. 155.

22 Naube, Eckhertz, p. 44. Wilden, in von Keusgen, *Omaha Beach*, p. 56.

23 Gockel, p. 31. Keller, pp. 11, 14, and 17; Winter and Hinevez, in Eckhertz, pp. 156 and 9.

24 Rommel, in G. Bernage, *Omaha Beach*, pp. 25–6. Von Keusgen, *Stützpunkt WN 62*, pp. 40 and 67.

25 Ziegelmann, taken from D. Isby, *The German Army at D-Day*, p. 125. Lützen, in Von Keusgen, p. 56. Heinz, Milano and Conner, in *Normandiefront*, p. 30.

26 Ebeling, in S. Zaloga, *Rangers Lead the Way*, p. 11. Kaufmann, in von Keusgen, *Pointe du Hoc*, p. 59. Marion, C. Ryan interview, July 30, 1958, Ryan Centre.

27 Keller, *Vom Omaha Beach Bis Siberien*, p. 19.

28 Bauch, Bongard, and Kuska, in Von Keusgen, *Stützpunkt WN 62*, pp. 77 and 56.

29 Gockel, p. 78. Winter, in Eckhertz, pp. 156–7.

30 André, in G. Bernage, pp. 75–6; and Lefebvre, pp. 123 and 125.

31 Wegner, Milano, and Conner, pp. 67 and 69–71; Naube, in Eckhertz, pp. 45–6.

32   Ziegelmann, 352 Div Telephone log, Wehrmacht times one hour behind Allied,
     amended to coincide with Allied time, 01.00 to 03.10, 03.14, 04.10 to 04.20. Pluskat,
     in C. Ryan interview, pp. 4–5. Bongard, in Von Keusgen, *Omaha Beach*, p. 75.

TWO: FORCE "O": MIDNIGHT TO 3:30 A.M.
The Funnel. Midnight to 3:00 A.M.
1   Officer and LCT executive officer, in C. L. Symonds, *Operation Neptune*, pp.
     249–50. Hendley, "D-Day: A Special Report," *Washington Times*, June 6, 1984.
2   Hall, in J. Balkoski, *Omaha Beach*, p. 59. Morison, S. Berger, taken from *Breaching
     Fortress Europe*, p. 117.
3   Shepherd, *Invasion. The Story of LCI(L) 92 in the Invasion of Normandy on June 6
     1944*, US Coast Guard account.
4   Shoemaker, in "Lasting Impressions of the Longest Day," *World War II*, June
     2004, p. 45; Capa, in R. Whelan, *This Is War! Robert Capa at Work*, p. 224. Silva,
     interview taken from A. Czogalla, *Invasion in der Normandie*, Spiegel TV, 2003.
     Ferrara, in J. E. Ewing, *29 Let's Go!* p. 37.
5   Staff officer and rumors, in J. Balkoski, *Beyond the Beachhead*, pp. 6 and 55.
     Martin, in ed. S. Kluger, *Yank: The Army Weekly*, June 30, 1944, p. 180; Capa,
     Slightly Out of Focus, p. 137.
6   Carroll, interview B. C. Pohanka, *Military History*, Feb. 1992, p. 37. Shoemaker,
     WW II Magazine, Jun 2004, p. 45.
7   Ehret, in M. Bowman, *Air War D-Day*, vol. 2, p. 14. Stone, ibid, p. 17. Ardery, in
     J. Balkoski, *Omaha Beach*, p. 88. Aanenson, taken from G. C. Ward and K. Burns,
     The War, p. 195.
8   Spaatz and De Russey, in Balkoski, pp. 76–7.
9   Stone, in Bowman, p. 17.
10   Eighth Air Force after-action report, July 1944, J. Balkoski, p. 79; Stone and Isgrig,
     in Bowman, vol. 2, pp. 8 and 17; Stephens, in M. Bowman, *Remembering D-Day*,
     pp. 88–89.
11   Gilbert, in Balkoski, p. 91; Patterson, in Bowman, vol. 2, p. 10.

GIs: Government Issue. 1:30 A.M. to 3:00 A.M.
12   Riley, in L. W. Getz, "The Face in the Surf," *World War II*, Jan. 2004, p. 40.
13   Wozenski, J. C. McManus, *The Dead and Those About to Die*, p. 40; Evangelist,
     taken from A. Kershaw, *The Bedford Boys*, p. 72; S. Berger, in *Breaching Fortress
     Europe*, p. 106. Thompson, ibid, p. 118. Combat engineer, in R. T. Bass, *The
     Brigades of Neptune*, p. 100.
14   Silva, interview A. Czagalla, *Invasion in der Normandie*, Spiegel German TV, 2003.
     Rarey, in H. Buckton, *Friendly Invasion*, p. 6.
15   Anglo-American cultural differences, J. Balkoski, *Beyond the Beachhead*, p. 40;
     A. Kershaw, p. 56.
16   Sexual escapades, taken from R. J. Kershaw, *Tank Men*, pp. 310–11. Peters, in
     Friendly Invasion, p. 12; girls, p. 129.
17   Hendley, *Washington Times*, June 6, 1984.
18   Saroyan, in Whelan, p. 208. Trabant, in A. Kershaw, *Blood and Champagne*, p. 116.
     Capa, in Whelan, p. 208.

19   Wilson, in L. Lefebrve, *They Were on Omaha Beach*, pp. 23–24.

20   Shoemaker, *World War II*, June 2004, p. 45; Wilson, ibid, pp. 26–28.

21   Wilson, in Lefebvre, p. 87. Shoemaker, WW II, June 2004 p. 45.

"Strictly Power." The Plan. 2:30 A.M. to 3:30 A.M.

22   Hendley, *Washington Post*, June 6, 1984; Capa, in Whelan, p. 222; Rich, in A. Kershaw, *Blood and Champagne*, p. 122; Carter, in J. Balkoski, *Omaha Beach*, p. 61.

23   Race to the foreshore figures taken from, R. J. Kershaw, *D-Day Piercing the Atlantic Wall*, pp. 34–35.

24   Gerow, in Balkoski, p. 21; Wilson, in Lefebvre, p. 28.

25   Gerow, in Balkoski, p. 24; Chase, ibid, p. 23.

26   Cawthon, *Other Clay*, p. 41; Taylor/Thompson, in J.H. Thompson, "D-Day's Cauldron," *Chicago Tribune* special, May 29, 1994.

27   Krieger, in Lefebvre, p. 52. MacPhee, ibid 86; Ford, p. 104; Guise, p. 21; Bognanni, pp. 64–65; Cawthon, p. 42.

28   Hangsterfer, in Balkoski, p. 26. Corlett, in J. Balkoski, *Beyond the Beachhead*, p. 124

29   Bradley, *A Soldier's Story*, pp. 256, 264, and 266.

30   Williams, in P. Winter, *D-Day Documents*, p. 45. "Bigot Top Secret," *Neptune Review* No 14, 09.00 May 14. Winter.

31   "Bigot Top Secret," *Neptune Review* No 17, 09.00 Hours, June 4, ibid, Winter. Williams, ibid, p. 48; Scott-Bowden, ibid, p. 50.

THREE: THE STORM BREAKS: 2:00 A.M. TO 5:00 A.M.
"Whole World Against Us" 2:00 A.M. to 4:55 A.M.

1   Ziegelmann, in D. Isby, *The German Army at D-Day*, p. 193.

2   Keller, *Vom Omaha Beach Bis Siberien*, p. 21.

3   Meyer, 03.15 352 Division telephone log; Airborne figures, taken from R. J. Kershaw, *D-Day: Piercing the Atlantic Wall*, p. 74; Keller, pp. 20–21; and H. K. von Keusgen, *Omaha Beach*, p. 86.

4   Lücking and Heinz, in Keusgen, pp. 73 and 81.

5   Naube, in H. Eckhertz, *D-Day Through German Eyes*, pp. 46–7. Wegner, in Milano, and Conner, *Normandiefront*, p. 74.

6   Severloh, *WN 62*, pp. 52–53; in Keusgen, *Stützpunkt WN 62*, p. 81; Pluskat, in C. Ryan Collection, Ohio University Archive, interview, pp. 5–6.

7   Crouch, in C. J. Anderson, *Screaming Eagles at Pointe du Hoc*, World War II, July 2001, p. 38.

8   Kirchhoff, Coulmain, and Le Devin, in Keusgen, *Pointe du Hoc*, pp. 82–83.

9   Kirchhoff, ibid, p. 87.

"Bacon and eggs on the edge of Eternity"—2:30 A.M. to 4:30 A.M.

10   Cawthon, *Other Clay*, pp. 47–48.

11   Branham, in 29th Division, *Diverse Eyewitness Accounts of Omaha Beach*, S. Trew collection.

12   Slaughter, *Omaha Beach and Beyond*, p. 99; Cawthon, ibid, p. 48.

13   Barnes, *Fragments of My Life*, pp. 61–2. Garcia, personal account, Trew; Cawthon, p. 42.

14 Wilson, in L. Lefebvre, *They Were on Omaha Beach*, p. 131.

15 Koch, in R. Miller, *Nothing Less Than Victory*, p. 276.

16 Slaughter, pp. 96–97 and 100–101; Barnes, p. 62; Gaskill, in G. R. Metcalf, *With Cross and Shovel*, p.105;. Stevens brothers, taken from A. Kershaw, *The Bedford Boys*, p. 118; Capa, *Slightly Out of Focus*, p. 139.

17 Cawthon, p. 44. Garcia, personal account; Barnes, p. 61.

18 Dallas, in R. Miller, p. 260.

19 Cawthon, p. 50; Slaughter, p. 106.

20 Jacobs, in M. Bowman, *Remembering D-Day*, p. 90; Patterson, in M. Bowman, *Air War*, vol. 2, p. 10; Gibson, in J. Balkoski, *Omaha Beach*, p. 92.

21 Isgrig, Meconis, and Stephens, in Bowman, *Remembering D Day*, pp. 66, 88, and 89. Tarcza, in Bowman, *Air War*, vol. 2, p. 52.

22 Isgrig, ibid, p. 66. Patterson, in Bowman, vol. 2, p. 10; Mitch, ibid, p. 9.

23 Jacobs, in Bowman, *Remembering D-Day*, p. 90.

24 Patterson, in Bowman, vol. 2, p. 10; Ardery, in Balkoski, p. 95.

25 Johnson, in Balkoski, p. 95; Healy, in Bowman, vol. 2, p. 29. Smith, in Balkoski, p. 96.

"A Series of Flashes on the Horizon." Bombardment. 5:50 A.M. to 6:20 A.M.

26 Severloh and Bongard, in Keusgen, *Stützpunkt WN 62*, p. 83; Severloh, *WN 62*, pp. 53–54; Gockel, *Das Tor Zur Hölle*, p. 79; Naube, in Eckhertz, p. 47; Winter, ibid, p. 158.

27 Heinz, in Keusgen, *Omaha Beach*, p. 84; Dubois, in Lefebvre, *They Were on Omaha Beach*, p. 127; Oxeant, ibid, p. 124; Simeth, in Milano, and Conner, *Normandiefront*, p. 76. Darondel, in M. L. Roberts, *D-Day Through French Eyes*, p. 122. Ferrary, ibid, p. 31. Oxéant, in Keusgen, p. 80.

28 Kwiatkowski, in Keusgen, p. 83; Lützen, ibid, p. 82; Winter, in Eckhertz, pp. 157–159; Naube, ibid, pp. 48–49.

29 Kwiatkowski, in Keusgen, p. 86. Severloh, interview, Czogalla, *Invasion in der Normandie*, Spiegel TV 2003; and *WN 62*, p. 54; Winter, in Eckhertz, p. 158. Heinz, in Keusgen, pp. 83–84.

30 Ygouf, in Lefebvre, p. 126; Scelles, in Keusgen, p. 85; and Lefebvre p. 127; Severloh, *WN 62*, p. 54; Broeckx, in Roberts, pp. 73–74.

31 Keller, in Keusgen, p. 86.

FOUR: DEATH RIDE: 4:15 A.M. TO 6:30 A.M.
A Wild Death Ride. 4:15 A.M. to 6:15 A.M.

1 Green, in R. Bailey, *Forgotten Voices of D-Day*, pp. 270–271; Slaughter, p. 103; Wilson, in L. Lefebvre, *They Were on Omaha Beach*, p. 132; Cawthon, *Other Clay*, pp. 50–51.

2 Barnes, p. 63; Capa, *Slightly Out of Focus*, p. 139; Murdoch, in R. Miller, p. 248.

3 Healey, in R. T. Bass, *The Brigades of Neptune*, p. 106; Garcia, personal account, Trew; Tarbit, in R. Bailey, *Forgotten Voices of D-Day*, p. 276; Shepherd, *Invasion. The Story of the LCI(L) 92 in the Invasion of Normandy on June 6 1944*, US Coast Guard account.

4 Ross, personal account; Davies, in Bailey, pp. 96–97; Garcia, personal account; Lewis, 29th Division diverse eyewitness accounts; Slaughter, p. 107.

5   Wilson, in Lefebvre, p. 132. Lewis, in RT Bass, *Clear the Way!* p. 22.

6   Bradley, *A Soldier's Story*, p. 267; and in ed. W. G. Ramsey, *D-Day Then and Now*, vol. 2, p. 321; Spaulding, in R. Kershaw, *D-Day: Piercing the Atlantic Wall*, p. 114; Slaughter, p. 107.

7   Woodward, Case, and Fitts, in J. C. McManus, *The Dead and Those About to Die*, pp. 69–71; Sledge, Barry, and Harkey and After-Action report, in J. Balkoski, *Omaha Beach*, pp. 100–103; diver information, *After the Battle*, p. 342; Skaggs, in McManus, p. 71.

8   Sabin, in Balkoski, p. 167; Green, Bailey, p. 272.

Sie Kommen! 5:00 A.M. to 6:30 A.M.

9   352 Div Telephone log, 04.52, 04.55, 05.04 and 05.20 hours.

10   Naube, in Eckhertz, *D-Day Through German Eyes*, pp. 49–50.

11   Wegner, Milano, and Conner, in *Normandiefront*, p. 76; Winter, in Eckherz, p. 160.

12   Gun and obstacle figures, taken from S. Zaloga, *The Devil's Garden*, Table 13, p. 130 and Table 14, p. 155.

13   Gockel, *Das Tor Zur Hölle*, pp. 80–84; Severloh, *WN 62*, pp. 54 and 56.

14   Heinz, in Keusgen, p. 95; Kwiatkowski, ibid, p. 96; Wegner, in Milano, and Conner, p. 77.

France Looked Sordid and Uninviting. 6:15 A.M. to 6:30 A.M.

15   Cawthon, p. 52; Barnes, p. 65.

16   Slaughter, p. 107; Bradley, *A Soldier's Story*, p. 268.

17   Capa, *Slightly Out of Focus*, p. 139; Itzel, in R. T. Bass, *The Brigades of Neptune*, p. 107; Barnes, p. 63.

18   Green, in Bailey, pp. 272–273.

19   Stevens, in D. Fortuna, "The Bedford Boys," *World War II* June 2004, p. 30; Capa, p. 140; Barnes, pp. 65–66.

20   Wilson, in Lefebvre, pp. 132–133. Silva, interviews; Dir C Carey, *Bloody Battlefield. Omaha Beach 6 Jun 1944*, UK Channel 5 TV; and C. Czogalla, *Invasion in der Normandie*, Spiegel TV 2003.

21   Green, in Bailey, p. 274.

22   Naube, in Eckhertz, p. 52; Wegner, in *Normandiefront*, pp. 78–79.

FIVE: FIRST WAVE FLOUNDERED: 6:30 A.M. TO 7:30 A.M.
Vierville Cliff Shoulder. Right. 6:30 A.M. to 7:20 A.M.

1   Thraxton, in L. Lefebvre, *They Were on Omaha Beach*, p. 140; Nider, ibid, p. 137.

2   Roach, in A. Kershaw, *The Bedford Boys*, p. 84.

3   Naube, in H. Eckhertz, *D-Day Through German Eyes*, p. 52; Nash, US Army Historical Division interview, J. Balkoski, *Omaha Beach*, p. 121.

4   Goranson and Rudder, in Balkoski, pp. 113–114 and 116; Salomon, interview, R. Kirk, *D-Day. H-Hour*, History Channel TV, 1994.

5   Robertson, in Balkoski, p. 126; Russo, ibid, pp. 124 and 128; Callahan, ibid, p. 127; Bingham, *Diverse Eyewitness Accounts of Omaha Beach*, 29th Division, unnumbered ms.

6   Heil, in Lefebvre, p. 79; Bartholomew, in R. T. Bass, *Clear the Way!* pp. 24–25;
     Ross, ibid, pp. 22–23. Demolition engineer, Sgt. R. Martin, article June 30, 1944,
     Yank, ed. S. Kluger, *Yank: The Army Weekly*, p. 182.
7   O'Neill, in Bass, ibid, p. 27; Evnetsky, in M. Bowman, *Air War D-Day: Bloody
     Beaches*, p. 40.
8   Slaughter, *Omaha Beach and Beyond*, p. 110.
9   Callahan, in Balkoski, p. 127; Bingham, in *Diverse Eyewitness Accounts*, Lowry, in
     Lefebvre, p. 155.
10   Naube, in Eckhertz, pp. 50–51. Sales, in A. Kershaw, *The Bedford Boys*, p. 181.
11   Nider, in Lefebvre, pp. 137–138; Feduik, in Bowman, p. 122.
12   Jarvis, in Balkoski, pp. 108–109; Feduik, in Bowman, p. 122; Agee, in Lefebvre, p. 188.
13   Wegner, in V. Milano, and B. Conner, *Normandiefront*, p. 83.
14   Dolan, in Lefebvre, pp. 154–155. Cawthon, *Other Clay*, pp. 52 and 37.
15   Moody, in G. Stern, *The Cover Up at Omaha Beach*, p. 46.
16   Goranson, Morrow, and Belcher, in *Roughing it with Charlie*. C Company History
     1945, pp. 28, 32, and 34.

Colleville Cliff Shoulder Left. 6:30 A.M. to 7:30 A.M.

17   Severloh, *WN 62*, p. 58.
18   Kwiatkowski and Plota, in von Keusgen, *Omaha Beach*, pp. 114–115, 118; Severloh,
     p. 58.
19   Selbach, in von Keusgen, *Stützpunkt WN 62*, pp. 90 and 92; Severloh, interview,
     A. Czogalla, *Invasion in der Normandie*, Spiegel German TV 2003. Gockel, *Das Tor
     Zur Hölle*, pp. 85–86.
20   Selbach, in von Keusgen, ibid, p. 92; Gockel, p. 85.
21   Official 1st US Division report, *16E on D-Day*, NND735017.
22   Wozenski, in R Miller, *Nothing Less Than Victory*, p. 293.
23   Silva, interview, C. Carey, *Bloody Battlefield*; *Omaha Beach 6 Jun 44*, LWT for
     Channel 5 UK TV. Quotations, taken from 16-E official report.
24   Riley, personal account, taken from *World War II*, June 1994.
25   Wilson, in Lefebvre, pp. 133–134; Fitzsimmons, 16-E D-Day report.
26   Garland, in Balkoski, p. 152; Wood, ibid, p. 150.
27   McManus, John C, *The Dead and Those About to Die*: Talton, p. 101; Gibbons,
     p. 102; Battle report, p. 99; Hurlbut in Balkoski, p. 151.
28   Capa, *Slightly Out of Focus*, pp. 139–140; Wozenski, in Miller, p. 293.
29   Capa, ibid, p. 141; Buell identified, in R, Whelan, *This Is War! Robert Capa at
     Work*, p. 234; veteran, taken from von Keusgen, *Omaha Beach*, p. 11.
30   This incident is based on exhaustive research by Lowell L. Getz, "The Face in the
     Surf," *World War II*, June 2004, p. 40.
31   Fitzsimmons, 16-E on D-Day narrative.
32   Wilson, in Lefebvre, pp. 164–166.
33   Message, HQ 1st Infantry Division, radio log USS *Ancon*, English Channel,
     June 6, 1944.
34   Trimpe, in Lefebvre, p. 162; Hemingway, in C Prime, *Omaha Beach. Tue 6 Jun
     1944*, p. 104.
35   Boardman, in McManus, p. 107.

36 Götsch, in von Keusgen, *Stützpunkt WN 62*, p. 95.

37 352 Tel Log reports bunkers out of action at 7:20 and 7:45 A.M. Selbach, Plota, and Krieftewirth, in von Keusgen, ibid, pp. 98–99.

SIX: POINTE DU HOC, "THE JIB": 6:40 A.M. TO 11:10 A.M.
The Cliff. 6:40 A.M. to 7:30 A.M.

1 Block, *2nd Ranger Battalion Narrative History, Apr 43–May 45*, US Military History Institute, p. 56.

2 Gabaree, in G. Sterne, *The Cover Up at Omaha Beach*, p. 11; Block, ibid, p. 55; Block was to be killed in action on Dec. 8. 1944 in Germany.

3 D Company, A. E. Baer Jr., *D for Dog*, p. 34; Kirchhoff, in von Keusgen, *Pointe du Hoc. Rätsel um einen deutschen Stützpunkt*, p. 92.

4 McClosky, in Sterne, p. 24; D Company, *D for Dog*, p. 33. Eikner, letter to W. G. Ramsey in April 1994, *D-Day. Then and Now*, vol. 2, p. 331.

5 D Company, ibid. Bains, S. Zaloga, in *Rangers Lead the Way*, p. 30; Davis and Stivison, in Sterne, pp. 102–103.

6 Kirchhoff, in von Keusgen, p. 94; Satterlee and bombardment, taken from Zaloga pp. 31 and 34.

7 South, in Sterne, pp. 101–102.

8 Karl and Kirchhoff, in von Keusgen, pp. 97 and 94–95.

9 Kerchner, in Sterne, p. 100; Davis, p. 103; Wintz, p. 100.

10 Kirchhoff, in von Keusgen, p. 97; Petty, in C. Ryan, *The Longest Day*, p. 173; South, in Sterne, p. 97.

11 Crouch and Goodgal, in C. J. Anderson, "Screaming Eagles at Pointe du Hoc," *World War II*, pp. 39–40.

12 Lomell, interview, in R. Kirk, *D-Day. H-Hour*, History Channel TV 1994 and Sterne, p. 99; Pots and South, in Sterne, pp. 98 and 102; Kirchhoff, in von Keusgen, p. 104.

The Plateau. 7:30 A.M. to 11:10 A.M.

13 Kirchhoff, ibid, p. 104; Lomell, in ed. M. Bowman, *Remembering D-Day*, p. 69.

14 Lomell, History Channel TV interview; Bowman p. 69.

15 Müller, in von Keusgen, pp. 111 and 106.

16 Lomell, TV interview, ibid. Kaufmann, in von Keusgen, p. 106.

17 Raaen, personal account, Trew and Balkoski p. 172; Coleman, in Sterne, p. 19; Edlin, ibid, p. 18.

SEVEN: WIN OR LOSE?: 6:45 A.M. TO 8:30 A.M.
The Center. Saint-Laurent-sur-Mer. 6:45 A.M. to 8:00 A.M.

1 Spalding, interview, US, Army 1st Div rear CP Herve Belgium, Feb. 9, 1945. p. 22; Murray, interview, *D-Day Plus 40*, BBC TV June 1984.

2 Buck, in Y. Henkin, *Uneasy Red*, p. 109; Murray, BBC interview.

3 Dawson and Miceli, group interview with Company 16-G, Aug. 22, 1944. Online.

4 Stine and Miceli, ibid.

5 Dawson letter to family, June 16, 1944, 1st Div Museum. Quoted Henkin, p. 109.

6 Wozenski, in R. Miller, *Nothing Less Than Victory*, pp. 293–4.

7   Arnold and Edlin, in J. Balkoski, *Omaha Beach*, p. 173; Schneider, ibid, p. 174.

8   Fuehr, in V. Milano and B. Conner, *Normandiefront*, p. 115; Winter, in H,
     Eckhertz, *D-Day Through German Eyes*, p. 160.

9   Epstein, Balkoski; p. 174; Snyder, G. Sterne, *The Cover Up at Omaha Beach*, p. 30.

10   Raaen, in Balkoski, pp. 174–5. Klein, interview; taken from R. Kirk, *D-Day.
     H-Hour*, History TV Channel, 1994.

11   Gray, in Sterne, p. 38. Brown, ibid, p. 28.

12   Raaen and Parker in Balkoski, p. 176.

13   Winter, in Eckhertz, p. 161. Gray, in Sterne, p. 36. Miller, personal account, Trew.

Leaders. 7:00 A.M. to 8:30 A.M.

14   Leveel, in M. L. Roberts, *D-Day Through French Eyes*, pp. 19–20.

15   Beike, in Eckhertz, pp. 170–171 and 178–179.

16   Duchien and Marion, interview, July 3, 1958, taken from C. Ryan Papers.

17   Ladder report, 352 Div Tel Log, 08.19 hours.

18   Ziegelmann radio traffic, in D. Isby, *The German Army at D-Day*, pp. 194–195 and
     352; Infanteriedivision *Invasionstag*, RH19 1X12.

19   Keller, in von Keusgen, *Omaha Beach*, p. 148.

20   Albert, in L. Lefebvre, *They Were on Omaha Beach*, p. 202; Hue, ibid, p. 161;
     Hardelay, pp. 197–198; Scelles, pp. 183 and 222–223.

21   WN 76 report, in Isby, pp. 194–195; Kwiatkowski, in von Keusgen, p. 146. Heinz,
     in *Normandiefront*, p. 84.

22   Wegner, ibid, p. 83; Severloh, *WN 62*, p. 65; Naube, in Eckhertz, p. 55; Ocker,
     taken from Isby, p. 196.

23   1st Div report, Note to Col. Gavalas, HQ 1 Div, June 8, 1944, enclosure to original
     Spalding interview. Lord, letter Jan. 19, 1988 to US Army Military History Institute.

24   Bingham, in *Diverse Eye-Witness Accounts of Omaha Beach*, 116th regiment, Trew.

25   Bare, in Bowman, *Air War D-Day*, p. 101. Corpse, taken from G. C. Ward and K.
     Burns, *The War*, p. 207; Hamilton, in Bowman, p. 103; Arnold, in Sterne, p. 45.

26   Carroll, interview, B. C. Pohanka, "Beach with No Cover," *Military History*, Feb.
     1992, p. 38.

27   Pinder was posthumously awarded the US Medal of Honor, in J C McManus,
     pp. 134–136.

28   Carroll, Pohanka interview, p. 39.

Stop the Boats. 8:30 A.M.

29   Hickman, in Balkoski, p. 241; p. 397 report, ibid, pp. 240–242; Lewis, in *Diverse
     Eyewitness Accounts of Omaha Beach*.

30   Cota, in Balkoski, p. 197.

31   Brown, in Sterne, p. 28; Burke, ibid, p. 40; Coughlin, ibid, p. 34.

32   Thompson, *Chicago Tribune* article, May 29, 1994; Lypka, in J C McManus, p. 178;
     Taylor and interview report, in Balkoski, pp.198–199.

33   Vyn, in Balkoski, p. 179; Walker, ibid, p. 180.

34   Shepherd, *The Story of the LCI-92 in the Invasion of Normandy on 6 June 1944*, US
     Coast Guard document.

35   Capa, in R. Whelan, *This is War! Robert Capa at Work*, p. 234.

EIGHT: THE CRISIS: 8:30 A.M. TO MIDDAY
Dilemmas. 8:30 A.M. to 11:00 A.M.

1   Shoemaker, "Lasting Impressions of the Longest Day," p. 46, *World War II*, June 1994; Bradley, *A Soldier's Story*, p. 270.

2   Hendley, "D-Day: A Special Report," *Washington Times*, June 6, 1984; Capa, *Slightly Out of Focus*, p. 148; Wilson, in L. Lefebvre, *They Were on Omaha Beach*, pp. 196–197.

3   Jarreau, in R. Whelan, *This is War! Robert Capa at Work*, p. 235; Shoemaker, p. 46. Hendley, *Washington Times*.

4   Miller, personal account; Nyland, interview, *D-Day Plus Forty*, BBC TV, June 1994; Raaen, in J Balkoski, *Omaha Beach*, p. 229.

5   Huebner and Mason, in J. C. McManus, *The Dead and Those About to Die*, pp. 193–195.

6   Bradley, pp. 271–272; Hansen and Dempsey, in N Hamilton, *Monty. Master of the Battlefield*, p. 611.

7   Sanders, *Gunfire Support at Omaha Beach*, Kindle edition, p. 1071; Harding and Gentry, in Y. Henkin, *Uneasy Red*, p. 89.

8   Wilson, in Lefebvre, p. 197; Lützen, Plota, and Severloh, in Von Keusgen, *Omaha Beach*, p. 147–148.

9   *Gunfire Support at Omaha*, Ramsey, Kindle edition, p. 1071; Beer, pp. 1060–1071; Boyd, pp. 1142–1154; Gaskill, in M. Bowman, *Air War D-Day. Bloody Beaches*, p. 98. Carroll, B. Pohanka interview, "Beach with No Cover," *Military History*, Feb. 1992.

10 Keeler, Knight, and Anderson, in J C McManus, pp. 205–206.

11 Gibbs and AA medic; J C McManus, pp. 204 and 206.

12 Winter, in H. Eckhertz, *D-Day Through German Eyes*, pp. 161–164.

13 352 Division telephone log 09.35. Report Ic to Ia. Wehrmacht time was one hour behind Allied.

14 Bradley, p. 271; Kean, in Hamilton, *Monty*, p. 613.

More Infantry. 9:30 A.M. to 1:00 P.M.

15 Beike, in Eckhertz, p. 179; Wurmheller, in Von Keusingen, *Omaha Beach*, p. 163; Breeden, *Diverse Eyewitness Accounts of Omaha Beach*; Eisemann and Dowie, in C. Ryan, *The Longest Day*, pp. 201–202.

16 Beike, in Eckhertz, pp. 179–183.

17 Heinz, in Von Keusgen, *Omaha Beach*, p. 160.

18 Keller, *Vom Omaha Beach Bis Siberien*, p. 22; Hentschel, in Von Keusgen, p. 159.

19 Combat Report, in M. Bowman, *Air War D-Day. Bloody Beaches*, p. 19. Ford, ibid, p. 16.

20 Keller, pp. 22–5.

21 Ford, in Bowman, p. 18; Riley, p. 40, *World War II*, June 2004.

22 Talley radio report, in J. Balkoski, *Omaha Beach*, p. 237.

23 Severloh, *WN 62*, pp. 69–70.

NINE: VILLAGE FIGHTING: 11:30 A.M. TO DUSK
Colleville East. 11:30 A.M. to 7:00 P.M.

1   Extracts from 352 Division telephone log, Wehrmacht time one hour behind Allied. Allied time used in text.

2 Ziegelmann, in D. Isby, *The German Army at D-Day*, p. 197; Scelles, interview, by P. Poutaraud and G. Badufle, April 21, 1994.

3 Pluskat, C. Ryan Papers, interview Pluskat, pp. 9–10; Kwiatkowski and Lützen, in von Keusgen, *Omaha Beach*, pp. 164–166.

4 Severloh, American veteran, von Keusgen, p. 11. "Beast of Omaha" interview, in A. Czogalla, *Invasion in der Normandie*, Der Spiegel German TV 2003.

5 Dawson, in J. Balkoski, *Omaha Beach*, p. 283.

6 Broeckx, in M. Roberts, *D-Day Through French Eyes*, p. 74.

7 Bauch Telephone reports, 352 Div telephone log, 12.35 and 12.48. Hentschel, in von Keusgen, pp. 167–168.

8 Gockel, *Das Tor Zur Hölle*, pp. 90–91 and 93.

9 Kwiatkowski, in von Keusgen, pp. 166–167.

10 Schnichels, Gockel, p. 88; von Keusgen, *Stützpunkt WN 62*, p. 124; Kwiatkowski, in von Keusgen, *Omaha Beach*, p. 167.

11 Wilson, in L. Lefebvre, *They Were on Omaha Beach*, p. 242.

12 Severloh, *WN 62*, pp. 70–72; Czogalla, *Der Spiegel* interview.

13 Dawson, *Group Interview with Company 16-G*, Aug. 22, 1944.

14 Mason, 1 Div HQ Notes to Col Gavalas, June 8, 1944, enclosure to Spalding doc. Slaughter, *Omaha Beach and Beyond*, p. 116.

15 Spalding and Bieder, in Balkoski, p. 286.

Vierville West. 10:00 A.M. to 1:30 P.M.

16 Andre, in Lefebvre, p. 234; Houyvet, in Roberts, pp. 98–99.

17 Hardelay, interview, by C. Zévaco and M. Hardelay, Nov. 21, 2003; Levoir, interview by D. Vincent and L. Alain, Dec. 2003, Omaha Beach Memoirs website.

18 Fulk, in Balkoski, p. 287. Chambrin, interview, by B. Veyrat and M. Campo, Dec. 15, 1993, Memoirs. Hardelay, in Lefebvre, p. 232 and interview by Zévaco and Hardelay. Jeanne, in Lefebvre, pp. 263–264.

19 Slaughter, p. 113; *McCork* log, in Balkoski, p. 277.

20 Naube, in H. Eckhertz, *D-Day Through German Eyes*, p. 57; Wegner, in V. Milano and B. Conner, *Normandiefront*, pp. 98–99.

21 Slaughter, p. 115.

22 Shea, in Balkoski, pp. 276–277 and 279.

23 Kraiss, *Kriegstagebuch der Führungs Abt AOK 7, 6 Juni 44, 12.00.* [13.00 Allied time]. Bradley, *A Soldier's Story*, p. 272.

Saint-Laurent Center. 11:30 A.M. to Dusk.

24 Heinz, in von Keusgen, *Omaha Beach*, pp. 160–161. Keller, *Vom Omaha Beach Bis Siberien*, pp. 25–66.

25 Krieger, in Lefebvre, p. 257; Van Roosen, in *Normandiefront*, p. 97; Garcia, in Balkoski, p. 299.

26 Wilch, in Balkoski, p. 302.

27 115th History, Balkoski, p. 302. Renée, interview, by M. Cook, S. Zévaco, and N. Bégue, Feb. 17, 1994. Andre, interview, by B. Tougard, Jan. 2004. Omaha Memoirs.

28 Cooper, in Balkoski, p. 305.

TEN: TENUOUS FOOTHOLD: 4:00 P.M. TO MIDNIGHT
Kampfgruppe Meyer. 4:00 P.M. to 11:55 P.M.

1. Aaenenson, in G. C. Ward and K. Burns, *The War*, p. 224.
2. Ziegelmann, *M.352 Infanteriedivision. 1 Invasionstag*. RH19IX/2 part document Bundesarchiv. Casualty figures: The *Panzer Lehr* Division lost 5 tanks, 84 armored half-tracks, and 90 wheeled vehicles moving between 120–200 km to the front between June 6–8. The *12th SS* lost 22 killed and 60 wounded covering 70 to 190 km over the same period. Figures from R. J. Kershaw, *D Day: Piercing the Atlantic Wall*, p. 200.
3. 352 Div Telephone Log 16.02, 16.10, 16.17 and 17.30 add hour for Allied time.
4. Bach, diary June 6, in J. Balkoski, *Omaha Beach*, p. 308.
5. Carroll, interview B. Pohanka, "Beach With No Cover," p. 40, *Military History*, Feb. 1992; Plager, in Balkoski, p. 312.
6. Branham, *Diverse Eyewitness Accounts of Omaha Beach*, Trew.

Pointe du Hoc. The Angle. Midday to Midnight.

7. Goodgal, p. 40, *World War II*, July 2001.
8. Kirchhoff, in von Keusgen, *Pointe du Hoc*, p. 111. Wegner, in Milano, and Conner, *Normandiefront*, pp. 107–108, 111–112, and 135.
9. Gabaree, in G. Stern, *The Cover Up at Omaha*, p. 115.
10. Gabaree, ibid, p. 117; Maimone, in R. Drez, *Voices of D-Day*, p. 265; Wegner, in *Normandiefront*, p. 145.
11. South, in Stern, p. 102.

Dusk to Darkness. 5:00 P.M. to Beyond Midnight.

12. Shepard, *Invasion, The Story of the LCI (L)-92 in the Invasion of Normandy on June 6 1944*, US Coast Guard doc.
13. Barnes, *Fragments of My Life*, pp. 66–67.
14. Heinz, in *Normandiefront*, p. 136.
15. Naube, in H. Eckhertz, *D-Day Through German Eyes*, pp. 59–60; Gockel, *Das Tor Zur Hölle*, pp. 98 and 99–100; Severloh, *WN 62*, p. 83.
16. Slaughter, *Omaha Beach and Beyond*, p. 117; Graham, in L. Lefebvre, *They Were on Omaha Beach*, pp. 249–250.
17. Krieger, in Lefebvre, p. 251; Graham, ibid, p. 250.
18 Jeanne, in Lefebvre, p. 254; Hardelay, p. 257; Renard, p. 254; Broeckx, in M. L. Roberts, *D-Day Through French Eyes*, p. 74.
19. Keller, *Vom Omaha Beach Bis Siberien*, p. 26; Lasater, in Lefebvre, p. 159; Shea, in Balkoski, p. 340; Perry, Stern, p. 75.
20. Lasater, Lefebvre, p. 159; Keller, p. 26.
21. Wheeler, in Lefebvre, pp. 251–252.
22. Cawthon, *Other Clay*, p. 67; Slaughter, p. 119.
23. Seidl, in *Normandiefront*, p. 115.

BEYOND 24 HOURS

1   Hathaway, Combat interview 337, *2nd/5th Ranger Bn Normandy Landings June 6–8, 1944*, US National Archives Gp No 407; Maimone, in R. Drez, *Voices of D-Day*, p. 265.

2 Roberts, in J. Balkoski, *Beyond the Beachhead*, p. 154.

3 Goodgal, in *World War II*, July 2000, p. 92.

4 Rudder, article, "Took My Son to Omaha Beach," *Collier's*, June 11, 1954.

5 Casualty figures, in J. Balkoski, *Omaha Beach*, Appendix 1, pp. 350–352; A. Beevor, *D-Day*, p. 112; Rooney, in G.C. Ward and K. Burns, *The War*, p. 210.

6 Stevens, in A. Kershaw, *The Bedford Boys*, pp. 174–175.

7 Casualties, in Beevor, pp. 49, 124, and 519; Renard, in L. Lefebvre, *They Were on Omaha Beach*, p. 259; Leroutier, interview by G. Mylène and V. Emilie, Dec. 2003, Omaha Memoirs. Hardelay, in Lefebvre, p. 273; Scelles, ibid, p. 280; Pottier, in M. L. Roberts, *D-Day Through French Eyes*, p. 146.

8 Casualties, in Balkoski, p. 351. Sales, in A. Kershaw, p. 179; Stevens, ibid, p. 184. Slaughter, *Omaha Beach and Beyond*, p. 118.

9 Stevens, in A. Kershaw, p. 220. Nance, taken from R. Goldstein article, *New York Times*, April 22, 2009.

10 Ziegelmann, in D. Isby, *The German Army at D-Day*, p. 204; Kraiss, 352 Div tel log 23.30 hours; Goth, in Von Keusgen, *Omaha Beach*, p. 191; Slaughter, in A. Kershaw, p. 181.

11 Silva and Severloh, interviews, A. Czogalla, *Invasion in der Normandie*, Spiegel TV 2003.

12 Wilson, in Lefebvre, p. 248.

13 Medical evaluator and Spalding, in J. C. McManus, *The Dead and Those About to Die*, pp. 295–296.

14 Ehlers, in G. C. Ward and K. Burns, *The War*, pp. 210–212.

INDEX

ACKNOWLEDGMENTS

I would like to thank Dr. Simon Trew from the British Royal Military Academy at Sandhurst for his generous help and support for this project, in his identification of much previously unsighted source material. I am truly grateful.